Harnessing the Corporate PC

Harnessing the Corporate PC
Guidelines for Profitable and Productive Personal Computing

Joseph L. Podolsky

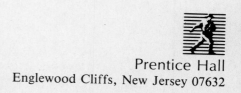

Prentice Hall
Englewood Cliffs, New Jersey 07632

Library of Congress Cataloging-in-Publication Data

PODOLSKY, JOSEPH L.
    Harnessing the corporate PC: guidelines for profitable and
productive personal computing/Joseph L. Podolsky.
    p.   cm.
        Bibliography: p.
        Includes index.
        ISBN 0-13-384181-2
        1. Industrial management—Data processing.   2. Microcomputers—Programming.   I. Title.
HD30.2.P63 1988
658'.05416—dc19

Cover design: *George Cornell*
Manufacturing buyer: *Paula Benevento*

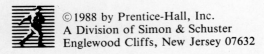 ©1988 by Prentice-Hall, Inc.
A Division of Simon & Schuster
Englewood Cliffs, New Jersey 07632

The publisher offers discounts on this book
when ordered in bulk quantities. For more
information write:

Special Sales/College Marketing
College Technical and Reference Division
Prentice-Hall, Inc.
Englewood Cliffs, New Jersey 07632

Printed in the United States of America

10 9 8 7 6 5 4 3 2 1

ISBN 0-13-384181-2 025

PRENTICE-HALL INTERNATIONAL (UK) LIMITED, *London*
PRENTICE-HALL OF AUSTRALIA PTY. LIMITED, *Sydney*
PRENTICE-HALL CANADA INC., *Toronto*
PRENTICE-HALL HISPANOAMERICANA, S.A., *Mexico*
PRENTICE-HALL OF INDIA PRIVATE LIMITED, *New Delhi*
PRENTICE-HALL OF JAPAN, INC., *Tokyo*
SIMON & SCHUSTER ASIA PTE. LTD., *Singapore*
EDITORA PRENTICE-HALL DO BRASIL, LTDA., *Rio de Janeiro*

*To my colleagues at Hewlett-Packard
and in the information system industry
from whom I gain knowledge and insight,
and to my family,
whose love and patience sustains me always.*

Contents

Preface   ix

PART ONE
USE OF PERSONAL COMPUTING FOR INDIVIDUAL TASKS   1

    Levels of Sophistication   1
    Changes in Task Content   2
    Back to the Basic Step   3

Chapter One   ***The Impact of Personal Computing in the Corporate Environment***   5
    Introduction   5
    How Innovation Is Implemented   5
    What Happens in Each Department   9
    References   9

Chapter Two   ***Corporate Guidelines***   11
    Assumptions   11
    Transition to the Sanction Period   12
    Structure of Corporate Guidelines   12
    Authority for Corporate Guidelines   12
    Guideline 2.1: Objectives of the Personal Computing Program   13
       Checklist: Guideline 2.1—Objectives of the Personal Computing
       Program   17

Guideline 2.2: Scope of Personal Computing Guidelines   19

Checklist: Guideline 2.2—Scope of Personal Computing Guidelines   23

Guideline 2.3: Responsibilities for Personal Computing   25

Checklist: Guideline 2.3—Responsibilities for Personal Computing   37

Checklist: Guideline 2.3 Continued—Justification for Personal Computing   39

Guideline 2.4: Guidelines for the Personal Computing Information Center   41

Checklist: Guideline 2.4—Guidelines for the Personal Computing Information Center   53

References   55

Chapter Three   **Basic Operating Guidelines**   **57**

Introduction   57

Guideline 3.1: Acquiring Personal Computing Equipment   57

Checklist: Guideline 3.1—Acquiring Personal Computing Equipment   63

Guideline 3.2: Ownership Issues   65

Checklist: Guideline 3.2—Ownership Issues   71

Guideline 3.3: Sharing Personal Computing Technology   73

Checklist: Guideline 3.3—Sharing Personal Computing Technology   81

Guideline 3.4: Personal Computing Security Guidelines   83

Checklist: Guideline 3.4—Personal Computing Security Guidelines   93

Guideline 3.5: Personal Computing Away from Company Facilities   95

Checklist: Guideline 3.5—Personal Computing Away from Company Facilities   99

Guideline 3.6: Nonbusiness Use of Personal Computing   101

Checklist: Guideline 3.6—Nonbusiness Use of Personal Computing   103

References   105

Chapter Four   **Control Guidelines**   **107**

Introduction   107

Guideline 4.1: Operational Controls for Personal Computing Users   108

Checklist: Guideline 4.1—Operational Controls for Personal Computing Users   123

Guideline 4.2: Personal Computing as Part of Total Quality Control   127

Checklist: Guideline 4.2—Personal Computing as Part of Total Quality Control   133

Guideline 4.3: Applying Personal Computing to the "Right" Tasks   135

Checklist: Guideline 4.3—Applying Personal Computing to the "Right" Tasks   145

References   147

Contents

PART TWO
USE OF PERSONAL COMPUTING IN COORDINATED SYSTEMS 149

References 152

Chapter Five

Coordinating Personal Computing Systems 153

Introduction 153

Guideline 5.1: Architecture of Coordinated Personal Computing Systems 155

Checklist: Guideline 5.1—Architecture of Coordinated Personal Computing Systems 167

Guideline 5.2: Logical Design of Coordinated Personal Computing Networks 169

Checklist: Guideline 5.2—Logical Design of Coordinated Personal Computing Networks 175

Guideline 5.3: Data Structures for Coordinated Personal Computer Applications 177

Checklist: Guideline 5.3—Data Structures for Coordinated Personal Computer Applications 193

Guideline 5.4: Host Computers in Coordinated Personal Computing Systems 195

Checklist: Guideline 5.4—Host Computers in Coordinated Personal Computing Systems 211

References 215

Chapter Six

Guidelines for Personal Computing Communications Networks 217

Goal of Communications Networks 217

Definitions 218

Local Computing versus Communication 218

Categories of Interapplication Communication 218

Advantages to Communications Networks 220

Standards 222

Chapter 6 Guidelines 222

Guideline 6.1: Logical Structure of Personal Computing Communications Networks 223

Checklist: Guideline 6.1—Logical Structure of Personal Computing Communications Networks 235

Physical Structure of Personal Computing Communications Networks 237

Checklist: Guideline 6.2—Physical Structure of Personal Computing Communications Networks 247

Management Considerations for Personal Computing Communications Networks 249

Checklist: Guideline 6.3—Management Considerations for Personal Computing Communications Networks 265

References 269

Appendix: Some Details about Communications Standards 271

Chapter Seven   **End-User System Development**   **277**

Introduction 277

Definitions 278

End-User Systems Development versus End-User Programming 278

Guideline 7.1: End-User Responsibilities in Developing End-User
Systems 282

Checklist: Guideline 7.1—End-User Responsibilities in Developing
End-User Systems 291

Guideline 7.2: Tools to Facilitate End-User Systems Development 293

Checklist: Guideline 7.2—Tools to Facilitate End-User Systems
Development 301

Guideline 7.3: Role of the PCIC in End-User Systems
Development 303

Checklist: Guideline 7.3—Role of the PCIC in End-User Systems
Development 309

References 313

Chapter Eight   **Where We Are: Where We Are Going**   **315**

Introduction 315

Status of Personal Computing in Corporate Environments 316

Artificial Intelligence in Personal Computing in Corporate
Environments 321

Decision Support Systems in Personal Computing in Corporate
Environments 324

Impact on Society from Personal Computing in Corporate
Environments 328

References 332

Appendix A   **Sample Forms**   **335**

Sample Form 3.1A: Personal Computing Equipment
Selection List 336

Recommended List 336

Approved List 338

Not-Recommended List 340

Sample Form 3.1B: Personal Computing Request and
Justification Form 343

Index   **345**

Preface

Personal computing has entered the corporate world like a wild stallion, beautiful to see, full of potential, inspiring both awe and fear. Like the stallion, personal computing can realize its potential only when tamed, and, if not tamed, personal computing (as with the stallion) may be troublesome, dangerous . . . and expensive to feed.

Personal computing brings the power and complexities of both computing and information systems out from raised-floor rooms onto every desk in the company. Therefore, the responsibility for taming this tool falls to everyone: senior managers, who must set the appropriate policies; information systems managers, who must provide the appropriate business and technical expertise; and personal computing users and their managers, who must make the daily decisions and perform the actual work that will prove the value of this powerful tool. The guidelines in this book are directed to all those people, all who share the responsibility for using personal computing to its full potential.

The guidelines offered in this book assume an organizational setting where many people work together in a department structure. The model used is an organization with geographically dispersed locations, but the guidelines can easily be scaled up and down to fit almost any organization—commercial, nonprofit, or government.

No one book can presume to provide complete knowledge of the vast, dynamic subject of personal computing. You should not implement these guidelines (or any others) on blind faith. This book, therefore, provides extensive background on the suggested guidelines so that they can be applied and modified intelligently. In addition, references are provided for each chapter so that readers can study subjects of interest further.

At the end of each guideline, I have included a checklist which serves two important functions. First, it provides a summary of the key points in the guideline. Second, and more importantly, the checklist provides a tool for both the users who are implementing personal computing and for their managers. Both can use the checklists to verify that the appropriate issues have been considered.

Note that the checklists should be used as outlines, not as whips. You may certainly wish to augment the guidelines (and therefore the checklists) with statements appropriate to your specific organization and situation. Equally important, you may wish to ignore or replace certain guidelines. The checklists allow you to do so consciously and with justification, not through oversight.

This book can be read from beginning to end like a novel, but skipping among the chapters may be more effective as you address particular issues.

Some of these guidelines may be appropriately incorporated into formal company policies, while others are simply effective operating practices, what amounts to "common sense" in this rapidly changing technology. Your goal should be to communicate these guidelines to your organization such that your organization maximizes the benefits from this personal computing revolution while minimizing potential concerns.

Personal computing has gained its strongest foothold in office applications, but the technology is gaining rapidly in all locations in the organization. The guidelines are therefore designed to apply to all functions within a company: factory, field, and laboratory environments in addition to office situations.

Some Definitions

Readers should note that I use the phrase "personal comput*ing*." This term is intended to encompass all systems that are used by individuals for doing their own work; personal computing, in this sense, is very similar to what is sometimes called "end-user computing."

From a hardware standpoint, personal computing includes both stand-alone personal comput*ers* and the use of a personal terminal connected to a larger "host" computer, programmed to allow each user to function independently. Most of the guidelines apply equally to all forms of personal computing. Differences are noted when appropriate. Further, these guidelines can be applied in most technical and organizational environments, so I have purposely omitted discussion of specific hardware and systems or application software.

Personal computing, as used in this book, also refers to "general-purpose" computing. The guidelines are not designed for use with single-purpose, dedicated machines such as word processors, "smart" telephones or copiers, or computer-driven machine tools or lab equipment (although some of the guidelines may also be appropriate for these applications).

"Conventional EDP" refers to all forms of information systems other than those included in personal computing. Conventional EDP is usually performed by professional information systems specialists who develop and operate systems for the benefit of others. Those "others" may use personal computing in addition to the conventional EDP systems. In fact, the programmers who develop the conventional EDP systems might well use personal computing to enhance their own quality and productivity.

"Department managers" are those people who manage the people who do the work of the company. They may be "line" or "staff" in an organizational sense. Working for department managers are "users" (department managers themselves can, of course, be users also). All of these people are the consumers of personal computing services in a company.

Evaluation of the impact of personal computing is particularly difficult because of the diverse and pervasive use of the technology in most organizations. In any case however, department managers, not technical EDP managers, must assess the value of personal computing in terms of the organization's primary objectives; guidelines to help with this are shown in Chapter 4.

The term "equipment" is used as a "catch-all" for all products involved in personal computing. Equipment includes hardware, software, supplies, documentation, and anything else the users might need specifically for personal computing tasks.

Organization of the Book

Part I is fundamental to all personal computing since it focuses on individual tasks. Basic guidelines are provided which must be considered by organizations regardless of size and technical sophistication.

Part II focuses on the guidelines needed as the organization integrates personal computing into coordinated systems. Such coordination is a major step for many organizations and may come slowly, but it is from these efforts that dramatic benefits from personal computing can be achieved.

Go to It

Personal computing is rapidly evolving as sophisticated technology is placed into practice. These guidelines will help you harness this tool, giving the people and departments in your organizations far greater strength. Note that the power is still in your people; personal computing changes the process in which that power is applied, and as with any effective tool, provides leverage, but personal computing is, by itself, inert.

Hopefully, these guidelines will help you apply your intellectual energies, not only merely to tame the personal computing stallion, but also to harness its energy in productive, profitable tasks. Go to it!

JOE PODOLSKY

Part One

USE OF PERSONAL COMPUTING FOR INDIVIDUAL TASKS
INTRODUCTION

Levels of Sophistication

In most companies, personal computing develops along two axes. First, the scope of use increases. Second, in any given department (or even by individual), the sophistication of use increases. Scope of use is described in Chapter 1, with personal computing moving through stages from experimentation to institutionalization. Scope of use is essentially a measure of how many people in a company are using the technology. It is important because even the most wonderful tools cannot accomplish anything until they are used.

Of equal importance, however, is the amount of resources that becomes available when a new technology is widely accepted. People help and learn from each other, forming a "critical mass" that generates chain-reaction enthusiasm. Further, managers often justify investment in support resources based on the numbers of employees that will be affected.

The second axis of development refers to *how* the technology is used. In personal computing, sophistication increases in two main steps, Personal Uses and Organizational Uses. Part I of this book addresses the Personal Uses and Part II addresses the Organizational Uses. Note that as shown in Figure I.1, Organizational Uses build on the Personal Uses base. That base must be solid if Organizational Uses are to be successful.

Within Personal Uses is first a Basic step and then a Control step. Organizational Uses can be divided into a segment involving coordinated systems and a segment involving end-user programming, both of which are dependent on a third segment, communications. Although these three segments can appear in a company or a department in sequence, they usually occur in parallel, by project, with communication issues as the major focus. These three segments address the ways in which personal computing links individuals and departments into larger systems within the corporation.

The first two steps, the Basic and Control steps, focus on the way personal

1

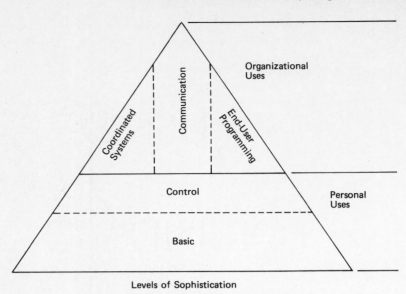

Figure I.1 Levels of sophistication.

computing affects individuals and their work tasks. Through these individuals, small working groups, organizational sections, and departments are also influenced by personal computing.

Changes in Task Content

In the Basic and Control steps, the actual content of what specific people do usually changes. Jobs that were organized along functional lines become more task oriented, focusing on appropriate business purposes rather than on intermediate functions.

For example, before personal computing, a large proposal might require the services of an accountant to do the cost analyses, a typist to put the proposal into final form, and a graphics specialist to draw the graphs, in addition to the marketing, manufacturing, and product specialists involved. Using personal computing, however, the line people can complete the proposal with minimum assistance from staff specialists. Cost analyses can be developed using spreadsheets, the typing can be accomplished on a word processor, and the illustrations may come from a graphics package, all operated by the people directly supporting the prospective customer. The final presentation can then be created by "desktop publishing."

Personal uses do not change business functions

In the Basic and Controls steps, the way the work is done may change, but the fundamental business purpose and product remain the same. In the example above, a proposal is written, albeit by different people and in different ways, both before and after personal computing. As people reach the Organizational Uses steps, however, the entire concept and/or form of the proposal might change; in some cases, the product offered may change. Information systems can become strategic company tools.

For example, the proposal might be sent to the customer in machine-readable form rather than on paper. Preprogrammed routines or spreadsheets might let the prospect review several different alternatives. A program might be included that displayed the product on the prospect's computer screen, allowing the prospect, perhaps, to manipulate the image until it meets expectations.

Different people, different needs

Some personal computing users, especially those who become involved in the experimentation and hobbiest phases, will want to learn and master the technology for its own sake, with little regard for appropriate business uses. The lack of "friendliness" presented by systems becomes an almost welcome challenge.

The majority of users, however, will want the technology to be essentially invisible, "user friendly." These people and most nontechnical managers are interested in what the technology can offer in terms of productivity, accuracy, and reliability, usually on the tasks now performed in the business. We want, of course, to best meet the needs of this second group; they are the ones who will ultimately justify the investment we make in personal computing.

While doing so, however, we are well advised at least to consider the needs of those who really enjoy exploring the technology. These people become the advisors and consultants to the others. They are the applications-oriented explorers who should be asked not only to consider technical innovation but also applications innovation, new ways of meeting basic customer needs through the use of personal computing.

The concepts of "efficiency" versus "effectiveness," "doing things right" versus "doing the right things," are discussed in Chapter 4.

Organization changes

As both levels of sophistication and scope of uses progress, the company itself will probably change its organization to adapt to the potential offered by personal computing. Organizations may become "thinner and shorter," with fewer levels of management and fewer support departments. Product and marketing focus will become more "vertical," closely matching product specifics with customer needs rather than bending products and customers until there is a match. Some elaboration of this view of the future is discussed in Chapter 8.

Back to the Basic Step

The levels of sophistication shown in Figure I.1 form a pyramid, each level building on previous levels, each no more stable than those below. As expected, therefore, the first, the Basic level, is crucial and forms the foundation for all subsequent activities. This firm base can be created by implementing the Corporate Guidelines described in Chapter 2, the Basic Operating Guidelines described in Chapter 3, and the Control Guidelines described in Chapter 4. All these guidelines should be issued together so that bad habits are not formed as increasing numbers of people begin to use personal computing.

Mixed enthusiasm

These initial guidelines will be greeted at best with mixed enthusiasm. The issuing of the guidelines represents the end of the Hobbiest period and the beginning of the Sanctioned period (see Figure 1.3). The hobbiests and experimenters will be grateful for the added support and attention, but they will miss the somewhat elite status that they once held, and they may resent the "restrictions" imposed by the guidelines.

People who have never used personal computing may also receive the guidelines with conflicting feelings. They will probably anticipate the opportunities with excitement, but will have apprehensions consisting of the fear of the unknown, and the perhaps legitimate concern that they will not be able to adapt to the new technologies.

Implementation process

The best way to calm this predictable unrest is to be as definitive and as organized as possible when issuing the guidelines. At least the skeleton of the Personal Computing Information Center organization (see discussion in Chapter 2) should be in place when the guidelines are issued. The mechanics for asking questions, for resolving undefined situations, and for commenting on both the guidelines and their implementation should be clear and open to all if, for no other reason, to give those concerned a "pressure valve" to release frustration and confusion.

The guidelines as issued should probably be relatively "loose" and realistic from the first, assuming that employees will not take advantage of decentralized authority and generalities. Realistic guidelines are written with the hope that they will usually be followed, with few and legitimate exceptions. Even at that, of course, modifications to reflect practice should be expected. Because they deal with basic issues, the guidelines in this part go to some effort to explain issues rather than merely stating policy, in the hope that they may be useful for education of all involved with personal computing.

Chapter One

The Impact of Personal Computing in the Corporate Environment

Introduction

Personal computing is a technology that will affect all organizations, large or small. This pervasiveness is inevitible because of the obvious advantages of this equipment in such common tasks as word processing and spreadsheet calculations, coupled with intense consumer marketing of such systems. You have only two choices: to manage the use of personal computing in your company, or to ignore this phenomenon, allowing it to affect your company in a haphazard manner.

How Innovation Is Implemented

All innovation follows an "S" curve similar to the one shown in Figure 1.1. Early in the life of the innovation, a few people experiment with it. As the innovation becomes better known, the number of people using it expands rapidly, finally slowing as some market saturation is reached. Often we are faced with a "family" of S curves, each overlapping as the latest model of the family of products obsoletes the earlier model (see Figure 1.2).

In a company, the implementation of personal computing follows an "S" curve similar to the one shown in Figure 1.3. It resembles the general curve shown in Figure 1.1 with a few major distinctions. The first portion of the curve, the Experimentation phase, occurs when a few adventurous souls begin "playing" with personal computing at work. They may purchase a system for a specific purpose and then find other uses for it; some might simply bring to work equipment they had at home.

The second phase occurs when the experimenters join together to share common interests. During this "Hobbiest" phase, the uses of personal computing are more organized, but on a voluntary, unmanaged basis. Hobbiests often align themselves with families of hardware of software, and form communities of interest,

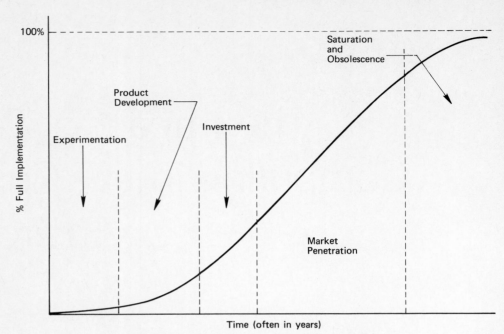

Figure 1.1 Technology implementation curve.

using their informal organization to experiment, promulgate successes, and enlist additional users to their communities. Toward the end of this phase, those using the personal computing equipment are convinced that the equipment can have a positive impact on the company, there are many success stories, and others in the company are showing interest in adopting the technology for wider use.

Up to this point, personal computing activities are usually informal, operating outside the formal hierarchy and with little assistance or interference by the com-

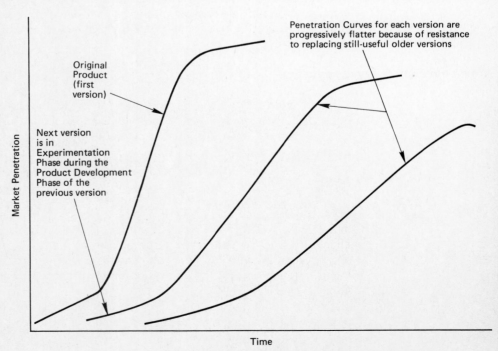

Figure 1.2 Product family curves.

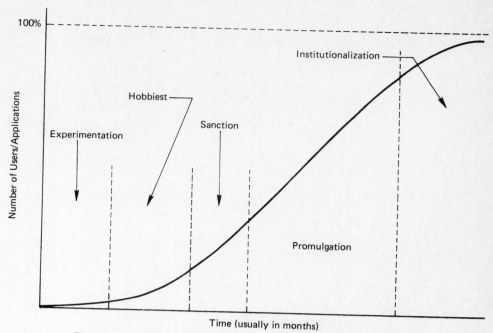

Figure 1.3 Stages in the acceptance of personal computing.

pany management structure. After the Hobbiest stage, however, comes the "Sanctioned" phase, where official notice is taken of the trend; resources are provided and rules are established. It is at this stage that guidelines such as those suggested in this book become appropriate. During this third phase, the Sanction period, the company gives its formal approval and support to the use of personal computing and encourages its use wherever appropriate in the company. The number of users begins to increase rapidly.

The next stage can be called "Promulgation." Everyone in the company can get involved with the new technology as long as the guidelines are observed, and the guidelines themselves take on the quality of living documents, evolving with changes in needs, applications, and technology. Promulgation usually follows an S curve. Personal computing proceeds slowly at first, with installations increasing rapidly as the concepts take hold and become, first, "fashionable" and then demonstrably useful. During the steep slope on the S curve, organizational changes and job adaptations occur. Activities outrun controls, and depending on the culture of the company, controls are either tightened or free reign is allowed to run its course. Either extreme, of course, has its problems, and the trick is to find the appropriate middle ground. Over time, the support services gain experience and competence and the continuing growth in personal computing is handled effectively.

At some point, however, the number of new installations begins to slow; everyone who needs personal computing is already involved, although the technology and related equipment may have changed several times. This stage is called "Institutionalization." Personal computing becomes part of the normal environment of company operations; it is "taken for granted." Guidelines and practice are usually synchronized because rate of change has slowed. In fact, the guidelines are rarely opened during this stage, since they are followed routinely by informal agreement.

Support services are now blended with the normal services provided by the company; people just assume the availability of the technology. In most companies, the use of copiers is an example of a technology that is in the Institutionalization phase. Very few companies are yet in the Institutionalization phase with personal computing.

TABLE 1.1

Characteristics of Phases of Implementing Personal Computing

Characteristic	Phase				
	Experimentation	Hobbiest	Sanction	Promulgation	Institutionalization
Number of users	Very few; slow growth	A few more; slow growth	More users; growth rate increasing	Many more; very rapid growth	Maximum number of users; slow growth
Official company involvement	None; studied ignorance	Begin formal investigation	Issues guidelines; organize PCIC	Full management; full PCIC support	None specific; part of normal operations.
Variety of applications	Many, but very shallow	Many shallow, a few with some depth	Many shallow, an increasing number with full support	Many, with full support	Maximum number, slowly expanding
Cost to company	Small, not visible	Small; measure investigation only	Large; should control as an investment	Large, but paid by departments	Large, but paid as part of normal operations
Benefits to company	Few; some people learning	Few; a bit more learning; scope defined	Users begin to benefit; support roles defined	Benefits increase rapidly; rapid changes	Changes institutionalized; benefits taken for granted

8

The types of support needed varies by stage. The major support mechanism, the Personal Computing Information Center (PCIC), is initiated during the Sanction stage and reaches full flower during promulgation. It is likely that the PCIC, as a separate organization, will whither during the institutionalization stage. The PCIC's major purpose as a "facilitator of change," will no longer be needed. It will have accomplished its purpose. Its activities will simply be absorbed by the company's normal operating units. Equipment selection will be handled by purchasing, training by personnel, and technical services by the EDP department.

The significant support provided by top management attention will also wane during the institutionalization phase. They will also take personal computing for granted and will focus their efforts on other high-priority issues.

Table 1.1 shows highlights of some of the characteristics of each phase.

What Happens in Each Department

In most companies, personal computing develops in two ways. First, the scope of use increases, and second, in any given department (or even by individual) the sophistication of use increases. The topic of sophistication of use is discussed in Chapter 3.

In fact, each department goes through the phases shown in Figure 1.3. Each goes through the phases, however, very rapidly until the department is at the same level as are most of the other departments in the company. For example, let's assume that the public relations department decides to acquire its personal computing equipment when the rest of the company is already in the Sanction phase. Someone in the PR department will be the experimenter, seeking out the needed knowledge to install the appropriate equipment. In a few days, perhaps with some technical help from friends in other departments, our experimenter has a few applications working and others in the department are gaining skills and confidence. The department is now in the Hobbiest phase.

In a few weeks, most of the people in the department, perhaps with significant help from others in the company who have been down this same road, are using the equipment well and along with everyone else are in the Sanction phase. This department is now a full member of the personal computing "club" in the company and proceeds up the curve at an appropriate pace.

REFERENCES

BILL BEERS, "Information-Resources Planning: Strategy for Success," *Today's Office,* November 1984, p. 20.

GARY D. BROWN and DONALD H. SEFTON, "The Micro vs. the Applications Logjam," *Datamation,* January 1984, p. 96.

RICHARD LEVITZ, "How to Control Microcomputer Power So All Organizational Levels Benefit," *AMA Management Review,* February, 1984, p. 22.

ROBERT M. POSTON, "IEEE Software Engineering Standards," *IEEE Software,* April 1984, p. 94.

JUDITH A. QUILLARD and JOHN F. ROCKART, "Looking at Micro Users," *Computerworld Office Automation,* August 15, 1984, p. 11.

PAUL A. STRASSMAN, *Information Payoff,* The Free Press, New York, 1985.

Chapter Two

Corporate Guidelines

Assumptions

The policies proposed in this chapter define one model for the controlled implementation of personal computing. The model is based on several assumptions:

- Company management wants to gain the benefits from standardized, controlled use of personal computing.
- The organization may have several geographically dispersed operations. Smaller companies with only single locations can simplify their guidelines to recognize the comparative ease with which policy coordination can be accomplished.
- The company, in its other policies, encourages local discretion and allows employees freedom in the way they do their specific jobs.
- Innovation and productivity are valued and encouraged.
- Communication among employees and among the operational entities is encouraged.
- A more traditional EDP department already exists, with its own guidelines and procedures. Those organizations that have no such department can still benefit from these guidelines, but the technical guidance that would otherwise come from the EDP department will have to be obtained from consultants or from the expertise of an in-house specialist hired or trained for this task.

The guidelines also mention, in a few places, scientific and manufacturing personal computing functions. The guidelines are not, however, written only for technical companies and can easily be adapted for organizations in almost any industry. It is important to note that personal computing is *not* limited to office automation, but can be applied successfully in *all* organizational functions.

11

Transition to the Sanction Period

The issuing of guidelines usually marks the beginning of the Sanction phase of the use of personal computing. The company is "officially" recognizing the importance of the new technology and is taking steps to control and facilitate its implementation. As noted before, the experimenters and hobbiests will have mixed feelings; they will enjoy the support and recognition now available, but will resent the structure, bureaucracy, and loss of status they had as pioneers. The transition to the Sanction phase may be smoothed if the efforts of the experimenters and hobbiests can be formally recognized and their knowledge harnessed by asking for and heeding their advice.

Structure of Corporate Guidelines

Four guidelines are suggested to set overall company policy. They should be reviewed in sequence since they build on each other.

The first (Guideline 2.1) defines the objectives of the personal computing program, setting the overall structure of what company managers would like to achieve with personal computing tools. This guideline is the foundation of all others and should be adapted to be consistent with the philosophies and culture of your company. All the other guidelines in the book "merely" describe ways of achieving these objectives and strategies.

Guideline 2.2 outlines the scope of personal computing. This is equivalent to a working definition of personal computing. The definition shown in Guideline 2.2 is purposely broad, but you should check to see if this broad definition creates overlaps and potential conflicts with other, existing policies. Consistency among policies is a virtue and either these new guidelines and/or the old ones should be modified to achieve a workable fit. If such a fit is difficult to achieve, you should at least state which guideline has priority in case of perceived conflicts.

The third guideline, Guideline 2.3, responsibilities, is the implementation of many of the assumptions mentioned above. The final responsibility for personal computing is clearly placed on the desk of user department managers, although responsibilities for technical advice and support are also defined.

Implementation of the corporate guidelines is accomplished primarily through the Personal Computing Information Center (PCIC), described in Guideline 2.4. The PCIC described in the guideline is an extremely useful concept, but it may be too elaborate and costly for many companies. Shown in this guideline are alternatives to the optimum PCIC model that may be more appropriate for some organizations. Note, however, that the functions assigned to the PCIC in the guideline must be provided somewhere or the personal computing objectives will not be reached.

Authority for Corporate Guidelines

The corporate guidelines should appear to be written by the company's highest administrative manager, usually the vice-president of administration or of finance or by the Chief Information Officer if such a person exists in your company. In fact, of course, the guidelines may be written by the chief information manager (CIM) or by a task force specially organized for this specific purpose. Having the vice-president's name in the byline, however, gives the guideline the required political clout and, in addition, ensures that the vice-president is involved with and committed to the policies.

Some organizations require that guidelines be "authorized" by the corporate officer with jurisdiction in this area. If possible, corporate guidelines on personal computing should be authorized at least by the company's chief operating officer or, if possible, the chief executive officer. This high-level signature gives wide credibility to the guidelines and provides the visible involvement and commitment of top managers.

Guideline 2.1: Objectives of the Personal Computing Program

Background

Companies have used computers in both administrative and engineering functions for many years. To manage computer-oriented activities properly, many have computer centers at corporate headquarters and remote locations. The remote centers are usually the responsibility of local management, although all centers are encouraged to follow defined standards and use systems which will allow data exchange among organizations. In addition, there is often functional/technical management at corporate headquarters which has the staff responsibility for coordinating the information systems efforts throughout the company, on a "dotted-line" basis.

Why are these guidelines needed? What has changed?

In recent years, two parallel technological breakthroughs have made it possible to consider making computing power available for personal use, in addition to the more-defined organizational uses. The first of these breakthroughs involves the individual use of "pieces" of larger computers through "time sharing." Low-cost terminals on people's desks give them the ability to use the larger computers to do work independent of how others are using the computer.

The second, more recent breakthrough is the development of low-cost, relatively powerful "personal computers." These are devices designed for use on individual desktops (some are even completely portable). Personal computers have made it economically feasible for millions of people to have a computer of their very own, either at their workplace or at their home, or both.

Complementing this development of personal computing "hardware" has been the development of computing "software," programs that allow people to use personal computing without knowing how to program and without requiring the services of a computer expert. These hardware and software technologies have created a phenomenon sometimes called "end-user computing," where people get their work done without the intervention of EDP professionals.

Purpose of corporate guidelines

The personal computing revolution has created vast opportunities . . . and potentially serious problems. Guidelines are needed so that the company can harness this potential while avoiding at least the most obvious pitfalls. As noted above, these guidelines create official recognition and sanction of this activity, a step that is needed for personal computing to become accepted in all areas of the company.

Responsibilities for personal computing

Responsibilities for personal computing lies with department managers. Managers are expected to mix the wisdom of the guidelines with business judgment, especially as rapidly changing technology offers new opportunities.

Some organizations may elect a more centrally controlled approach, requiring their managers to follow written guidelines explicitly. In these situations, the central policy writers will be challenged to keep current on both the changing needs in the company and how dynamic personal computing technology can best meet those needs. I prefer and recommend the more decentralized philosphy suggested in these guidelines.

Guideline maintenance

Because of the dynamic and individual nature of personal computing all employees should be encouraged to submit suggestions on how these guidelines may be improved.

Guideline distribution

Often, introductory, philosophical guidelines are buried with attention paid only to the more pragmatic, practical papers. The objectives and strategies, especially for personal computing, are too important to be ignored. Managers must understand the strategies and objectives when faced with situations not explicitly covered by the guidelines.

It is especially important that this first guideline, the objectives and strategies, be included with all distributions of any personal computing guidelines, not only when the guidelines are first written but also when they are distributed to employees who become interested in personal computing later.

Statements of guidelines

1. *Increase the productivity of individuals and the departments in which they work.*
2. *Focus on the basic purposes and functions of the business.*
3. *Encourage individual and group innovation.*
4. *Increase communication among employees.*
5. *Provide continuing security for company assets.*
6. *Use personal computing for business purposes, not for recreation or for non-company-related projects.*

Increase productivity—Personal computing can change the way individual tasks are accomplished and also the way in which those tasks weave together to accomplish the work of a group. The goal is to do more work and better work for the same or lower costs.

This objective stresses the need for productivity both for individuals and for the small groups in which they work. The measure is cost: better work for the same cost or the same work for lower costs. Another measure might be more work for only small increases in costs.

One typical scenerio is that personal computing raises costs in the short run as people learn the technology. When, however, the work load increases, personal computing allows the same number of people to handle the increased tasks.

Personal computing productivity is often best measured for a group rather than for an individual. Personal computing often allows jobs to be totally restructured, creating impressive synergy within small groups.

Focus on the basic purposes and functions of the business—In some cases, personal computing changes the way in which groups should be organized. This phenomenon is discussed extensively in Chapter 4. Managers should be prepared to make these changes based on an understanding of the fundamental functions of the business and with concern for the effects of these changes on the individuals involved as they relate to their internal and external customers.

Many of the functional divisions of work that are followed in companies result from the specialization of data or of computational skills inherent in manual tasks. Personal computing can break down these barriers. For example, certain accounts-payable operations might automatically be triggered by a receiving operation, without the intervention of additional people.

These new functional organizations can often be seen by listing the basic processes required of the business, regardless of size. All processes other than those listed are "overhead" costs which are subject to restructure when the technology permits. Many personnel, accounting, and quality assurance jobs are ripe for restructure, as are administrative tasks in line functions such as marketing and manufacturing and research/development (R & D).

It is also possible to increase greatly the productivity of line functions, although organizational restructuring may be less likely. Interestingly, personal computing may be most useful in increasing the performance of those people who are already very good, since (1) the range and impact of those people can be expanded, and (2) they may more readily take advantage of the new technology. Clearly, however, overall average productivity of a group may be increased through the consistency, accuracy, and speed offered by personal computing.

Encourage individual and group innovation—Personal computing gives people the tools to do tasks in ways limited only by their imaginations. Managers should help people set objectives that are consistent with those of the group. The company should also allow people to maximum freedom to accomplish those objectives in their own way.

All the improvements mentioned above are by-products of innovation. I believe that we achieve the best results when we help people set general goals and then give those people the freedom to achieve those goals in their own ways. We must, however, monitor the processes that people use and advise them on ways in which others have been successful so that overall group knowledge and practice continually rises.

Management by objectives existed, as a philosophy, long before the coming of personal computing. In some functions, large systems actually limited discretion because the work was structured and paced by the systems. Personal computing can return control to individuals so that each can best achieve the agreed-upon objectives.

Increase communication among employees—Two problems sometimes occur when people are given freedom to use their own methods: first, people may not know of better methods developed by others, and second, several people may be working on similar problems creating unnecessary duplication of efforts. Both these problems can be mitigated by publicizing the "best practices" which people have developed, to help people know what others are doing and to make known methods readily available to all. These methods may be publicized via newsletters and conferences where people can "show and tell." This communication creates information-based economies of scale and economies of knowledge that provides a competitive edge.

Communication is important, not only on methods, but on business topics as well. Personal computing can allow important information to flow more rapidly among people in the company so that all can work together to provide the best possible products and services to customers.

For example, personal computing can give people access to electronic mail and computer-readable files. This means that information can be sent to appropriate people faster and the information can be more timely and accurate. Further, the costs of maintaining the files can be reduced, since only one copy need be maintained, and that in electronic form. Also, the costs of copying, distributing, and filing all that paper can be significantly reduced.

Provide continuing security for company assets—It is important to accomplish the objectives shown above while maintaining security at least at the levels that existed before the use of personal computing. Personal computing creates types of assets new to the company; these include personal machine-readable data, personal programs, and related methods and documentation. It is appropriate to recognize, catalog, and protect these new assets.

Further, personal computing gives many more people the power to compromise traditional financial and material assets. Just as personal computing gives individuals leverage for business tasks, it also gives them the ability to do more mischief. Security is discussed more fully in later chapters.

Note, too, that the measure of effectiveness mentioned in the guideline is the level of security that existed *before* the use of personal computing. Personal computing should not be allowed to cause security to deteriorate; nor, however, will personal computing, by itself, improve weak security situations.

Use personal computing for business purposes, not for recreation or for non-company-related projects—This objective is especially important when justifying additional personal computing capabilities. Personal computing should not become merely the latest gadget or status symbol; managers should have a clear understanding of how the personal computing capability will be used before approving additional expenditures.

Because of all the publicity about personal computing and because of the "fast-track" image given by the media to personal computer users, personal computing can easily become a fad or a status symbol. Personal computing must be treated as a tool, a powerful tool, but one that is not appropriate for all situations and all people.

As noted above, I feel that it is the responsibility of department managers, with the best advice available, to decide where and for whom personal computing is appropriate.

This objective also implies that the justification for personal computing not consider its applicability to other aspects of the employees' lives. Recognize, however, that once employees have mastered personal computing for business uses, they will also use it for home uses and for work they do as volunteers for nonprofit organizations. Within limits, this is positive, because it allows employees to integrate personal computing into all aspects of their lives and usually be much more productive at work. Guidelines 2.3 talks more about nonbusiness uses of personal computing.

The use of games on business personal computing equipment raises similar questions. Within limits, games are probably positive: they help people overcome any shyness they may have with the equipment, they can be good training aids, they can provide constructive models for how useful business systems should look, and they can simply be a good way of taking a work break. Games are not, however, the reason for getting business personal computing, should not be considered in justifications, and should not be allowed to interfere with the basic work that needs to be accomplished.

CHECKLIST

Guideline 2.1
Objectives of the Personal Computing Program

	YES	NO	N/A
1. Is the focus of the personal computing program on increasing the productivity of individuals and the departments in which they work?			
2. Does the personal computing program focus on the basic purposes and functions of the business?			
3. Does the personal computing program encourage individual and group innovation?			
4. Does the personal computing program include features designed to increase communication among employees?			
5. Does the personal computing program include provisions that provide continuing security for company assets?			
6. Is the personal computing program justified, based on uses of personal computing for business purposes, and not for recreation or for non-company-related projects?			

Guidelines 2.2: Scope of Personal Computing Guidelines

Background

Until recently, computers were so expensive that they were restricted to centralized corporate or divisional use. In addition, the programming and the use of those computers was so complex that highly trained specialists were required to "translate" the business needs expressed by users into systems and programs that would run on the computers.

Because of the expense invested into these data processing resources, needs of individual users were often balanced with overall company efficiencies. Further, since EDP departments were usually cost centers, their budgets were set without regard to actual, varying business conditions. Both these limits often force users to wait long for services from busy EDP departments.

In addition, many companies have policies that prohibit users from purchasing EDP services from outside the company, from a commercial service company or software developer. This gives the company EDP department a virtual monopoly, but with cost limits in place, the EDP department has no way of filling the unrestricted demand.

All this is being changed. The first breakthrough was the development of low-cost terminals and software that allowed, through the terminal, individual use of pieces of large computers. Even more important, however, is the still evolving development of the low-cost, single-user "personal computer." As the costs of capable hardware decrease, software writers are developing programs which make that low-cost power accessible, not only by highly trained EDP experts, but also by those who are the business experts, the users.

This combination of low cost, high performance, ease of use, and small size gives us opportunities to transform the way we work in ways limited only by our imaginations, changing the way we work and the structure of the organizations in our companies.

Note, in particular, the factors listed in the foregoing paragraph. These factors are, to a large extent, the basic definition of personal computing; that is, personal computing occurs when computational and/or data processing equipment is (relatively speaking) low in cost, small in size, high in performance, and easy to use.

To the extent that one of these factors cannot be met, personal computing becomes compromised. For example, the "ease-of-use" factor has been the hardest to accomplish, primarily because the technology of software has not matched that of hardware. To compensate for this, these guidelines suggest the organization of "expert advisors," the Personal Computing Information Center (PCIC). As personal computing becomes sufficiently "friendly," this organization will change and will eventually disappear.

Purpose of this guideline

Given the evolution described above, it is important to define clearly the scope of these guidelines, to differentiate between the existing policies governing the large corporate and division EDP functions and "personal computing." Note that these definitions are purposely broad to allow for the maximum flexibility required as technology and applications rapidly change.

Guidelines are living documents

Personal computing users should be encouraged to share with others innovative applications of personal computing. One way of facilitating that sharing is to encourage people to contact the chief information manager (CIM) and the vice-president, administration so that guidelines on scope can be expanded. A request to hear about unusual applications serves two additional purposes: first, it emphasizes the ongoing interest and involvement of the CIM and the vice-president, administration; second, it clearly gives permission (and the implication of positive recognition) for innovative applications.

Statements of guidelines

1. *Personal computing is defined as the use of computing and data processing equipment by individuals (users), for their own purposes, without the intervention of computer experts.*
2. *If in doubt, it is preferable that situations be treated as "personal computing," governed, therefore, by personal computing guidelines.*
3. *Personal computing is usually considered an administrative tool, but these guidelines can be applied to all functional organizations, specifically including scientific and engineering personal computing and workstations used in operational activities such as manufacturing.*
4. *Portable and special-purpose computing and data processing tools are included in the definition of personal computing.*
5. *Having presented an extremely broad definition of personal computing, it is important that each manager apply these guidelines wisely, in ways appropriate to the situation.*

Note that this basic definition includes "computing and data processing equipment." The major differentiating feature is the ability for a user to function without intervention from an "expert," either programmer or operator.

At any moment in time, it is possible to specify, in a particular company, what "personal computing" is. Rapid changes in needs and technology outstrip the speed with which guidelines can adapt; therefore, the guidelines are generalized and are not equipment specific.

If in doubt, it is preferable that situations be treated as "personal computing," governed, therefore, by personal computing guidelines. This gives priority to personal computing guidelines over others, which, for example, may define traditional EDP.

Personal computing guidelines place significant authority squarely in the hands of user managers, while traditional policies usually give authority to the expert staff groups. The effect is to give users a powerful tool with which to negotiate with the staff groups. This may not sit well with staff groups, and the concept needs to be reviewed with all concerned.

Personal computing is usually considered an administrative tool, but these guidelines can be applied to all functional organizations, specifically including scientific and engineering personal computing and workstations used in operational activities such as manufacturing. Personal computing must *not* be considered synonymous with "office automation." Personal computing extends across all functional areas, for, in fact, many of the most profitable applications of personal computing are in operational areas.

Portable and special-purpose computing and data processing tools are included in the definition of personal computing.

These guidelines are applied to equipment regardless of the cost of the equipment; whether or not the equipment is classified as capital or expensed equipment by accounting policies is not relevent to the application of these personal computing guidelines. Clearly, small and portable computing tools increase the potential for individual uses, so that portable, transportable terminals, data collection devices, computers, and even some sophisticated calculators fall within these guidelines.

Portable computers can be applied to many organizational functions, but they are especially useful in work away from company facilities. Salespeople, for example, can use portable computers in a variety of ways:

- Insurance salespeople can evaluate and cost alternative plans together with the customers right in the customers' offices or homes.
- All salespeople can communicate with company central computers to receive quotations and/or to check on the status of previously placed orders.
- Salespeople can place orders and even receive confirmations while still working with a customer.
- Salespeople can complete administrative paperwork, such as expense reports and call reports, without returning to their office.

Other people can use portable computing also. Here are a few examples:

- Repair technicians, while working at a customer site, can communicate to company central computers for diagnostic and procedural assistance and can automatically process administrative transactions.
- Auditors and engineers working at field sites can use portable computers both for personal computation and for communication with larger company systems.
- Manufacturing people can use portable computers to follow specific projects in job-shop environments, where it may not be possible to place conventional terminals in fixed locations.

In absolute terms, some personal computing equipment can be quite expensive; if, however, it is appropriate when compared to alternative tools and is available for use without expert controls, the tool can be considered part of personal computing.

These guidelines can be applied to a wide variety of familiar office, laboratory, and production equipment, depending on how the equipment is used. Examples include "smart telephones," electronic typewriters, copiers, printers, plotters, micrographics equipment, electronic test equipment, and electronic measuring equipment.

At the other extreme of sophistication, these guidelines may also be applied to computing applications which link individuals together as part of a larger network. Examples imclude such things as electronic mail, information reference systems, electronic bulletin boards, and on-line phone directories.

These examples show the other end of the personal computing spectrum. There is no question that networks and communications require the involvement of experts. The operation of individual network nodes can, however, meet the requirements of personal computing. The best example of this is probably the telephone.

Having presented an extremely broad definition to personal computing, it is important that each manager apply these guidelines wisely, in ways appropriate to the situation. Common sense must be the foundation of all applications of guidelines in general, but such sense is particularly vital in the rapidly changing world of personal computing. Usually, the simplest applicable rules should be followed, especially with equipment clearly covered by several different guidelines. For example, if telephones are being used only for voice communication, it is probably incorrect to manage them under personal computing guidelines. When, however, telephone systems become part of data communication networks and are integrated with computational equipment, these guidelines should probably be applied.

CHECKLIST

Guideline 2.2
Scope of Personal Computing Guidelines

	YES	NO	N/A
1. Has personal computing been defined as the use of computing and data processing equipment by individuals (users), for their own purposes, without the intervention of computer experts?			
2. Do company policies provide that, when in doubt, it is preferable that situations be treated as "personal computing," governed, therefore, by personal computing guidelines, rather than conventional information systems policies?			
3. Are personal computing guidelines applied to all functional organizations, specifically including scientific and engineering personal computing and workstations used in operational activities such as manufacturing, as well as administrative and office functions?			
4. Have portable and special-purpose computing and data processing tools been included in the definition of personal computing?			
5. Having presented an extremely broad definition of personal computing, do the guidelines leave ultimate decisions in the hands of managers who are expected to apply these guidelines wisely, in ways appropriate to the situation?			

Guideline 2.3: Responsibilities for Personal Computing

Background

Definition of responsibilities for personal computing must specify the narrow path between anarchy and bureaucracy. The uses of personal computing must be structured to allow the company to function as one organization while still giving individuals the freedom to innovate.

Defining "standard responsibilities" runs the risk of implementing bureaucracy. Balancing coordinated activities with freedom to innovate is tough to achieve, but just the effort is usually extremely beneficial.

The benefits of designating responsibilities come mainly from having "champions" of personal computing to encourage people to accept and master the technology. Similarly, these responsible people can resolve disagreements and set standards which will enhance the benefits that an organization achieves, while minimizing the frustrations.

Purpose of this guideline

This guideline states who is responsible for the major aspects of the company's personal computing program. There are three areas of concern:

- Responsibility for business management of personal computing
- Responsibility for personal computing support functions
- Responsibility for administration of these guidelines

The third area of concern, administrative responsibilities for the guidelines, is almost mechanical. The first two topics, however, are consistent with and implement the strategies discussed in Guideline 2.2. First, the responsibilities for personal computing is granted to department (user) managers, and second, those managers are given the support they need to make personal computing successful.

Responsibility for business management of personal computing

1. *The responsibility for planning, operating, and controlling personal computing belongs to the managers of the departments in which personal computing is used.*
2. *Employees who wish to use personal computing and managers who approve purchases should carefully consider:*
   a. *The reasons for using personal computing*
   b. *Alternatives involved in personal computing*
   c. *Some of the potential negative consequences*

Personal computing in all areas of the company is incorporated into the business functions of the company. Therefore, it is appropriate that the managers who are generally responsible for the company's operations also take responsibility for personal computing.

In addition to responsibilities for the application of personal computing, department managers should be specifically responsible for the physical security of personal computing equipment and for the security of related programs and data. In exercising their responsibilities, managers should be guided by:

- The normal expense and capital authorization limits
- The advice provided in company guidelines

- The advice provided by the company's chief information manager (CIM) and the manager of the Personal Computing Information Center (PCIC)

All this advice is both useful and important and, under normal circumstances, should be followed. In case of doubt, however, the advice of the CIM may supersede the guidelines. The final responsibility for personal computing, however (as for all other functions), regardless of advice, lies with the department management.

Some department managers may have some difficulty in properly implementing their personal computing responsibilities. Planning and operating technical tools are functions familiar to many managers; personal computing adds some new challenges, but the differences are straightforward. Controls and security considerations, however, are new to almost everyone.

Therefore, advice should be provided. One form of advice is provided by the approved expense budget. Some companies set special, more relaxed expense limits in order to encourage personal computing implementation. I prefer a more strict approach, asking managers to meet their financial goals, making whatever trade-offs they choose, within the established, normal expense limits. In fact, a case could be made for holding managers to even tighter overall department expense limits (in the long run, at least), expecting that personal computing creates unbudgeted efficiencies.

Advice also comes from operating guidelines and from experts, inside or outside the company. The advice of people is generally more current and adaptive than that written into guidelines, but in the end, after all is read and heard, the department managers still bear responsibility for their own decisions.

Having said that, of course, decisions that are made contrary to the advice of guidelines or experts may involve political as well as technical considerations; since personal computing is new and not fully understood, its use often has high visibility. High visibility increases the opportunities for decisions to be made based on non-technical (but perhaps very valid) considerations.

Employees who wish to use personal computing and managers who approve purchases should carefully consider the reasons for using personal computing, alternatives involved in personal computing, and some of the potential negative consequences.

Situations appropriate for personal computing

- Where the work can be performed just as well or better and at lower cost by personal computing. The best examples of these applications are word processing, graphics, spreadsheets, and simple, frequently performed calculations (such as loan calculations in a finance department or mortgage calculations in a real estate office).
- Where the quality of the work performed will be improved by using personal computing. Improvements are usually in the areas of increased accuracy, increased consistency, and more rapid completion of the job. All these quality improvements usually also result in lower costs, since the work needed to correct errors is reduced.
- Truly personal applications, such as list keeping, calendars, and card files. (But see comments below about work better done manually.)
- Applications where personal computing can integrate tasks and enrich jobs. For example, in a construction office, one person can both calculate and prepare, in presentation form, complex bids using properly programmed personal computing systems.
- Where having a personal computer or terminal on people's desks gives them

access to company communication facilities. If communications is the only goal, the least expensive equipment that will meet the need should be chosen, unless the communications capability is the "bait" used to lure a reluctant employee into the world of personal computing.

These five reasons can be subjected to vigorous numerical justification or to subjective intuition. As with most other applications of computing/data processing, specific return-on-investment values are difficult to calculate and even more difficult to justify.

In spite of this, many serious mistakes can be avoided if, when an employee requests personal computing equipment, the manager asks two simple questions:

What do you plan to do with the personal computing equipment?

What are the alternatives for accomplishing the same business purposes?

Again, however, a balance must be struck. Employees should be asked to think about what they plan for the equipment, but the questions should not reinforce resistance to personal computing. Many people already have a natural concern about trying new tools; the justification process should be a filter, not a barrier.

Alternative solutions

Manual systems. The job is done with no automated help at all. This is a good alternative for one-time jobs, for jobs that have not yet been well defined, or for jobs that take only a short time to do manually. For example, simple calendar functions are usually much easier to do on paper forms.

Personal computing is a gentle form of automation, but it is automation nonetheless. Tasks which are not well defined or which are not repetitive may be difficult and uneconomical to automate. On the other hand, personal computing is useful for investigating system specifications when used as a tool for creating prototypes for conventional EDP applications.

Conventional EDP. The task is designed and programmed by the EDP department. This is a good alternative for jobs that affect multiple departments, affect significant company assets, or require a significant investment in design and programming. Conventional EDP is also considered when the job requires writing on or modifying a data base used by many departments.

It may be a serious mistake to assume that *all* automated tasks are best done with personal computing. Some of the situations that favor conventional EDP are shown above, but when in doubt, the best arbitrator is probably the CIM, who has responsibility for both conventional EDP and personal computing support.

Personal computer versus time sharing. Is the job done best by a stand-alone computer or by a terminal connected to a large, shared computer? Using the shared approach is appropriate when all personal computing users need the same programs, when many people need access to common data files, when there is great benefit in electronic communication among people (although local area networks, linking personal computers, could satisfy the communication requirement).

The choice between the two basic types of personal computing is technical, economic, and political. Technically, time-sharing systems are somewhat more intimidating. Users of terminals must abide by the protocols set by the central computer; having access to the central computer gives users great power but often at the cost of technical sophistication.

The use of stand-alone personal computers is indicated when there is a need for transportability or portability, when personal computers can, at reasonable cost, lighten the work of overloaded central computers, when the reliability inherent in having several personal computers available has advantages over the use of a single, shared computer.

From a technical standpoint, the best compromise is often a personal computer that is also attached to a central computer as a terminal. These so-called workstations give users access to the power and communication capabilities of "host" computers while allowing them the flexibility of a stand-alone computer. This versatility is usually, however, somewhat more expensive than an ordinary personal computer, and technical support must be provided for both personal computers and for time sharing. Personal computers, in general, are more expensive than terminals, especially for upkeep, if not for initial cost. They give, however, more flexibility and control to individuals.

Politically, using terminals and time sharing gives far greater control to central systems management. Individual terminals are also less susceptible than personal computers to many of the negative consequences discussed below. Note, however, that even when effective time sharing for personal comput*ing* is provided, personal comput*ers* will inevitably begin to appear, as portables, as "loaners from home," or as "holdovers" from college. Forbidding them will, at best, drive them underground.

Multiuser personal computers versus stand-alone systems.   When several terminals are hooked to a single central processing unit (CPU), regardless of the size or cost of that CPU, the CPU is considered a "host" system and is controlled by normal EDP guidelines (even though the terminals may represent personal computing).

Connecting personal computers via networks are, however, considered personal computing (see Part II). This distinction is made because of the need for sophistication and control needed by host systems. Networks, of course, require similar sophistication and controls, but the individual computers can, when appropriate, operate independently.

Attaching terminals to a computer requires that ("host") computer to have systems software and technical management to provide adequate time-sharing capabilities. This is true regardless of the size and cost of the host. In fact, small, inexpensive hosts are often more difficult to manage because they lack some of the sophisticated programs and hardware features available on computers designed for time sharing. Multiuser systems can sometimes be justified if they are dedicated to a specific purpose; examples include inquiries against a common file or shared data-entry systems.

A more flexible solution is communication between several "equal" personal computers through networks; such a network is called a "peer" network. In their simplest form, these networks can be linked with telephone lines, with each node containing a device allowing the node to connect to the line. This device is called a "modulator-demodulator" or "modem" for short, and often requires that users dial the telephone number of another node to establish the connection with that node.

More powerful systems, called "local-area networks," allow direct communication among computing applications within a building or on an academic or industrial campus. In addition, broadband (e.g., ×.25) communication allows efficient systems linkages even among remote locations. All of this is discussed more fully in Part II.

Potential negative consequences

Creeping costs.   The costs of personal computing for any individual far exceed the initial cost of the hardware and software. The costs of additional software, additional peripheral equipment, supplies, reference texts, and training aids may accumulate over time to significant amounts; the initial purchase is the "razor," while these future costs are the "blades."

These additional costs are very hard to track and control because the incremental amounts are very small (and can be authorized by the lowest-level managers) and because they are "buried" in accounting records as "supplies" or "miscellaneous expensed equipment." The costs that add up most quickly are those for software. Typical prices are below $500 and can add up rapidly. The real key is to keep track of these costs. Probably the best way is to motivate your accounting department to establish an account code for software so that all charges can be accumulated and reported. Then the only hole is the petty-cash system, and most software costs more than petty cash will allow.

Books are rarely a problem, since even the most avid reader will be hard-pressed to spend more than a few hundred dollars per year, and, even at that, books can be and usually are shared wih other employees.

Magazine subscriptions give few problems for the same reasons; in addition, many magazines are free to qualified subscribers. On the other hand, since magazines make money by selling their subscription list, magazine subscriptions generate incredible amounts of unrequested junk mail, often duplicates, since vendors mail to subscribers from several magazines. All this junk mail can create a substantial load on a company's mailroom. It may make sense, therefore, to have policies such as these:

- Have magazines (and, therefore, junk mail) mailed only to home addresses.
- Insist that employees request that publications not place their names on lists sold to others.
- Have mailrooms deliver only mail (other than magazines) with first-class postage.

I generally view financial controls over publications as pennywise but pound foolish. Employees eager enough to read are acquiring very inexpensive training. Similarly, allowing them to manage these relatively inexpensive items communicates an interest in their development and trust in their judgment. The cost of losing and replacing even one professional will offset any savings gained on publications for years to come.

Formal training can be quite expensive but is also quite visible, since the employee usually needs time to attend the classes or seminars. Besides the costs of training, care must be taken to assure equity among employees, since training is often considered a privilege.

The point of all this is *not* to encourage you to deny these resources to your employees; in fact, these expenses are usually very justifiable. These resources are, however, costly, and therefore, must be anticipated and managed.

Making "programmers" out of "business people." Some personal computing users become so fascinated by this tool that they spend their time writing or modifying programs rather than focusing on their job. Having access to personal computing can encourage even the most antitechnical employee to become an amateur programmer. Usually, any "playing" on company time passes quickly and probably will improve the ability of the employee to use personal computing productively.

Some users, however, suffer from a more sustained preoccupation as software experimenters. They have a compulsion to try any packages which they find, whether or not the packages pertain immediately to business use of personal computing. Again, some of this play is probably healthy, but too much may offset any productivity gains expected and may even cause resentment from other employees who feel that the personal computing users are "getting away with something." If the problem persists, some management counseling is probably appropriate.

Employee fear.   Personal computing can cause two types of concerns to employees. First they may suddenly feel inadequate. Many may have felt successful using older methods but fear that they will never master the new technologies. Second, other employees may fear that their job will be eliminated, and even if their employment is guaranteed, they fear that their careers will be damaged when they are thrust into unfamiliar tasks.

Of the two types of fears mentioned, the first, the fear of being unable to master the new technology, is easier to deal with. The personal computing work can be presented as a growth opportunity, and the training provided, accompanied by strong support from the employees' supervisors will usually quiet the concerns.

The fear of unemployment or, at the least, of job displacement is a more difficult issue. The circumstances will vary greatly depending on the company, on the types of employee relations that have existed in the past, and, most of all, on the individual employee. If unions represent part of the work force, their contract terms will also be a consideration.

In general, I feel that open communication is probably the most effective strategy. If employees will be asked to change jobs, make that known and support the change with training and whatever other assistance is appropriate. Immediate reductions in staff are rarely caused by the use of personal computing.

On the other hand, it is quite fair to expect that the existing employees can cope with additional growth and that new employees need not be added as rapidly as may have been needed before. Similarly, employees who leave the company in the course of normal attrition may not need to be replaced.

Status symbols.   Once one person in a group gets a personal computer or terminal, there is great pressure to get others for everyone, regardless of the legitimate need. The desire to participate in personal computing for status reasons has both good and bad facets. The positive aspect is that this desire may facilitate the implementation of personal computing. The desire for status may overcome any fear of computing or resistance to change. On the other hand, personal computing status symbols may go to the wrong people, leaving fewer resources for more appropriate users.

Status also becomes an issue with regard to the latest equipment. People may want the latest piece of hardware or software without regard to their actual need. This creates "premature obsolescence" of existing equipment and not only needlessly spends company funds but also creates unneeded training and support costs for the new equipment. Sometimes people order software and never remove the product from its protective shrink wrapping. The most effective way of dealing with this issue is to consistently follow the established justification and audit procedures.

Control problems.   Personal computing can make good people more productive; it can also increase the power of anyone bent on mischief. Stories of computer crime and computer criminals are well known; there is no question that the potential for mischief is serious and must be considered.

There are essentially two approaches to these problems, both discussed more fully in later chapters. First are technical solutions such as passwords, monitors, logs, locks, and encryption. The other approach is sociological and, as such, is no different than control problems in nonpersonal computing situations. Control can best achieved by hiring honest employees, by managing them fairly, and by organizing so that any problems that do occur are found quickly and localized.

Some combination of these approaches is usually best, with the emphasis placed depending on the company's culture. More formal, structured, centralized companies probably lean toward technical measures, while companies with less formal structure and more decentralized management can probably take advantage of sociological solutions.

Legal liabilities. Use of personal computing presents a unique set of legal liabilities. One problem is centered around the easy duplication of proprietary software. If an employee, using company funds, or reimbursed by the company for a purchase, violates the software copyright, the company may become liable for resulting damages.

Another type of problem can be unauthorized generation of official company documents. For example, a stock broker could generate an official-looking research report without the knowledge of the appropriate managers. A misled client could easily sue the brokerage firm for damages. This type of problem is really a control issue, discussed more fully later.

The proprietary software issue is far more common. The basic rule should be that all employees are expected to obey the law with regard to the appropriate use of proprietary software packages and all managers are responsible for assuring proper conduct. In addition, when personal computing hardware is purchased either from the Personal Computing Information Center or through normal purchasing channels, the buyer should be asked to specify what software will be used with the hardware.

The company's internal audit staff might also conduct random audits of personal computing users to verify that software is being used legally.

Unless special agreements are negotiated (see the discussion of site agreements below), personal computing packages are sold for use on only one specific computer. Some vendors state that their software can be used only on one computer at a time, but that the software can be moved from computer to computer, as needed.

The problem is that the software is usually easy to copy with no trace or trail, at minimal cost. Because it is easy, software "pirating" is considered to be widespread, and some software vendors are suing large companies for violation of the software copyright.

Actual enforcement methods will vary greatly depending on the company, but the minimum measures are those shown in the guideline: use of random audit and checks to see that software is purchased along with hardware. Neither of these is foolproof, however, and management attitude is probably the most critical element. If managers "wink" at software copyright violations or if they are unreasonable when authorizing the purchase of copies of software for each user, you can be sure that software piracy will take place.

Systems management concerns. The personal computing users must take responsibility for all sorts of technical concerns which are usually handled by data processing professionals in conventional EDP facilities. These concerns include such things as making backup copies of files, maintaining security, using operating systems and utility software, and dealing with hardware and software failures.

One of the clear benefits of personal computing via time sharing rather than through the use of a personal computer is that, when time sharing, it is usually economical to have a dedicated, competent "system manager" who is responsible for hardware and system software maintenance, for security, for solving technical problems, for making backup copies of files, and so on. Even then, users must usually take responsibility for what they do in their own accounts.

When dealing with stand-alone personal computers, *all* the technical responsibilities fall to the users. Granted, the problems are usually considerably less complex than those faced by multiuser computers, and if one computer "breaks," it is possible to just borrow another. Technical advice can also be provided by the Personal Computing Information Center.

In either case, personal computing users must learn more about some arcane subjects than they had anticipated; and this situation should be considered when implementating personal computing. The problem is most acute in organizations where the technical aptitude of the workers is low, and the turnover is very high, for example, nonprofit organizations, small retail stores, and fast-food stores. If automation is appropriate for these types of organizations, it is best provided by highly specialized systems which *decrease* rather than increase user flexibility.

Ways of mitigating all these concerns are discussed elsewhere, but they should be considered from conservative viewpoints while reviewing personal computing justification.

Having considered all these positive reasons, alternatives, and potential negative concerns, individual department managers must decide whether personal computing is appropriate for their employees, whether the potential benefits from personal computing outweighs the potential problems. Department managers should get the best technical advice available, but the decisions are too critical to be left to the technicians. See Guideline 2.4 for ways in which the Personal Computing Information Center can assist with the justification and evaluation of personal computing applications.

Implementation suggestions—By now, it is, hopefully, clear that personal computing is no panacea, and has the potential of causing significant problems. As you proceed, I suggest these steps:

- Read and understand the guidelines offered in this book. Tailor them for your organization, implement them, and follow up to be sure that they are being used.
- Go slowly. Try personal computing first in a pilot organization. Analyze the experiment and adjust additional implementations to take advantage of what is learned from the pilots.
- Learn from "bootleg" personal computing activities. Personal computing is so pervasive that it is impossible to completely deny your employees access to it, but you can learn from these "nonauthorized" uses and channel future activities.
- Especially at first, at the beginning of the Sanction period, plan to provide as much support as is economically possible; except from an economic viewpoint, it will be almost impossible to offer more than the users need. For the first year, perhaps two, treat personal computing support costs as an investment. After personal computing becomes more fully established, normal economic justification procedures can be and should be applied.

Rights of possession versus rights of ownership

3. *Personal computing equipment, even though used by individual employees, officially belongs to the department in which the employee works.*
4. *All data developed by personal computing belong to the company and are subject to the same rules of control, security, and records retention as are company data developed in any other automated or manual manner.*

Whenever an employee transfers to another department, the personal computing equipment should remain behind unless the managers involved make specific arrangements for a transfer following the asset transfer rules set by accounting.

When employees work with tools assigned specifically to them, they soon feel a sense of personal ownership. This is true of a mechanic's wrenches, a photographer's camera, a chef's knives, and is certainly true of personal computing equipment. When the employee moves on, these is a natural desire to take along those familiar tools.

The written rule should take the most conservative, restrictive viewpoint; as shown in the guideline, the "real" owners of the tools are the departments that paid for them, and the departments have the "legal" right to keep them, even as individual users transfer. In actual practice, however, whether or not to allow employees to take their personal tools when they leave requires decisions that are best left to the discretion of department managers; consistency is desirable, but the actual circumstances usually vary so much that each requires separate thought. For example, if an employee leaves to join a competitor, you most certainly will deny transfer privileges. If, however, an accountant transfers to another accounting department inside your company, you might very well allow the equipment to go also.

The specific decision is also dependent on whether or not the equipment will be used after the employee leaves. If the equipment will sit idle, you might feel more generous about allowing the transfer, since you will not incur the expense of replacing the equipment.

Sometimes, the reverse situation occurs: transferring employees do not want to take equipment, and the department wants them to take it. This usually happens when the equipment is slightly obsolete, and whoever orders new equipment will receive an updated (often less expensive) version. In this case, the equipment should remain with the legal owner, the department, unless other arrangements are negotiated.

Although all the examples given above imply hardware, remember that these comments apply to software also (remember that software is included in the definition of "equipment"). If you allow a software package to transfer, you may need to purchase a new copy if you still need that software after the employee leaves. Making copies for use by both the transferring employees and the departments they leave usually violates the software copyright and license agreements and is, therefore, illegal.

All data developed by personal computing belong to the company and is subject to the same rules of control, security, and records retention as are company data developed in any other automated or manual manner. Whereas there is much room for discretion in the transfer of equipment, there is none in the transfer of data. Files of data, whether in human- or machine-readable form, belong to the company and the department and should be kept, used, or stored as required by the company's records retention policies.

Ownership of employee-written software

5. *Software written by employees belongs to the company if **any** of the following conditions apply:*
   a. *The software was written using company resources or equipment.*
   b. *The software was written during the employee-author's normal working hours.*
   c. *The software is useful for the company's business functions.*

The question then arises as to the ownership of software to which one of the conditions apply. Note that, most often, if none of the conditions above are met, the company will probably not even "officially" know that the software exists; actual knowledge will be obtained becuase the employee in some way tells others in the company about the software.

There are several alternatives, but two seem most appropriate. First, the company can simply ignore the situation. The software simply belongs to the employee-authors; the benefits, costs, responsibilities, and potential liabilities are all theirs. Even with this seemingly simple approach, the company should state this as policy so that neither the employee-authors nor their customers for the software have any different expectations.

Under the second approach, software written by employees on their own time, on their own equipment, and on applications apart from the company's business belongs jointly to the employee and the company. Under this joint ownership structure, the company may implement the software for internal use only with no royalty payments to the employee-author; all other rights and liabilities associated with the software, including the right to market the software outside the company, belong solely to the employee-author.

There is a temptation to take a very strict line and say that any software written by the employee, at any time, on any equipment, when in the employ of the company belongs to the company. Such a hard line may not be appropriate because:

- The position may not be legally enforceable (or may require expensive litigation to enforce).
- Valuable, creative employees may resent unfair infringement of the company into what they consider to be their private affairs.
- For the company to take advantage of the latent value of the software may be unreasonably expensive, especially if the company is not in the business of marketing software and/or has no obvious use for the software in this normal business.
- A software vendor, as does any vendor, takes on certain legal liabilities for the maintenance of the product, for its fitness for use, and for certain damages that a customer might incur in the use of the product. A company might not be anxious to face these responsibilities in areas removed from its normal business.

A guideline such as the one suggested might well take a strong, company-biased position. I strongly advise, however, that if your company owns employee-written software (by virtue of this guideline) and you have no use for or interest in the software, you give the employee ownership of the software in return for the employee assuming all costs and potential liabilities for the software.

For example, assume that an accountant working for a real-estate development company uses the company-provided personal computer to write, on personal time, a program for commodity speculation. Under the guidelines, the company would own the software, but it would be sensible for the company to sell the ownership rights and liabilities to the employee for a nominal sum.

Responsibilities for support functions

6. *The chief information manager (CIM) is responsible for establishing a Personal Computing Information Center (PCIC), which, in turn, is responsible for providing personal computing support to users.*

To maximize the potential inherent in personal computing requires significant technical support, far beyond that available in most departments of the company. The CIM is charged with the responsibility for providing appropriate support. The CIM provides this support through the Personal Computing Information Center (PCIC), which reports to the CIM. This short paragraph simply introduces the

PCIC as the primary company support mechanism for personal computing. Guideline 2.4 is devoted to details of the PCIC.

A good PCIC will probably guarantee the effective implementation of personal computing; it is, however, an investment that some companies may be unable to make. Here are some lower-cost (but probably less effective) alternatives:

- Assign PCIC responsibilities to the normal EDP development people. The drawback to this is that these people are already overworked, with a huge backlog of projects, and have a sufficiently difficult time keeping up with changes in information systems technology. Since each personal computing application is, by itself, a relatively tiny project, personal computing users will probably not get the warm attention they need. Further, the information systems people may have difficulty in keeping up with the extremely rapid changes in personal computing technology. Finally, information systems people, familiar with the economies of scale inherent in large systems, may be unable to encourage or appreciate the benefits of personal computing.

- Ask a local computer store to act as the PCIC, both for a retainer and for the profits it will generate by providing your company with personal computing equipment. The limitations here are relatively obvious and derive from the fact that the interests of the computer store people may diverge from those of your company. They may push equipment which gives them a higher profit rather than that best suited to your needs. Further, their people are less likely to really know or appreciate your internal organizational considerations and priorities, especially where geograhically remote locations are involved. The store people are also less likely to coordinate personal computing activities with those of conventional EDP.

In spite of these problems, using a store as the PCIC may be satisfactory for a small company or may be a good temporary solution while personal computing policy is evolving.

Administrative responsibilities

7. *The PCIC is responsible for establishing, distributing, and maintaining personal computing guidelines.*
8. *Local managers may authorize exceptions to corporate guidelines and may, in fact, issue local guidelines that supersede corporate guidelines.*

Guideline maintenance—Because of the dynamics of personal computing technology, guidelines should probably be reviewed semiannually and revised as necessary. All employees should be urged to suggest additions and modifications to these personal computing guidelines. The suggestions should generally be sent to the manager of the Personal Computing Information Center (PCIC).

Guideline distribution—To accomplish their purpose, guidelines must be read. The only limitation on distribution should be cost, and again, remember that the publication of these guidelines is really a very small part of the overall investment needed to promulgate personal computing.

The initial distribution is usually to all managers in the company who have authority, as shown in general accounting records, to buy capital equipment or who can sign for expenditures of $1000 or more. Guidelines are also issued to all members of the company's information systems departments.

After the initial distribution, simply give guidelines to employees who request or approve requests for personal computing equipment and also to anyone likely to give advice regarding personal computing. If the implementation of personal computing is accomplished by department or by geographic entity, these guidelines might appropriately be distributed and reviewed at the personal computing orientation or "kickoff" meeting. The guideline distribution is controlled by the PCIC. The PCIC maintains a list of all guidelines holders for use in distributing modification releases and for use in PCIC communication activities.

Note that the assumption in all of this is that personal computing guidelines will be in "hard-copy" (paper) form. As personal computing becomes widely used, it may be much more efficient to distribute both the guidelines and revisions in electronic form, either on "floppy" disks or via electronic mail or networks. Electronic distribution, in addition to being rapid and cost-effective, also allows updates to occur more frequently. On electronic media, as in paper form, specific subjects can be quickly located using indexes. In addition, on electronic media, searches can often be made simply by scanning for key words or phrases.

Personal computing guidelines are generally not confidential, and distribution is not restricted in any way; in fact, wide distribution is encouraged to increase compliance. On the other hand, people who really do not need the guidelines should not request the guidelines or should ask the manager, PCIC to remove them from the distribution list just to save the company the cost of copying and distributing unneeded paper.

In some companies, policy manuals are controlled, with a specific numbered copy assigned to specific individuals. This does not seem necessary with personal computing guidelines. The PCIC wants to know who has copies only so that updates and announcements will reach interested people.

Guideline authorization—Personal computing guidelines should be authorized by someone with appropriate influence and credibility. A high-level authorizer also demonstrates the commitment and involvement of top management.

Local managers may authorize exceptions to corporate guidelines and may, in fact, issue local guidelines that supersede corporate guidelines. These exceptions and local guidelines should be issued in writing and a copy of the exception or local guideline should be sent to the CIM as soon as possible, before the local guidelines are published, if practical.

The wording of this last guideline strongly implements decentralized control over personal computing. It allows local managers to supersede these guidelines, requiring only that the CIM be notified, possibly after the exceptions have been implemented. The CIM may be able to deal with any potential problems only retroactively.

Stronger provisions, giving more centralized control, are easy to draft, if desired. Here are some alternatives, in order of increasing strictness:

- Exceptions can be allowed but must be approved by the CIM before they are implemented.
- No exceptions are allowed, but the CIM may approve special provisions for specific departments within the text of the company-wide guidelines.
- No exceptions are allowed and all departments and divisions must follow the same guidelines.

CHECKLIST

Guideline 2.3
Responsibilities for Personal Computing

	YES	NO	N/A

1. Have the responsibilities for planning, operating, and controlling personal computing been assigned to the managers of the departments in which personal computing is used?

2. Do employees who wish to use personal computing and managers who approve purchases carefully consider:
   a. The reasons for using personal computing?
   b. Alternatives involved in personal computing?
   c. Some of the potential negative consequences?

3. Does personal computing equipment, even though used by individual employees, officially belong to the department in which the employee works?

4. Does all data developed by personal computing belong to the company, subject to the same rules of control, security, and records retention as are company data developed in any other automated or manual manner?

5. Do the personal computing guidelines state that software written by employees belongs to the company if any of the following conditions apply:
   a. The software was written using company resources or equipment?
   b. The software was written during the employee-author's normal working hours?
   c. The software is useful for the company's business functions?

6. Is the chief information manager responsible for establishing a Personal Computing Information Center (PCIC), which, in turn, is responsible for providing personal computing support to users?

7. Is the PCIC responsible for establishing, distributing, and maintaining personal computing guidelines?

8. May local managers authorize exceptions to corporate guidelines and, in fact, issue local guidelines that supersede corporate guidelines?

CHECKLIST

Guideline 2.3 (continued)
Justification for Personal Computing

	YES	NO	N/A

Situations Appropriate for Personal Computing

1. Can the work be performed just as well or better and at lower cost by personal computing?

2. Will the quality of the work performed be improved by using personal computing?

3. Are these truly personal applications such as list keeping, calendars, and card files?

4. Are these applications where personal computing can integrate tasks and enrich jobs?

5. Will personal computers or terminals on people's desks give them access to company communication facilities?

Alternatives Solutions
Have these alternative solutions been considered?

6. Manual systems

7. Conventional EDP

8. Personal computer versus time sharing

9. Multiuser personal computers versus stand-alone systems

Potential Negative Consequences
Have these potential negative consequences been considered?

10. Creeping costs

11. Making "programmers" out of "business people"

12. Employee fear

13. Status symbols

14. Control problems

15. Legal liabilities

16. Systems management concerns

39

©1988 by Prentice Hall, A Division of Simon & Schuster Inc., Englewood Cliffs, NJ 07632

Guideline 2.4: Guidelines for the Personal Computing Information Center

Background

As noted above, in the discussion of Guideline 2.3, the technical support required to realize the potential of personal computing exceeds the capabilities of most departments in the company. This necessary support is provided, ideally, by an organization, reporting to the chief information manager (CIM), called the Personal Computing Information Center (PCIC).

The PCIC provides the structure to both control and promulgate the use of personal computing in efficient and economic ways. In addition, the PCIC is expected to provide guidance with the flexibility and responsiveness to technical change that cannot be achieved with written guidelines.

Purpose of this guideline

This guideline outlines goals for the PCIC and the types of functions it provides. This list of functions is not exhaustive; the PCIC is expected to continue to evolve and offer services appropriate to both the technology and to the needs of their users (the other departments in the company) as technology and needs change.

PCIC organization

1. *The PCIC reports to the CIM; it is part of the company's EDP organization but is separate from the other development and operations groups in EDP (see Figure 2.1).*
2. *To assist the PCIC in fulfilling its purposes and functions, and to assist the CIM in managing the PCIC, a PCIC steering committee is appointed.*
3. *Within the first month of each fiscal year, the PCIC steering committee publishes a report showing the effectiveness of the PCIC during the previous fiscal year.*
4. *As the work load demands, and as economic considerations permit, PCIC representatives are located in divisions and sales administration offices. These representatives are administered directly by local EDP managers with a functional "dotted line" to the manager, PCIC.*

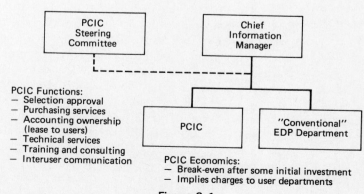

Figure 2.1

The CIM is responsible for all EDP activities in the company, and personal computing, while having some unique properties, has much in common with conventional EDP. Of equal importance, personal computing and conventional EDP must be coordinated for the company to obtain maximum benefits. The best compromise, then, to balance the need for coordination with the need for specialization is to have the PCIC separate from the conventional EDP organization, but also reporting to the CIM.

To assist the PCIC in fulfilling its purposes and functions, and to assist the CIM in managing the PCIC, a PCIC steering committee is appointed. The steering committee should be appointed by the company's highest-ranking administrative officer and should consist of the CIM, the manager, PCIC, plus at least five and no more than nine user representatives. The steering committee should meet at least quarterly to provide advice to the CIM on PCIC functions. The CIM is chair of the committee. The company's administrative officer should periodically rotate users assigned to the committee and fill any vacancies that may arise.

The functions of the PCIC are set so that, among other things, the PCIC has some of the characteristics of a stand-alone business. This should help give the PCIC a healthy market orientation and make it more responsive to users' changing needs. There are, however, several major differences. First, the PCIC has certain specified functions, designed for the good of the overall company, not necessarily for the good of the PCIC. Further, the PCIC has a virtual monopoly on the company's personal computing business and can, therefore, adopt practices that a stand-alone business might find uncompetitive.

To achieve the appropriate user orientation under these circumstances, a steering committee is appointed. While the steering committee is chaired by the CIM and the manager of the PCIC is also on the committee, the bulk of the committee consists of user representatives. These representatives are rotated periodically so that viewpoints remain fresh and objective.

Within the first month of each fiscal year, the PCIC steering committee publishes a report showing the effectiveness of the PCIC during the previous fiscal year.

This requirement for an annual report is a way of encouraging the PCIC to maintain high, public visibility. The annual report will certainly be read by the top managers and by the user community. The requirement for writing the report will also be an incentive to the steering committee to maintain positive control over the PCIC.

As work load demands and as economic considerations permit, PCIC representatives are located in divisions and sales administration offices. These representatives are directly administered by local EDP managers with a functional "dotted line" to the manager, PCIC.

The PCIC is able to provide support for personal computing functions for the geographic site on which it is located. Services to remote sites are provided by mail with traveling consultants, telephone hot lines, and similar services.

As needs increase, however, it may be appropriate and economically feasible to locate "satellite" PCICs at remote locations. These may begin with one or two representatives trained at the first PCIC and eventually evolve to full service facilities.

As the remote sites grow, however, the management principles should remain constant. The remote PCIC representatives should be administratively managed by the local EDP managers or if there are no EDP managers, by some other appropriate manager.

Functional responsibility, however, rests with the manager of the central

PCIC, to assure high-quality, consistent, and coordinated services to the remote sites. Further, since the PCIC steering committee helps manage the central PCIC, it also shares in the functional responsibility of the remote services.

Goals of the PCIC

5. *The basic goal of the PCIC is to help its users (departments in the company) achieve the personal computing objectives and strategies described in Guideline 2.1.*
6. *The PCIC uses economic incentives, technical advice, education, training, and persuasion rather than formal authority to achieve its goals.*

The PCIC achieves the first goal by helping people in the company better understand and use personal computing and by using standards, guidelines, and economies of scale to maximize cost-effectiveness. The PCIC also has an obligation to company management to balance the unconditional use of personal computing with appropriate considerations of efficiency, effectiveness, and economy.

These general statements emphasize the balance that the PCIC must strike between helping employees and their departments with the needs of the company. The balance is between flexibility and efficiency, individuality, and economies of scale. It is a narrow line to walk. Further, since much of the power of personal computing lies in communication between people, the PCIC is responsible for coordinating personal computing communication, especially with regard to interaction with other data processing, computing, and communication activities in the company.

As the technology becomes economically available, the PCIC is also responsible for integrating personal computing with audio and video telecommunications. Communication, as used here, has two meanings. The first is communication in the media sense, transferrring information among people in traditional forms such as newsletters and training. The PCIC has some important responsibilities in communicating information about personal computing to users and also among them, in order to share good ideas.

The second meaning refers to electronic communication, usually data communication. The primary responsibilities for data communication do not belong to the PCIC; they belong to other departments inside EDP. The PCIC is responsible, however, for the coordination of personal computing activities with data communication technology. The PCIC links its customer-users with the data communication specialists.

In some cases, the two meanings blend, with interpersonal communication taking place over electronic media. Training can be interactive via personal computing; newsletters can be distributed via electronic mail; reference material can be studied via videotext.

The PCIC uses economic incentives, technical advice, education, training, and persuasion to achieve its goals; it is a staff organization and does not have direct authority over functions of user departments. The PCIC will therefore succeed only if users want to do business with it. The PCIC must offer the products and services wanted by users at prices that are competitive to alternative sources. This "free-market" approach gives an entrepreneural flavor to PCIC operations and gives the customer-users real value. In fact, of course, as mentioned in the discussion about the steering committee above, neither the PCIC nor the users operate in a true free market, but even an attempt at free-market activities is better than falling back to pure bureaucratic operations.

Responsibilities of the PCIC

7. *The PCIC performs the functions stated below; the list is a guide. The actual functions change from time to time as determined by the CIM; the manager, PCIC; and the PCIC steering committee:*
   a. *Equipment selection*
   b. *Purchasing personal computing equipment*
   c. *Marketing personal computing services*
   d. *Application justification and evaluation*
   e. *Equipment support*
   f. *Training and consulting services*
   g. *Accounting and inventory control*
   h. *Pricing arrangements for users*
   i. *Self-sufficient operations*
   j. *Standardization*
   k. *Management of purchases for employees' personal use*
   l. *Management of obsolete equipment*

Equipment selection—The PCIC establishes both Recommended and Approved lists of hardware and software used in the company. Recommended Equipment (the term "equipment" is used in these guidelines to include hardware, software, and related materials and supplies) is that with which the PCIC has favorable experience and which fits into the company's personal computing strategy and standards. The PCIC provides its full range of services only for Recommended Equipment.

Approved Equipment is that which the PCIC feels will work well in some applications or situations, but may have more limited or specialized uses than does Recommended Equipment. The Approved list may also show equipment which looks good on paper but with which the PCIC has insufficient experience. Another use for the Approved list is for obsolescent equipment which is gradually being replaced in the company with newer, Recommended Equipment. Users of Approved Equipment must generally provide their own support, since the PCIC provides limited or no services for Approved Equipment.

The PCIC may also designate certain hardware or software as "not recommended" if the PCIC has negative experiences or references. Users are strongly urged not to use equipment on the Not-Recommended list. The PCIC updates these lists whenever appropriate, but the goal is to balance technical sophistication with the benefits of consistency and standardization.

By maintaining a list of equipment appropriate for the company, the PCIC can achieve some form of economies of scale while allowing degrees of freedom, especially in the use of the equipment. Also, the PCIC can become knowledgeable in the equipment it recommends. Obviously, the trick is to offer enough of a variety on the recommended list to satisfy most user needs, while keeping the list manageably small.

The Approved list is a halfway point for equipment. It is a place to put promising equipment whose value is yet to be established, and also may be a home for obsolescent equipment which is still used only by those not yet converted to something new.

The Not-Recommended list is crucial. This list is a specific warning to users. Users who purchase "not recommended" equipment should be subject to organizational criticism.

In the rapidly changing world of personal computing, there is also an infinitely long "nonlist" of equipment about which the PCIC has no comment, usually because it has never heard of it. It is appropriate for users to bring attractive-sounding equipment to the attention of the PCIC in hopes that the equipment will work its way to Recommended status.

Purchasing personal computing equipment—The PCIC, working with the company purchasing department, negotiates with manufacturers and dealers for the most favorable price and terms for Recommended Equipment. At the discretion of its manager, the PCIC may elect to maintain an inventory of Recommended Equipment; the decision to maintain inventory is based on volume pricing and delivery-time considerations. Whenever possible, such inventory is on consignment, so that the company's funds are not spent until needed.

In performing these functions, the PCIC takes on the characteristics of an in-house computer store. In fact, the PCIC can actually enter into dealership arrangements with vendors and wholesalers so that the PCIC can offer full services and favorable prices to its customer-users.

Under these circumstances, users "purchase" equipment, as needed, from the PCIC using the company's internal transfer system. The PCIC, in turn, actually purchases the equipment from appropriate sources in economical lots or through blanket purchase agreements. Most companies would be well advised to assign an experienced buyer from the company purchasing department to assist the PCIC in the negotiation of these arrangements.

Ideally, of course, the PCIC would not tie up the company's assets in personal computing inventory, but as with any retail operation, a trade-off must be made between offering "off-the-shelf" service by carrying inventory versus carrying no inventory and having to wait for deliveries. An excellent compromise, where appropriate, is to have the equipment in stock on consignment. In any case, the PCIC should negotiate the right to return unused equipment to the vendor if it has not "sold" internally after a designated period.

The most logical alternative to this arrangement is to have agreements with local computer stores to offer similar purchasing services. This certainly lowers the financial commitment involved in the PCIC, but also reduces the control that the PCIC can exercise in promoting standards and consistency and in enforcing reasonable justifications.

If a noncompany retail store is used, it is important that the PCIC receive from the store complete information about the transaction so that the PCIC can follow-up with the appropriate support services. The best way of assuring this is to require that users have the PCIC countersign the purchase request so that the PCIC knows about the transaction as it is occurring and can follow up if complete information is not returned.

Another alternative is to have a complete PCIC store at large company facilities, but to have retail store agreements to support sales offices or smaller, remote facilities that can not be supported as well by a company PCIC.

These arrangements are used for hardware and software, and also for supplies, reference materials, furniture, and accessories unique to personal computing needs and which are not economically available through normal purchasing channels. Clearly, hardware and popular software packages should be offered by the PCIC. Equally important is the need to offer cables, specific personal computing supplies such as floppy disks, print wheels and ribbons, and reference material to support Recommended Equipment.

Although it is convenient for the user-customers to be able to do all their shopping at one place, it may not be economical for the PCIC to offer continuous forms, furniture, filing equipment, and other supplies that can easily be obtained from conventional sources. It would be a good service, however, for the PCIC to have special discount arrangements with certain commercial stores which offer these supplies, and the PCIC can either refer users to these stores or actually place orders at these stores on behalf of the users.

Software acquisitions/site licenses. Software acquisition presents some special considerations. Software is protected by copyright laws. In addition, most software package "sales" are represented as lease or licensing agreements, so that the vendors do not give up full ownership rights to the buyers. In particular, vendors (lessors/licensors) prohibit the buyers (lessees/licensees) from copying the software and providing it to other users.

These lease agreements are usually described on the outside of the software packages and are considered, by the vendors at least, in effect when the user opens the protective wrapping on the box. Most software lease terms allow one copy of the software to be made for backup; any other copies are considered illegal unless special arrangements are made with the vendor.

Whenever possible, the PCIC should negotiate with software vendors to allow multiple copies of the software to be used by the company for fixed or discounted prices. These agreements are called "site licenses" and are usually one of two types:

1. Volume discount arrangements where the licensor simply offers lower prices as more packages are purchased (licensed). For example, the licensor may offer the first 10 packages at list price, numbers 11 to 20 at 10 percent discount, 21 to 50 at 15 percent discount, and 51 up at 20 percent discount. This arrangement is common with personal computer software sold in package form. Sometimes time limits are applied to this arrangement; for example, the volume discount may apply only to packages purchased (licensed) in a given year.

2. Right-to-copy arrangements which give the licensee the right to copy the software from one system to others. Often, the licensor will provide the licensee with labels for the duplicate copies of the software, but the licensee must provide the physical media (disks or tapes). Sometimes, the licensor provides a copy of the software documentation for the duplicates; most often, the licensee is merely given one copy of the documentation for every 10 copies, or the licensee is simply granted the right to copy the documentation as well as the software. Right-to-copy arrangements are particularly valuable when a software package is available on a computer network and can be invoked by remote computer nodes. Without the right-to-copy arrangement, the customer would be in technical violation of the copyright law whenever the program was run on the network by a computer other than that on which the software was originally installed.

Site licenses are also important in classroom settings where software may be used on multiple personal computers by many students in an environment where it is difficult to monitor and control the use of software packages. These issues should be raised when considering volume discounts and/or site licenses:

- The price of multiple units of the software itself.
- Rules for using a single software package on different computers.
- Rules/cost for copying the software to other (customer-supplied) media for use on multiple computers.
- Rules/cost for having the software available for use by many people on a time-sharing computer.
- Rules/cost for having the software embedded in other customer-developed software and widely distributed within the company. This is an issue for vendor-supplied tools, utility programs, or subroutines.

- Rules/cost for having the software available to multiple users on a network.
- Rules concerning support; how many different users can ask for help.
- Rules/cost for copies of training materials, keyboard templates, and other documentation.
- Agreement as to how upgrades and modifications to the software will be distributed.
- Cost and rules for other products from the same vendor, especially products that are designed for use together with the software being licensed.
- The length of time during which the license is in force, especially the length of time over which units are counted for volume discounts.

When negotiating site licenses, the customer (licensee) should seek these advantages:

- The license and/or volume discount should apply to the entire company, not to just a division or location.
- The license and/or volume discount should be extended over the longest period of time possible. For example, some vendors try to limit the discount to packages bought in a given year; it is better, obviously, to negotiate a longer period.
- The licensing and/or discount should be applied to all versions of the basic package and, if possible, to all software in the vendor's family of products. For example, if the vendor offers a word processing package, a file management package, and a report writer, negotiate to have the license/discount apply to all of those products, not just one.
- If the software is to be used on a network, permission to do so should be explicitly stated in the agreement to prevent any future misunderstandings.
- Sometimes vendors limit the number of people who can request services or ask questions about the software. The customer should negotiate for as many such "systems managers" as needed, especially if the software will be used in a number of geographically separate locations.

If some type of site licensing agreement is not reached, each user of the software must purchase or lease the package individually, at an individual price. This may not be as bad as it seems. Some packages may be available from mail-order distributors at individual prices which are lower than those offered by a vendor's site license. The PCIC can support honest behavior in a number of ways:

- By requiring that all orders for hardware must also have orders for software appropriate to the task stated in the equipment justification
- By refusing to supply utility software or services that will copy protected software
- By offering software at discounts such that there is little economic incentive to illegally copy software
- By negotiating site licenses, again reducing the economic incentives to illegally copy software

Marketing personal computing services—As part of its free-market orientation, the PCIC promotes its services in company publications or in specially designed advertising materials so that people know what is available. In addition, in accordance with guidance from the PCIC steering committee, the PCIC may make special efforts to implement personal computing in specific functions or specific company locations. These special efforts may include focused advertising, seminars, and training, or even special promotional discounts.

As with any advertising, some is strictly informational and can be included in the company's normal internal publications. In addition, however, special brochures explaining general or specific services should be published. Price promotions are, of course, especially attactive, but may lower the PCIC revenues and, therefore, should be used with caution.

Other approaches are to bundle software and hardware, offer training along with other sales, and offer complete systems (computers with peripherals) at a cost lower than that of the individual components. Anything that offers value to users should be promoted.

Demonstration centers.   The PCIC may also maintain demonstration centers at designated company facilities. Recommended Equipment is demonstrated, and prospective users may ask questions and try specific products. The demonstration centers are also good places for the users to try alternative software packages to determine which seem to best suit their needs.

These demonstration facilities are useful as both sales and training centers. The only problem may be the scheduling of the equipment so that the two uses do not conflict. Demonstration centers are also useful for training PCIC personnel and for trying to duplicate user problems in an attempt to determine solutions.

Placing orders.   Orders are placed at the demonstration centers or any other PCIC facility or by company mail or telephone. To facilitate placing orders, the PCIC periodically publishes catalogs stating prices and expected delivery times (subject, of course, to changes dictated by vendors).

For those employees at remote sites (and even for those local people who prefer to walk with their fingers), the PCIC should offer mail- and phone-order services. These are best supported by a catalog detailing both Recommended Equipment and any "specials" currently being promoted by the PCIC. These catalogs are very convenient but should be analyzed carefully to assure that they are cost-effective, because they are expensive to produce and maintain.

Application justification and evaluation—At the request of department managers, the PCIC staff reviews proposed applications for personal computing equipment to validate or develop justification for the application. Further, department managers may ask the PCIC to periodically evaluate the effectiveness of personal computing applications in their departments.

As has been mentioned before, the primary responsibility for the effective use of personal computing rests with the department managers. The PCIC, however, should assist the managers by asking prospective personal computer users several simple questions. The answers to these questions should be evaluated by the department managers with the advice of the PCIC.

These questions and answers are recorded and used later for follow-up evaluations of the personal computing application. Here are some typical questions:

- What business tasks do you intend to accomplish with this personal computing equipment?
- What do you expect to be the benefits (show both tangible and intangible benefits) from your use of personal computing?
- What alternatives to personal computing have you considered for this task?
- What alternative types of personal computing equipment have you considered for this task?
- What costs, in addition to the equipment now being ordered, do you expect to incur for this task over the next 12 months?

Department managers are also responsible for evaluating personal computing applications. Again, the PCIC can offer technical assistance to the managers. The best bases on which to conduct the evaluation are first, the expectations set by the answers to the questions above, and second, comparisons with other employees doing similar tasks with and without personal computing.

Equipment support—The PCIC maintains an equipment support service that installs Recommended hardware and system software. It also has the capability to make adjustments and simple repairs. The PCIC has established blanket contracts and service agreements to accommodate more serious repairs. The PCIC maintains a number of system components that may be loaned to users whose hardware is being serviced. The PCIC also maintains a "hot-line" over which users can call with problems or questions about Recommended Equipment. Telephone hot-lines or hot-lines on electronic mail are also excellent for providing informal ongoing support. The PCIC offers support only for Recommended Equipment. It may elect to offer limited support for Approved Equipment, but it must be careful not to invest in noneconomical support resources to the point of diminishing the support for Recommended Equipment, which is its primary responsibility. (Support for Approved Equipment is most often available when the Approved Equipment in question is obsolete hardware which previously was recommended.)

The PCIC is able to provide all equipment installation services. The PCIC should be able to unpack the equipment, connect various peripherals to CPUs, connect terminals to host computers, and configure the hardware and software, as needed.

PCIC technicians should also be able to adjust systems and to diagnose and repair simple problems. For anything beyond its capabilities, the PCIC should refer the equipment to specialists.

Training and consulting services—The PCIC offers training classes for personal computing hardware and software. The PCIC also offers consulting services to help users define their requirements, specify configurations, decide what software is appropriate, and specify applications. The PCIC, however, does *not* write, modify, or maintain programs for users. If users need programming assistance, they request it from normal EDP channels.

These small paragraphs cover a lot of territory, since training and consulting services are major activities of the PCIC and will be primary ways of affecting personal computing usage in the company. Equally important is the provision that the PCIC will not perform programming tasks; the PCIC is not staffed either for program development or for program maintenance. Further, if special-purpose programs must be written, the task may not be appropriate for "personal computing," in the sense that such users no longer have control over their own tasks.

Usually, the EDP department offers programming services, and its specialists, along with the users, may, in fact, decide to implement the programs on personal computing equipment. At the appropriate time, the PCIC may become involved in recommending appropriate equipment, but the PCIC should leave application systems development to others.

Accounting and inventory control—For accounting visibility and inventory control, all personal computing equipment is brought into the company through the PCIC. Equipment is either capitalized or expensed as required by accounting rules. All software, however, is expensed.

If possible, all equipment should, on the accounting records, belong to the PCIC. This gives the PCIC rights and obligations with regard to keeping PCIC inventory records and tracking applications. The PCIC then keeps its own records with regard to which department has actual possession of specific units.

All the capitalization or expense accounting transactions are carried out in the PCIC location, even though the PCIC passes those charges along to the users via the company's internal allocation system (see below). If users move equipment among departments or individuals, the PCIC (which should know about the move for business reasons regardless of accounting ownership), as accounting owner, has leverage in obtaining information about the transfer.

The recommendation that software be expensed is a very conservative viewpoint and should be considered carefully by the company's tax counsel. The policy to expense software is usually appropriate for stand-alone packages and for office software products, but there may be good reason to capitalize software that is used for engineering and/or manufacturing applications, especially if that software is bundled with capitalized hardware or is part of a large, capitalized project.

Accounting and inventory transactions are created at time of equipment installation in the user department. When the PCIC installs the equipment in the department that ordered the system, either the asset or expense is transferred to the using department. At the option of the using department, the PCIC will also "lease" the equipment to the user.

The users transfer internal funds to the PCIC to pay for the personal computing equipment and become the functional owners of the equipment. The users can pay in a single transaction or through a lease agreement with the PCIC (See additional comments under "Pricing arrangements for users" below.)

Note that the flow of funding from the users to the PCIC may not match exactly the "real money" payments the PCIC makes to vendors. In the early years of the PCIC, this policy may increase the investment required in the PCIC.

The PCIC maintains records showing what equipment is located in what department and assigned to what individual.

For all the business reasons shown in this chapter, the PCIC maintains complete and accurate records as to which department and which individual is in possession of what personal computing equipment. The accounting policies discussed above give the PCIC the leverage it needs to keep its records up to date.

Some companies may wish to take a more relaxed attitude with regard to tracking personal computing usage, leaving control solely in the hands of department managers. Even in these companies, the PCIC will want to keep whatever records it can so that it can send newsletters and promotion materials to those users, but the PCIC can use voluntarily obtained distribution lists for these purposes, rather than accounting records.

Keeping complete and accurate records is expensive and time consuming, but it can be profitable if the lists are well used for PCIC marketing. They are also useful in case of need to transmit warnings rapidly because of faults found in either hardware or software.

Pricing arrangements for users—The PCIC tries to charge users prices that are lower than list prices but high enough to recover total costs. If the lease option is chosen, the PCIC sets a monthly charge such that recovery of costs, including an appropriate interest charge, is achieved in 24 months or less.

The PCIC also sets appropriate charges for its training and consulting services. In some cases, the PCIC elects to "bundle" services with equipment for one price. PCIC pricing must be such as to provide users with incentives to purchase equipment voluntarily from the PCIC. If PCIC prices are too high, gradually users will purchase from lower-cost, outside sources, and this entire support and control mechanism will deteriorate.

One attractive pricing mechanism is the equipment lease. The PCIC should set the lease interest rate low enough to create attractive monthly rates. Lease rates, of course, are a function of the length of the "write-off" period; longer periods provide lower lease rates. On the other hand, a fairly short recovery period, three years, is suggested because of the rapid rate at which personal computing equipment becomes obsolete.

Self-sufficient operations—The PCIC is expected to be economically self-sufficient on a quarter-to-quarter basis. This means that the PCIC strives to break even. Excess revenues or deficits are transferred to or from an appropriate company overhead account quarterly. In the first year of its operation, however, the PCIC is subsidized by the company according to a financial projection prepared by the PCIC steering committee and approved by the company's chief financial officer. The PCIC is charged for its expenses and is allocated overhead in the same manner as are other EDP departments. All these provisions are designed to keep the PCIC "lean and mean." Only by avoiding nonproductive overhead will the PCIC be able to compete successfully with outside computer stores.

Note that pressure should be placed on the PCIC to remain market oriented as measured by short-term (quarterly) financial results. Nor is the PCIC encouraged to build up a "war chest" by being allowed to keep any "profits." However, the PCIC is not restricted by an annual preset budget, as a traditional cost center might be. Rather, the PCIC is allowed to vary its expense levels as long as those levels match the revenues received.

Note, also, that we should expect at least one year of investment (negative cash flow), and this flow should be controlled by a budget approved by the PCIC steering committee. The steering committee should also approve any investments needed after the first year and should scrutinize any unusual changes in the PCIC's quarterly income and expenses. In general, the PCIC steering committee is responsible to both the user community and to company management to assure that the PCIC meets its goals at the lowest reasonable cost to the company after all internal transfer costs are eliminated.

Standardization—The PCIC balances the need for innovation with the economies that are derived from standardization. Although personal computing is, by definition, personal, the company and the individual employees benefit from the maximum possible sharing of software and data. This balance between innovation and standardization is achieved by allowing the maximum individuality with regard to personal uses of hardware and software; when, however, the personal computing links with other company systems or with other employees using personal computing, standards set by the PCIC and by EDP are observed. The standards set for data control and for security are especially important.

Management of purchases for employees' personal use—The primary function of the PCIC is to serve the personal computing needs of employees while working on company business. Whenever possible, however, the PCIC also provides services to employees who wish to purchase personal computing equipment for their use at home and, if possible, to the immediate families (dependents) of employees.

Some employees will be authorized (by their department managers) the use of company-owned personal computing equipment at home. The PCIC, of course, will support this equipment as it does any other company-owned equipment. If economically possible, however, the PCIC should also support employees' personal computing purchases for their own noncompany uses. The PCIC should not, however, appear to be going into competition with local computer stores. Therefore, it should not carry, for employee purchases, any equipment that is not justified by company requirements. For example, it would not be appropriate to stock low-cost game machines even if other members of the employee's family might want to purchase such machines.

In some remote geographic locations, the PCIC may be the most sophisticated personal computing facility in the area, and nonemployees may wish to acquire equipment at the PCIC. Unless such activity is closely related to the company's normal business, I would strongly recommend that the company resist the temptation to go into what is essentially the retail computer dealership business.

Normally, the PCIC would charge employees the same prices as those used for company purchases plus any marginal costs that are unique to providing services for employee purchases. Employees, of course, are required to pay "real money" for their purchases. The PCIC may work with the company payroll department to allow payroll deductions for employee purchases.

Management of obsolete equipment

Compatibility and conversion.   One of the factors in personal computing is that hardware and software become obsolete very rapidly. To the extent possible, the PCIC recommends new equipment that is compatible with old. Compatibility is most critical for data, but is also desirable for programs. Whenever appropriate, the PCIC offers the services necessary to convert from one generation of personal computing to the next.

This section points out a primary danger of the rapid changes in personal computing technology. As users move from one set of equipment to newer tools, programs and data that functioned on the old equipment may not work properly on the new systems. The PCIC can use the Recommended List to encourage the use of only that equipment which allows reasonable system migration from one personal computing generation to the next. For major changes, the PCIC may be required to obtain and provide special systems that will convert old systems to formats accepted by the new ones.

Obsolete equipment.   As new hardware becomes available, the PCIC, at its discretion, can take back the old equipment. The transfer is made at the book value of the equipment. The PCIC then disposes of the equipment in any appropriate ways, under the general supervision of the PCIC steering committee. As the "book owner" of personal computing equipment, the PCIC takes back physical possession of the equipment when it is no longer needed by the department users. If the PCIC does not have another customer-user, the equipment can be considered for disposal outside the company. Acceptable disposition methods include sale to used computer dealers, donations to schools or nonprofit agencies, and sale to employees.

The management of obsolete equipment is a potential problem in the PCIC and requires careful, ongoing oversight by the PCIC steering committee. It could be a conflict of interest, for example, for employees to purchase obsolete equipment themselves and then resell the equipment to brokers at a profit. On the one hand, the PCIC should not have in its inventory much used equipment which is unlikely to have future use in the company. On the other hand, the PCIC should not be suspected of disposing prematurely of valuable company equipment, especially if that equipment is purchased for nominal sums by employees. This is an area where advice from internal auditors may be appropriate.

CHECKLIST

Guideline 2.4
Guidelines for the Personal Computing Information Center

	YES	NO	N/A
1. Is the PCIC part of the company's EDP organization, reporting to the CIM, but separate from the other development and operations groups in EDP?			
2. Has a PCIC steering committee been appointed to assist the PCIC in fulfilling its purposes and functions, and to assist the CIM in managing the PCIC?			
3. Within the first month of each fiscal year, does the PCIC steering commitee publish a report showing the effectiveness of the PCIC during the previous fiscal year?			
4. As the work load demands, and as economic considerations permit, are PCIC representatives located in divisions and sales administration offices?			
5. Are these representatives administered directly by local EDP managers with a functional ''dotted line'' to the PCIC manager?			
6. Is the basic goal of the PCIC to help its users (departments in the company) achieve the personal computing objectives and strategies described in Guideline 2.1?			
7. Does the PCIC use economic incentives, technical advice, education, training, and persuasion rather than formal authority to achieve its goals?			

8. Does the PCIC perform the functions shown below? (The list is a guide. The actual functions change from time to time as determined by the CIM, the PCIC manager, and the PCIC steering committee:
  a. Equipment selection
  b. Purchasing personal computing equipment
  c. Marketing personal computing services
  d. Application justification and evaluation
  e. Equipment support
  f. Training and consulting services
  g. Accounting and inventory control
  h. Pricing arrangements for users
  i. Self-sufficient operations
  j. Standardization
  k. Management of purchases for employees' personal use
  l. Management of obsolete equipment			

53

REFERENCES

JOHN BARKLEY and LYNNE S. ROSENTHAL, *Issues in the Management of Microcomputer Systems,* National Bureau of Standards Publication 500–125, September 1985.

DAVID BRAY, "Using Personal Computers at the College Level," *Computer,* April 1984, p. 36.

"Corporate Executives' Guide to Personal Computing," *Computer Decisions,* special issue, March 15, 1984.

"Creating an Information Center Strategy," *EDP Analyzer,* February, 1987.

ROBERT DELAET, "Documentation: The Time-Saver," *Computerworld,* November 5, 1984, p. ID/35.

TOM EWING, "Information Centers: A Hive of Activity," *InformationWEEK,* April 14, 1986, p. 30.

DAVID GABEL, "Keeping Corporate Computers Personal," *Personal Computing,* March 1984, p. 68.

RICHARD T. JOHNSON, "The Infocenter Experience," *Datamation,* January 1984, p. 137.

PETER G. W. KEEN and LYNDA A. WOODMAN, "What to Do with All Those Micros," *Harvard Business Review,* September–October 1984, p. 142.

JOANNE KELLEHER, "Information Centers, Their Choice: Justify Existence or Go out of Business," *Computerworld,* August 11, 1986, p. 51.

ALICE LaPLANTE, "Corporate Micro Labs Offer Solutions," *InfoWorld,* April 28, 1986, p. 47.

ALICE LaPLANTE, "The Rise and Development of the Information Center," *InfoWorld,* September 1, 1986, p. 27.

LATON McCARTNEY, "Truce Declared in DP-User War; Reconstruction Begins," *InformationWEEK,* August 5, 1985, p. 30.

LINDA O'KEEFFE, "Assessing PROFS," *Datamation,* February 1984, p. 185.

JANET O'MARA, "Building an Information Center That Works," *ICP Data Processing Management,* Autumn 1984, p. 24.

JANET O'MARA, "The Information Center, the Nucleus of Productivity," *ICP Business Software Review,* August–September 1984, p. 53.

WILLIAM E. PERRY, *The Micro-Mainframe Link: The Corporate Guide to Productive Use of the Microcomputer,* John Wiley & Sons, Inc., New York, 1985.

LAURENCE J. PETER, *The Peter Pyramid,* William Morrow & Company, Inc., New York, 1986.

JOHN O. SAUNDERS, "Planning PC Upgrades," *Computerworld,* April 16, 1986, p. 49.

JIM SEYMOUR, "Site Licensing: Ready . . . or Not?" *Today's Office,* April 1986, p. 19.

DAVID SHAY, "Selling the Idea," *Computerworld Office Automation,* February 15, 1984, p. 41.

KEVIN STREHLO, "Why the Big Corporate Battle over Personal Computers?" *Personal Computing,* May 1984, p. 65.

JAMES M. TEETERS, "Service Plan Provides PC Insurance for Columbus Mutual," *Today's Office,* September 1985, p. 49.

LEE WHITE, "New Life for the Info Center," *Computerworld,* May 14, 1986, p. Focus/15.

LAURIE YOUNG, "The 'In' Place to Buy Micros," *Computerworld,* November 5, 1984, p. ID/31.

Examples of how information centers have been implemented in specific companies are reported frequently in the technical press. In 1984, *Information Systems News* (now *InformationWEEK*) published a weekly column called "Personal Computer Strategies" describing various information centers. For example:

JOHANNA AMBROSIO, "Chase (Manhatten Bank) Offers 1-Stop Support," May 21, 1984, p. 68.

RICHARD S. DAVIS, "Grumman Center Spurs PC Use," July 2, 1984, p. 52.

PHILIP J. GILL and PAUL E. SCHINDLER, JR., "PCs Get Chevron's 'Full Serve'," January 23, 1984, p. 56.

PAUL E. SCHINDLER, JR., "Del Monte: PCs Controlled," January 9, 1984.

In addition, a special April 14, 1986 issue dedicated to information centers, *InformationWEEK* briefly describes personal computing activities at organizations such as American Can Co., Chase Manhatten Bank, Johnson & Johnson, Levi Strauss & Co., Metropolitan Life, Pfizer Pharmaceuticals, Polaroid Corp., Portland Gas & Electric Co., and the U. S. Veterans Administration.

Here are a few more articles that describe the ways in which specific companies have implemented personal computing:

RICHARD METZ, "Boeing's PC Practices," *Datamation,* January 15, 1986, p. 85.

SHARON GAMBLE RAE, "Micro Management: Flying High at Boeing," *Business Software Review,* January 1986, p. 22.

CHARLES RUBIN, "Blossoming Productivity Linked to Micros," *InfoWorld,* May 20, 1985, p.31.

Chapter Three

Basic Operating Guidelines

Introduction

These guidelines implement the corporate guidelines and fill in much appropriate detail. They are basic to all work with personal computing and should be distributed with or immediately after the corporate guidelines, early in the Sanction period. These guidelines cover these issues:

Guideline 3.1: Acquiring Personal Computing Equipment
  (See also Appendix A)
    Form 3.1A: Personal Computing Equipment Selection List
    Form 3.1B: Personal Computing Request Form.
Guideline 3.2: Ownership Issues
Guideline 3.3: Sharing Personal Computing Technology
Guideline 3.4: Personal Computing Security Guidelines
Guideline 3.5: Personal Computing Away from Company Facilities
Guideline 3.6: Nonbusiness Use of Personal Computing

Guideline 3.1: Acquiring Personal Computing Equipment

Fundamental philosophy

1. *Employees are encouraged to acquire and use personal computing equipment when it is appropriate for business reasons, as judged by their department managers.*

This simple sentence makes three key points that set very fundamental philosophies:

- The company wants employees to adopt personal computing in their work.
- Personal computing should be used for business purposes.
- The judgment of appropriateness of use is left to department managers, not to staff departments or top management, nor to the employees themselves.

These philosophies emphasize that while recognizing the individuality inherent in the choice of personal computing equipment, there are economic and logistic reasons for channeling individual choices toward designated equipment.

Further, since personal computing represents a substantial investment, the justification and evaluation of personal computing applications requires considered management attention. Similarly, guidelines for the accounting treatment of personal computing equipment are also appropriate, so that the equipment receives proper and consistent treatment in financial records and so that, from the accounting records, analyses of personal computing usage can be obtained.

The philosophy explicitly chooses the need for this uniformity over the benefits that might come from a totally *laissez-faire* policy which allowed people to do "their own thing." It is over this point that the "hobbiests" will probably feel confined. Yet, without it, the vast majority of people in the company will never benefit from personal computing.

Guidelines for acquiring personal computing equipment

Remember that "equipment" is used here to include personal computing hardware, software, and supplies. Primary topics are:

- What equipment is acquired
- What justification is appropriate
- What accounting procedures are followed

Selecting equipment

2. *Equipment is selected from a Personal Computing Selection List (a sample is shown as Form 3.1A in Appendix A). The Selection List shows Recommended, Approved, and Not-Recommended equipment.*
3. *If at all feasible, equipment should be selected from the Recommended List. Approved equipment is acceptable if there is nothing on the Recommended List that is functional or economically equivalent. Not-Recommended equipment should not be selected.*

You will immediately note that a large class of equipment is ignored: equipment that is on none of the three lists. The PCIC cannot have a firm opinion on all the personal computing equipment that has, does, or will sometimes exist, so the guideline is set in the affirmative; select recommended equipment! As a practical matter, if someone wants to buy equipment on none of the lists, the matter can be referred to the PCIC, which can investigate further if the need is sufficiently strong. Ultimately, purchase of such equipment should be approved by department managers with advice from PCIC managers.

The Selection List usually begins as an informal list and, as demand increases and as the PCIC becomes more sophisticated, the Selection List may evolve to a catalog, complete with application explanations and illustrations. If a user decides, with the department manager's permission, to obtain some equipment on none of the lists, the PCIC should request that the user provide the PCIC with an evaluation of the equipment to give guidance to others who might ask about the same equipment in the future.

Pricing and availability on the selection list—Published prices and availability are obviously subject to change. The PCIC should probably adopt a last-in-first-out pricing philosophy, which means that even units in inventory bought at a different price are transferred to users at prices reflecting the current market.

Since personal computing equipment prices generally fall, this policy encourages the PCIC to keep a small inventory so that it need not incur significant losses when it "writes down" inventory to market value. Small inventories, however, may mean slow availability. The manager, PCIC must make these types of business decisions, recognizing that users, if they get sufficiently dissatisfied with PCIC service, will begin to buy equipment from outside sources.

Selection List criteria—The criteria used to place equipment on one of the sections of the Selection List should be well defined and carefully considered, since the Selection List is a fundamental personal computing standard. Although the criteria should be both technical and specific, there are certain very general considerations both for hardware and software that can be categorized into five attribute groups: fitness for use, usability, reliability, performance, and supportability.

It is beyond the scope of this text to elaborate on the definition of these attributes, but one portion of the fitness-for-use category, compatibility, is of particular concern in equipment selection. "Compatibility" simply means that equipment should work together easily if you want them to work together. Typically, for example, compatibility between business and scientific personal computers may not be an issue if they are rarely used together. On the other hand, compatibility between a personal and a host computer may well be important if the personal computer is to be used as a workstation connected to the host.

In general, compatibility can be evaluated at three levels: data, program, and hardware. Each of these levels can be further detailed; for example, data have both a format and a physical realization on a medium. If formats are compatible, we can probably transfer files among computers on communication lines, even if the computers use different data storage media. Even given format compatibility, if the two computers in question have different collating sequences (e.g., do numbers sort before or after letters?), some translation may be needed before the data can be used by both systems.

Finally, compatibility is only one factor. Depending on the application, other attributes, such as performance or usability, may weigh more heavily in the actual equipment selection. On the other hand, as new equipment becomes available to replace old, compatibility may be paramount so that the investment in software and data will not need to be repeated.

Selection criteria are both complex and technical, especially in the rapidly changing personal computing marketplace. Therefore, it is appropriate that the criteria be proposed and maintained by the manager, PCIC and be ratified by the CIM and the PCIC steering committee.

Buying from the PCIC

4. All equipment is purchased through the Personal Computing Information Center (PCIC). The PCIC delivers the equipment from its stock, if possible, or orders the equipment from predetermined vendors.

This statement is straightforward: users should buy everything through the PCIC. The PCIC, in turn, has control over the way it chooses to meet the demand. In fact, one of the major performance measures for the PCIC should be its ability to deliver ordered equipment by the date requested by the users.

Personal computing equipment is acquired by completing a company internal order form and a personal computing justification form (see sample Form 3.1B in Appendix A). Both these documents are sent to the PCIC. The PCIC, working with the purchasing department as necessary, returns the appropriate copy of the internal order with the anticipated delivery date shown.

Users should be buffered from outside vendors and deal only with the PCIC. All purchasing from outside vendors will be done by the PCIC. Users, therefore, acquire their equipment from the PCIC using whatever internal order or internal transfer mechanism exists in the company.

As a practical matter, the PCIC should maintain a supply of blank justification forms and be prepared to assist users in completing them. The users then have the forms signed, complete the internal order forms, and return the whole package to the PCIC. In some cases, where particular equipment is scarce, the PCIC might even have an informal "reservation" system, holding equipment for a short period while a user gets the paperwork processed. The PCIC should maintain a file of these justification forms for use in evaluations and for studies on the uses of personal computing.

Justification

5. *In addition to the internal order form, users also complete a justification form (a sample is shown as Form 3.1B in Appendix A).*
6. *The PCIC does not evaluate the justification shown on the form. It merely verifies that a justification exists and has been approved by the department manager.*
7. *The justification will, however, be used for these purposes:*
   a. *To help the user determine the appropriate equipment to acquire*
   b. *To form the basis of an evaluation to be made by the PCIC, 6 to 12 months after installation*
   c. *For the PCIC to use to collect statistics on how personal computing is used in the company*

Note that although the PCIC does not have the authority to pass judgment on justification, PCIC experts can and should suggest different equipment from that ordered if they feel that what the user ordered may be inappropriate.

The business benefits used to justify the equipment usually fall into one or more of these categories:

- Accomplishes the same work in less time and at lower cost.
- Accomplishes the same work at higher quality. (For example, the work might have fewer errors or be ready more rapidly. As an aside, higher-quality work usually also results in lower costs due to the elimination of error-correcting rework or inaccurate estimates while waiting for complete information.)
- Reorganizes tasks to improve the efficiency of the department.
- Increases innovation and creative approaches to the work being performed.

Personal computing can often accomplish some of these benefits by helping users focus on basic business tasks rather than on "second-order" tasks which were necessary under older methods. For example, detailed reports might be eliminated in favor of personal computing programs which allow searches of the basic data, reporting only what is needed. Chapter 4 discusses the concepts of "first-order" and "second-order" tasks in more detail.

Ongoing services

8. *Users should request all support services directly from the PCIC. The PCIC should have the capability to perform training, application support, and hardware maintenance minor repairs, but it should establish blanket agreements with appropriate service vendors for significant repair tasks.*

The PCIC will assist employees in the appropriate use of software packages and will help employees adapt the packages to the specific applications. Depending on the scope of the assistance, the PCIC may charge users for these consulting services. The PCIC also assists users in evaluating and selecting the appropriate hardware and software for their applications.

As described further in Guideline 3.3, the PCIC also offers classes for employees in the operation of Recommended hardware and software. Fees for these classes are also usually charged. The PCIC maintains a personal computing–oriented library of reference books/manuals and periodicals and invites users to use the materials at the PCIC. Borrowing the materials is not permitted. Except for those manuals specifically offered by the PCIC, users obtain texts and periodicals through normal purchasing channels.

One important service, often overlooked, is that of a reference library. There are so many books and periodicals in the personal computing marketplace that it is both impossible and expensive to have each user purchase their own materials. Further, the materials are so specialized and of such uneven quality that there is a high risk that money will be wasted unless the users can preview what they are ordering. The PCIC should, as a service to both the users and as continuing education for the PCIC staff, keep up to date on the literature and offer users opinions on the value of various publications for specific purposes. Users should, of course, have at their desks the references they need and use often. Some companies may wish to offer this service through the PCIC also, but I suggest that these types of purchases be made through normal company channels, and may even be best handled by the petty-cash system.

The PCIC offers the users "one-stop shopping" for all their personal computing needs, but economics will suggest that except in the largest organizations, many of these services will be purchased from outside vendors. The request for even these outside services, however, should be channeled through the PCIC so that the PCIC can monitor requests.

In general, the PCIC should try to offer internally those services which are closely linked to the company's business while leaving equipment-specific services to outside vendors. Thus equipment selection and application-oriented services belong at the PCIC, whereas hardware repair and general training can best be obtained from others.

Equipment ownership

9. *From an accounting viewpoint, all personal computing equipment is purchased by the PCIC, and the equipment is carried on the PCIC asset lists, with appropriate expense and depreciation charges applied to the PCIC accounts.*
10. *The PCIC, however, transfers the equipment to the department that actually ordered the equipment.*

The PCIC maintains an inventory, by serial number when possible, showing what equipment is where. The PCIC should become expert on the appropriate bookkeeping for these transactions. Tax treatment is a major factor, and the PCIC should, with the appropriate legal and accounting assistance, know exactly how to process each transaction. Users need not become concerned with the technicalities.

Equipment "leases"—Equipment, the cost of which is "small" ($1000 is a reasonable amount), may be paid for in a one-time fund transfer to minimize accounting transactions. In general, however, the PCIC should "lease" the equipment to users by charging the user department a monthly fee that recovers both the cost of the equipment and anticipated service costs. The monthly charges are set based on an interest rate and payback period recommended by accounting. Because of the speed with which personal computing equipment becomes obsolete, the payback period should be relatively short; three years is reasonable.

When the equipment is "leased" from the PCIC in this way, the user agrees:

- To lease the equipment for at least one year.
- To be financially responsible for the physical safety and security of the equipment; unusual damage or equipment loss is charged immediately to the user department. (However, the PCIC may purchase insurance covering all the company's personal computing equipment. In this case pro-rated premiums should be charged to users as part of the equipment lease.)
- To be responsible for the use of software in compliance with legal agreements/requirements.
- To be responsible for security of equipment and data so that the personal computing facilities are not misused from either a legal or an ethical viewpoint.

Users should be asked to agree to some very simple lease terms to assure that they understand both the financial and physical responsibilities involved. If you feel that it is necessary, the terms mentioned in the guideline could even be drafted into a quasi-legal form and signed by the users for emphasis. Rather than deal with another piece of paper, however, I recommend that the lease terms be well publicized and verbally explained to any first-time users and, of course, be included in published guidelines.

Inventory control

11. The PCIC should know, however, where all the equipment is physically located. The PCIC keeps files of the internal orders and the justification forms, but it should probably also keep an inventory in a machine-readable data base.

This data base can be used to answer questions such as: "Who has equipment X?" "What equipment is in department 1234?" "How much money has been spent on personal computing equipment in the last year by department 1234?" And by processing the inventory file along with a personnel file: "How much has been spent on personal computing equipment by department per employee?" These and other questions give both the PCIC steering committee and the chief information manager the means of measuring and monitoring the implementation of the personal computing program.

CHECKLIST

GUIDELINE 3.1
Acquiring Personal Computing Equipment

	YES	NO	N/A

1. **Fundamental Philosophy**

   Are employees encouraged to acquire and use personal computing equipment when it is appropriate for business reasons, as judged by the department managers?

2. **Selecting Equipment**

   Is equipment selected from a personal computing selection list showing recommended, approved, and not-recommended equipment?

   If at all feasible, is equipment from the recommended list selected? (Approved equipment is acceptable if there is nothing on the recommended list that is functional or economically equivalent. Not-recommended equipment should not be selected.)

3. **Buying from the PCIC**

   Is all equipment purchased through the Personal Computing Information Center (PCIC)? Does the PCIC deliver the equipment from its stock, if possible, or order the equipment from predetermined vendors?

4. **Justification**

   In addition to the internal order form, do users also complete a justification form?

   Does the PCIC evaluate the justification shown on the form? (It should not. The PCIC should only verify that a justification exists and has been approved by the appropriate department manager.)

   Is the justification, however, used for these purposes?
   a. To help the user determine the appropriate equipment to acquire
   b. To form the basis of an evaluation to be made by the PCIC, 6 to 12 months after installation
   c. For the PCIC to use to collect statistics on how personal computing is used in the company

(Continues)

63

5. On-going Services

   Do users request all support services directly from the PCIC?

   Does the PCIC have the capability to perform training, and application support, and hardware maintenance minor repairs, and has it established blanket agreements with appropriate service vendors for significant repair tasks?

6. Equipment Ownership

   From an accounting viewpoint, is all personal computing equipment purchased by the PCIC, and carried on the PCIC asset lists, with appropriate expense and depreciation charges applied to the PCIC accounts?

7. Inventory Control

   Does the PCIC, however, physically transfer the equipment to the department that actually ordered the equipment, and maintain records showing what equipment is where?

   Does the PCIC keep files of the internal orders and the justification forms, and an equipment inventory in a machine-readable data base?

Guideline 3.2: Ownership Issues

Why ownership is an issue

1. *Personal computing equipment and users become symbiotic. The major warning, however, is that hardware, even with programs and data, may be essentially useless to the owner department without the specific people who know how to use them all. And those people may be substantially handicapped without their specific equipment. Redeveloping software and procedures can be time consuming and expensive, even for the same person who developed them the first time.*

Ownership is usually clear with regard to most equipment and materials in the company. Personal computing equipment raises some special problems because:

- The equipment is assigned to and used for long periods of time by only one person. For example, when that person is away from the office, the equipment usually sits idle.
- The equipment is relatively transportable. (Some personal computing is, in fact, designed for portability.)
- Part of the equipment, the software, is "invisible" and easily transferred among media and locations.
- Data created by the personal computing users may also be "invisible," portable, and in nonstandard formats designed for the specific personal computing application.
- Procedures and documentation for using the personal computing equipment in applications are usually informal and incomplete, if they exist at all.
- Having become familiar with the equipment (often people become dependent on it), employees use it for nonbusiness purposes.

All these factors combine to create a relationship, a sense of ownership, between people and their machines that is unusual in the normal business world. Employees become dependent on their personal computing systems and become, at least temporarily, less capable of functioning if their specific system is unavailable to them. Similarly, the equipment may be relatively useless to the company without the specific employee who uses it. The hardware and software packages can be used by others, but the specific business results from a specific person/personal computing combination is often (usually) extremely difficult to replicate.

Purpose of this guideline

Suggestions are offered here on legal and functional ownership of hardware, software, and data. Ownership of programs and data developed in nonbusiness situations is discussed in Guideline 3.6.

Defining these ownership relationships does *not* improve the ability of the company to continue to operate a particular personal computing application without the employee who developed it; only the use of standards and appropriate documentation will accomplish that. This guideline will, however, speak to the physical possession of the equipment and to the ownership of the software and data developed in the past and ensure that the company receives the appropriate returns from its investment in both the employee and in personal computing.

This guideline is intended to define issues that are inherent in the nature of personal computing and discuss how some of these "side effects" can be mitigated so that the company can receive the return it expected from its investment and also deny any benefits from those investments to competitors.

Accounting ownership

2. *As mentioned in Guideline 3.1, the PCIC owns all hardware from an accounting viewpoint and maintains a central set of records, showing who has physical possession of the equipment.*

The equipment may also be transferred among departments without affecting accounting records, although the PCIC inventory records are updated whenever equipment changes locations (see "Inventories of personal computing equipment" below). The PCIC also maintains the appropriate insurance coverage on all personal computing equipment. The cost of that insurance is built into the rates which the PCIC charges to user departments. Often, a company's blanket insurance will cover the hardware and sometimes the software. Insurance on data or even to pay for the recovery of data is available but applies usually to well-controlled EDP centers. Coverage for personal computing data is usually not practical.

User department responsibilities

3. *The user department has functional and physical possession and financial and security responsibilities for the personal computing equipment.*

All practical ownership rights and responsibilities belong to the users. From a functional standpoint, they, not the PCIC, are responsible to see that the equipment is used appropriately and legally. Users are responsible for using the equipment in appropriate business ways and for ensuring that the equipment is both physically and functionally secure. The user departments take appropriate measures to keep the equipment from being damaged or stolen. User departments also take appropriate measures to prevent the equipments' use for illegal activities (see Guideline 3.4). User departments are also responsible for paying the agreed-upon PCIC charges.

Software purchases

4. *Software is usually purchased/leased by users directly, preferably from the PCIC.*

Purchase software for personal computing is almost always expensed rather than capitalized; therefore, accounting records for these packages are rarely kept. Software packages are ordered from the PCIC whenever possible so that the PCIC can, for consulting and training purposes, know which departments use which software. With the knowledge of the PCIC, however, users can order software directly from vendors or from retail dealers.

Although all ownership rights and responsibilities, including accounting responsibilities, if any, belong to users, the PCIC is still involved as the purchasing conduit and needs to track those purchases so that it maintains an understanding of the users needs. This may be difficult since, as a practical matter, users can and will acquire their own software from all sorts of sources. The PCIC will probably want to use periodic surveys to determine what software the users really use.

As with hardware, user departments exercise all rights and responsibilities with regard to software ownership. In particular, users are responsible for following the explicit and implicit lease provisions with regard to copying the software and/or with regard to multiple system use. These provisions may vary among packages, especially those for which site usage agreements have been negotiated.

Ownership of user-developed software and data

5. *Computer programs and related documentation developed by users or by others specifically for users belong to user departments. Data developed by users, regardless of the software involved, also belong to user departments and are subject to at least the same security as paper data.*

See Guideline 3.4 for additional comments on personal computing security. As noted above, the programs become an asset to the company only if they are usable by someone other than the person who wrote it. This usability is usually a function of the quality of the program documentation, which, in personal computing, may be low. Nonetheless, the company owns the code and whatever documentation exists and can, at its discretion, prevent its sale or use for the benefit of others, whether that be the employee or other companies.

Data are defined as any organized set of numbers, letters, or symbols on which the programs operate. Data include materials entered into the systems, the permanent and temporary files used during processing, and the electronic or paper information displayed as results of processing. Data usually have values independent of the software that created them; the data can often be used by programs other than those which originally created them. The user departments have ownership rights and responsibilities for the data in all forms, including but not limited to data in paper form, on fixed or removable disks, on backup tapes, or even in computer memories.

The primary obligations of ownership of programs and data involve security and retention. Security involves allowing access to only those authorized; this is discussed in Guideline 3.4.

Usually, the user who writes a program does so in an iterative fashion with small modifications made as needed. The problems occur because users rarely follow professional programming standards and rarely take the time to document the programs. Thus, if others wish to use the program, it may be difficult. Further, because of poor program structures, significant maintenance may be difficult, even for the user-programmers themselves, much less for others.

The data developed by such programs are much easier to document, are often understandable by inspection of knowledgeable people, and can be processed by other programs, and therefore may have value even without the programmer whose program originally built them. The assumption should always be that the department retains the programs and data even when the user-programmer leaves. Often, the user-programmer is allowed (since floppy disks are so easily transported, it is practically impossible to prevent program removal) to take a copy along to the new job, but even this might be prohibited in cases of competition or confidentiality. If the user-programmer gives adequate notice of the departure, often someone else can be trained to run the system and, at least minimum documentation can be written.

Retention issues

6. *Personal computing data and, where appropriate, software should be retained the same length of time as applies to comparable paper documents.*

Retention implies keeping data for exactly the correct length of time. Keeping documents too long can be as serious a mistake as early disposal. This correct time is defined by company policy in accordance with government regulations and generally accepted accounting principles.

Retention is usually considered an issue only with regard to data, since the data can usually be used independent of the program. In some applications, however, the data and programs are tightly linked. For example, the data of a product designed by a computer-aided-design (CAD) system may not be usable without the specific CAD package. In these cases the retention rules are applied to both the data and the programs (and the program documentation).

If data are not kept long enough, a company can fall into violation of audit and government regulations. Such records may have to be rebuilt at great cost or the company becomes subject to expensive penalties. Because of this, companies tend to keep data "forever."

This policy, however, causes two other problems. First, keeping all those records is expensive, and maintaining some system so that the records can be retrieved is even more costly. Second, some companies found themselves in litigation in which the courts ordered them to produce whatever records they had even if they were records that need not have been kept. Had the records been destroyed, there would have been no penalty. Therefore, companies should retain records for just as long as needed but no longer. Department managers are responsible for following record retention rules. Note that these rules pertain to records in all their media forms (e.g., paper, floppy disk, tape, or microfiche).

Inventories of personal computing equipment

7. *PCIC maintains inventories of personal computing equipment to facilitate support efforts and allow study of the costs and effectiveness of personal computing, in general, and of the relative performance of different types of personal computing.*

Accurate inventories are also necessary for verifying compliance with legal restrictions on software package usage and, if necessary, for investigating alleged breaches of security involving personal computing. The PCIC should do the best it can at maintaining inventories of who has what hardware and software. In most large organizations, however, it is going to be difficult to be completely accurate with hardware and almost impossible with software; the equipment is simply too portable and can easily be obtained from sources other than the PCIC.

There is, however, value in maintaining as good an inventory as possible. The inventory provides the PCIC with a customer list and becomes useful for internal market research, usage analysis, and economic evaluations. The inventory lists also form the base for the distribution of newsletters and other interuser communications. The inventory is, of course, also the basis for paying lease charges to the PCIC. Complaints about the accuracy of the charges are often a good source of inventory corrections.

Inventory records will be accurate only if the users keep them up to date. The only way that will happen is if the update process is convenient and if there are adequate incentives and some penalties associated with the update. The forms for update should be simple and readily available. If electronic mail is installed, updates could be completed without paper at all. The incentives are in the form of services from the PCIC and users groups who depend on the PCIC inventories for their lists. The penalties come in the form of whatever sanctions may result from problems found during audits.

As mentioned above, the PCIC has accounting ownership for all personal computing hardware. This gives the PCIC the right and capability of maintaining inventory records showing what hardware is located where. It also minimizes the paperwork involved in moving personal computing equipment among user departments; PCIC records are changed, but accounting records are not affected.

Annually, the PCIC should send to department managers a list showing what personal computing equipment the PCIC thinks is located in that department. The department managers should update the lists and return them to the PCIC. "Excess" equipment can then either be returned to its original owner or can be added to the inventory of the new location. "Lost" equipment will result in an accounting write-off which will be charged to the department that lost the equipment.

Internal audits should check the accuracy of the PCIC's inventory as a small part of their routine. Software, especially, should be spot checked both to know what is there and to verify that only legal copies are in existence.

CHECKLIST

Guideline 3.2
Ownership Issues

	YES	NO	N/A

1. Why Ownership Is an Issue

Has a guideline been issued describing the rights specific employees have to their specific personal computing equipment? (Personal computing equipment and users become symbiotic. The major warning, however, is that hardware, even with programs and data may be essentially useless to the owner department without the specific people who know how to use them all. And those people may be substantially handicapped without their specific equipment.)

2. Accounting Ownership

As mentioned in Guideline 3.1, does the PCIC own all hardware from an accounting viewpoint, and maintain a central set of records showing who has physical possession of the equipment?

3. User Department Responsibilities

Does the user department have functional and physical possession and financial and security responsibilities for the personal computing equipment?

4. Software Purchases

Is software usually purchased/leased by users directly, preferably from the PCIC?

5. Ownership of User Developed Software and Data

Do computer programs and related documentation developed by users, or by others specifically for users, belong to user departments?

Do data developed by users, regardless of the software involved, also belong to user departments and are they subject to at least the same security as paper data?

6. Retention Issues

Are personal computing data and, where appropriate, software retained the same length of time as applies to comparable paper documents?

(Continues)

71

	YES	NO	N/A

7. Inventories of Personal Computing Equipment

Does the PCIC maintain inventories of personal computing equipment to facilitate support efforts and allow study of the costs and effectiveness of personal computing, in general, and of the relative performance of different types of personal computing?

Guideline 3.3: Sharing Personal Computing Technology

Basic policy

1. *Users should be given both permission and encouragement to work with others in the use of personal computing.*

This team spirit, a feeling of exploring unknown territory together, is a major piece of the "fun" in personal computing, while adding to the efficiencies and effectiveness of company operations.

One of the dangers in personal computing is that people will continually "reinvent" or rediscover techniques already well known to others. This problem is more acute in personal computing than in other technologies because personal equipment users may not ask questions, fearing to display their lack of competence. Some users feel a need to "master their machine" by learning to develop programs rather than learning to use the equipment as tools for mastering the departments' work. Still other users remain apart from personal computing's potential because of fear of change and lack of even the knowledge on how to get started.

Also, unless the company takes aggressive action to cause personal computing users to relate to each other, natural organizational boundaries will remain communication barriers. The costs and frustration that can result from this fear and from unnecessary duplication of effort can be avoided if the company encourages the sharing of personal computing knowledge. Additional benefits come from synergy, usually within a department, but sometimes across organizational boundaries. From this synergy comes healthy organizational change.

Cost avoidance comes, of course, from not having each person reinvent everything from scratch. A certain amount of individual "exploring" is probably acceptable as a means of individual learning, but especially as the technology inside the company becomes mature, new users should be encouraged to take needed training, perhaps even as a prerequisite to receiving their own equipment. In fact, the training may help them decide exactly which equipment is best for them.

Role of the PCIC

2. *The PCIC has the basic responsibility to encourage sharing of personal computing technology, to keep users updated as technologies change, and to minimize the learning curve for all users.*

3. *However, other resources, such as users' groups, are valuable and should be encouraged as long as they are self-funding.*

As time passes, however, other sharing resources will also become popular within the company. User groups, for example, will develop their own charters and their own programs to meet the needs of their members. These resources are valuable and should be encouraged as long as they are self-funding. See comments about users groups below.

Training

4. *Training is a fundamental "sharing" mechanism and is therefore one of the primary functions of the PCIC.*

Generally, training is focused on specific hardware or software; general concepts courses are also popular, and as more personal computing is installed, courses oriented toward specific applications are also useful. The PCIC is responsible for personal computing training in the company. The customers for this training are the end users in departments that have installed personal computing equipment. Training is offered on general computer concepts, on the use of specific hardware and or software products, and on specific applications of personal computing. Seminars are also held on the management issues raised by personal computing, focusing primarily on implementation, staffing, organization, and control topics.

The PCIC, at its discretion, may charge for courses individually or may bundle the training into its charges for personal computing equipment. Training also allows people with similar interests to meet each other and develop effective informal relationships for communication and cooperation.

One important area often ignored is that of management education with regard to personal computing. With the help of organizational development specialists, it is often useful to hold seminars on how best to implement personal computing and how best to take advantage of its capabilities. Later seminars might also focus on how to cope with the changes that result directly or indirectly from the technology.

The PCIC, since it is expected to operate at "zero cost," must charge for its training services. During the Sanction period, when personal computing is new to the company, it probably makes sense for the PCIC to "bundle" the cost of training with the cost of the equipment so that users will be motivated to take the courses. Later, when users are more sophisticated and have a better appreciation of the benefits of training, the PCIC can "unbundle" the training. Then, equipment charges can remain competitive with those from outside vendors, and the training offerings can establish their own "market."

Another common approach is to bundle introductory courses with the equipment but to offer advanced or "elective" courses on an optional, charge-per-course basis.

Although some of the courses are developed by the PCIC itself, others may be acquired from hardware and software vendors or from commercial vendors of training seminars and materials. The PCIC should also take full advantage of the offerings of local high schools and colleges and of the seminars offered by professional associations.

Training coordination—The PCIC should designate one of its staff as training coordinator. When the PCIC is small, this may be a part-time job, but it is important to have someone with training as a designated responsibility. Besides arranging the classes discussed in other paragraphs, the training coordinator might even develop some computer-based training tailored for the company using some of the authoring systems currently available. In addition, the training coordinator is happy to meet with users to develop curricula tailored to their specific needs.

Although some users will prefer taking courses as the needs arise, others will accomplish more if they follow a prescribed curriculum which requires that they take a variety of courses in a sequence that provides cumulative growth. The training coordinator should design such a curriculum even when the courses are from a mixture of vendors and use a mixture of media.

The PCIC training coordinator maintains a catalog of all the classes and training materials offered by the PCIC. In addition, the training coordinator has brochures and catalogs showing what is available from sources outside the company.

Requests for types of training not currently available from the PCIC are welcomed since they alert the PCIC to unmet needs. All requests should be directed to either the training coordinator or to the PCIC manager.

Training sources—Especially when the PCIC is small, it may be much more economical to make use of the extensive network of noncompany training resources that are available on all aspects of personal computing. Often, a long-term arrangement can be established to offer a degree of consistency. Training services are also often offered by computer stores, by hardware and software vendors, and by consultants.

The main drawback to outside training, of course, is that it is usually not tailored to your company's specific situation. Consistency in both the curriculum and the teaching style may also achieve uneven results.

Classes can be taught in-house even by outside vendors. In-house classes save students' time and cost and also give the students a chance to develop relationships that can form a useful informal network. On the other hand, classes outside the workplace are less prone to frequent interruption, and the students from one company can meet those from others and exchange fresh ideas.

The PCIC should not expect to select people who may attend outside classes or seminars. Selections should be made by department managers, but the PCIC can be a resource to show what sessions are available and even have evaluations from past students for reference.

Classroom training is only one of the tools available to the company. Training that uses the power of the computer is a natural fit with personal computing, and the PCIC should offer software packages that provide this training. Also, one of the criteria used for the selection of recommended software should be the types of training materials available with the package.

One of the common concerns regarding computer-based training methods is that the student has no one to whom to direct questions. The guideline suggests the use of proctors to provide this human interaction. A related approach would be to assign a "mentor" for each portion of the curriculum. This mentor would not need to be present whenever the student was working but would be "on-call" in case any questions arise.

The PCIC may also offer several types of self-paced training materials:

- Various forms of computer-based training materials which allow the student to use personal computing equipment to interact directly with the lesson. Some of the classes are totally self-contained, while others allow interaction between a "proctor" and the student when assistance is needed.
- Video-based lessons of two types: the conventional videotape class works well for fixed lectures or demonstrations; a newer form of training uses videodisk technology, often with a personal computer, to allow the student more control over the pace and direction of the lesson.

Computer- and video-based training materials are particularly appropriate for use at company sites that do not have a PCIC. The PCIC training coordinator arranges the distribution of the materials to distant locations. In addition, however, instructors are willing to hold classes at distant sites, at the request and expense of the site. The PCIC is also willing to make available its lesson plans and other training materials so that EDP people, personnel trainers, or other competent instructors can present the classes at the distant sites.

The PCIC training coordinator has a variety of tools that can be used for remote training. Obviously, self-paced methods are useful; instructors can also make trips to hold a series of courses; it is more costly but also usually more effective to bring students from distant locations to a central facility for training. As a feasible, but last resort method, lesson plans and training materials can be sent to remote sites where someone can "stay a day ahead of the class" and teach the course.

Personal computing standards

> 5. *Standards are established to communicate to the "best practices" discovered by others, and to establish common practices so that systems developed independently can still function together ("interface" standards).*

Personal computing standards are mostly of the "best practice" variety, although standards to allow systems to interact are discussed in the guidelines on communication (see Chapter 6). All of these guidelines are essentially standards for personal computing, although in a narrower sense, the major standard affecting personal computing is the choice of hardware and software, as discussed in Guideline 3.1.

General standards for systems development are usually published by the company EDP department. These general standards also apply to original systems developed using personal computing, but usually do not discuss the creative application of software packages, which is the more common form of "systems development" for most personal computing users.

Standards have generally not reached their positive potential in the data processing industry. Programmers tend to believe that whatever they do is, by definition, best practice. Interface standards have been much more successful because they are essentially self-enforcing; those who do not follow the standards cannot use the interface.

In conventional EDP, best practice standards have been most successful when they have been enforced through peer pressure at walkthroughs and inspections. This tool is less available to personal computing users since the projects are usually individual. As noted above, these guidelines are in themselves a set of best practice standards; many of the guideline provisions are easily enforceable; others are not, and some should be left to the discretion of local managers who can use walkthroughs and peer pressure as needed.

There is a cost to develop and implement standards; the price of not using standards, however, is in duplicate development of methods and in far higher costs in systems operation and maintenance. It is worthwhile, therefore, to take the trouble to tailor and implement guidelines such as these.

Technical standards for personal computing are best linked to those used by the company's conventional EDP staff.

The company EDP department may also maintain a "data dictionary" which defines the format and usage of files that are used by more than one function in the company. The data dictionary is an important standard because it permits various systems to share use of data with minimum duplication and confusion. If personal computing users plan to use any of the data that are included in the data dictionaries, those users should become aware of these standards so that they can use the data properly and also be informed whenever changes are made.

Users' groups

> 6. *Users' groups should be established to provide an effective means of encouraging people who have common interests to work together in ways not constrained by the company's formal organization.*

A general users' group for all personal computing users are usually inappropriate, since the scope of such groups would be too broad. Groups could be formed, however, around families of hardware and around software packages. The most successful and enduring groups, however, are those which organize around specific application; users can discuss how best to apply the latest in personal computing technology to their individual needs.

The PCIC provides staff assistance to users who wish to form and operate groups. Funding for the users' groups operations, however, comes from "dues" from user departments. Individual users' groups are expected to be self-funding. The PCIC should, however, provide advice on users' group operations, provide and prepare distribution lists and mailing labels for those users who might be interested in the group, and of course, the group can use company conference facilities for meetings.

Users' groups should be voluntary organizations, with their own leadership and organization and should be completely self-funding and independent of the company's support. On the other hand, the company really benefits from the enhanced communication that occurs through users' groups. It is appropriate, therefore, for the company, usually through the PCIC, to help the groups get started and to provide information and staff services to the group at a low or no-cost basis. The PCIC also uses its inventory records to help users' groups reach people who might be interested in joining the groups.

Reference library

7. The PCIC maintains a library for reference only; people are encouraged to visit the library but may not remove materials from it. People who wish to use materials at their desks should borrow them from other library facilities or buy them through normal purchasing channels.

The PCIC library contains current books on personal computing topics, all PCIC publications and catalogs, magazines and newspapers on personal computing topics, and copies of the most current documentation on Recommended Equipment. The PCIC is also open to suggestions for additional materials to be kept in its reference library.

Although an important part of the PCIC's communication mission is well fulfilled by having manuals, texts, and periodicals available for review and reference, it is usually prohibitively expensive to provide a full-service "lending" library. Employees are encouraged, therefore, to obtain their individual copies of books through normal channels. If the company already has a lending library established for other functions, it is, of course, appropriate to have the PCIC work with this facility to provide services to users. The reference library may also contain various types of electronic media such as videotapes or videodisks. The library might also maintain a subscription to public data networks and data bases for reference use.

Newsletters

8. The PCIC publishes a periodic newsletter for all personal computing users.

The newsletter should have two major sections, a general section for all users plus specialty sections sent only to personal computing users in that application area. For example, there could be three specialty sections: office personal computing, engineering and scientific personal computing, and programmer support personal computing.

The general section contains information about significant PCIC events, significant changes to the Selection List, information about new and revised guidelines, and announcements of classes, meetings, or other events, inside or outside the company, of interest to the personal computing users. The specialty sections contain anything that is of unique interest to people using personal computing for the specialty application. In particular, however, these sections contain examples of how personal computing is used for various applications. These sections talk about the people who do the work as well as the technology involved, and interested users are encouraged to communicate directly with each other.

Although the specialty sections are focused toward those people whom the PCIC has identified as being in that specialty, people can subscribe to more than one specialty. Thus engineering managers might want the specialty news about their technical field, but also might be interested in news about spreadsheets and project management systems. To control too many subscriptions, a charge per specialty can be imposed, perhaps with the first specialty free.

Newsletters, of course, are not only the domain of the PCIC. In particular, users groups might decide to publish newsletters of their own, or they might elect to develop one of the specialty attachments for the PCIC publication. Newsletters are not only excellent ways of transferring information among interested users, but they are also a good way to ensure that the PCIC has a current list and correct addresses of users.

The PCIC is responsible for the content of the newsletter and must answer, as it does for all other responsibilities, to the CIM and to the PCIC steering committee. Therefore, although everyone in the company is encouraged to submit articles, final editing may be done by the PCIC staff. This censorship should be imposed rarely, if ever. In fact, the need for censorship probably indicates a more significant management failure, but in cases of sensitive issues, the final responsibility and authority rest with the PCIC.

Consulting

9. *The PCIC offers, for fees charged to the user departments, consulting services on the use of personal computing. These services are most appropriate to help a user over a specific barrier or solve a specific problem. Consulting services are not appropriate for long-term personal computing operations.*

Consulting is particularly useful when introducing personal computing into a department or when making a dramatic change in the environment or equipment. Consulting services are very useful for one-time or infrequent tasks, especially those that require specialized expertise. Consultants, however, are usually too expensive to use for routine work. Consultants can bring to the users experience and expertise and can also put users into contact with others who may have faced similar problems.

PCIC management should be aware, however, that people who are knowledgeable in a subject are not necessarily good consultants. Consulting requires excellent analysis and communications skills in addition to subject knowledge.

Consulting is also available on a phone hot-line basis. This hot-line service is provided for a fixed monthly fee charged to the users.

Expert services

10. *While consulting is designed as a "rifle shot" to solve a specific problem, the PCIC offers ongoing "expert services" in specific technical areas so that the users need not each replicate this expertise.*

11. *These expert services are retained by monthly service contracts offered to users or on a "time and materials" basis.*

The primary "expert service" offered by the PCIC is equipment maintenance and repair (serious problems may be contracted to repair service outside vendors by the PCIC as part of the charges to the users). Additionally, however, the company EDP department often offers to personal computing users two other expert services, one in custom systems development and one in communications (data, voice, and video). Users are encouraged to suggest the need for additional services to the manager, PCIC.

Access to specialists is one of the most important services offered by the PCIC. Certain common problems might be resolved directly by PCIC generalists, but most of the time, the PCIC will merely channel the request to a specialist, inside or outside the company. Sometimes, if the company already has sophisticated electronic maintenance services in-house, the PCIC can contract with the in-house service to provide the required expertise.

The PCIC should encourage people to call PCIC for service, not the vendor, even though they know that PCIC will call in the vendor. In this way, the PCIC can keep statistics on both problems and repair services so that the PCIC can evaluate the performance of both equipment and vendors.

CHECKLIST

Guideline 3.3
Sharing Personal Computing Technology

	YES	NO	N/A

1. **Basic Policy**

   Are users given both permission and encouragement to work with others in the use of personal computing?

2. **Role of the PCIC**

   Does the PCIC encourage sharing of personal computing technology, to keep users updated as technologies change, and to minimize the learning curve for all users?

   Are the other resources, such as users' groups encouraged as long as they are self-funding?

3. **Training**

   Is training considered a fundamental "sharing" mechanism and established as one of the primary functions of the PCIC?

4. **Personal Computing Standards**

   Are standards established to communicate to the "best practices" discovered by others, and to establish common practices so that systems developed independently can still function together ("interface" standards)?

5. **Users' Groups**

   Have users' groups been established to provide an effective means of encouraging people who have common interests to work together in ways not constrained by the company's formal organization?

6. **Reference Library**

   Does the PCIC maintain a library for reference only?

   Are people encouraged to visit the library, and use the materials at the library? (People who wish to use materials at their desks should borrow them from other library facilities or buy them through normal purchasing channels.)

7. **Newsletters**

   Does the PCIC publish a periodic newsletter for all personal computing users?

(Continues)

8. Consulting

Does the PCIC offer, for fees charged to the user departments, consulting services on the use of personal computing? (These services are most appropriate to help a user over a specific barrier or solve a specific problem. Consulting services are not appropriate for long-term personal computing operations.)

9. Expert Services

While consulting is designed as a "rifle shot" to solve a specific problem, does the PCIC offer on-going "expert services" in specific technical areas so that the users need not each replicate this expertise?

Can these experts services be obtained either by monthly service contracts or on a "time and materials" basis?

Guideline 3.4: Personal Computing Security Guidelines

Minimum policy

1. The company should control this equipment in the same manner that other company assets are controlled. Similarly, data developed by personal computing should be controlled as are other company documents, whether in paper or machine-readable form.

It is tempting to dismiss personal computing security with this statement, which forms a minimum policy for personal computing security. Unfortunately, the nature of personal computing raises a large number of unique security issues. Note also that the security provisions described in this guideline are designed for normal business applications, not for high-security situations or for military "mission critical" applications.

Personal computing security issues

Note that we must be concerned with two distinct types of security issues, damage to personal computing assets and problems caused by the use of personal computing equipment. Here are a few of the issues:

- Personal computing hardware is portable and easily sold.
- Software and data can be transported either on easily concealed floppy disks or invisibly communicated via telephone lines.
- The speed and data processing power of personal computing can be applied to criminal tasks with the same efficiency and effectiveness that is applied to legitimate business operations. Further, this power can be applied privately.
- The use of personal computing is itself a valuable commodity that can be diverted ("stolen") toward nonauthorized (if not illegal) purposes.

The key point here is to emphasize that with personal computing, security is not merely business as usual. The minimum policy provides that security with personal computing should be no worse than security was before. It is possible but not probable that security will improve when personal computing is implemented because of the general increase in concern about security. In general, however, with the implementation of personal computing, companies will be required to work harder to just maintain the security status quo.

Remember, also, that security and user "friendliness and convenience" often are mutually exclusive. Since a major aspect of personal computing involves ease of use, security provisions should be imposed only when really necessary and then to the minimum extent consistent with the value of the assets at risk.

Often it is more cost-effective, from the standpoint of the overall personal computing program, to provide maximum convenience and friendliness, thereby encouraging appropriate personal computing use. Protection from misuse of personal computing will come from the integrity of good employees. In addition, some company assets can be covered by insurance, which would provide financial reimbursement in case of security breach.

One good strategy might be to leave the operation open until problems occur, and if they do, gradually impose tighter controls.

The decision on the scope and nature of security used is made by department managers with the technical advice of PCIC and EDP department experts. The published security guideline should be authorized by the chief information manager (CIM) and probably countersigned by the manager of security and the head of internal audit so that both of those people are knowledgeable about the guideline and committed to its concepts.

Basic guideline

2. *State the policy unequivocally: Violations of security in this company are expressly forbidden. The absence of "adequate protection" is in no way to be viewed as an excuse for violations to occur.*

One of the reasons that computer security is difficult is that computer crime has become a game where breaking into a system is viewed as merely an intellectual challenge; the attitude is, "If you can't keep me out, I have a right to get in." This guideline explicitly states that the absence of protection is not permission to violate security and that the company does not view violations as a game. Having said all that, everything shown below is explanation and elaboration.

Violations

3. *Security violators are subject to normal due process disciplinary personnel procedures.*

Some companies, however, may want to toughen these guidelines by stating unilaterally that security violators will be subject to dismissal. One characteristic of computer security violations is that even though the results of the violation are known, the violation method might not be known. Therefore, sometimes penalties are softened if the violator reveals the method so that general security can be improved.

Violations of security should be reported to the company security manager or to the vice-president, administration. Although it is desirable that people reporting violations identify themselves, it is more important to detect and correct the problems; therefore, serious anonymous reports should be thoroughly investigated.

Since there is a stigma against "tattletales," acceptance of anonymous reports is explicitly mentioned. Clearly, however, it is preferable to know who witnessed the violation so that the person can aid in the investigation, be available as a legal witness, and as appropriate, be given a reward for reporting the security breach.

The issues discussed below give examples of violations and describe precautions to be taken. However, the list below is not meant to be inclusive, and violations other than those shown below may be as or more serious, depending on the specific circumstances.

Security of personal computing equipment

4. *In sequence:*
   a. *Discourage attempts at theft or destruction.*
   b. *Prevent theft or destruction if attempted.*
   c. *Recover the equipment promptly if stolen.*
   d. *If all else fails, recover the financial value of the equipment.*

Note that the four steps are sequential; protection first and compensation last. As mentioned before, the definition of "equipment" includes both hardware and software. "Security" in this section refers to both theft or unauthorized use of personal computing equipment or blatant destruction of the equipment.

There is nothing innovative in the methods suggested in this section of the guideline. An important point is that personal computing documentation needs protection as much as do the more obvious machine-oriented assets. The principles can and should be applied in sequence to all types of personal computing equipment.

Backup to the documentation must also be protected. Documentation backup is usually maintained on a computer file or in microfilm/fiche form. The computer files may be protected as data, while the microfilm can be secured as are other human-readable documents.

The cost of recovering lost or damaged equipment can be covered by insurance. Users who are interested should discuss the subject with the CIM. Insurance is offered by some carriers to compensate for business interruption and for data reconstruction in cases where data are damaged. These coverages, however, are usually placed on data in conventional EDP environments, where controls are more formal than they usually are in personal computing environments. Those personal computing users who feel that insurance has a role in their security plans are best advised to integrate their plans with those of conventional EDP so that the coverages and procedures are as consistent as possible.

Hardware

- Be sure that normal company security applies to personal computing hardware. This includes simple periodic checks of work locations by security people, and use of property passes.
- Lock the equipment; some units actually need key locks to turn them on. Units can be locked to desks.
- Clearly label the equipment with asset tags or some type of difficult-to-remove identification. An identification number scratched into the equipment is often appropriate.
- Record the serial numbers of the equipment.
- Be sure that the hardware is covered by the appropriate insurance.

Note that the protection methods mentioned follow the sequence of the principles. Note also that there is nothing "high tech" here. Personal computing can be protected in the same ways that you might protect a typewriter, portable copier, or laboratory instrument.

Software: purchased and developed—These are ideals for which to strive; the portability of software makes the achievement of these security goals extremely difficult.

- Keep records of who has what software. If the software package has a serial number, record it. Make reasonable attempts to keep track of copies of the software as well as originals or masters.
- Make a backup copy of the software for protection; keep a record of the location of the backup copy. Software master media also need protection. Usually, that is accomplished by making and using working copies, while the masters are kept secure for backup. Most software lease agreements allow the making of only one working copy. If the master does become damaged, some vendors will replace it for a nominal fee if the damaged master is returned.

Some vendors "copy-protect" their software to discourage unauthorized distribution of the software via illegal copying. This copy protection, however, can cause significant inconvenience for people who load working copies to a hard disk or who make working copies for operational security. Additionally, some vendors offer their software in copy-protected form for one price while offering the same software without the copy protection for a higher price.

Finally, utility programs are available which defeat some of the common copy-protection schemes. PCIC experts might use these programs appropriately to help users who have had trouble with copy protection, but general use of such programs should be discouraged to inhibit illegal software copying activities.

- Software in its machine-readable form is indistinguishable from data and can be secured in the same way (see the section on data security).

Software, of course, needs protection both from mischief and from illegal use. In general, the types of controls suggested by this guideline work for both motives, but controls preventing the unauthorized access of the software are especially important if the software is stored on a host machine.

Procedures and documentation: paper and machine-readable (e.g., Computer-Assisted Instruction, Help commands)

- Keep the documentation and training materials for the system, both for programmers and users, as secure as the program code.
- Documentation that is in human-readable form should be subject to the same security procedures as other documents of similar security classification. These documents are usually in paper or film form (e.g., microfiche, videotapes). The types of security usually applied include such things as clear labeling of security classification, special handling, logging of distribution, numbered documents, and of course, locked storage with access only to those people with an appropriate clearance and a need-to-know.
- Documentation in computer-readable form should be treated with security provisions described in the section on data security.

Data: paper and machine-readable—Data in three "stages" must be considered when discussing security. Appropriate controls must be placed on the data entered into the system ("input" data), the machine-readable files both during the processing and while in storage waiting to be used again ("machine-readable files"), and reports and displays of data (information) after processing ("output" data). Each of the three stages presents different risks and requires different treatment.

Control of data is like the classic chain; overall security is only as strong as the control of the weakest link. Most EDP people focus their attention on control of machine-readable data, but users should also insist on adequate control of data in both its input and output stages.

Input data.   Some types of computer crime simply involve entering fraudulent transactions into a legitimate, routine process. For example, an employee might enter an invoice for goods not received so that a check is issued to a conspiring vendor.

The best way of dealing with threats to input data security is through normal accounting controls. For example, have procedures to ensure that properly approved purchase orders, invoices, and receiving documents are all present before a check is issued. Keep in mind, however, that most of these controls are based on the assumption that collusion among employees is rare and that one employee will provide a check on the other. When personal computing is involved, however, we may be tempted to give, for the sake of efficiency, more authority to a single person, since via personal computing, people may have the power and skills to perform entire procedural sequences without the assistance (and the checking) of others.

There is no easy answer; security versus job integration is a trade-off which, like many others, must be balanced by the department managers. One possible alternative might be to program the personal or host computer to do at least some of the checking and to flag, log, and report potential security violations.

Unless the data themselves are classified, input data are rarely encrypted. If necessary, of course, a personal computer is an excellent tool for automatic encryption or decoding of data, away from human sight, for further processing, thus allowing confidential processing to be accomplished by people without clearances.

Machine-readable files. As a basic precaution, all machine-readable files should be copied ("backed up") periodically so that the "gremlins" that live in all computers do not "eat" an important file. These backup steps seem unnecessary and are often overlooked by novice personal computing users—until the first time an accident destroys a critical file. In fact, one of the advantages of time sharing on a host system versus personal computers is that files on a time-shared system are usually routinely backed-up by professional operators.

Depending on the sensitivity of the files and the capabilities of the system used, other security measures can be taken. First, the physical volumes (disks or tapes) should be dated and labeled both in machine-readable ("internal") form and externally; the external label should be different from the machine-readable version. All programs that use the files should, of course, check both the date and the internal label and all operating procedures should require checking the external label. The internal label should also contain a record count and a control total that is also verified by the programs.

The next level of security is provided by password protection, where a user or a program run by the user must provide a password before the program can open the file. These passwords, must, of course, be kept secret and changed periodically. File labels and passwords are not common on personal computers but are usually available on host computers used for shared personal computing operations.

The most secure method of protecting files from unauthorized access is by encrypting the file in a way that can be decoded only by specially controlled programs. A variation of this technique is to compress the file such that expanded, usable versions are available only to programs with certain capabilities. Remember also to protect the files in all their forms; working and backup copies must be protected and the data must be protected while it is in the computer, especially if the computer is connected to others via communication lines.

Just as EDP professionals often ignore human-readable data, users are often negligent in their treatment of machine-readable data. Conventional EDP operations are usually meticulous in backing-up files; personal computing users are sanguine until they get burned.

Note the suggestion that a data file, to be secure, should have both external labels for proper identification by human beings, and internal labels for proper identification by programs, and that the two labels should be different. This difference is another security protection; a programmer who does not have access to the program documentation will not be able to process the label merely by reading the external label. The label, however, is not a password. Usually, programmers can easily bypass labels to read the files.

Encryption is a powerful protection, but it is the ultimate step in increasing the cost of processing and in making the data inconvenient to use. Sometimes data can be left human readable and be encrypted within the machines by having automatic code/decode routines within every program that interacts with people.

Files themselves are not the only point of vulnerability. Clever programmers can attach routines to operating systems which steal or damage data during those fleeting microseconds that the data are in the memory of the computer itself. This puts a higher priority on encrypting at an input processing stage so that the data are most often processed in encrypted form.

Machine-readable media must also be disposed of in a secure manner. Worn-out magnetic disks and tapes can still be read with special programs and sensitive equipment. Disks that are cleared or tapes that are "scratched" usually still contain most of the data last recorded; merely the directory or label data has been removed. Media that once contained confidential data should be cleared by special programs which destroy all the previous data, or be placed in special devices that destroy the data by exposing the media to a strong magnetic field.

Output data.   Output data in machine-readable form can be treated as any other file described above. Similarly, human-readable forms of output, typically paper or film, can be treated as are other classified human-readable documents, following the company's standard procedures.

Several special precautions are appropriate, however. First, because of the potential high volume of output, special secure files are often needed. Also, when output displays are used, the user must be sure that unauthorized people do not have access to the screens while they are being used. Finally, records retention and destruction procedures must be followed with special care, if only because of the typical large volume of computer output.

Most users who work in high-security environments are familiar with procedures that control output documents, especially those in paper form. The only novelty presented by personal computing is the fact that data are often displayed on a video screen rather than in paper form; therefore, visual access to those screens need also be controlled. The open-office environments popular in many industries tend to exacerbate visual access problems.

One problem caused by personal computing is that official reports, produced normally by conventional EDP, can now be simulated by someone with personal computing capabilities. If this is a problem, conventional EDP can use special, controlled-use paper that is marked in some distinctive way to differentiate official reports from any of even identical format produced by personal computing.

Data communication—Data transmitted among computers are vulnerable via various forms of "taps," usually another computer placed somewhere in the communications channel. These factors are discussed a bit more below and in the guidelines on data communication in Part II.

There are only two reasonable protections against data communication access; they can be used individually, but are most effective when they are used together.

- Data are encrypted in some way so that they are incomprehensible without the "decoder" program.
- Documentation about the data is kept secret so that unauthorized users, even if they obtain the data, do not have the knowledge necessary to interpret them correctly.

Communications channels are also vulnerable to interruption. Everyone using data communication should therefore, have alternative transmission plans or channels, resorting, if necessary, to the physical transfer of disks or tapes (or, perish the thought, even paper), if all else fails.

Security from personal computing equipment

5. *Implement:*
   a. *Personnel controls*
   b. *Operational controls*
   c. *Access controls*
   d. *Encryption*

Personal computing power can be used as a tool for mischief as easily as it can be used for legitimate business functions. The steps discussed below will not protect the company from a well-trained, persistent criminal, but as with locks on doors, will discourage casual, "playful" pranks, and perhaps, even encourage purposeful criminals to ply their "trade" elsewhere. As mentioned above, these controls increase the difficulty of using systems, and the value of the resources protected must be balanced against both the tangible and intangible costs of the inconveniences imposed.

Although security of equipment and data is a relatively routine extension of existing practice, security from personal computing poses unusual difficulties because of the power that can be applied "invisibly" and from remote locations. Further, damage can be done without leaving any trail simply by copying valuable information and using that information for seemingly legitimate transactions.

This section of the guideline makes no pretense at being a complete discussion of security issues, but it does describe some of the issues. Those involved in systems that are vulnerable to attack are well advised to obtain expert advise on the subject.

The misuse of personal computing poses these dangers:

- Destruction of assets
- Disruption of normal services
- Unauthorized use of resources
- Software/data alteration
- Privacy violations

Controls to enhance security from personal computing—The measures discussed below are listed in order of their importance and priority and should be implemented in the order shown.

Personnel controls.   The controls shown above use technology to fight technology. Usually, however, the most effective controls are those that focus on people. Simple procedures are very effective; for example, people in critical jobs should be rotated regularly; when employees terminate, their accounts and passwords should be deleted from the host computers; and passwords, especially those that allow access to broad system capabilities, should be changed frequently, at random periods.

It is a cliché, but it must be said: "People commit crimes, not computers." Personnel controls, therefore, must be basic to any security plan. Without this as a base, all else becomes very weak. Personal computing makes personnel controls even more important than they are in conventional EDP, since personal computing gives a great deal of power to a much wider variety of people than does conventional EDP. Note also that personnel controls may be implemented without harming personal computing's precious need for convenience.

Operational controls.   The EDP operations departments at most companies have many procedures, developed over years of experience, to protect the EDP resources from accidental or deliberate damage. Personal computing users are strongly encouraged to discuss operational controls with the EDP operations manager and tailor the controls to suit individual needs.

These are the types of controls that can be implemented:

- File backup procedures
- File volume library control
- Internal and external file labels
- Batch and processing controls
- Transaction and activity logging

Simple external labeling and file backup procedures should be followed by all personal computing users, just for protection against accidents. More sophisticated procedures can be established if they are needed, again with the help of experts.

Access Controls.   The goal here is to limit access to computing resources only to authorized people. The system checks for authorization by asking for and verifying the legitimacy of a password. Both data and programs can be checked this way. Passwords are, in effect, keys to locked vaults and should be treated with the same respect that one would treat a valuable key.

Another way of verifying the authenticity of users is to have the host system check that the terminal being used is allowed to perform the functions being requested. A variation of this is often used in communications systems when users call in over phone lines. Systems can be obtained that examine a table to locate the correct phone number for the person attempting access. The system hangs up on the caller and calls back to the authorized user. This type of access control is particularly useful for systems that are vulnerable from attack by "hackers" who randomly call until they reach a computer.

Password and callback controls are particularly effective if used properly, together with personnel and operational controls. Passwords, of course, are useful only if they are kept secret. The stories of seeing passwords taped to terminals or of having passwords appear on distributed reports are legend.

A new threat to password security comes from the availability of word processing dictionaries in machine-readable form. Clever hackers can simply program their personal computer to try every word in the dictionary. Therefore, it is important to use passwords that are not real words and are long enough (greater than five characters) to discourage someone simply attempting all possible permutations and combinations of available characters.

Passwords and allowed use of only designated terminals both increase the complexities of using systems and should, therefore, be used with those trade-offs in mind. Callback systems can also create occasional problems if a legitimate user wants access to the system from a different location than that to be called, but callback is a powerful deterrent to "hacker attack."

The controls mentioned above provide active barriers to potential trespassers. It is also important to log all accesses to systems and data bases. These logs are routinely used for usage charges and for operational performance analyses, but the logs can also provide important clues if unauthorized access is suspected.

All activity on a time-shared system should be logged, no matter what, to provide the basis for performance analyses and for allocating costs to appropriate users. These logs can also be quite useful when tracing a potential security violation. Logs on personal computers are, however, quite rare. Many operating systems do date and time-stamp files as they are saved, and they may give some clues to activity.

Encryption.   The next level of defense is to encode the computer files in such a way that they will be illegible to anyone who does not have the proper decoding key. This technique is most appropriate for data that are easily accessed. The most common example is that of data which are transmitted over common carrier lines and can easily be tapped. Encryption is the best, albeit most inconvenient defense available to us. As encryption is expensive to implement properly, it should be used only when other security methods seem inadequate.

Privacy violations

6. Deliberate violations of privacy in the company should be explicitly prohibited as a separate statement apart from other security considerations.

Violations of privacy simply allow data about people to become known when those data are deemed by the individual and the company to be confidential. Privacy issues are another novelty of personal computing. People often enjoy learning "harmless secrets" such as the salaries of others or what is said in their personnel records. There are laws that must be followed with regard to certain privacy issues, but more important is the need for basic respect for each other. Further, it is a small step from a "harmless" invasion of privacy to much more serious tampering of data.

The files most at risk are, of course, personnel and payroll records. These files should be protected as described above; in addition, great care should be taken to retain only those data really needed, and even current data should be "on-line" only when absolutely necessary for processing.

Personal computing, especially time sharing, is vulnerable to a much more incidious type of privacy attack. When all employees conduct much of their business over electronic media it is technically possible for someone to "eavesdrop" electronically and monitor a person's activities. In fact, unless a personal computing device is specially shielded, technicians with appropriate spectrum analysis equipment can "read" the electronic emissions from that device at some distance.

Anyone using electronic devices, especially those using communications equipment, is vulnerable to detection and monitoring by someone using other electronic devices. This is a significant concern of media such as cable television even more than it is in personal computing.

Again the purpose here is not to provide either a diatribe on the subject of privacy violations or a technical primer on its prevention. Rather, personal computing users should be aware of this potential problem, forbid its practice, and obtain the appropriate expert assistance if significant prevention measures must be implemented.

Security responsibilities

7. *User responsibilities. Users themselves are primarily responsible for security. Employees should respect and follow security provisions and should encourage others to do the same both by their words and examples.*

8. *Department management responsibilities. Managers should create the environment needed to encourage users to comply with security provisions.*

9. *Audit responsibilities. Audits by external and/or internal auditors should routinely include the verification of compliance with security guidelines.*

10. *PCIC responsibilities. The PCIC provides the technical expertise and equipment needed to implement security guidelines.*

11. *Responsibilities of others. All employees are urged to abide by and encourage and support all appropriate security activities.*

User responsibilities.   Users themselves are primarily responsible for security. Employees should respect and follow security provisions and should encourage others to do the same both by their words and examples. This paragraph emphasizes that the primary concern for security belongs not to some staff "police force" but to the users and department managers. They can and must get technical advice from auditors and from experts in the PCIC and in the conventional EDP department, but the basic responsibility is theirs nonetheless.

Department management responsibilities.   Managers should create the environment needed to encourage users to comply with security provisions. Managers should provide positive examples in their individual actions, but should also verify

that their employees are following security guidelines and should provide the resources needed for implementing reasonable security measures.

Audit responsibilities.   Audits by external and/or internal auditors should
routinely include the verification of compliance with security guidelines. The audit
reports should include any suggestions on how security might be improved.

PCIC responsibilities.   The PCIC provides the technical expertise and equipment needed to implement security guidelines. As needed, the PCIC provides consulting and training in security issues and also includes security considerations when
screening equipment for its Selection Lists. The PCIC may also offer on the Selection List specific hardware and software for use in security applications. The PCIC
also assists the auditors in developing appropriate tools for effectively verifying security. These tools are also available to any users who wish to monitor their own
security performance.

Responsibilities of others.   All employees are urged to abide by and encourage and support all appropriate security activities. Security is a responsibility of all
employees, whether or not they are specific users of personal computing. Even those
not directly involved in personal computing have the responsibility to encourage
compliance and report violations. For example, if the janitorial staff finds classified
materials or passwords in the trash, it might be wise to report this to their supervisor,
who in turn could bring it to the attention of appropriate people. This is not to say
that everyone should "spy" on others. When security is an issue, however, everyone
should at least be alert.

CHECKLIST

Guideline 3.4
Personal Computing Security Guidelines

	YES	NO	N/A

1. **Minimum Policy**

   Does the company control this equipment in the same manner that other company assets are controlled?

   Similarly, are data developed by personal computing controlled as are other company documents, whether in paper or machine-readable form?

2. **Basic Guideline**

   Is the policy stated unequivocally: Violations of security in this company are expressly forbidden? (The absence of ''adequate protection'' is in no way to be viewed as an excuse for violations to occur.)

3. **Violations**

   Are security violators subject to normal due process disciplinary personnel procedures?

4. **Security of Personal Computing Equipment**

   Are security processes implemented in the following sequence?
   a. Discourage attempts at theft or destruction
   b. Prevent theft or destruction if attempted
   c. Recover the equipment promptly if stolen
   d. If all else fails, recover the financial value of the equipment

5. **Security from Personal Computing Equipment**

   Have you implemented the following processes?
   a. Personnel controls
   b. Operational controls
   c. Access controls
   d. Encryption

6. **Privacy Violations**

   Has a separate statement been issued, separate from other security statements, explicitly prohibiting deliberate violations of privacy?

(Continues)

93

	YES	NO	N/A

7. Security Responsibilities

Have these security responsibilities been defined?

a. User responsibilities. Are users themselves primarily responsible for security? (Employees should respect and follow security provisions and should encourage others to do the same both by their words and examples.)

b. Department management responsibilities. Are managers held responsible for encouraging users to comply with security provisions?

c. Audit responsibilities. Do audits by external and/or internal auditors routinely include the verification of compliance with security guidelines?

d. PCIC responsibilities. Does the PCIC provide the technical expertise and equipment needed to implement security guidelines?

e. Responsibilities of others. Are all employees urged to abide by and encourage and support all appropriate security activities?

Guideline 3.5: Personal Computing Away from Company Facilities

General

1. *The normal equipment selection process described in Guideline 3.1 is followed with regard to equipment purchased for use away from company facilities; the equipment selected is appropriate to the specific application in addition to being appropriate for use in a portable or remote mode. The equipment is subject to the same type of justification as is equipment used at company offices.*

Technology has advanced to the point of economically allowing personal computing to occur far from the company facilities. There are two general methods: employees can communicate with a host computer from their home or a remote site via data communication facilities; alternatively, employees can use a stand-alone computer at the remote site and eventually transfer their work product either on paper or in machine-readable form.

One variation on this second situation is the use of portable computers, which can be used in almost any environment and are particularly suitable for use while traveling or while working in areas away from electric outlets. Gradually, personal computing technology is advancing to the point that the equipment can be available wherever a person happens to be. It may be economically feasible for some employees to have equipment at home or at temporary job sites or even to carry a basic equipment set while traveling.

Use of personal computing away from company facilities presents the same types of issues discussed elsewhere with, however, some special considerations. This guideline discusses those considerations.

Hardware Control

2. *As with all equipment, the PCIC records who has received the hardware and where it will be physically located.*

3. *Portable equipment is also assigned to a specific user; the locations recorded by the PCIC are the users' "home base."*

If equipment is permanently transferred to other locations or users, the person receiving the equipment notifies the PCIC as soon as possible. Temporary moves or loans need not be reported; the permanent user is still considered responsible for the equipment. Portable equipment is also assigned to a specific user; the locations recorded by the PCIC are the users' "home base," even though the equipment may be most often physically located in users' briefcases or automobiles.

Portable units are often assigned to equipment "pools" and given, as needed, to different users. In this case, the equipment records assign the equipment to the manager and location of the pool. The pool managers are responsible for the actual location of the equipment at any given time.

Pools of personal computing equipment are useful when the equipment is needed only for certain jobs and can be used by different people. This might be appropriate for salespeople or service technicians who wish to carry equipment on certain client calls.

Software control

4. *The rules for appropriate and legal use of software packages are the same for remote users as they are for users in company facilities; all other guidelines pertaining to software use also apply.*

The PCIC, to assure proper compliance, is particularly careful to verify that for every hardware unit provided to users, the appropriate software is also legally obtained. When hardware is placed in a pool, the manager of the pool is responsible for compliance with the guidelines pertaining to the proper use of software and for assuring that legal copies of the software exist for each pool unit in use.

It is more difficult to control software when it is associated with hardware that moves around, but the basic rules are the same as they are for fixed equipment. Spot checks to see that software is used correctly is about the only reasonable form of audit.

Pools of hardware create special problems with regard to the legal use of packages. If possible, it is best to assign specific software to specific units, but it may be reasonable to have enough software packages for all the hardware units that are in actual use at any given time.

Security Considerations

5. *Guideline 3.4 regarding controls and security also applies to equipment in remote use.*

Physical control of the equipment is of particular concern; the users and managers to whom the equipment is assigned are responsible for the security of the hardware, software, and data, and are, in general, responsible for compliance with Guideline 3.4. Since remote users are the most frequent users of dial-in data communication lines, the precautions described in Guideline 3.4 with regard to security from personal computing are of particular importance.

The control of equipment is of particular concern, since the equipment is usually away from any type of controlled environment. The users themselves must, therefore, take responsibility for physical security of the hardware, software, and data. Similarly, remote equipment poses the greatest threat to security from personal computing, and most of the provisions shown in Guideline 3.4 are specifically oriented toward such equipment.

Personal Use

6. *Use of personal computers for nonbusiness purposes is permitted as long as their use in no way conflicts with the company's general code of business conduct (see also Guideline 3.6).*

Personal use of personal computing equipment is a common, almost inevitible situation. In writing guidelines, we have three alternatives: We can forbid personal use, we can permit personal use, or we can ignore the issue.

Forbidding it establishes unenforceable provisions that will most certainly be ignored. Permitting it may encourage some users to abuse their privileges and spend company time on personal projects. Therefore, I recommend that the issue be ignored unless obvious abuses become visible and that nothing be said about this subject in your guidelines. Guideline 3.6 discusses this subject in more detail.

If, however, you do feel the need to discuss personal use in this guideline, be sure to refer to whatever published code of conduct exists in your company. Use of personal computing equipment for personal projects may raise a number of ethical questions which are discussed further in Guideline 3.6.

Personal computing used by "home workers"

7. *Employees who routinely accomplish most of their work in their homes and use personal computing are subject to the same guidelines as their colleagues working at company locations.*

8. *Department managers may authorize the assignment of personal computing equipment for home use to employees who normally work at company facilities.*

Department managers make particular efforts to maintain contact on general topics as well as on topics that pertain to the employees' specific tasks. This includes all the communications that come from the PCIC. Further, home workers are urged to contribute to the PCIC suggestions on how the uses of personal computing in home work situations can be improved. Working at home using personal computing equipment is feasible in a growing number of jobs and is particularly convenient for parents with young children or people who are mobility impaired.

Supervisors of home workers must take special care to maintain two-way communication. We usually do not realize how much review and guidance occurs on informal bases until we become obligated to do all communication formally.

Although department managers may authorize the assignment of personal computing equipment for home use to employees who normally work at company facilities, this practice is not encouraged because of the expense and issues of potential "favoritism" that can be raised; however, it may be appropriate for people who are "on-call" during nonworking hours and who could use personal computing to complete their "on-call" tasks.

Use of company-owned personal computing equipment at home may also be authorized for temporary periods to enable employees to complete a specific, time-sensitive project. When the project is over, the equipment should be returned. Departments where people have frequent needs for taking equipment home may wish to establish a pool of equipment from which equipment can be obtained on a rotating basis.

If employees have their own (employee-owned) equipment at home which is compatible with the company systems, department managers may authorize the employees to acquire, at company expense, the necessary equipment to allow the employees to communicate with other company systems and increase their productivity and flexibility. Since the costs of this equipment are relatively low, the justification for this type of "home work" may be less critical.

CHECKLIST

Guideline 3.5
Personal Computing Away from Company Facilities

	YES	NO	N/A

1. General

Is the normal equipment selection process described in Guideline 3.1 followed with regard to equipment purchased for use away from company facilities?

Is the equipment selected appropriate to the specific application in addition to being appropriate for use in a portable or remote mode?

Is the equipment subject to the same type of justification as is equipment used at company offices?

2. Hardware Control

As with all equipment, does the PCIC record who has received the hardware and where it will be physically located?

Is portable equipment assigned to a specific user? (The locations recorded by the PCIC are the users' "home base.")

3. Software Control

Are the rules for appropriate and legal use of software packages the same for remote users as they are for users in company facilities? (All other guidelines pertaining to software use also apply.)

4. Security Considerations

Is guideline 3.4 regarding controls and security also applied to equipment in remote use?

5. Personal Use

Is use of personal computers for nonbusiness purposes permitted as long as their use in no way conflicts with the company's general code of business conduct?

(Continues)

99

	YES	NO	N/A

6. Personal Computing Used by "Home Workers"

Are employees who routinely accomplish most of their work in their homes and use personal computing subject to the same guidelines as are their colleagues working at company locations?

Do department managers have the authority to assign personal computing equipment for home use to employees who normally work at company facilities?

Guideline 3.6: Nonbusiness Use of Personal Computing

General

1. *The personal use of personal computing equipment is probably inevitible and probably cannot and should not be completely discouraged.*

As employees become familiar with and dependent on personal computing for their business tasks, they will want to use these facilities for the work they do for volunteer organizations and for their personal chores. Further, since personal computing is, by its nature, private, supervision of these activities is virtually impossible.

There are two different types of nonbusiness uses. Most of this guideline is oriented toward the nonbusiness use of company-owned equipment. However, some employees are willing to purchase personal computing equipment for their own use; this guideline also discusses how the employee and company can work together in this situation. There are, however, some potential problem areas, and these are covered in this guideline by grouping situations into "acceptable" and "unacceptable" categories.

Primary guideline

2. *As with most other issues regarding personal computing, the department managers are also responsible for the logical administration of nonbusiness uses of personal computing.*

3. *In addition, however, the department managers and the employees should be particularly aware of the provisions of the company's code of business conduct and be especially sure that the code is being followed in both letter and spirit. (If your company does not have a code of business conduct, this might be the incentive necessary to write one.)*

Ownership of data and software produced by employees is discussed in Guideline 3.3; these ownership provisions should be reviewed by all employees who consider use of personal computing equipment for nonbusiness projects. Various types of ethical conflicts can arise while using personal computing equipment, and these should be resolved by reference to the company's code of business conduct. Some examples of potential ethical conflict include doing work for competitors, or doing work for customers for personal rather than corporate gain, or doing work that distracts employees from their normal duties.

Generally acceptable situations

4. *Situations are acceptable as long as they do not cause ethical conflict and as long as they do not create added costs or legal liabilities for the company.*

The following are situations in which nonbusiness use of personal computing equipment is generally acceptable.

- Personal computers or workstations used in local mode may be used on the employees' time for nonbusiness purposes as long as the use does not inhibit others from performing company work.
- As mentioned in Guideline 3.5, department managers may approve employees' use of company-owned equipment to link employee-owned hardware with company facilities.

- Employees must abide by the legal restrictions pertaining to the use of software. In general, these rules merely tie a specific copy of the software to a specific hardware unit without regard to purpose or use. In these cases, the software normally assigned to the hardware being used could also be used for nonbusiness projects (as long, of course, as the projects meet the other requirements described here).

Generally unacceptable situations

5. *If a situation does not meet the criteria for acceptability by the definition above, it is probably an unacceptable situation.*

Some circumstances can be hybrids; for example, it may be acceptable to use a personal computer for a personal project as long as the employee provides all the supplies. The following are situations that are generally unacceptable.

- Employees may not use scarce resources needed for company business for nonbusiness purposes. This specifically includes the use of host computer resources such as disk space and computer time.
- Employees may not use company-owned expendable supplies for nonbusiness projects. Employees may, however, purchase these supplies from the PCIC (at prices set for these transactions by the PCIC; see comments about PCIC purchases below). This applies especially to such things as printer supplies and floppy disks.
- Employees may not use the technical services offered by the PCIC at company expense. The PCIC may, however, at its discretion and price, offer selected services to employees working on nonbusiness projects.
- As mentioned above, employees may not use company personal computing equipment in situations that create conflict of interest between the employee and the company or in situations in which the employee violates the company's code of business conduct.

PCIC support of employee-owned equipment

6. *At the discretion of the PCIC steering committee, the PCIC may offer its services for employee-owned equipment or for the employee purchase of equipment for appropriate prices.*

The prices set for these services should be sufficient to cover both the actual cost of the equipment and some of the overhead associated with the PCIC operation. Cost plus 10 percent is probably close, but accounting management should set the prices.

Availability is a more sensitive issue. If equipment is scarce, the PCIC may put employee purchases at the back of the waiting list; or a first-come-first-serve rule may be used. Often, the best compromise is a rule that puts employees to the back of the list until a designated time (e.g., three months) has passed, after which the employee order pops to the top.

CHECKLIST

Guideline 3.6
Nonbusiness Use of Personal Computing

	YES	NO	N/A
1. General Has management accepted the fact that the personal use of personal computing equipment is probably inevitible and probably cannot and should not be completely discouraged?			
2. Primary Guideline As with most other issues regarding personal computing, are the department managers held responsible for the logical administration of nonbusiness uses of personal computing? In addition, however, are the department managers and the employees particularly aware of the provisions of the company's code of business conduct, and are they sure that the code is being followed in both letter and spirit?			
3. Generally Acceptable Situations Are situations considered generally acceptable as long as they do not cause ethical conflicts and as long as they do not create added costs or legal liabilities for the company?			
4. Generally Unacceptable Situations Are situations considered generally unacceptable if they do not meet the criteria for acceptability defined above?			
5. PCIC Support of Employee-Owned Equipment Does the PCIC steering committee have the authority, at its discretion, to allow the PCIC to offer its services for employee-owned equipment or for the employee purchase of equipment at appropriate prices?			

REFERENCES

RANDY L. ALLEN and MICHAEL BERKERY, "Conducting the Cost/Benefit Analysis," *Small Systems World,* October 1984, p. 38.

ROBERT G. ANDERSON, DAVID R. WILSON, and DAVID C. CLARK, "Foiling Snoopers: Use See-Through Security," *Management Information Systems Week,* April 7, 1986, p. 40.

SANDRA D. ATCHISON, "These Top Executives Work Where They Play," *Business Week,* October 27, 1986, p. 132.

TRUDY BELL, "How to Market and Protect the Software You Write," *Personal Computing,* January 1984, p. 221.

AUGUST BEQUAL, "A Security Checklist," *Computerworld,* December 23, 1985, p. 33.

WILLIAM M. BULKELEY, "Courts Expand the Copyright Protection of Software, but Many Questions Remain," *The Wall Street Journal,* November 18, 1986.

WILLIAM M. BULKELEY, "Uncovering the Hidden Costs: Want the Real Price Tag on That Office Computer System? Just Start Multiplying." *The Wall Street Journal,* June 12, 1987, p. 14D.

ROBERT P. CAMPBELL, "Survivability: More than Redundant Lines and Hardware," *Telecommunications Products and Technology,* December 1986, p. 26.

"Encryption," *Proto,* published by AT&T, Vol. 4, No. 4, 1986, p. 5.

ANNE R. FIELD and ZACHARY SCHILLER, "Electronic Data Could Make Trouble for the Law," *Business Week,* October 27, 1986, p. 128.

LOUIS GIGLIO, "Computer Security Priority: Protecting against Inside Jobs," *InformationWEEK,* August 19, 1985, p. 28.

ROBERT L. GRAHAM, "The Legal Protection of Computer Software," *Communications of the ACM,* Vol. 27, No. 5, 1984, p. 422.

MICHAEL HAMMER, "The OA Mirage," *Datamation,* February 1984, p. 36.

DORAN HOWITT, "Electronic Perks: Companies Help Employees Buy Personal Computers," *InfoWorld,* December 31, 1984, p. 30.

IRENE E. ISAAC, *Guide on Selecting ADP Backup Processing Alternatives,* U.S. Department of Commerce, NBS Special Publication 500–134, November, 1985.

STANLEY A. KURZBAN, "Careers in Computer Misuse—Not So Appealing After All," *Computers and Society,* ACM Special Interest Group on Computers and Society, Vol. 15, No. 4, Winter 1986, p. 7.

TED LANDBERG and STANLEY WINKLER, *Starting and Operating a Microcomputer Support Center,* National Bureau of Standards Publication 500–128, October 1985.

ED LANDRY, "Making Office Connections Work at John Hancock," *Computerworld,* April 14, 1986, p. 65.

ERIK LARSON, "Working at Home: Is It Freedom or a Life of Flabby Loneliness?," *The Wall Street Journal,* February 13, 1985, p. 31.

MERJA HELEN LEHTINEN, "How Secure Is Your Factory?" *Managing Automation,* May 1986, p. 31.

LAWRENCE J. MAGID, "With 'Ollie-Ware,' Purging Documents Is Easier," *San Jose Mercury News,* August 9, 1987, p. 3E.

EDITH MYERS, "Should Data Be Insured?" *Datamation,* October 15, 1984, p. 78.

DAVID NEEDLE, "Telecommuting: Off to a Slow Start," *InfoWorld,* May 19, 1986, p. 43.

DONN B. PARKER, "The Many Faces of Data Vulnerability," *IEEE Spectrum,* May 1984, p. 46.

ROBERT PARKER, "How Grumman Harnessed Microcomputer Power," *Training,* April 1986, p. 39.

Password Management Guideline, Department of Defense Publication CSC-STD-002-85, 12 April 1985.

TEKLA S. PERRY and PAUL WALLICH, "Can Computer Crime Be Stopped?" *IEEE Spectrum,* May 1984, p. 34.

Personal Computer Security Considerations, National Computer Security Center Publication NCSC-WA-002-85, December 1985.

LARRY PRESS, "Debugging Spreadsheets," *Abacus,* Vol. 2, No. 3, 1985, p. 54.

LISA RALEIGH, "Buyers Copy Software in Legal Gray Area," *San Jose Mercury-News,* March 17, 1985, p. 11F.

PETER G. SASSONE and A. PERRY SCHWARTZ, "Cost-Justifying OA," *Datamation,* February 15, 1986, p. 83.

JOHN SAUNDERS and NAOMI KARTEN, "How to Evaluate Micro-Based Systems," *Computerworld,* November 26, 1984, p. ID/17.

DAVID STAMPS, "Pioneering: It Hasn't Been Easy," *Datamation,* February 15, 1986, p. 62.

DAVID STAMPS, "Who's Maintaining the Micros?" *Datamation,* April 15, 1986, p. 83.

HERB SWARTZ, "Telecommuting's Expansion Poses Host of Legal Questions," *InformationWEEK,* April 15, 1985, p. 38.

LEE THE', "Take Charge of Your Software," *Personal Computing,* January 1985, p. 121.

JOHN VOELCKER and PAUL WALLICH, "How Disks Are 'Padlocked'," *IEEE Spectrum,* June 1986, p. 32.

JEFFERY WALDEN, "Cracking Down on Micro Crime," *Business Computer Systems,* October 1984, p. 40.

PETER WALDMAN, "Those Dangerous Liaisons, Managers Who Fall for Their Office PCs Could Be the Downside of the Computer Age," *The Wall Street Journal,* June 12, 1987, p. 16D.

FRED W. WEINGARTEN, "Electronic Surveillance and Civil Liberties," Testimony before the House Judiciary Subcommittee on Courts, Civil Liberties, and Administration of Justice, *Computers and Society,* ACM Special Interest Group on Computers and Society, Vol. 15, No. 4, Winter 1986, p. 13.

"Where Will Applications Be Developed?" *EDP Analyzer,* Vol. 21, No. 12, 1983

Chapter Four

Control Guidelines

Introduction

In the basic guidelines, we set the foundation on which other personal computing applications can be built. In the first level of sophistication, personal computing helps employees do the work that they have always done, except in different, more efficient ways. In this chapter, guidelines are provided to help employees use the personal computing tools in ways that improve control, control over personal computing, control over established processes, and finally, control over the tasks to performed to help the company achieve continued success. "Control" is usually associated with security, restrictions, and constraints. As used in this chapter, however, control takes on its other meaning, to advise and manage, as in "controlling a ship."

In this chapter we look at how personal computing can help provide controls to accomplish two major management goals; first, to "do things right," and then, a harder task, to identify and "do the right things." Guideline 4.1, "Operational Controls for Personal Computing Users," provides assistance in the control of personal computing itself. It seems appropriate that users should learn to manage their personal computing processes before attempting to apply personal computing as a tool in more complex business situations.

In Guideline 4.2, "Personal Computing as Part of Total Quality Control," the concepts of total quality control (TQC) are introduced in the context of personal computing applications. TQC concepts can be applied for all processes, either to improve an existing process or to evaluate new processes designed to address fundamental business functions.

Then, in Guideline 4.3, "Applying Personal Computing to the 'Right' Tasks," we directly address the issues involved in using personal computing to change the types of work that is done, to eliminate tasks that are no longer needed because of the powers of personal computing, and to evaluate the role that personal computing plays in this restructuring.

This series of guidelines is moderately technical and, therefore, is appropriately written or reviewed by the chief information manager (CIM) and other administrative managers, specifically accounting and internal audit. Quality managers, in those companies which have that function, should also become involved with these guidelines.

Guideline 4.1: Operational Controls for Personal Computing Users

Similarities to conventional EDP controls

The controls outlined in this guideline are similar to those developed over years of experience for conventional EDP applications. At best, however, they are a subset of those controls and should *not* be considered sufficient for use in conventional EDP applications.

From an operational control standpoint, the primary difference between personal computing and conventional EDP is the small number of people and organizations (usually one) involved in an individual personal computing application. This factor reduces the need for many conventional controls, while making it difficult to implement some of the separation–of–function controls which are usually a key portion of conventional controls.

General goal

1. *Give those people who are responsible for results the maximum amount of direct control over the processes that produce those results.*

As implied above, in personal computing, all control tasks become the responsibility of users; EDP specialists are not directly involved. The goal is to give those people who are responsible for results the maximum amount of direct control over the processes that produce those results.

Personal computing usually reduces the number of people and the number of steps involved in a process. Because of this, the control needs of personal computing applications, although similar to those appropriate for conventional EDP, differ greatly in detail. It is unrealistic (and usually unnecessary) to expect most users to implement operational controls in the same way that those controls are implemented by EDP professionals. Some controls, however, are both appropriate and necessary for personal computing applications.

Department managers must decide when these controls are sufficient, and more important, when more sophisticated controls should be implemented with professional assistance, as needed.

Basic guideline

2. *Controls are the responsibility of the department managers who supervise personal computing users. Advice on personal computing controls may be obtained from the manager, Personal Computing Information Center (PCIC), from the chief information manager (CIM), and from the internal audit department.*

Owner, custodian, user concepts

3. *Every system should have one "owner"; the system may have several "custodians" and many "users." In personal computing applications, these three roles may be fulfilled by one person, but the responsibilities for each role must, nevertheless, be understood.*

The responsibilities of each are defined next.

These concepts become important when more than one person uses a specific system or where data are shared by several people or systems. By determining the owner, custodian, and users of each system resource, personal computing users become aware of the network of responsibilities and authority that surrounds systems and can participate in the communications needed to assure that departments coordinate their activities.

The vice-president, administration designates the owner of selected company-wide system resources. Owners have the authority to designate custodians. Users are rarely designated, as such, although the custodians will often maintain records of users to facilitate communication of changes and allocation of charges.

Responsibilities

4. *The owner has responsibilities for all logical and financial decisions concerning the resources.*
5. *The custodian of a resource is that organization which, following the owner's direction, implements processes that use the resource.*
6. *Users employ the resource in their routine business.*

Owners, custodians, and users have different responsibilities for systems resources. System resources are the programs, documentation, data, and codes that are the fundamental components of the system.

Note that these roles are defined by department (or department manager) rather than by individual. This not only allows for individual job turnover, but it also provides department managers the freedom to reorganize their departments to adapt to changing conditions without modifying these fundamental systems–resource relationships.

- The owner has responsibilities for all logical and financial decisions concerning the resources. One department is the owner of the resource. For example, only the owner of the product number code has the right to authorize changes to product number formats. The owner is also responsible for developing and maintaining the policies and procedures that are followed by all organizations involved with the system.
- The custodian of a resource is that organization which, following the owner's direction, implements processes that use the resource. There can be several custodians for each resource.
- The most common custodians for conventional systems are the EDP department and accounting. In personal computing applications, the custodian and user are often the same, even for those systems owned by other departments.
- Custodians perform their duties as authorized by the owners. For example, an EDP system may be built to show the relationships of various product codes as they are linked together to form a high–level assembly. Similarly, accounting can be asked to collect financial data in categories consistent with various product number groupings.
- Users employ the resource in their routine business. There are usually many users of each resource. For example, marketing and R&D are typical users of product codes.

Fundamental to all controls is the concept that designated people have specific responsibilities with regard to a system and play specific roles in its operation. Owners, of course, are the key players because it is they who control resources, set priorities, and exercise management authority. This usually is not a big deal in personal computing applications, since the systems are very localized and all roles are played by one person or, at most, several people in one department.

Typically, owners are identified first. Then the owners designate the custodians. Users identify themselves by becoming "customers" of the system (although at least some of the customers/users must be identified when the system is built). Sometimes, however, especially for systems that have been in existence for a long time, the custodian is obvious, but the one specific owner is not; there appear to be many owners. In this case, it behooves the custodian to locate and designate a single owner or for the custodian department to establish itself clearly as both owner and custodian.

As personal computing becomes more pervasive, however, the applications may begin to directly affect company-wide systems and resources. Then, to assure the appropriate control and integrity, specific owners should be designated. Owners are usually suggested by the CIM, but the actual designation should come from the senior administrative officer.

It is quite common for a department to play multiple roles. This is especially true in personal computing situations, where, for example, individuals commonly initiate and maintain data (ownership tasks), develop systems that are structured around the data (custodial tasks), and use the data for making decisions and completing transactions (user roles).

It is essential, however, for personal computing users to identify the owners, custodians, and users for each resource that is used or modified by other departments; such identification is usually unnecessary, however, for those resources that never leave the personal computing user's own department.

For example, if an accountant uses personal computing to develop a product cost analysis which is submitted to the manufacturing manager, the accountant is acting as a custodian (and perhaps a user) of product codes, but is probably the owner (and custodian and user) of the personal computing software. The manufacturing manager is a user of the codes (and may even be its owner).

The point is that the accountant cannot change the format of the product code and is obligated to use it with the constraints imposed by the owner. If the accountant needs a revision, in order, for example, to consolidate data on "families" of products, the accountant must request the revisions from the owners. Similarly, the owner, before granting these revisions, should assess the impact the changes might have on other custodians and users.

Even when only one person is involved in all parts of a system, there are different roles to play at different times. This is not an important consideration when the system is used for just a short time, but it becomes useful when applications are used for routine operations either by a single person or by several people.

Report authenticity—One of the unique issues raised by personal computing is that of authenticity and integrity of computer-prepared reports. When reports are produced from conventional EDP systems, those reports are usually granted a higher status than that of manually prepared documents because the readers assume (often incorrectly) that the system has been carefully reviewed and tested for accuracy and consistency. In fact, although we all would like improvements in conventional systems, they are usually subjected to at least a minimum set of technical and user testing. Such is not the case, almost by definition, with personal computing systems. One person can produce very formal and official-looking reports with no testing and review at all. It is a case of "reader beware."

One way of helping the developers of personal computing applications toward increased integrity in their systems is to implement the separation of roles described in this guideline section. The owner, custodian, and user each view the system from a different viewpoint and with a different set of expectations; these viewpoints are, of course, most objective when the individual roles are taken on by separate individuals, but this defined separation of viewpoints is useful even when taken by the same person at different times.

It is still, however, up to those who try to form business judgments based on the information shown on computer reports to verify independently the integrity of the data shown. Usually, that verification is based on some sort of "rule of thumb" to provide a check on reasonableness and consistency.

Some companies, to allow easy differentiation between "official" computer reports prepared by conventional systems and ad hoc personal computing reports, prepare official reports on special paper which is available only to the EDP professionals. The "reader beware" policy, however, is probably the best, regardless of the source of the reports, since even "official" reports may have integrity problems.

Equipment controls

7. Personal computing equipment is owned by the PCIC; the personal computing users fulfill both custodial and user roles.

As custodian, the personal computing users maintain complete lists of the equipment assigned to them, including the product and serial number of all hardware and the name, number (if any), and version of all software. These lists are necessary for reconciliation with accounting and PCIC lists and are also vital in case the equipment is lost or destroyed. As custodians, personal computing users are also responsible for the security and control provisions outlined in Guideline 3.4.

As has been thoroughly discussed before, the PCIC should be the legal "owner" of the hardware, leaving the user departments to fulfill the custodians and user roles. This straightforward "accounting" policy in fact implements an important "separation–of–function" control mechanism.

This guideline section highlights, however, the responsibilities, with respect to equipment, which the custodian must assume. They are merely the "commonsense" provisions that should be followed by everyone who has been entrusted with the use of a valuable resource owned by someone else.

User responsibilities include whatever is necessary to keep the equipment in working condition and technically current. Equipment users should, of course, have hardware defects repaired; if software defects are detected, they are reported to the PCIC, which, as appropriate, will report the defects to the vendors. Users are responsible for implementing "bug fixes" or "workarounds" so that the software can be used.

Periodically, vendors issue updates to both hardware and software systems. Users are responsible for installing these updates and for testing their applications to verify that the applications still work correctly.

These updates may sound routine and easy to do, but in fact, may be quite complicated. In some instances, systems that worked well before the "fixes" may need (sometimes major) adjustments to work on the updated system. Therefore, one major user responsibility is to retest and revalidate the accuracy and integrity of key systems after making changes to the hardware and software, even if the changes appear innocuous. The PCIC should also test changes to recommended equipment and warn users of any possible problems.

Personnel and organizational controls

8. The basic control is to put the power of personal computing only into the hands of those who can be trusted to use the power constructively and responsibly.

Toward that end, department managers may set rules defining which employees in their departments may apply for personal computing privileges. If such rules are adopted, however, it is essential that they be applied uniformly and consistently to all employees. One common rule is to require that employees be employed by the company for six months before they are eligible for full personal computing privileges.

It is also important that personal computing users understand the power and implications of this technology. It may be appropriate, therefore, for department managers to require that before users obtain personal computing equipment, they attend the "Introduction to Personal Computing" course offered by the PCIC. This course should cover the fundamentals of personal computing technology, procedures, business, and ethical issues, but is usually not a substitute for courses on specific equipment or applications.

Access controls, as described in Guideline 3.5, are always appropriate, especially for data. At the very least, data and programs that are on removable disks should be kept in locked containers when not in use. When reasonable, passwords should be used to restrict access to data and programs.

Be open and flexible—While controls over who has access to personal computing power must be exercised very judiciously, in my opinion, errors, if they occur, should be made on the side of openness and flexibility rather than on the side of restrictiveness. In those organizations, however, where employees have direct control over negotiable assets (cash, stocks, bonds, etc.), controls should probably be more restrictive, going, if appropriate, to the point of requiring that all personal computing users be bonded.

When restrictions are imposed, it is essential that they be imposed equitably. The use of personal computing is a privilege that can have a direct bearing on career success, and, therefore, could be interpreted as a means of discrimination (or, on the positive side, a means of affirmative action).

Require introductory courses—Requiring that all users have at least an introductory course in personal computing is a particularly good control, albeit somewhat expensive. This will assure that every user has at least been exposed to some basic technical, procedural, and ethical concepts. Therefore, problems are less likely to be caused by "sins of omission."

If this guideline is adopted, however, the PCIC should assure that people can attend the basic course conveniently and promptly. Long waiting lists or expensive trips to remote sites will simply encourage people to ignore the rule, or, worse yet, bypass the PCIC to obtain equipment. Therefore, introductory courses should be available at all company sites or, better yet, should be available in self-paced, perhaps computer-based form.

Separate functions—In multiuser applications, the classic control, separation of functions, is appropriate. In particular, the systems design and programming functions should be separated from operational responsibilities. At each "handoff" from person to person, data controls can be implemented to assure that the processing is being performed correctly and to flag erroneous operations if any occur. Typically, the following functions are separated: the initiation of a transaction, the authorization of transactions, the recording and processing of transactions, and the custody of the assets to which the transactions refer.

The need for the security provided by this separation of functions must be balanced, however, with the loss of effectiveness to be gained by integrating functions via personal computing into the job of a single employee. Individuals performing key processing tasks should be rotated periodically. A side benefit of this policy is that the knowledge of specific personal computing applications is periodically transferred among individuals. This usually also encourages improved documentation. If appropriate, personal computing users with key processing responsibilities may be bonded to provide the company with financial protection.

The controls described in this section are appropriate to routine transaction processing, for conventional EDP as well as personal computing. One time or ad hoc applications usually ignore this type of control. While separation of functions in the operational process flow is important, rotating assignments may be even more useful. Rotation not only provides control but also has the positive side effects of distributing knowledge and encouraging documentation.

Routine jobs and schedules

9. *Schedules are required from all personal computer users who are developing applications or processing transactions.*

Typically, the custodian and users of the application provide schedules and progress reports to the owner. Owners who are dissatisfied with the schedules or progress may apply additional resources or incentives, or change the process with which the work is accomplished, or simply change the schedules.

Schedules are appropriate for tasks which are new or which are performed aperiodically. When tasks must be performed at the same time in a particular period, they may be scheduled as "routine jobs," with schedules set and resources dedicated on a predicted basis each period. For processing that requires data submitted by several organizations, the system custodian usually specifies data "cutoff" dates and times so that the data from the different sources are comparable.

Schedules serve four functions:

- They provide incentives and pacing for individual tasks.
- They are means of coordinating the work of different people.
- They are used to coordinate the application of resources with the process used to complete the task.
- They are used as the measure against which actual progress is measured to display status and to predict variances from the schedules.

In personal computing, the first function is often most important, since much of the work is performed by a single employee, with minimum resources. In more complex, multiperson tasks, schedules for coordinating efforts are appropriate. Schedules are also appropriate for routine jobs.

When security is an issue, processing schedules, even for routine jobs, may be varied and kept secret to minimize any threat of interference. Otherwise, schedules, and progress against those schedules, are displayed prominently, both to provide maximum motivation and to communicate status to all concerned. In conventional systems development, schedules are usually honored in their violation; actual dates almost always exceed original estimates, often by large amounts. Sometimes, then, users, when developing systems themselves, take the opportunity to "just do" the work without a commitment to a time frame.

As the guideline suggests, to have no schedule is probably an overreaction. Schedules are important, even for tasks that have no need for coordination with others, to provide pacing and expectations against which progress can be measured.

Schedules are desirable but perhaps optional in personal computing development, but they are almost mandatory in any form of multiple-person operational activity. The work performed by personal computing applications is almost always part of larger tasks, and the schedules serve as a means of coordinating the various work elements.

Schedules also provide a time frame for use in operational improvements, as described later in Guideline 4.2. These time frames are also important to audit trails and give analysts index points with which to calibrate events.

Documentation

10. Some minimum documentation is always appropriate.

11. The PCIC can encourage good, consistent documentation by publishing an outline with sample and blank forms.

Documentation is another subject that has suffered from its image in conventional EDP, and as a result, personal computer users tend to overreact negatively and take the opportunity to ignore documentation completely.

Documentation in personal computing applications is usually less extensive than that appropriate for a well–managed conventional EDP system, and there is a natural tendency to write essentially no documentation, since "I will always remember what I did." Were it only so. You may remember what you did for six hours, maybe even for six days, but by six weeks or six months vital details exist only if written. Further, documentation is vital for converting a personal computing application from an individual effort to a company asset. Therefore, some minimum documentation is always appropriate.

Documentation of personal computing applications development serves these needs:

- To communicate what the application does
- To describe the interfaces needed with other systems
- To describe how the system may be modified
- To describe how the application is operated
- To allow managers to verify that the application has been built in accordance with "official" standards

During system operation, documentation is needed to show when the system was used, who ran it, and what data were used. Documentation of all problems encountered in the process is also important. The following types of documentation are appropriate for most personal computing applications:

- A brief, general description of the application
- A listing and explanation of codes and transactions that are accommodated by the application
- Procedures for handling and correcting errors
- Procedures for handling exceptions
- A listing and explanation of the formulas and algorithms used in the application
- A description of the files used in the application
- A description of the displays and reports produced by the application
- Procedures needed to assure that the application has completed its process correctly
- Trouble reports
- Problem resolution reports
- An operating schedule

- An operations log
- Any special operating instructions
- Data/report retention/destruction schedules
- Examples of transactions being processed

Most personal computing documentation is informal, kept simply in a labeled notebook. The PCIC can encourage good, consistent documentation, however, by publishing an outline with sample and blank forms.

Documentation is usually in paper form, but personal computing technology is appropriately used to improve the productivity of the documentation process. At the very least, the documentation should be prepared using word processing software. Personal computing can also be used to display operations documentation and capture and record the needed reports concerning the actual run on electronic logs.

Documentation can also be produced only in electronic form. The most common form of "electronic documentation" is a file of "help" commands with which the user can explore all topics. Sometimes, "tutorials" are also available "on–line."

Documentation is important for all production applications, even those that use software packages. When using software packages, the documentation supplied by the vendor will often be adequate to describe the technical aspects of the system, but documentation must still be written to describe how the package is used in this particular application.

Generally, the system custodian actually writes and maintains the documentation, under the direction of and with funding by the owner. Standards for personal computing documentation may be published by the PCIC, but department managers are responsible for the contents of the documentation for each specific application.

Documentation should be developed as early as possible during the development of the application. Almost every three months, the custodian should review the documentation to update it based on operational changes that may have occurred. Documentation is routinely reviewed by internal audit, but primary enforcement of documentation needs must be accomplished by periodic reviews by department managers and peers.

Requirements for documentation should be set and funded by systems' owners, but the actual work is performed by the custodians. Sometimes users are asked to write their own documentation; this may be effective if the work is closely supervised by the appropriate technical people.

In any case, the custodian has the responsibility of reviewing the documentation periodically to verify that the documentation is still complete and accurate. Production systems have a way of "evolving" through actual use, and care must be taken to see that the documentation is maintained along with this "evolution."

Change controls

12. A minimum set of controls are appropriate over changes to personal computing applications.

In conventional EDP applications, a major control over changes to programs or to processing procedures involves clear separation of operation and development functions. Such separation is desirable in personal computing applications, but it is usually not practical because of the individual nature of personal computing. Certain control steps are appropriate, however, in personal computing applications:

- Changes to systems are managed as projects and subject to the same types of controls as any new project.
- Changes should be documented in writing.
- All changes must be approved by the owner, although approval of changes to processing can be delegated to custodians.
- The nature of the change, the reasons for making it, and the change implementation schedule are all communicated by the custodian to all users in time for the users to prepare for the effects of the change.
- All changes must be tested in the same way that new applications are tested; in addition, however, the entire application must be tested after each change to verify that new errrors have not been created by the change.
- All program names should be by a revision control number which is updated every time a change is made to the program and displayed whenever the program is run.
- All documentation is updated to reflect the changes. The documentation should refer to the revision numbers to which the documentation applies.

One of the facts of life in information systems is that more money is spent on maintaining systems than is spent in originally developing those systems. Because of this, great emphasis is (or should be) placed on building those systems in ways that will facilitate economical maintenance, even at the cost of other factors, such as performance or speed of development.

One of the corollaries to this substantial cost of maintenance is that conventional EDP departments are so busy maintaining old software that they have no time to work on new applications. This "excess demand" creates long backlogs in most EDP departments, which, in turn, builds frustration in users. Interestingly, this frustration is one of the major reasons for the popularity of personal computing; given the long backlogs, users would do work themselves rather than waiting for their EDP department to do it for them.

The problem, of course, is that this solution carries its own seeds of destruction; to the extent that systems become successful (i.e., useful and well used), those systems must be maintained as business needs change, creating, even in the personal computing milieu, the cost and complexities of maintenance.

One solution is to build "disposable" systems, systems which are of such low cost that it is cheaper to build new ones than fix old ones. Some personal computing applications, especially those using spreadsheet and data base packages, are indeed easy to rewrite, although paradoxically, systems built on those base packages are usually also easy to change.

Given all this, it is quite likely that changes to personal computing applications will be needed, and as noted in the guideline, these changes should be documented and controlled at least as well as new projects. The types of controls described in the guidelines are really minimums; if changes become a large part of the personal computing work load, it will be wise to consult with the CIM to adopt the change controls used in your company's conventional EDP efforts.

Regression controls

13. *Regression errors can be detected and corrected by having a standard set of test data which is processed through the system every time changes are made. This regression test base should, of course, be updated whenever new features are added to the system.*

Modifications to systems can fix problems and add features, but they can also create new, unexpected errors. These errors cause the system to "regress." Regression errors can be detected and corrected by having a standard set of test data which is processed through the system every time any changes are made. This regression test base should be updated whenever new features are added to the system.

File protections

14. File controls are appropriate primarily for personal computing applications that are used in routine operations.

Again, these guidelines are a simplified subset of what is usually appropriate for conventional EDP; in specific circumstances, the CIM may feel the need to recommend additional file controls.

- All machine–readable files should be labeled externally in human–readable language and internally in machine–readable language. The internal and external labels should be *different*. (If the labels are different, the external label gives no help to someone attempting unauthorized access to the file.) The labels should identify the physical media with a permanent "volume number" and the application–oriented logical files with a "file name" in the format acceptable to the computer's operating system.
- A log should be kept showing which logical files are on which volumes.
- The date each file is created or last updated should be shown on both the internal and external labels and on the log.
- Whenever practical, the file should have a machine–readable "end–of–file" label which contains both a record count and a control total. Every program that reads the file should balance the records processed to the controls; every program that writes to the file should create new control totals.
- Password control over files should be used sparingly. Passwords provide additional security but also greatly reduce the convenience inherent in personal computing. In time–sharing computing, account and user passwords usually provide sufficient security for normal situations without additional passwords applied to individual files.
- In general, when necessary, passwords can be used to grant reasonably free read–only access to files, while update authority can be restricted.
- All personal computing users should get in the habit of copying files frequently. They should copy files from the volatile computer memory to disk periodically during the day and definitely every time they leave their desks. One incident in which several hours of work are lost because someone tripped over a power cord will reinforce this habit.
- Files should be copied regularly for backup in case the primary file is damaged. The copy should be on a different physical volume from the primary file. In applications where transactions are applied to an "old" master file and a "new" master file is produced, several "generations" of old masters and transactions should be saved for backup.

  Once on disk, duplicate copies become very cheap insurance. Especially in the relatively uncontrolled environments in which most personal computing takes place, accidents can and do happen. Those accidents destroy hard work unless the files have been copied and saved, preferably on a medium (e.g., tape, floppy disk) different from that which contains the original. The backup medium should be labeled and dated and stored separately from the original.

Hard disks, which are not removable and which contain millions of bytes of information, pose special problems. Hard disks are very reliable and, if care is taken, will rarely cause file loss. On the other hand, some basic precautions are appropriate:

- Remove from the hard disk any program (e.g., a disk format program) which can destroy all the data on the disk.
- Keep on the hard disks only programs or data that are duplicated elsewhere. For example, some people keep only working copies of programs on their hard disks, with the master copies kept elsewhere on removable media. All files can also be kept on removable media.
- The contents of the hard disk can be copied periodically either to a larger computer to which the personal computer is connected or to special tape drives developed specifically for backing-up hard disks. A few tape drives can serve a great many personal computing users; the PCIC can offer a backup service in which it loans a backup tape drive to users; alternatively, the PCIC could actually bring the tape drive to the user and perform the backup. In either case, the user purchases and stores the backup tape itself (although for critical applications, the PCIC could offer the use of a secure, fireproof vault for storage of hard disk backup tapes).

Process controls

15. Process controls are usually specified by the owner of the application but detailed and implemented by the custodian. Processing controls are particularly important when several people are involved in the work flow.

The purpose of process controls is to coordinate the efforts of several people, to provide the basis for analyzing and correcting problems, and to provide the basis for analyzing and improving the process. When one person runs the entire process, as is often the case in personal computing applications, process flows and associated controls are often ignored. This is a mistake, for several reasons:

- The person running the system usually gets data from one group of people and reports results to still another group. Those three parties form a process in which all three have expectations of each other, which, in turn, need controls.
- Process descriptions are important parts of the systems documentation needed for helping others understand how the system operates.
- If the output of the system turns out to be in error, the person must be able to determine where and how the problem occurred.

Here are some appropriate process controls:

- Processing should be performed on a predetermined schedule.
- All processing steps should be logged; the logs should be preprinted and have space to record when each step was taken, what media volumes are used, and who performed each step. As noted above, these logs are usually on paper, but they can also be kept in electronic form using a personal computing application.
- Transactions that are entered into the process ("input" transactions) should be controlled with both record counts and totals of significant fields. The system should verify the control totals at all stages of the process.

- If the input transactions are entered in several batches, the batch numbers are logged and verified.
- Reports produced by the system should also contain control totals, which allow the users to verify that the processing has completed correctly.
- Key fields, those used to identify transactions, should be verified by a "self-checking" number embedded in the field which is recomputed and checked by each program step.

Wherever possible, the process controls should be gathered automatically. For example, the transaction controls and the logging of steps can all occur under program control and, in fact, with no paper copies being produced unless needed. The process control data can be posted to a separate log/control file which is printed only if needed for analysis.

Error controls

16. *The ultimate goal of error control is to understand why and how the error occurred and to alter the process so that the error will not occur again.*
17. *All programs in production systems must check data and processing for unexpected situations. If a data error is detected (e.g., numeric data where alpha data are expected), the transaction must be reported to someone for correction.*
18. *In addition to detecting errors, the system must assure that the corrected transactions are resubmitted to the system.*

All programs in production systems must check data and processing for unexpected situations. Correction of some situations can be accomplished by the program itself; for example, most program languages allow the program to detect if a file read has failed and automatically attempt a reread. If a data error is detected (e.g.,numeric data where alpha data are expected), the transaction must be reported to someone for correction. In addition to detecting errors, the system must assure that the corrected transactions are resubmitted to the system.

- All types of data (input, process, output) should be checked for both format and validity by all programs in the system.
- Errors should be removed from the main processing system and placed on a "suspense file," which is then controlled in the same way that all other system files are controlled.
- Control totals on the main system should be adjusted to reflect the removability of the errors.
- Specific procedures must be written to review the error transactions that are placed on the suspense file and to provide the ability to correct the transactions and resubmit them to the main system. All transactions made to and from the suspense file should be dated.
- Corrections to transactions should always create an offset to the error; the incorrect transaction should never be eliminated or changed in place. Following this practice will greatly enhance future investigations into the specific processing that affected error corrections.
- The system owner should establish rules stating the time allowed to correct data errors. The system should automatically provide the owner with a report showing any errors not cleared within the specified time.

- To monitor the performance of the system, the system owner and custodian should receive routine reports showing statistics about system errors. This report should show the number of errors detected, by type, and the average time it takes to clear errors, also by error type. Any user/operator deviations from the documented procedures should also be noted. Process improvements can be made based on these statistics and notes.

Error control is an area of systems design that creates problems even for trained, experienced information systems professionals. Most analysts have little trouble detecting errors and reporting them. The problems come with the three next steps: first, the transaction controls must be corrected to reflect the file as it exists with the errors removed; second, the errors must be routed to the process or persons who will correct them; and third, the errors must be resubmitted to the system, updating the appropriate process controls.

The error management process (really a "subprocess") must be considered and tested carefully and subjected to its own process controls, as described in this guideline. The focal point of this subprocess is the "error suspense file." This file becomes the "master file" for the errors from this system and should be managed and updated with the same respect as that shown to the systems main master file. It is important, therefore, that this "error master file" (the suspense file) be "updated" with offsetting transactions rather than changing errors "in place."

Since this is such a fragile area, the role of the custodian becomes quite important. As noted in the guideline, the custodian must review error registers and take particular note of errors that are not cleared in a reasonable time. It is also useful to record errors in statistical categories so that trends can be analyzed.

As noted above, reasons for errors should be understood and corrected, with the ultimate goal being to eliminate errors completely. Often, the best way to understand the error process is to capture and analyze the transactions used to offset (correct) the original errors.

Audit trails

19. *Audit trails must be maintained showing all steps in the system process, when those steps occurred, and who was involved, to allow investigators to verify the process and determine if and where errors were created.*

Some errors cannot be detected by the system but are detected by users later. It is important to maintain adequate records showing all steps in the system process, when those steps occurred, and who was involved. These records, called audit trails, allow investigators to verify the process and determine where errors were created.

Audit trails are useful for detecting errors and identifying who made the errors and where the errors occurred, and equally important, audit trails are also useful for identifying, measuring, and improving the system process. Audit trails can be used to verify that improvements are, in fact, occurring. Many mistakes occur, not in routine processing, but in the handling of transaction errors/corrections and exceptions. It is important, therefore, that steps taken in these parts of the process be particularly well recorded.

As mentioned above, system users should correct errors through the use of transactions that offset the error, rather than making modifications directly to the original incorrect transaction. Following this practice greatly facilitates future reviews and audits.

Audit trails should simply be the sum of the process control records collected routinely. These records become audit trails when a problem is being studied. The focus for controls should be on process improvements, but the tension associated with audits will usually make people more aware of the significance of controls and, therefore, encourage a certain amount of discipline.

Interestingly, personal computing systems are inherently more difficult to audit than are manual or conventional EDP systems. In manual systems, where paper is used, the collection of paper records can be filed and is available for use in a later audit. In conventional EDP, reports and paper console logs can also be used for investigations.

Future investigations are also easier when there are "old" and "new" master files, written to separate files, as is usually the case in a classic batch sequential file update in a conventional EDP system. An auditor can easily trace the changes by comparing the old and new records.

Direct-access files that allow updates in place are much more difficult to analyze. Personal computing systems rarely keep old and new files unless the system users, following custodians' directions, take specific steps to do this. I strongly recommend this practice; floppy disks are much cheaper than the time and aggravation involved in reconstructing old files.

Rather than depending on the operations skills of a system's users, the developers can simplify potential reconstructions by never updating records in place but always using and recording correction transactions as "journal entries" against the original transactions. This is probably a good policy to follow in all systems, but it is especially appropriate for personal computing systems, where it is so easy to erase old files or transactions, thereby destroying the trails needed for audit or reconstruction.

In addition, in personal computing, reports most often merely appear on video screens; the few records kept are usually written on reusable media such as floppy disks. If these records are to be available for future studies, the personal computing system custodian should take great care to maintain library records of media and to reuse the media in accordance with a carefully considered media retention policy. This implies that the physical media be permanently numbered, both internally and externally, so that the files on the media can be related to a specific disk or tape.

Identification code controls

20. Personal computing developers should **not** *invent identification codes when standard codes exist. The codes used in personal computing applications should be the standard, company-authorized codes.*

Data format controls

21. Personal computing users should **not** *invent data formats when standard formats exist. When technically feasible, personal computing users should use the same data dictionaries as those used in conventional EDP applications.*

Duplication of codes or data formats not only is a waste of time and money but creates incompatibilities between systems and the data that flow among them. In addition, if standard codes or formats are not used, the reports and analyses made from these systems will, at best, require additional explanation and, at worst, confuse and mislead readers. Standards such as these are ultimately the responsibility of the vice-president, administration, but the specifics are usually delegated to the accounting department or to the CIM.

When technical differences between personal computing and conventional

EDP equipment require format changes, the conversions should be well documented. Further, if possible, all the conversions of formats should occur in a single program (a "gateway"), allowing all the other programs in the system to be at least internally consistent. Proper standardization of identification codes and data formats also greatly facilitates coordinated personal computing systems, discussed in Part II.

CHECKLIST

Guideline 4.1
Operational Controls for Personal Computing Users

	YES	NO	N/A

1. General Goal

Do those people who are responsible for results have the maximum amount of direct control over the processes that produce those results?

2. Basic Guideline

Is the responsibility for controls given to the department managers who supervise personal computing users?

Can advice on personal computing controls be obtained from the manager, PCIC; from the CIM; and from the internal audit department?

3. Owner, Custodian, User Concepts

Are systems' owners and custodians explicitly defined?

Are their responsibilities well defined and understood? (Every system should have one owner; the system may have several custodians and many users. In personal computing applications, these three roles may be fulfilled by one person.)

4. Responsibilities

Are the following responsibilities understood?

a. The owner has responsibilities for all logical and financial decisions concerning the resources.

b. The custodian of a resource is that organization which, following the owner's direction, implements processes that use the resource.

c. Users employ the resource in their routine business.

5. Equipment Controls

Is all personal computing equipment owned by the PCIC?

Do the personal computing users understand and accept their dual role as both custodian and user?

(Continues)

123

6. Personnel and Organizational Controls

   Is the power of personal computing being placed only into the hands of those who can be trusted to use the power constructively and responsibly?

7. Routine Jobs and Schedules

   Are schedules required from all personal computer users who are developing applications or processing transactions?

8. Documentation

   Is some appropriate, minimal documentation always required?

   Does the PCIC encourage good, consistent documentation by publishing an outline with sample and blank forms?

9. Change Controls

   Have an appropriate, minimal set of controls been defined for changes to personal computing applications?

10. Regression Controls

    Are regression errors detected and corrected through the use of a standard set of test data which is processed through the system every time any changes are made? (This regression test base should, of course, be updated whenever new features are added to the system.)

11. File Protections

    Are file controls appropriately set for personal computing applications that are used in routine operations?

12. Process Controls

    Are process controls usually specified by the owner of the application but detailed and implemented by the custodian? (Processing controls are particularly important when several people are involved in the work flow.)

13. Error Controls

    Has the goal of error control been defined as follows: To understand why and how the error occurred and to alter the process so that the error will not occur again?

    Do all programs in production systems check data and processing for unexpected situations?

If a data error is detected (e.g., numeric data where alpha is expected), is the transaction reported to someone for correction?

In addition to detecting errors, does the system assure that the corrected transactions are resubmitted to the system?

14. Audit Trails

   Are audit trails maintained showing all steps in the system process, when those steps occurred, and who was involved, to allow investigators to verify the process and determine if and where errors were created?

15. Identification Code Controls

   Are guidelines established suggesting that personal computing developers should *not* invent identification codes when standard codes exist? (The codes used in personal computing applications should be the standard, company–authorized codes.)

16. Data Format Controls

   Are guidelines established suggesting that personal computing users should *not* invent data formats when standard formats exist? (When technically feasible, personal computing users should use the same data dictionaries that are used in conventional EDP applications.)

125

Guideline 4.2: Personal Computing as Part of Total Quality Control

There is a specific assumption in this guideline which is carefully stated in the first line of the fundamental principle section: that the company has decided to use total quality control (TQC) as a basic management philosophy. If this is not the case, you may wish to bypass this guideline. Better yet, you may wish to read the guideline, implement it for personal computing, and then gradually implement TQC in other company processes.

Note that the use of TQC is not a fad or a one-time "quick-fix" program. Rather, TQC is a definitive way of management and can and should be applied to all forms of organizational activities and processes. This guideline barely scratches the surface of TQC; the full implementation of TQC in a company requires top management commitment and ongoing, in-house expert leadership.

Fundamental principle

1. *Total quality control (TQC) is a set of business practices that has been adopted by our company. Personal computing is an important tool that helps employees move these concepts from theory into "real-world" practice.*

State that total quality control (TQC) is a set of business practices which has been adopted by the company, and mention the role of personal computing. The reasons behind a company's commitment to a TQC program are based on several fundamental assumptions:

- Processes should be focused on the needs of external and internal customers.
- All the work performed by employees can be described as part of a process.
- All processes can be continually improved.

This guideline focuses on the use of personal computing in support of other TQC efforts in a company; Guideline 4.3 focuses on the effectiveness of the personal computing process itself.

Elements of TQC

2. *Perform the following steps in order.*
   a. *Choose an operation to improve, based on customer requirements.*
   b. *Describe the work, task, or project as a process.*
   c. *Identify measurement points in the process.*
   d. *Specify metrics at each measurement step.*
   e. *Collect data for each metric at each measurement step.*
   f. *Analyze the data and prioritize areas that appear, according to the data, to need improvement.*
   g. *Evaluate alternatives for improving the process.*
   h. *Implement improvements/changes.*
   i. *Monitor the process.*

The elements of TQC, as used in this guideline, are illustrated in Figure 4.1 and include the following steps in the order shown:

Choose an operation to improve based on customer needs—Focus on those activities that provide the highest leverage (i.e., most results for the effort/cost invested) on tasks which will most help your customers. Selection of the "right" activ-

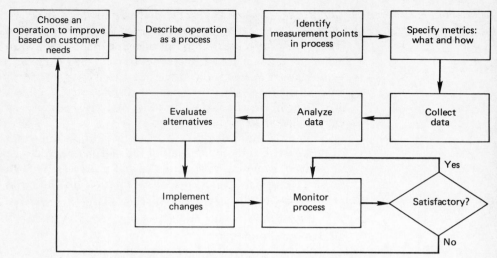

Figure 4.1   Operations improvement flowchart.

ity to improve is similar to "doing the right things," discussed in Guideline 4.3. Use data whenever possible to determine which operation needs work.

Note the focus on processes that affect customers. One of the major benefits of the TQC methodology is that employees must identify their customers and, through analysis and interviews, determine what it is that the customers really want.

Analysis of customer needs is as crucial as is the methodology for meeting those needs. Especially with regard to information systems, customers may not know or be able to articulate their true needs; prototyping methodologies are, therefore, often appropriate. Personal computing technology is particularly useful in these situations.

Describe the work, task, or project as a process—Often, managers describe themselves as "results oriented," stating that the "ends" are what really count and that the "means to the ends" are less important. The TQC methodology asks instead that managers become "process oriented," focusing on results but in terms of the processes that produce those results, and on intermediate measures in those processes.

Identify measurement points in the process—Here are some of the characteristics of measurements that are appropriate for TQC:

- They measure process performance, not just output.
- They are measurements at significant points in the process. Significance is usually based on the location of the step in the process. Typically, significant points are at the beginning and the end of the process, at any bottleneck, at points where significant resources (labor, material, capital) are added, or at points where responsibilities in the process change. It is in this characteristic that a "results orientation" is reconciled with the process orientation; "results" are really performance measures taken at a prespecified point in the process.
- The appropriate data can be collected easily and economically.
- Repeated measurements are possible and will provide consistent information that will highlight exceptions and trends.
- The results of the measurements are clear and easy to communicate.
- The measurements can be compared to an ideal.

Specify metrics at each measurement step—Specify both what to measure and how it should be measured. Measurement tools/instruments should be selected, people trained to use them, and appropriate procedures written.

Collect data for each metric at each measurement step—Data should be collected in economical and consistent ways and in a form that facilitates analysis. All the people involved in data collection should have some training, which should include, at a minimum, these topics:

- An overview of the TQC process, so that the data collectors understand why data collection is important.
- A discussion of the specific measurements being taken, why the measurement is appropriate, and how the data will be analyzed. Typical and reasonable results should be shown, but care must be taken to avoid creating biases in the minds of the collectors.
- Specific training on how to use the measurement equipment, on how to record the data, and on the procedures and methods to be followed.

Automated data collection methods and tools should be used whenever economically feasible. Such automation may not lower cost, but it will almost always increase the accuracy, reliability, and consistency of the data.

Analyze the data and prioritize areas that appear, according to the data, to need improvement—All the data should be gathered by a person trained in data analysis techniques. In addition, this person should have participated in the training of the data collectors and understand any problems that the data collectors (and, therefore, the data itself) may have.

The technology of data analysis in a TQC context is known as statistical quality control (SQC); many statisticians, people with professional training in statistics, are specializing in this technology and are useful in establishing and monitoring TQC efforts. As with other applications, however, the basic responsibilities still rest with the department managers.

Since analyses often compare results for different periods, the analysis person should be sure that the data are processed for comparable periods; usually, this implies the enforcement of specific cutoff times. Depending on volume, the analysis person might collect data at interim periods, performing a summary analysis when a major report is due. Frequent collections and interim analyses allow faster feedback and therefore more rapid process improvements. Typical SQC tools are control charts, scatter plots, checksheets, Pareto charts, and histograms.

Evaluate alternatives for improving the process—Alternatives should be discussed with everyone involved in the operation and measurement of the process. Managers and individual contributors should have equal voice. If any opinion is given preference, it should be that of the people who will actually implement the proposed changes. Alternatives can be displayed and evaluated using such tools as process flow diagrams, cause–and–effect diagrams, and experiments where changes are made and statistically evaluated.

Implement improvements/changes—The implementation of process modifications should be made with the same care that was taken with the initial process installation. It is particularly important to update the process documentation and to provide all the necessary training. Pilot or parallel processes may be appropriate. Once the process has been modified, it is also necessary to review and modify, if necessary, the process measurement points and methods.

Monitor the process—The data collection and analysis should be performed frequently until the process is operating in a stable, satisfactory manner. Stability implies that the measurement data routinely fall within specified boundaries; those boundaries are set by managers based on their expectations of what is satisfactory for this process at this time.

Once the process is satisfactory and stable, the frequency of data collection and analysis can be reduced. Process improvement resources can then be focused on other priority processes, or if resources are available, attention can be directed to this same process to improve it still further, the ultimate goal being "perfection."

Applying personal computing to TQC

3. Personal computing can be justified and should be applied as a tool to improve the implementation of TQC principles in the company.

4. Personal computing can be used to accomplish changes in:
   a. Products being provided to the customer
   b. Processes themselves
   c. The ways in which processes are being used

Examples of each of these would be: products being provided to the customer: improved reports, at lower cost, more frequently; the processes themselves: compressing several steps into one, thus increasing accuracy and throughput time, while lowering costs; and the ways in which the processes are being used: by providing improved instructions at each process step.

The suggestions shown in this guideline for accomplishing TQC should be viewed only as examples; users, following the TQC principles mentioned above, should develop their own, specific applications. In addition, system custodians might develop TQC methods for all system users, and owners might request and provide the resources needed to make TQC an integral part of the applications.

Reduce costs—The most common personal computing applications work on producing the same results or products more efficiently. These typically reduce costs, at least in the long run, and are easily justified on this basis. From a TQC standpoint, we also focus on the quality benefits, usually accuracy and reliability, which come from using personal computing.

Change products and/or services—It is more difficult, but usually more profitable, to find ways in which to change the actual product or service being delivered. This allows personal computing to affect the company revenues as well as its costs.

Both internal and external products can be changed. For example, rather than producing long accounting reports, a general accountant can use personal computing to prepare, instead, a detailed data base containing the same set of financial records. The users of the accounting reports can then develop personal computing applications to search the data base for the transactions and relationships that are of interest.

Change customer–oriented processes—We can also use personal computing to change the way we work with customers ("external" products). In service businesses, such as banks, travel agencies, and public accounting firms, personal computing can be used to change the way in which the services are delivered. Customers can actually use their own personal computing applications to work with the vendor; for example, many banks offer bill–paying services where customers can use their personal computers to transfer money from their bank account to that of a vendor, totally bypassing the normal check–writing process.

Manufacturing companies must use a bit more creativity in finding ways in which personal computing can directly increase revenues. Here are some suggestions:

- Personal computing systems can be given to customers for use in placing orders directly with the vendor, bypassing the normal order–taking process. The ease of doing business may increase order volume from customers using these systems.
- Customers can be sold or given personal computing applications which help them better use the vendors' products. For example, a semiconductor manufacturer may sell a customer a design system that helps the customer select the appropriate component for a given application.

This subject is discussed further in Guideline 4.3.

Personal computing as a measurement tool

In addition, personal computing may be used as part of the measurement and evaluation process. For example:

- To collect data from the process
- To analyze and report the data collected
- To simulate and evaluate the effects of alternative process steps
- To monitor the process
- To provide automatic control for process management equipment

Applying TQC to the personal computing process

5. *Use of personal computing is itself a process that can be improved using TQC principles; personal computing can be used to monitor personal computing processes.*

For example, when developing personal computing applications, we can use text editors to help write programs, store and retrieve subroutines and data layouts from personal computing libraries, and actually use personal computing to execute series of programs. We have discussed before how personal computing can be used appropriately in operational support roles.

Further, personal computing can be used to ensure improved meeting of customers' real needs by using personal computing systems as application prototypes or as interim solutions until what is needed and what is provided converge.

To summarize: Virtually everything in business can be viewed as a process oriented toward improving customer satisfaction, and personal computing can and should be applied to the improvement of the process itself and of the products produced by those processes.

CHECKLIST

Guideline 4.2
Personal Computing as Part of Total Quality Control

	YES	NO	N/A

1. Fundamental Principle

Has the company adopted total quality control (TQC) as an important busines practice?

Is personal computing recognized as an important tool that helps employees move these concepts from theory into "real world" practice?

2. Elements of TQC

Has the company adopted the following methodology to implement TQC philosophies?

a. Chosen an operation to improve, based on customer requirements

b. Described the work, task, or project as a process

c. Identified measurement points in the process

d. Specified metrics at each measurement step

e. Collected data for each metric at each measurement step

f. Analyzed the data and prioritized areas that appear, according to the data, to need improvement

g. Evaluated alternatives for improving the process

h. Implemented improvements/changes

i. Monitored the process

3. Applying Personal Computing to TQC

Is the implementation of TQC principles viewed as a reasonable justification for personal computing?

Is personal computing being used as a tool to improve the implementation of TQC principles?

Is personal computing being used to accomplish changes in:

a. Products being provided to the customer

b. Processes themselves

c. The ways in which processes themselves are being used

(Continues)

133

4. Applying TQC to the Personal Computing Process

Is the use of personal computing itself viewed as a process that can be improved using TQC principles?

Is personal computing used to monitor personal computing processes?

Guideline 4.3: Applying Personal Computing to the "Right" Tasks

As noted in Guideline 4.2, the key to TQC is not only that processes should be improved, but that we should focus on those things important to our internal and external customers. This guideline speaks specifically to the use of personal computing as directly as possible in the support of customer–related activities. This process is sometimes described as applying information systems to "strategic" needs of the enterprise.

Fundamental principle

1. *Personal computing can significantly improve the company's processes by focusing on first–order tasks, bypassing or eliminating second–order tasks.*

As described in Guideline 4.2, personal computing is appropriately used as part of the improvement of work processes; personal computing can help "do things right." It is usually more important, although more subtle, to apply personal computing to "doing the right things." The "right things" are those that help meet the real needs of our customers and are evaluated using the customers' measures and expectations. Although our primary customers are those people and companies that buy our products and services, for the purposes of this guideline, everyone in the company can be said to have customers, even if, for some, the customers are other company employees. In this guideline, these "right things" are called "first–order tasks," tasks that are fundamental to the success of the business. Tasks have developed to support internal rules or bureaucracy are called "second–order tasks" and should be avoided, if possible.

Personal computing can significantly improve the company's processes by focusing on first–order tasks, bypassing or eliminating second–order tasks (although personal computing may also be justified by allowing the second–order tasks to be accomplished more efficiently than can be done manually).

Focus on first-order tasks

2. *We can and should apply personal computing to first-order tasks.*

The terms "first-order tasks" and "second-order tasks" are used as simply another way of looking at the issue of direct customer support. In fact, no company of any size can operate only with first-order tasks. A payroll system, for example, needed by all but tiny businesses, is a second-order task. Thus it is valuable and appropriate to apply personal computing to those second-order tasks. In fact, most personal computing (and conventional EDP) applications have been focused on second-order tasks.

The "news" is that we can and should apply personal computing to first-order tasks. Convention EDP is usually buried within the support organizations in the company, and therefore information systems professionals rarely have the opportunity to focus on first-order tasks. Personal computing, however, in the hands of marketing, sales, and engineering people whose normal jobs are in first-order tasks, can and should be applied to first-order tasks.

In large, functionalized companies, paperwork often becomes a "substitute" for business realities, and goals are set in terms of the paperwork accomplishments. To the extent that these "paper realities" can be eliminated and replaced with contact with actual customers, products, and services, companies will be more successful.

It is common in these businesses, especially those that are geographically dispersed, to work with the actual customer at one location, build the product in another location, and perform the administration surrounding both the production and sale in still a third location. These locations are tied together by a steady stream of paperwork.

The paperwork, usually completed forms, take on lives of their own, and processing these forms often becomes the goal for many departments. Departments in which this is happening can usually be identified by the performance measures used to evaluate the employees. If the measures are something like "to complete 50 forms per day," it is fairly clear that this department focuses on the paper, not the underlying business effect.

It probably is not possible or even desirable to eliminate all second-order tasks, but it is probably always appropriate to *try* to eliminate the tasks. The attempt should be made by all employees, focused on the tasks under their control. A clerk may influence eliminating an entire form or, perhaps, simply some data elements on a form; a plant manager, however, might see ways to consolidate work and actually reorganize the work flows of several departments.

A specific example of this capability is desktop publishing, where the number of steps between the writer and final publication of a document is reduced significantly. Desktop publishing has been made possible by software that facilitates the creation of final copy (words), and of high–quality illustrations, and then allows one person to electronically merge the copy and illustrations. The invention of graphics printers allows that same person to actually produce the final document, choosing appropriate print fonts, printing the final copy in color or in black and white as needed.

Desktop publishing reduces costs, but also shortens the time needed to prepare documents. This joint capability will eventually allow documents to be economically prepared for specific customers and products. For example, a computer manufacturer could deliver to a customer reference documentation tailored to that customer's specific hardware and software configuration, rather than the generic documentation now provided. This documentation tailoring provides increased value to the customer and a competitive advantage to the vendor.

Personal computing, as noted in the guideline, can help by replacing the paper with electronic media; doing this probably reduces cost for both processing and filing the document. More can potentially be saved, however, when, using its communications and file access capabilities, personal computing actually changes the ways in which the work is performed.

For example, an important first-order task is the entering of customer orders into a company's manufacturing process. This order–entry process usually requires the use of volumes of paperwork to record the sale and schedule the products' manufacture and shipment. The processing of all this paperwork is a typical second-order task.

Personal computing can, when linked in appropriate systems, eliminate these second-order tasks. Orders can be entered electronically from the personal computing tools used by salespeople, transmitted to the appropriate manufacturing site, scheduled by a production controller using personal computing, and shipped by personal computing used by the finished–goods manager. The only paper needed may be the packing slip and, later, an invoice. Desktop publishing eliminates the intermediate steps and paper drafts involved in coordinating the activities of a writer, illustrator, layout person, and printing specialist.

Another example is the organizing of a customer support center. The first-order task is to provide training to customers, answer their questions, and solve any problems they might have with our products. Establishing procedures and forms and setting accounting and personnel policies are all important, but they are second-order tasks. Many of these second-order tasks can be bypassed if the customer support representatives have personal computing applications which automatically perform those second-order tasks still needed (e.g., payroll, customer billing) and eliminate the need for complicated forms and procedures.

Decision support systems

3. *Personal computing is also involved in first-order tasks when the application provides the company with business advantages not easily duplicated by competitors.*

"Decision support systems" (DSSs) are one way of providing the company with business advantages; these systems are, in effect, personal computing applications for senior executives. Personal computing systems that help executives focus on first-order tasks can also be called "decision support systems." These are discussed a bit more below and in more detail in Chapter 8.

Purpose of this guideline

4. *This guideline states the need to identify the basic functions of the business and describes some of the ways in which personal computing can be applied to these ("first-order") functions rather than merely improving the efficiency of "second-order" tasks. The guideline also describes methods for evaluating personal computing applications.*
5. *Sometimes simply stating that this approach is both valid and desirable provides employees with motivation to use personal computing to focus on first-order tasks.*

First-order tasks first

6. *In those applications and departments where the choice exists, personal computing should be applied to the first-order tasks involving "real" (outside) customers, rather than the first-order tasks involving internal customers.*

Note the emphasis, although it may appear obvious that while first-order tasks can refer to internal as well as external customers, those tasks that work with external customers have higher priority.

Identifying first-order tasks

7. *Determine how a task increases revenues, decreases costs, or provides competitive advantages.*
8. *Methods for increasing revenues:*
   a. *Increase the volume of customers' purchases.*
   b. *Increase average prices.*
   c. *Increase market share.*
   d. *Improve customer services.*
9. *Methods of decreasing costs:*
   a. *Lower costs of raw materials.*
   b. *Increase inventory turnover rates.*
   c. *Decrease manufacturing cycle time.*
   d. *Reduce manufacturing costs.*
   e. *Reduce costs of complying with government requirements.*
   f. *Decrease employee turnover.*

10. Ways to provide a competitive advantage:
   a. Identify and focus on optimizing the use of scarce resources.
   b. Increase the speed with which new products or products tailored for specific customers can be developed.
   c. Provide specific valuable services that competitors cannot easily duplicate.
   d. Provide executives with decision support systems.
   e. Reduce the number of organizational layers between the customer and the satisfaction of the customers needs.

Examples of methods for increasing revenues:

- Increase the volume of customers' purchases. For example, a system might be devised to analyze the historical pattern of customers' purchases to offer attractive price breaks for increased business volumes.
- Increase average prices. For example, salespeople could use a personal computing application for calculating appropriate prices on volume purchases of commodity items, using algorithms established by company marketing analysts.
- Increase market share. For example, a market researcher might develop a personal computing application that collects sales and price information on all competitors and helps the researcher develop a strategy to increase market share with minimum price erosion.
- Improve customer services. For example, personal computing applications can give salespeople the capability of responding rapidly to even complex customer requests for price and availability quotes.

Ways in which revenues can be raised are usually more obvious in those departments that work directly with external customers. Most ways of increasing revenues from customers involve obtaining more of the business that now goes to competitors. Developing new demand for a product or for totally new customers usually requires a great deal of marketing creativity. When there are essentially no competitors, it is probably more appropriate to focus personal computing on reducing costs. This type of "monopoly" may exist because of technical or geographic factors, or because of regulation (e.g., utilities, government organizations).

The most common form of monopoly, however, is the one that an internal vendor holds over internal customers. For example, anyone who wishes to purchase items must use the company's purchasing department. Usually, all EDP services must be obtained from the company EDP department, although some companies allow, at least in principle, the option of obtaining services outside the company if there are compelling reasons to do so.

It is usually particularly inappropriate for internal vendors to try to increase revenues from internal customers even when accounting systems allow this. For example, many EDP departments charge their internal users for the work performed for those users. It is better for the company for the EDP department to focus on providing increased services at lower costs rather than focusing on increasing revenues from its internal, captive customers.

Examples of methods of decreasing costs:

- Lower costs of raw materials. For example, a purchasing manager might collect data on many vendors performance and negotiate purchases only with those with the most prompt delivery performance and the highest quality in different price categories.

- Increase inventory turnover rates. For example, a manufacturing manager can calculate accurate parts usage history and keep on hand the minimum inventory needed, based on history, adjusted by demand fluctuations.
- Decrease manufacturing cycle time. For example, manufacturing engineers might use personal computing to simulate various shop-floor loading strategies, selecting the optimum routings for different manufacturing product mixes.
- Reduce manufacturing costs. For example, personal computing can be used to directly control process equipment, increasing the speed and consistency of production.
- Reduce costs of complying with government requirements. For example, the various government forms can be maintained in a personal computing system, requiring the entry of only those data that vary among reporting periods.
- Decrease employee turnover. For example, computer-based instruction systems can be used to keep employees up to date at minimum cost and time commitment.

For given levels of performance and quality, it is appropriate, in all organizations, to attempt to decrease costs, regardless of the revenue implications. Even in those organizations, such as some consultants or some government contractors, in which revenues are based directly on the incurred costs, keeping the costs down will usually improve the companies' long-term relations with the customers.

Cost, however, is a *primary* factor only if low costs are integral to the business strategy of the company or product line. The vendor should try to lower costs only when such action does not compromise other critical factors, such as quality or delivery time. In fact, an appropriate use of personal computing would be to improve quality or delivery time while keeping costs relatively constant. Interestingly, focusing on quality issues often lowers costs as a by-product by eliminating scrap, rework, and other wasteful operations.

Examples of ways of providing competitive advantage:

Identify and focus on optimizing the use of scarce resources. For example, use operations research algorithms to calculate low-cost, high-quality mixes of scarce materials.

Increase the speed with which new products or products tailored for specific customers can be developed. For example, computer-aided-design tools, coupled with appropriate data bases, can produce custom variations on standard designs very rapidly.

Provide specific valuable services that competitors cannot easily duplicate. For example, using personal computing together with communications and data base systems, our salespeople could offer next-day availability of our standard products even if the products must be shipped from warehouses in different parts of the country.

Some companies are able to increase market share by using personal computing applications to create a unique technical relationship between themselves and their customers. Usually, these applications somehow optimize scarce resources: for example, reduce design time, lower the use of expensive materials, lower the involvement of skilled engineers or executives, or reduce delivery times.

This section, again, while totally appropriate with regard to external customers, may cause problems if applied as a "competitive advantage" to internal customers. In internal relationships, cooperation, not competition, is the higher value; it is usually inappropriate to compete openly with another internal vendor, even in an attempt to provide higher value to an internal customer.

All this speaks to the sincerity of motivation rather than the appearance of action. Internal vendors should always try to optimize their resources and those of their (internal) customers, but should do so from a sincere desire to contribute more effectively to overall company performance, not merely to appear to be "showing up" sister company departments.

Provide executives with decision support systems. DSSs allow executives to use data bases, usually built by conventional EDP systems, in flexible, unstructured ways. The data bases used may be key company files or may be files that are accessible on public information utilities containing industry-wide or even national economic data. Generalized programs such as spreadsheets, and modeling can be used to analyze the data as needed for use in such applications as acquisitions/divestitures, long-range planning, investment decisions, market research, or research and development.

DSSs are tools that improve the use of the scarce resource known as excellent managers. There are two possible goals:

- To increase the amount of work performed by skilled managers
- To increase the number of people who can perform skilled management tasks

In general, the state of the art is such that we are able to approach the first goal even though we are less successful with the second. Personal computing can reduce the amount of clerical work needed to support management decisions and increase the speed with which decisions can be made. Personal computing may even give a manager access to more complete, more timely data on which to make decisions. The managers, however, are still needed to actually make the decisions.

More people will be able to make complex decisions if we are ever able to create "artificial executives" through the use of "artificial intelligence" technologies. Some routine decision making can be simulated by using special-purpose algorithms or "expert" programs which attempt to imitate what is done by the human manager, but even these sophisticated programs fail or mislead when circumstances surrounding the decision vary.

Reduce the number of organizational layers between the customer and the satisfaction of the customers needs. In a typical manufacturing company, for example, an order goes from a customer to a salesperson to an order processing person to factory production control to inventory control to manufacturing to shipping-with lots of staff activities along the way.

Shortening this process lowers costs for the company but also allows the company to satisfy the customer's needs more rapidly (and sometimes in a more tailored fashion), thus providing the customer with increased value and the company with competitive advantage.

How to apply personal computing to business tasks

11. *Determine whether and how a proposed personal computing application can be defined as a first-order task.*
12. *Determine what must be done, both technically and politically, to remove the barriers.*

If it is apparent that the task being automated is really a second-order task, determine what barriers prevent focus on the first-order tasks. Typical barriers are these:

- Organizational separation/functionalization
- Geographic separation

- Timing differences
- Government rules/regulations
- Company-imposed rules/policies
- Short-term versus long-term goals

Note that what is being defined in this guideline section is not a formula, but a process by which second-order tasks can be bypassed. The first step in the process is to specify what barriers are perceived.

Next, we should at least go through the exercise of defining the "ideal" situation, describing how the process would flow with all the barriers removed. Then it is possible to break the problem into its technical and political components and address them accordingly. Determine what must be done, both technically and politically, to remove the barriers. Usually, the technical problems are addressed more easily than organizational/political issues; technical issues should, therefore, be addressed first.

Personal computing applications can often help resolve technical issues by demonstrating how a problem can be solved. Managers can then focus on the political issues. For example, when a customer requests information on product availability, salespeople usually complete quote request forms which are processed both at the sales office and then at the factory.

The technical barriers involve the ability of the remote salesperson (or even the customer!) to inquire directly into a factory inventory. The organizational barrier is a separation of function between the field and factory, where the field people are interested in solving the immediate needs of specific customers while the factory is trying to lower costs and meet the long-run needs of many customers.

Personal computing can be used to help solve the technical problem. Demonstrating the ability for the field salespeople to easily and accurately read a factory's inventory files may encourage managers to solve the real political problem of divergent goals between the field and factory managers.

Generally, personal computing applications can help remove technical barriers by creating "electronic bridges" between organizations or data bases that may be separated in space or time. Depending on the culture of the company, personal computing can create more power in local organizations (my preference) or can allow central groups to exercise their power more competently than can be done without such systems. The political/organizational issues are not easily solved, but removing the technical excuses often exposes those problems, allowing open discussion that will provide the best opportunity for eventual resolution.

How to evaluate personal computing applications

13. *Set appropriate expectations. When the personal computing application is first justified, users should state their expectations or goals in business terms.*
14. *Perform the evaluations. Department managers are primarily responsible for evaluations.*
15. *Evaluation criteria. Business and productivity performance should be compared to expectations, stated in comparison to targets, history, and/or internal/external competition.*

Setting appropriate expectations—When the personal computing application is first justified, users should state their expectations or goals in business terms. These expectations (or a revised set of them) become the basis for future evaluations. Sometimes, of course, the expectations will be set by the department manager; for example, the manager may state that the user must increase productivity by 20%.

Expectations should be set for both individuals and for user departments; often, using personal computing, an individual's work load may increase, but the department becomes more productive, because, for example, a departed employee may not need replacement. Technical goals can also be set for the application. These goals can be set in terms of "attributes" such as functionality, usability, reliability, performance, and supportability.

Expectations may be set against three different types of goals: against a preset target, as compared to historical performance, or as compared to what similar functions are accomplishing elsewhere in the company or in the industry outside the company. The major point to emphasize here is that some sort of expectations should be set. The exact nature of the expectations is usually less important than the fact that they exist; expectations can be improved with experience.

Expectations are often best recorded on a matrix with functions along the left axis and attributes for column headings. Performance and technical goals can then be recorded in each cell.

Performing the evaluations—Department managers are primarily responsible for evaluations. They may receive help, however, from internal auditors, external auditors, consultants from the Personal Computing Information Center (PCIC) or from the conventional EDP group. Where possible, the department managers should solicit positive or negative feedback from the customers served by the personal computing application. Ideally, this feedback will be collected in an organized fashion, using, for example, a structured annual survey or questionnaire. If possible, the same questions should be asked each year so that differences in performance can be tracked. Individual users should also be encouraged to perform self-evaluations using checklists provided by the auditors or by the PCIC.

Evaluations of DSSs are usually made by the executives who use the systems, since criteria for the types of problems faced by these executives are usually highly subjective. Typical measures for these types of problems involve stock price changes, long-term growth in revenues and earnings, stability of period to period results, and long-term economic value of the company.

As with almost everything, the evaluation fulcrum is the department manager. In this function more than others, however, managers can and should call on expert advice. Many industrial engineers and consultants specialize in performance evaluation, and internal advisors, especially in audit departments, are specialists in key areas.

Using these experts gives department managers ways of working with their employees in objective ways, with no fear of unfair bias or preference. The experts can "hit and run," while the department managers must "live" with the effects of the evaluations and the corrections that result from them.

Evaluations are, of course, best when the results can be objectively measured and compared. This may be possible in operational situations but is virtually impossible in DSSs or in executive processes. Managers should, instead, set their own goals and be measured by their ability to meet their own expectations.

Evaluation criteria—Business and productivity performance should be compared to expectations, stated in comparison to targets, history, and/or internal/external competition. Business measures include such things as revenues, costs, or asset values. Although these can be set in absolute or relative dollar terms, such things as customer satisfaction can be measured using surveys, focus interviews, or other market research tools. The criteria, of course, for these surveys are the customers' needs, expressed in terms of their needs and expectations. Productivity measures include performance stated as rates per time period, or time or effort (e.g., person-days) needed to reach a given milestone.

If technical expectations were set, the application should also be compared against those goals. Even if specific technical targets were not set, evaluators may judge the application in terms of how it meets the users needs. For example, if it is apparent that many inexperienced people regularly use the application, it would be appropriate to comment on the usability of on–line reference materials such as "help" commands.

Evaluation criteria are also subject to "first-order" and "second-order" effects, where first-order criteria are those that reflect "real-world" measures rather than internal measures. It is not always clear, however, what measures are important, even in the external world. Most stock analysts have complex tables of indicators that vary by industry and sometimes by company. Therefore, as noted above, appropriate executives should be asked to set the goals, and performance can be measured against those expectations.

Recognize also that employees must sometimes take the risk of "doing what's right," not blindly "doing what's expected." Obeying orders rigidly is usually needed in military combat but is rarely appropriate in business activities, especially when employees deal directly with complex decisions.

Evaluating the personal computing program itself

16. It is also necessary to evaluate the personal computing program itself. As with applications, the best criteria are oriented toward customer and business processes.

Internal customers of personal computing are the users of the technology. Therefore, it makes sense for the evaluations to be made by the custodians of personal computing, the PCIC and the CIM. For example, one difficult but important area to evaluate is the social and morale effects that personal computing applications have on the users. Surveys and structured interviews can probe these areas but should be written and administered by experts in sociological research.

Reports comparing actual performance against expectations are usually prepared by the custodian and directed primarily to the owners of the systems (processes) involved. Copies of the performance reports are also usually distributed to users. Performance reports should be sufficiently frequent to be useful in adjusting performance but not so frequent that they are a nuisance. Costs of the performance reports should be included in the costs of the overall process and subject themselves to questions of cost-effectiveness.

It is difficult to define a "successful" information system. From a technical basis, however, here are some measures:

- The system should be reliable in the sense that given stimuli (inputs) give uniformly predictable results (outputs).
- The costs of the system's operation remain within predicted and acceptable ranges.
- The system is adaptable; it can be easily modified to accommodate a wide range of functions and a wide range of operating loads.

Since personal computing creates emotional as well as technical change, evaluation of sociological change is important. It is also important to use only professionals at sociological research to perform the evaluation, because poor research can give not only inaccurate results but can also create discomfort and nervousness among employees.

Prompt and accurate feedback of all results are needed so that performance can be adjusted as necessary. Personal computing applications can be developed for the express purpose of providing and displaying performance feedback, even on personal computing applications themselves. There is something strangely human about this self-evaluation; we are less "the cobblers mending their children's shoes" and more of "the doctors healing themselves."

CHECKLIST

Guideline 4.3
Applying Personal Computing to the 'Right' Tasks

	YES	NO	N/A

1. Fundamental Principle

Are personal computing applications significantly improving the company's processes by focusing on first-order tasks, bypassing or eliminating second-order tasks?

2. Focus on First-Order Tasks

Is personal computing being applied to first-order tasks?

3. Decision Support Systems

Is personal computing involved in first-order tasks in which the application provides the company with business advantages not easily duplicated by competitors?

4. Purpose of This Guideline

Have company managers identified the basic functions of the business and described some of the ways in which personal computing can be applied to these (''first-order'') functions rather than merely improving the efficiency of ''second-order'' tasks?

Do managers also understand methods for evaluating personal computing applications?

Has this philosophy been stated so that employees are motivated to use personal computing on first-order tasks?

5. First-order Tasks First

In those applications and departments where the choice exists, has personal computing been applied first to the first-order tasks involving ''real'' (outside) customers, rather than the first-order tasks involving internal customers?

6. Identifying First-Order Tasks

Have first-order tasks been identified and prioritized based on how the task increases revenues, decreases costs, or provides competitive advantages?

Can these methods be used to increase revenues?

a. Increase the volume of customers' purchases
b. Increase average prices
c. Increase market share
d. Improve customer services

(Continues)

Can these methods be used to decrease costs?

a. Lower costs of raw materials
b. Increase inventory turnover rates
c. Decrease manufacturing cycle time
d. Reduce manufacturing costs
e. Reduce costs of complying with government requirements
f. Decrease employee turnover

Can these methods be used to provide a competitive advantage?

a. Identify and focus on optimizing the use of scarce resources
b. Increase the speed with which new products tailored for specific customers can be developed
c. Provide specific valuable services that competitors cannot easily duplicate
d. Provide executives with decision support systems
e. Reduce the number of organizational layers between the customer and the satisfaction of the customers needs

7. How to Apply Personal Computing to Business Tasks

Can managers determine whether and how a proposed personal computing application can be defined as a first-order task?

Can managers determine what must be done, both technically and politically, to remove the barriers?

8. How to Evaluate Personal Computing Applications

Are appropriate expectations being set? (When the personal computing application is justified first, users should state their expectations or goals in business terms.)

Are department managers primarily responsible for evaluations?

Is actual business and productivity performance compared with expectations, stated in comparison to targets, history, and/or internal/external competition?

9. Evaluating the Personal Computing Program Itself

Is the personal computing program itself subject to evaluation? (As with applications, the best criteria are oriented toward customer and business processes.)

REFERENCES

LAWRENCE BERNSTEIN and CHRISTINE M. YUHAS, "Taking the Right Measure of System Performance," *Computerworld,* July 1, 1984, p. ID/1.

WILLIAM BOWEN, "The Puny Payoff from Office Computers," *Fortune,* May 26, 1986, p. 20.

RICHARD G. CANNING, "The System Development Spectrum," *EDP Analyzer,* April 1986.

Computer Control Guidelines, The Canadian Institute of Chartered Accountants, Toronto, 1970.

"Computerized Publishing Technology," An advertising, application, and product insert to *Datamation,* December 15, 1986.

"Computer Publishing Technology," special report in *Datamation,* April 1, 1986.

PHILIP B. CROSBY, *Quality Is Free,* McGraw-Hill Book Company, New York, 1979.

Data Processing Control Practices Report, The Institute of Internal Auditors, Inc., Altamonte Springs, Fl., 1977.

"Electronic/Desktop Publishing: Now a Management Strategy," *Modern Office Automation,* May 1977, p. BC22.

WERNER L. FRANK, "Personal Computers: Performance Paradigms," *Software News,* November 1984, p.16.

MARK GOLDSTEIN, "Power to the People, Evolving the Computer Revolution, *Industry Week,* May 12, 1986, p. 81.

JAMES V. HANSEN, "Audit Considerations in Distributed Processing Systems," *Communications of the ACM,* Vol. 26, No. 3, 1983, p. 562.

BILL INMON, "Rethinking Productivity," *Datamation,* June 15, 1984, p. 185.

BONNIE McDANIEL JOHNSON, *Innovation in Office Systems Implementation,* Department of Communication, Univ. of Okla., National Science Foundation Report No. 8110791, 1985.

ALICE LaPLANTE, "Consultant Finds Micro Costs Well-Justified," *InfoWorld,* October 6, 1986, p. 41.

MARTIN LASDEN, "Facing Down Groupthink," *Computer Decisions,* May 6, 1986, p. 52.

HOWARD MILLER, "End Users Drive Benefit Analysis," *Computerworld,* August 10, 1987, p. 59.

"Office Automation Restructures Business," special report in *Business Week,* October 8, 1984, p. 118.

WILLIAM PAT PATTERSON, "Unease in the Electronic Office," *Industry Week,* April 14, 1986, p. 51.

JIM PRUITT, "Software That Helps Reduce Costs and Improve Service," *Telecommunication Products & Technology,* May 1987, p. 63.

KENNETH G. RAU, "Performance Management; Tracking Information Systems," *Computerworld,* August 20, 1984, p. ID/17.

DAVID G. ROBINSON, "Synchronizing Systems with Business Values," *Datamation,* June 15, 1984, p. 152.

PETER J. ROSS, "The Personal Computer as an Integral Part of the Office," *The Office,* May 1984, p. 38.

RICHARD J. SCHOENBERGER, *Japanese Manufacturing Techniques,* The Free Press, New York, 1982, p. 47.

PAUL G. SCHREIER, "Personal Business: Targeting the Engineer's Desktop," *Electronic Business,* November 15, 1984, p. 108.

PAUL A. STRASSMANN, *Information Payoff: the Transformation of Work in the Electronics Age,* The Free Press, New York, 1985.

Part Two

USE OF PERSONAL COMPUTING IN COORDINATED SYSTEMS

Up to this point, the discussion of personal computing has focused on the tasks performed by individuals. Coordination of individual work efforts, of course, is necessary, even if the work is performed with personal computing, but that coordination is really no different from that needed for all other task methods; in fact, it is quite common to compile into one project, conventional EDP, personal computing tasks, and manual procedures.

In addition, with personal computing focused on individual tasks, the job descriptions of professional/technical employees probably remain the same as they were before personal computing, although the job descriptions of clerical/secretarial workers may, in fact, be modified to include the personal computing technology and processes. Systems administration may become a new job classification, although the specific duties will vary among departments. At some point, however, it is highly useful to coordinate individual tasks electronically. See the Levels of Sophistication pyramid shown in Figure I.1 on page 2.

Coordination can be accomplished in several ways:

- Linked conventional EDP systems. This is an extremely useful technology, but is outside the scope of this book.
- Personal computing applications linked through a central host. This is the technology of "on-line" systems, a reasonably well-understood and important tool, and is discussed in Chapter 5.
- Personal computing applications linked through a set of hierarchical central nodes. For example, several personal workstations can be linked to a departmental system, which, in turn, is linked to a divisional host, which, in turn, is linked to a corporate mainframe. Although this situation superficially resembles the personal-computing-to-central-host situation, there are significant differences that will be considered in Chapter 5.
- Personal computing applications linked through a topological network on an "equal" basis. This implies the ability for any personal computing node to

149

contact another without the direct intervention of a host. This technology is the youngest and the least mature. Guidelines for this technology are offered in Chapter 6.

Users of personal computing networks must concern themselves with the details of data communication, a technology that is even younger and more arcane than personal computing itself. Yet the marriage of these two sciences can bring incredible basic changes in the way companies meet needs of customers and, in fact, in the types of products and services offered. Data communications is also discussed in Chapter 6.

For the sake of convenience, we will call these last three types of systems, "linked" or "coordinated" personal computing systems or applications. Linked personal computing systems have these potential benefits:

- Speed of information transfer. Electronic data communication is usually significantly faster than physical movement of paper.
- Accuracy. Electronic copies are more accurate than manual copies, but an appropriate goal is to have no copies at all; data should be in only one physical location but should be electronically available to any authorized user.
- Cost savings. Saving time saves money, of course, but there are significant, tangible costs to be saved in such mundane areas as filing space, records retention, and mail delivery. Further, if we are, in fact, successful in eliminating all duplicate copies of data, whether or not in electronic form, we save, not only the costs of the multiple storage media, but also the costs of reconciling and refreshing the multiple files.
- Decentralization of work. Tasks are often centralized to take advantage of the synergy that results from frequent, informal interaction. Centralization also provides economies of scale and of technical, specialized expertise. Centralization, however, often removes the workers from the stimulating direct contact of the factory or marketplace.
- Electronic work coordination can allow us to "have our cake and eat it, too," by allowing key participants to remain geographically and organizationally dispersed while retaining rapid, informal contact. Similarly, expensive, scarce resources can be located in only one place but made available to other locations via communications facilities.
- Leveling the organizational pyramid. Status symbols, body language, office configurations, and other indications of "rank" or "power" are invisible over electronic media, leaving, instead, the substance of the transaction.
- Allows/encourages elimination of "second-order" multiorganizational tasks and sometimes allows/encourages the actual elimination of second-order organizations. Electronic task coordination gives us the opportunity to reexamine the tasks themselves and the organizations performing those tasks and to restructure them in more effective and efficient configurations. Generally, the comments made in Chapter 4, relating to individual personal computing, are also applicable in coordinated activities.
- Creates the possibilities of totally new products or services. Examples include electronic mail, computer conferencing, public "data bases," and electronic shopping.

These potential benefits, of course, create some issues:

The technology itself is expensive.   There are substantial one-time costs that may take several years to recover. In addition, there are new categories of ongoing expenses different from (and usually in addition to) those in conventional coordination tasks.

All these expenses, of course, will hopefully be offset by increased efficiency and effectiveness. However, while the new costs are relatively obvious and easy to specifically identify and collect, the savings are often intangible, long term, and vague. Proper funding of these areas requires "strategic viewpoints" rather than focus on short-run returns on investment.

Costs of implementing change. A major portion of the costs involved in coordinating personal computing applications involves the time and people who must plan and implement the organizational shifts that probably will occur. A significant part of the change management goes to help employees who suddenly feel obsolete and must be retrained and/or relocated. Similarly, there are costs involved with relieving the emotional stresses on those people who must be moved into different jobs or even different career paths.

Technology is still young. Because of this, the technology suffers rapid change, with "better" equipment being announced every week. Further, standards are emerging slowly; equipment may be difficult to interface or may be totally incompatible. To compound the problem, because of all these changes, even "experts" in the field may have many different "right" answers. All this tends to create potential problems that translate into the potential for large, unexpected costs to correct "errors." This problem can, at least partially, be mitigated by writing off the equipment costs (hardware and software) on the company's accounting books as rapidly as allowed by tax regulations.

Loss of audit trails and paper history. The signficant savings that result from the elimination of paper transactions also places the responsibility for controls on the electronic system. As described in Chapter 4, it is possible to create audit trails while using personal computing, but it requires special effort, effort which is above that normally needed to complete the application in the most expeditious way.

Some organizations, typically government departments, academic and research institutions, nonprofits, and even some large corporations, open themselves to public view. The journalists and historians who write about these organizations often depend for their data on the routine correspondence that flows through all organizations. When all this correspondence is in electronic form, it is much easier to hide, more difficult to understand even if it is located, and, of course, easier to destroy, either accidentally, or in accordance with a desire for efficiency, or simply to hide or disguise something that has become an embarrassment. Similarly, it is difficult to authenticate electronic data, even if they are found; the usual verifications, such as handwriting analysis, and examination of papers and inks, are no longer valid with regard to electronic media.

A corollary to this problem is the loss of historical documentation. Personal correspondence and memoranda are the grist of the historian's mill. As more of this material is placed on electronic media which are eventually recycled ("scratched" and reused), private documents will remain private, never to be discovered and displayed by future investigators.

Conflict with existing company culture. Many of the advantages described for coordinating personal computing applications assumes that company management *wants* to disperse functional activities and to allow informed decisions to be made at local facilities. Some companies may have good reason for keeping controls tightly centralized, and the management policies and company culture support this highly centralized style.

On the one hand, the advent of coordinated personal computing is an opportunity to reconsider the organizational structure and to opt for more distributed activities. If, however, after that consideration, the central control culture is ratified, coordinated personal computing applications should be structured to follow, not conflict with the style. This may mean that only a small subset of the technology is used, resulting in the prospect of only a small subset of the potential benefits.

Coordinated personal computing is not a substitute for personal contact, not a total substitute for travel. Although electronic communication increases speed, lowers costs, and allows less formal interactions, it does not replace the types of relationships that are created when people meet, share nonbusiness experiences, share meals, and observe, firsthand, the environments in which each works. These personal meetings, however, need not be as frequent as they now occur, and much money, time, and personal wear-and-tear can be saved by sending data rather than people.

The trade-offs created by the search for these benefits and the consideration of these issues result in what might be called a "conflict of priorities," local priorities versus those organizationally and geographically distant, individual priorities versus those of others, and personal computing application priorities versus those of other systems.

REFERENCES

"Computers Pose Challenge to Government Archivists," *San Jose Mercury-News,* August 26, 1984, p. 14A.

ANNE R. FIELD and ZACHARY SCHILLER, "Electronic Data Could Make Trouble for the Law," *Business Week*, October 27, 1986, p. 128.

THOMAS HILL, "A Strategy for Success with Office Systems Software," *Computerworld,* December 3, 1984, p. ID/11.

SUSAN E. KOCH, "The Interactionist Perspective on Computer Implementation," *ACM Computers & Society*, Winter 1986, p. 18.

ROGER SCHELM, "Planning for Tomorrow's Information Processing Needs," *Small Systems World,* November 1984, p. 25.

JOHN WELD, "The Emerging Legal Thicket of Electronic Bulletin Board Operators and Users," *ACM Computers & Society*, Winter 1986, p. 10.

Chapter Five

Coordinating Personal Computing Systems

Introduction

For the purposes of this chapter, information systems are categorized as follows:

- Batch. Transactions are grouped together and processed at prescheduled intervals through a computer, usually in a central facility.
- Central/conventional on-line. Transactions are entered into central information systems by users. If the transaction is made at the same time as the event occurs, and the transaction is processed immediately, the system is considered "real-time."
- Independent personal computing. All steps of the information systems application are performed by the user using either a personal computer or a terminal linked to a central computer.
- Linked personal computing through central host. Personal computing applications may communicate through a central computer to which all personal computing users are connected.
- Linked personal computing through hierarchial hosts. Personal computing users are connected to local hosts, which are in turn connected to other local hosts and to central systems.
- Linked personal computing through networks. Each personal computing application can connect itself to any other system in the network without going through other systems.

See Figure 5.1 for more information on the characteristics of these various forms of systems linkages. The definitions above refer to the logical way in which the information systems are connected. They physical flow may be different.

In the first three types of information systems, batch, on-line, and personal computing, the logical process flow and the physical flow are identical. For example,

153

	Control Rules	Character of Linkage	Speed of Communication	Appropriate Applications
Batch systems	Program, system, EDP operations	Rigid, predefined	Slow, reports, manual	Where paper is required (payroll checks, invoices); periodic jobs (general ledgers)
Conventional on-line systems	From central system	Predefined, but nodes can be added	Fast, along defined channels	Structured activities (order entry, personnel transactions, shipments)
Independent personal computing	Local, individual users	None or physical movement of media	None or slow	To support the work of individual employees; to give individual employees more power
Personal computing linked through central host	Shared	Predefined, but nodes can be added	Fast, along defined channels	Decentralized activities (production tracking, order quotations, depreciation calculations)
Personal computing linked through hierarchical hosts	Shared	Predefined to "local" host; flexible among hosts	Rapid to local hosts; speed among hosts a function of communication channel	Applications requiring shared resources (high-speed printers, microfilm equipment); where hierarchical data are needed (accounting summaries)
Personal computing linked through topological networks	Completely egalitarian	Totally flexible	Limited only to communication channel rules and speed	Work-sharing applications (mail, project coordination, information sharing)

Figure 5.1 Linkage characteristics of information systems.

in on-line systems applications, the data flow logically from the users to a central processing system and flow physically from terminals on users' desks to a central host on which the central processing occurs.

In networked applications, however, the physical flow may be different from the logical flow. In fact, ideally, the application should not even be aware of the physical flow; that is, the physical flow should be "transparent" to the information system application.

Definitions

Batch systems. Transactions are all accumulated and then processed at one, scheduled time, usually within a specialized EDP department. The results from the processing are usually displayed in paper reports which are then distributed to users.

Conventional on-line systems. Transactions are entered from terminals on users' desks and processed on a central ("host") computer, either immediately (in "real time") or periodically. This host computer is usually in a specialized EDP department. Results of the processing may also be displayed on the users' terminals.

Independent personal computing. The applications are completely managed and controlled by users via personal computers or terminals. Typically, the systems owners, custodians, and users are the same individual employee. Data remains with the local application and usually are not available to other information systems or other personal computing applications.

Personal computing linked through central computers. As much processing as possible is performed in line departments using personal computing. Results are used locally and are also sent to a host computer for use by others. Local personal computing applications may also request, from the host computer, data produced by others.

Personal computing linked through hierarchical hosts. The hosts described under independent personal computing are themselves capable of electronically calling other hosts or being called by those hosts, as needed by the personal computing applications attached to the "local" hosts. The "local" hosts act as a type of switchboard for data needed by personal computing applications.

Personal computing linked through a topological network. Personal computing applications can each electronically call other systems directly without the intervention of a series of hosts.

The logical connection of the information systems usually depends on geographic and/or organizational considerations, while the physical flows are dictated by technology considerations. As the technology evolves and is changed for reasons of efficiency and economy, the overlaying information system application logical flow may remain constant.

At the current state of the art, however, it is not possible to separate the logical and physical flow completely. Therefore, Guideline 5.2 discusses physical considerations, while the others in this chapter focus on logical issues.

From an organizational viewpoint, systems can be categorized in still another way. Systems can be considered as global, shared, or local. These categories are defined in Guideline 5.1. The concept of global, shared, and local systems provides a convenient structure in which responsibilities and resources can be assigned. For example, global systems are most often owned and operated by central information systems groups. Shared systems are often supported centrally, although they may have been originally developed at a remote site. Local systems, of course, are developed at local sites, but they are also often shared via mechanisms such as corporate or user-group-contributed libraries. Funding for the systems is also an issue, and in a decentralized company, can be allocated to local profit centers even if the systems are operated at corporate headquarters.

Before the advent of coordinated personal computing, global and shared systems were almost always conventional, often batch, systems. Individual personal computing was applied almost exclusively to local systems. Coordinated personal computing, however, is a technology that can be well applied to global situations, where the data entry and reporting can be processed locally, with the data flowing through a "data highway" and "data switching system" through central facilities.

Guideline 5.1: Architecture of Coordinated Personal Computing Systems

It is important to have some sort of a plan by which personal computing is coordinated. This plan is called an "architecture."

Responsibilities for the design and maintenance of the architecture

1. The chief information manager (CIM) is responsible for both the design and maintenance of the architecture.

The CIM will, of course, depend on the technical advice of many other systems professionals, primarily for expertise on data bases, data communications, and hardware/software capabilities. Paramount to the technical considerations, however, are the needs of the company's user community. For help in these areas, the CIM must work with company functional managers. For example, a marketing systems architecture must be coordinated with marketing functional management; accounting/administrative architectures must be coordinated with administrative managers.

Satisfying the needs of the individual functions, however, is only the first step. Next, the various functions must be coordinated to maximize communication and minimize redundancy. This interfunctional coordination must occur under the leadership of the CIM. The tools the CIM has for this are common company-wide codes and data bases.

Contents of the architecture

The details of each of these issues are far beyond the scope of this text, but shown below are some of the issues that must be considered in a system architecture.

- Customer needs. Describe the functions to be accomplished by the system in terms of basic (first-order) business needs as seen from the customers' viewpoint. Describe the organizational structure and major cultural conditions. Sometimes a strategic planning model using a mission statement or an "objectives, strategy, tactics" format is useful.
- Data bases. Describe the files to be used as reference (master files) and those which will reflect events that occur (transaction files). Describe the physical and logical relationship of files and who has authority to update them. Discuss timing conditions.
- Communication networks. Describe how data will be communicated among the geographic sites in the company. Also consider how data will be communicated across time, where it will be stored for future processing, and how it will be made available for use on a routine or special request basis.
- Hardware. Describe the types of computing hardware to be used in the system. Include not only types of central processing units but also peripherals such as tape drives, disk drives, terminals, and workstations. Consider, as appropriate, special-purpose machines such as multiplexers and file servers.
- Systems software. Describe the operating system to be used by the system, the programming languages to be used, and the utility programs to be available to system custodians and users.
- Applications systems. Describe the systems that will be used to fulfill the customer needs. This section is the one most often seen in current system descriptions with flowcharts, module descriptions, and so on. Describe the systems in terms of their global, shared, or local usage (see below).
- Conventional EDP systems. Describe the role of conventional EDP system in the architecture. Show which application systems will be developed in conventional EDP environments.
- Personal computing systems. Describe the way personal computing will be used in the architecture. Relate the systems as closely as possible to customer needs. Describe how personal computing will be used as part of the applications systems design.
- Support/maintenance strategy. Describe how the system will be supported during its initial implementation and during its useful life. Describe who (which organizations) will support the systems, how support will be funded, and what policies will govern the systems support.

Objectives for coordinated personal computing architectures

2. *Consider the following objectives:*
   a. *Functionality*
   b. *Reliability*
   c. *Supportability*
   d. *Adaptability*
   e. *Performance*

These objectives are interdependent; trade-offs can, however, be made. It is important, therefore, for you to prioritize these objectives for any given application so that decisions are made consistent with those priorities:

- Functionality. How well does the architecture do the task required by the application? What are the features that are incorporated in the system both from a user/customer and from a technical viewpoint?
- Reliability. What is the likelihood that the systems in the architecture will "break" (i.e., stop functioning properly)? What provisions are being made to minimize breakdown?
- Supportability. How easy are the systems in the architecture to change? How independent are the systems from each other from a defect standpoint? Will a flaw in one system collapse the entire architecture? How quickly can repairs to the systems be made?
- Adaptability. How easily can the architecture adapt to environmental changes? The most common changes that must be considered are changes in hardware used in the system and changes in the organizational structures on which the systems are built.
- Performance. How well does the architecture perform under varying work loads? At what volume point will the system degrade? Can changes be made in system hardware components that will easily adapt to increased volumes without changing the architecture or proprietary software? What happens if volumes decrease? What happens to operating costs at very low or very high transaction volumes?

Global, shared, and local systems

3. *The owners of systems should categorize them into global, shared, or local groups, depending on organizational scope.*

One architectural design that is particularly useful for linking decentralized organizational units is that of global, shared, and local systems. The owners of sytems should categorize them into global, shared, or local groups, depending on organizational scope.

A *global* system is one that is operated in only one location for the benefit of the entire company. To be truly global, a system must be not only centralized, but also must be sufficiently broad in its scope to satisfy the needs of the entire (sometimes diverse) enterprise.

A *shared* system is one that is operated locally but developed and maintained centrally. Often, only an operating version of the system (object code) is distributed so that the local operators cannot make changes that will make the local system incompatible with the common shared version. Another strategy is to allow changes only to reports or to other output functions, but not to input, processing, and data management functions.

Shared systems are particularly appropriate when they are designed to work with global systems. For example, the company might have a global corporate order management system, with shared order management systems provided to factories and to sales offices.

Local systems are developed and maintained locally. Any needed interfaces with other company systems are the responsibility of the local developers. Local systems can be operated on a local computer or on a time-shared central computer under local control.

Inevitably, in any large organization, local systems create redundancy and duplication under the blanket statement, "my problem is just like yours, except. . . ." Often, these duplications can be mitigated somewhat by having contributed libraries or at least abstracts of local systems available to all decentralized locations. Each location can use or, at worst, modify someone else's program to minimize duplication. The CIM can create these contributed libaries.

See Table 5.1 for a summary of the characteristics of global, shared, and local systems. These categories are useful because they create a rational framework in which to make ownership and funding decisions. In most cases, the appropriate category is reasonably clear; however, the chief information manager should arbitrate marginal cases.

System management

> **4. Representatives of the owners and users of global and shared systems should be formed into an advisory council that establishes policies and priorities with regard to the systems' functions.**

Custodians for these systems, usually professional EDP people, should be "staff" to these councils. All costs of shared systems should be allocated to users based on a formula that bills users in direct proportion to their usage. Global systems expenses are usually billed to a corporate function; allocation of local systems is at the discretion of local managers.

Personal computing is changing the structure of information systems, but not necessarily the way they are managed and funded. For example, currently, most global systems are built as conventional EDP systems; many are batch or conventional on-line in structure. New global systems, however, could be built as personal computing systems linked in any one of the three ways described above. The ownership and funding of those systems, however, need not change.

Together with the structural changes, however, comes a temptation to alter the way in which the systems are supported and modified. For example, conventionally structured global systems are usually supported centrally. When the global system has been changed to a linked personal computing structure, local end users may want the ability to modify their local systems.

This tendency must be carefully controlled. Local modifications of system outputs (reports, displays) are usually reasonable, but local variations in the way data are entered or in the data bases must be carefully considered, since such changes may affect other portions of the network.

If local operations really are significantly different, the global system can simply specify a data interface, a gateway. Gateways are discussed more completely below and are mentioned again in Guideline 5.3 and in Chapter 6.

TABLE 5.1

Hierarchy of Information Systems

System Type	Purpose	Characteristics	Owner	Custodian	User	Support	Funding
Global	To process and control transactions which must be managed in the same way everywhere in the company	Operated centrally, or, if some operations occur locally, the systems is linked by a network; usually, a conventional EDP system	A corporate department, sometimes with council of users as advisors	A corporate EDP group or local operations controlled by corporate	Everyone in the company involved in the function	Central	Central or allocated
Shared	To provide local organizations with systems which work with the global systems in a way that provides economic leverage	Operated locally but developed and supported centrally; often, a conventional EDP system but could be a linked personal computing system	A corporate department, usually with council of users as advisors	A corporate support function	Local organizations	Central	Allocated or by a usage formula
Local	To meet the systems' needs unique to each local organization	Systems developed, maintained, and supported locally, although some systems might be distributed by "contributed libraries;" often, personal computing systems	Local end users	Local EDP departments or end users	Local end users	Local	Local

159

Directories

5. *To transfer data and/or to perform shared processing, the company should maintain directories of the electronic addresses of people, application custodians, and data bases which are available for shared processing.*

Maintenance of these directories is the responsibility of the chief information manager.

Directory addresses—Clearly, to transfer electronic data among workstations, as in an electronic mail system, for example, there must be an addressing scheme known in electronic form to the system. These are usually in the form of a node or device address.

If at all possible, the addresses that are seen by people should be as easy as possible to use, with the network performing any necessary translation. For example, for a message system, a person's name should be sufficient, and the directory should look up the network address. In a voice mail system or in a system that has an electronic phone calling function, a directory of phone numbers is probably also necessary.

Addresses can be hierarchical. For example, the company-wide directory may contain only a person's building number or organization code. At the local building, a more detailed directory can route the message to the exact node used by the addressee.

Files (either programs or data) require more precision. Files normally may be located on a "system" (a computer or some other data manager like a "file server"), and within that system by file identification within a user account and/or group. File addresses can be embedded within an application or set up so that the requests can be made or altered each time the job is run. Security can be applied to these addresses so that certain data are available only to authorized addresses. Files can be identified by name, by number, qualified by date and time.

Still more flexibility can be achieved by having each application call for files only by a unique name, allowing a network directory to route the request to a specific hardware file. Such flexibility, however, means that some group, preferably within the conventional EDP group, must maintain the directory and maintain the list of file names used by all the applications that have access to the network. Sharing data within a network is a complex subject that is treated more completely in Guideline 5.3.

Criteria for application structure—The type of system linkage (see the five categories in Figure 5.1) best for any given application is a matter for professional judgment. The decision should be made by the system's owner and custodian with, as necessary, the advice of the CIM.

The criteria checklist shown in Table 5.2 may help define the issues and should be reviewed for all linked applications. The nine criteria shown in the table raise issues that usually are most relevant, but other criteria may be added to the list to accommodate specific situations. In addition, depending on the situation, the various criteria may be given different weights. Similarly, the "Significance" classifications are purposely stated in subjective terms, since the issues raised are relative. The checklist is therefore a useful tool, but it is only an aid to professional judgment.

Standard business codes

6. *A good way to achieve the consistency required for coordinated systems is to standardize and control some minimum set of business codes that affect global systems or affect transactions that flow among company entities.*

TABLE 5.2
Checklist for System Linkage Architecture

					Personal Computing		
Criteria	Significance	Batch Systems	Conventional On-line Systems	Independent Personal Computing	Linked Through Central Host	Linked Through Hierarchical Hosts	Linked Through Topological Hosts
Output schedule	Firm	×	×	×	×	×	×
	Flexible		x	×		×	×
	Dynamic		×	×			×
Input schedule	Firm	×	×	×	×	×	×
	Flexible		×	×		×	×
	Dynamic		×	×			×
Number of users	Many	×					×
	Moderate	×	×		×	×	×
	Few	×	×	×	×	×	×
Data volume	Large	×	×		×		×
	Moderate	×	×	×		×	×
	Small		×	×		×	×
Security requirements	High	×		×			
	Moderate	×	×	×	×	×	×
	Low	×	×	×	×	×	×
Location of most current data	Central	×	×		×		
	Few			×	×	×	×
	Many			×	×	×	×
System life expectancy	Long	×	×		×	×	×
	Moderate	×	×	×	×	×	×
	Short			×			×
Organizational scope of system	Global	×	×		×	×	×
	Shared	×	×	×	×	×	×
	Local			×	×	×	×
Amount of ongoing support anticipated	Large	×	×		×	×	×
	Moderate	×	×		×	×	×
	Small	×	×	×	×	×	×

7. *The company's chief administrative officer is usually responsible for selecting the codes to be standardized.*
8. *For each standardized code, the chief administrative officer must also designate an "owner" for the code.*

The potential cancer in all coordinated systems is inconsistency. As soon as identical items or transactions are identified in different ways by different systems, those systems can no longer communicate without expensive and usually ineffective reconciliation. One way to achieve this consistency is through a costly, centralized bureaucracy, but that often brings with it an arthritis which stifles flexibility, innovation, and mobility.

A better way to achieve the required consistency is to control some minimum set of codes that affect global systems or affect transactions that flow among company entities. These "standard business codes" are relatively few in number, but must be controlled consistently. A sample list of these standard business codes is shown in Figure 5.2.

The company's chief administrative officer is usually responsible for selecting the codes to be standardized. Once the selection is made, it is crucial that everyone involved with systems in the company know that these codes have been standardized and that the standard codes must be used, or, as necessary, modified in accordance with a specified procedure.

For each standardized code, the chief administrative officer must also designate an "owner" for the code. The owner must:

- Specify the description and format of the code.
- Specify the content of the code.
- Establish and manage the process by which any aspect of the code may be modified.
- Communicate the code to other system owners, custodians, and users throughout the company. This is both a proactive and a reference task. The codes should be published periodically, but systems developers should also know whom to call for up-to-date information on specific codes.

  One good way of accomplishing this communication is to have a well-maintained machine-readable master file for each standard business code. This file, of course, would be readily available for "read-only" reference by other systems in the company.
- Monitor compliance with the code standard and suggest enforcement procedures, as appropriate.

Data elements provide the basis for identifying, classifying, and summarizing data to provide meaningful information for business management. Data used by multiple functions and organizations must therefore have common and standard definitions, meanings, formats, and in many instances specified content to ensure integrity of the data used to generate that information. Basic business codes are the foundation set of elements required for the presentation of consistent information to top management about key aspects of the business and for legal reporting purposes.

Basic business codes consist of the key set of data elements that are used either singly or in specifically defined combinations (data groups) to manage the *company's information* on a uniform and consistent basis. They must have one, and only one, name and meaning throughout the organization. Moreover, they must conform to a common set of format rules for the data to retain the same meaning. In addition, these rules must be accepted throughout the enterprise.

The criteria for identifying this set of basic business codes are:

1. The specified set of data elements must be identified as being owned by the company.
2. Each element must have a specified corporate owner.
3. Ownership responsibilities must be clearly defined and communicated.

Owners are responsible for:

1. Specification of the description and format of the element.
2. Specification of either the content or establishment and implementation of procedures for assignment of the content.
3. Communicating changes to the custodians and users.
4. Decisions involving any change in specification of an element.
5. Monitoring compliance.

Figure 5.2   Basic business codes.

Basic Business Codes

Category/ Function	Identifiers/Classifiers	Corporate Owner
Assets	Asset number	Administration
Customer	Customer number	Marketing
	Customer purchase agreement number	Marketing
	Customer support agreement number	Marketing
	Customer type code	Marketing
	Family number	Marketing
	Dun's number	Marketing
	Sales order/section number	Marketing
	Order type code	Marketing
	Repair order number	Marketing
	Repair type code	Marketing
	Miscellaneous charge code	Marketing
	Invoice number	Administration
	Internal order number	Administration
Materials	Part number	Manufacturing
	Part preferred code	Manufacturing
	Part category code	Manufacturing
	Part status	Manufacturing
	Part item type	Manufacturing
	Drawing number	Manufacturing
	Unit of measure	Manufacturing
People	Employee number	Administration
Products	Product number	Manufacturing
	Model number	Manufacturing
	Option number	Manufacturing
	Product support suffix	Manufacturing
	Serial number	Manufacturing
Suppliers	Supplier number	Manufacturing
	Supplier status	Manufacturing
	Purchase order number	Administration
	Purchase agreement number	Administration
	IC Invoice number	Administration
Legal and management reporting	Entity	Administration
	Subentity	Administration
	District	Administration
	Department	Administration
	Account	Administration
	Subaccount	Administration
	Corporate subaccount	Administration
	Work force	Administration
	Product type	Administration
	Product line	Administration
	Subproduct line	Administration
	World-country code	Administration
	Political subdivision	Administration
Quality	QA failure code	Manufacturing
	Warranty code	Manufacturing

Figure 5.2 (*Continued*)

Gateways

9. *Gateways should be used whenever appropriate.*

10. *Completely written gateway modules will be provided as part of shared systems, at least for the most common interface situations.*

11. *Standards for gateways are managed by the conventional EDP department, in particular, by the section that manages data communication technology.*

Gateways are program modules that translate data from one format to another. Although such a transformation may be useful in even a stand-alone batch system, the gateways usually interconnect different portions of a network, in addition to reformatting data. Typically, a gateway is used between the communication portion of the network and one of the processing nodes. When used in this way, the "receiving" gateway strips the data of control or address fields needed only for the network, while the "sending" gateway adds the appropriate fields to the body of the data.

A given processing module usually has a specific data format which it uses during the processing, but that module may have several different gateways attached to it, each translating that module's data format to or from a format needed by some other part of the system (see Table 5.3).

The beauty of the gateway concept is that it separates the processing modules from the specifics of the data format. In doing so, it also loosens the coupling between various processing modules. Thus changes can be made to some modules with less concern about the impacts on other modules.

Use of gateways—Gateways should be used whenever appropriate. Gateways are particularly useful for global and shared systems. Therefore, gateways specifications will be written by system custodians and provided to owners and custodians of other systems on request.

In addition, completely written gateway modules will be provided as part of shared systems, at least for the most common interface situations. Standards for gateways are managed by the conventional EDP department, in particular, by the section that manages data communication technology.

Gateways are most useful when the company has global systems to coordinate, communicate, and summarize corporate-wide transactions, from distinctly different local systems. Companies with uniform local operations (e.g., franchises, airline ticketing stations) are usually best operated in a uniform way by local modules of the global system. Where the local entities are different, however, as in the case of a diversified manufacturer or retailer, the local systems should be tailored to local needs but should be required periodically to present data to the gateway or to receive data from it.

TABLE 5.3
Characteristics of Various Data Structures

Structure Type	Sequential Processing	Direct Access	Media	Space Usage	Access Flexibility	Appropriate Applications
Serial	Best	Worst	Any, tape or disk	Best	Only in sequence by preset key	High master file activity
Indexed	Good	Fair	Disk	Good	Direct or serial by preset keys	Need occasional direct access by one key
Hierarchical	Poor	Good	Disk	Fair	Direct by preset keys	Direct access needed on several keys
Relational	Poor	Good	Disk	Fair	Direct by any data element	Direct access needed on any data element
Random	Poor	Good	Disk	Poor	Direct by preset key	Direct access needed on one key

Getting the data to and from the gateway becomes a local responsibility. A shared system may be offered to both perform local functions and interface with the gateway, but the local entities are free to develop their own systems as long as they satisfy the gateway requirements. Many shared systems will simply include the needed gateways as modules of the shared system.

Gateways allow for flexibility in complex networks, but clearly, standardization among gateways will lower the maintenance costs of the overall system. These standards should be common to both conventional EDP systems and linked personal computing systems. Therefore, these standards should be managed by specialists in the conventional EDP department. One technique for achieving higher levels of standardization is a concept called "application packets," described in Guideline 5.3.

CHECKLIST

Guideline 5.1
Architecture of Coordinated Personal Computing Systems

	YES	NO	N/A
1. Responsibilities for the Design and Maintenance of the Architecture Is the chief information manager (CIM) responsible for both the design and maintenance of the architecture?			
2. Objectives for Coordinated Personal Computing Architectures Have the following attributes been considered? a. Functionality b. Reliability c. Supportability d. Adaptability e. Performance			
3. Global, Shared, and Local Systems Have the owners of systems categorized them into global, shared, or local groups, depending on organizational scope?			
4. System Management Have representatives of the owners and users of global and shared systems formed an advisory council that establishes policies and priorities with regard to the systems' functions?			
5. Directories To transfer data and/or perform shared processing, does the company maintain directories of the electronic addresses of employees, application custodians, and data bases which are available for shared processing?			
6. Standard Business Codes Has the company established a minimum set of standard business codes that affect global systems or that affect transactions that flow among company entities in order to achieve the consistency required for coordinated systems? Is the company's chief administrative officer responsible for selecting and maintaining the codes to be standardized? For each standardized code, has the chief administrative officer designated an "owner" for the code?			

(Continues)

	YES	NO	N/A

7. Gateways

Is the gateway concept used whenever appropriate?

Are completely written gateway modules provided as part of shared systems, at least for the most common interface situations?

Are standards for gateways managed by the conventional EDP department, in particular, by the section that manages data communication technology?

Guideline 5.2: Logical Design of Coordinated Personal Computing Networks

Background

Once the organizational setting of the system is clear, the system must be designed in terms of a general structure showing how and where data will reside and how and where processing will occur. This design is often called the "systems architecture."

When the designers have decided that one of the linked structures discussed in Guideline 5.1 is appropriate, they must then define both a "logical" and a "physical" architecture for the resulting network. The logical structure, the structure as it appears to users, regardless of the physical construction actually used, should be defined first and is the subject of this guideline. In fact, the logical structure often remains relatively constant over time while the physical structure changes to take advantage of advances in technology.

Networks

Systems are linked together by structures called "networks." Networks, in turn, are made up of "nodes," which are processing stations at which data may enter or leave the network. Nodes may also be points at which data remain within the network but are transformed or processed in some way. Nodes are connected by some type of communications linkages.

Networks can be described in terms of either their physical or their logical structure. This guideline speaks primarily about the logical implications of personal computing networks. The physical structure of networks is the "skeleton" that holds up the logical network functions. As the skeleton, it should be invisible, but like a skeleton, it defines and forms the logical "flesh" stretched over it. Chapter 6 is devoted to the physical structure of networks and communications and to the policies that will create a useful structure for personal computing networks.

Networks are usually described in terms of their topology (see Figure 6.4). In a "ring" structure, nodes are linked and can communicate only with their immediate neighbors. Communications with nonadjacent nodes must pass through intermediate nodes.

Another common structure is a "star," where each node can communicate only with a central "host" node. Communication between nodes can be accomplished only through the host. Sometimes the host of one star is linked to the host of another star, and the nodes can communicate with each other through those host linkages. Such networks are called "hierarchical" because, in the most common structure, department hosts are connected to divisional hosts, which are, in turn, connected to corporate hosts, following the organization's hierarchical structure.

The most complex networks allow their nodes to communicate freely with any other node, merely by addressing that node. Such a network is usually simply called a topological network.

Interface levels

To facilitate the efficient interfacing of systems built by different vendor and user organizations, the International Standards Organization (ISO) has developed the seven-layer Open System Interconnect (OSI) model. These layers are:

7. Application
6. Presentation
5. Session

4. Transport
3. Network
2. Data link
1. Physical

There are logical and physical components of each layer, but this guideline focuses primarily on the top three layers, while Chapter 6 focuses on the bottom four layers.

Servers

Some nodes are physically or logically structured to provide specific services for other nodes. These service nodes are called, with unusual logic, "servers." Each server usually has a designated function that is either too expensive to provide individually to each node or which provides data or linkage services that several nodes should share. As noted in the guidelines below, it is important to distinguish between those servers that are established only for economic reasons versus those that provide a logical function in the network, independent of cost. Advances in hardware cost/performance might eliminate the need for economic servers, but the need for logical servers will remain, independent of server costs.

For example, special-purpose printers or plotters may be designated as servers for use by several processing nodes for economic reasons. However, a data base that should be used by several nodes can be located and maintained on a single node, with that node becoming a "logical" server for the processing nodes which need to use that data base.

Conventional EDP as a server—Many of the provisions in this guideline are appropriate for conventional EDP as well as for personal computing. In fact, it is becoming quite common to mix the two types of computing as networks expand. From a logical standpoint, conventional EDP systems become another type of server, providing specific functions to the network. These functions may include large data bases, communication switching services, or fast and/or sophisticated processing capabilities.

Basic Rules

1. *Data should be entered into the network only once.*
2. *Data should be stored in the network in only one place.*
3. *Edits on entered data should occur as soon as possible after the data are entered, immediately if possible.*
4. *The responsibility for correcting input data belongs to the people who enter the data.*
5. *Data should be formatted into reports only on the specific request of a user.*
6. *Each node in the network should be as autonomous as possible and should therefore have as many capabilities as economically feasible.*
7. *Use of logical servers should, however, be maximized. The most common logical servers are shared data bases and communication services.*
8. *ISO standards should be followed whenever possible.*

To illustrate these rules, let's examine the process of revising a purchase order. The purchase-order revision should be entered by the buyer who made the revision. In this example, linked personal computing can be considerably more efficient than conventional EDP systems. In conventional systems, the buyer might need to complete a form which is then given to a data-entry person for keying into the system. Even with a conventional on-line system, the buyer is at the mercy of the schedules and condition of a central computer.

In a linked personal computing system, the buyers have their purchase orders on a file in their local computer. When a revision is necessary, the buyers recall the basic purchase order, make the necessary revisions, edit them, and release them for further processing on the network, without need for additional paperwork or the people needed to process that paperwork. Edit errors are flagged by the local computer, and the transactions are corrected immediately by the person knowing most about the situation.

Note that this example illustrates not only the efficiencies possible with personal computing, but also the dangers. With conventional EDP, transactions pass through several people and are usually recorded in several intermediate forms and files. Clear audit trails are possible.

With linked personal computing, all the data are handled by one person and stored in only one place, an efficient but risky practice. Routine backup of files and audit and supervision of transactions becomes imperative.

Data should be formatted into reports only on the specific request of a user. Preformatted reports such as those common for batch systems should be suggested to users, but the users should be given great freedom to design their individual report formats. Inquiry-type programs, in which the users ask for what they specifically need at a specific time, are preferred. These are sometimes known as ad hoc reports.

Ad hoc reports are usually produced through some type of inquiry or report-writer software. Even without such software, however, users specific needs can be met by allowing users to chose from among a menu of predefined formats. This tailoring capability is especially useful in on-line network applications (although I think that it is equally important in conventional EDP batch applications).

Each node in the network should be as autonomous as possible and should therefore have as many capabilities as economically feasible. Facility servers (e.g., shared printers, plotters, etc.) should be used only when necessary for economic reasons. The point is, of course, that the success of personal computing is largely because of the power that it gives so-called end users. Any move to diminish their autonomy will blunt the potential power of personal computing.

This is also a situation that changes rapidly as prices fall. For example, letter-quality printers were early examples of economically appropriate servers, but lower-priced impact, ink-jet, and laser printers make it reasonable to give a printer to individual nodes.

The PCIC should take responsibility for alerting users to price–performance breakthroughs and should advise on the compatability issues needed to take advantage of the lower-cost devices. Note that economy is the issue for equipment servers but not for "logical" servers, as discussed below.

Use of logical servers should, however, be maximized. The most common logical serves are shared data bases and communication services. These servers are part of the logic of the network, used to minimize redundancy, allow control, or provide appropriate linkages.

Economics can and should be allowed to drive the system's architectural strategy. For example, when a dramatic price–performance shift occurs, allowing full communication from each node rather than using hierarchical hosts, the entire network architecture might be redesigned. The economics to be considered, however, are not only the costs of the equipment but also the costs of the redevelopment and implementation, which are usually far higher than those of the hardware.

ISO standards should be followed whenever possible. Where ISO standards have not yet been adopted, or where there are conflicts or ambiguities, the chief information manager is responsible for setting the standard to be used in the company. Two standards need be considered, government standards such as ISO and industry standards. Each, however, can require interpretation.

Government standards may vary from country to country, sometimes requiring some type of conversion process as data cross national borders. Industry standards are commonly issued by professional societies such as the Institute of Electronics and Electrical Engineers (IEEE). However, large companies (IBM is the best example) often adopt different standards, which must be considered.

Sometimes the industry standard is simply that format used by the company which achieves the largest market share. In fact, one of the best reasons for a vendor to seek market share is to achieve acceptance of that vendor's standards.

ISO levels to be used

9. *Systems should be linked as high as possible on the ISO model so that maximum flexibility for implementing new technologies is retained without changing the logical structure that is perceived by the systems' users.*

It would be optimum to link systems only at the highest level, the application level. As a practical matter, however, most systems involve at least the application and presentation levels. Below that, from the session level down, hardware and operating system considerations become progressively specific and limit flexibility.

Network structures to be used

10. *Network structures should begin simply and become more sophisticated as applications and technical competence increases.*

Therefore, applications should begin with star structures, and, as appropriate, progress to ring and topological structures. Network structure constrains both functionality and performance. For example, using a relatively simple star structure, any user node can communicate with any other node, subject, however, to the availability of the central node. Communicating with another node directly may be far more rapid, but the network software needed may be far more sophisticated.

One form of central node used for star structures is the digital PBX, which switches data communication in the same way that voice communication is switched. Thus, as with voice, the users feel that they can communicate with anyone on the network directly (which, from a "logical" viewpoint, they can) even though, physically, all communication flows through a central switch.

Using workstations versus terminals

11. *Consistent with basic rule 6, workstations should be used whenever economically feasible.*

The exception might be where workstations encourage the existence of redundant data bases, thus violating rules 2 and 7. When a terminal is used as a node, it must be provided processing and data storage services by some other node, usually a central node/host. This places rules 1 and 3, input and output control, at the mercy of both the central node and the communication network; the potential reliability of the network thus suffers. These circumstances clearly make workstations attractive, economic considerations aside.

As has been discussed before, however, the further full capabilities are decentralized, the less the control that can be imposed by the central organization. Both data and processing redundancies become essentially inevitable, and security and control problems become more acute.

Here again the overall culture of the organization must be considered, and network form should follow the functions and values that exist in other aspects of the organization. If there is no clear trend, however, I suggest that maximum flexibility, growth, and synergy result from maximum decentralization, and these policies generally encourage this viewpoint.

Using logical servers versus using dedicated equipment

12. Data base servers should be used to facilitate the sharing of data among nodes that would otherwise need to duplicate files to accomplish their tasks.

However, local files unique to a node should not be placed on a server unless motivated by economics. When considering the costs of node facilities versus servers, calculate the initial costs of the equipment and the "costs of ownership"; the costs of maintenance, supplies, and space; and so on. Also calculate the costs in labor hours that will be required to convert the application to the local mode and the technical knowledge that will be needed to support the local node versus the server.

Using servers is an appropriate way to implement rule 2. This does not mean, however, that all data should be on servers. When high-capacity "hard" disks were expensive and floppies were limited in their capacity, the temptation was to use a hard disk server for storing the private files from several personal computers. Doing this, however, turns the personal computer into a "smart terminal" and limits the amount of flexibility available.

Costs and technology have evolved to where it is usually feasible to give each node enough storage for local files. Therefore, use of data servers should be limited to applications where data sharing or control is required. Facility servers should be used when it is not economically feasible to give the facility to all nodes that need to use the facility. Again, the goal should be to make each node as autonomous as is economically feasible. Thus, if an expensive, high-speed plotter is set up as a server, it may be appropriate to give at least some of the nodes lower-cost, lower-capability plotters as well. Communication services are a particularly appropriate function for a server.

Communication technology is trailing other aspects of personal computing. Appropriate systems are still relatively expensive and difficult to use. The expertise needed to use networks properly is in particularly short supply, and this situation alone may be the factor that suggests a server approach rather than a local facility.

Local nodes should, therefore, probably have only those communication facilities needed to link to the network, while all network controls are centrally located and centrally managed. Most local nodes should also have a modem that allows the nodes some flexibility in reaching public or private networks other than those established by the companies' communication specialists.

Responsibilities

13. The establishment and support of networks for voice, data, and video communications are the responsibility of the chief information manager (CIM).

The CIM should ensure that the network is capable of services to both conventional EDP and personal computing. As a practical matter, the CIM should establish a separate section within the EDP department to deal with communication technology. In addition, because of the need for specified interfaces, networks should be centrally managed, with relatively little local discretion allowed.

Policies for servers should be established by the Personal Computing Information Center (PCIC) and be updated frequently as technology and cost–performance points change. These PCIC policies may be overruled by the owners and custodians of specific systems to implement sharing or control functions in those systems.

System owners and custodians establish the rules when, for data sharing or for control reasons, servers are to be used regardless of cost. Even in these cases, however, the PCIC may recommend appropriate equipment. Where economics is the only issue, however, PCIC guidance, together with advice from the EDP communications specialists, is probably the best way to deal with this rapidly changing technology.

CHECKLIST

Guideline 5.2
Logical Design of Coordinated Personal Computing Networks

	YES	NO	N/A
1. Basic Rules			

1. Basic Rules

Have these basic rules been considered?

a. Are data entered into the network only once?

b. Are data stored in the network in only one place?

c. Do edits on entered data occur as soon as possible after the data are entered, immediately if possible?

d. Does the responsibility for correcting input data belong to the people who enter the data?

e. Are data formatted into reports only on the specific request of a user?

f. Is each node in the network as autonomous as possible and therefore have as many capabilities as economically feasible?

g. Has the use of logical servers, especially shared data bases and communication services, been maximized?

h. Are ISO standards followed whenever possible?

2. ISO Levels to Be Used

So that maximum flexibility for implementing new technologies is retained without changing the logical structure that is perceived by the systems' users, are systems linked as highly as possible on the ISO model?

3. Network Structures to Be Used

Are network structures begun simply and allowed to become more sophisticated only as applications and technical competence increase?

4. Using Workstations versus Terminals

Consistent with basic rule 1f, are workstations used whenever economically feasible?

5. Using Logical Servers versus Using Dedicated Equipment

Are data base servers used to facilitate the sharing of data among nodes that would otherwise need to duplicate files to accomplish their tasks?

(Continues)

	YES	NO	N/A

6. Responsibilities

Are the establishment and support of networks for voice, data, and video communications the responsibility of the chief information manager?

Guideline 5.3: Data Structures for Coordinated
Personal Computer Applications

Background

Data structures are important for all information systems, and for most conventional EDP systems, the data are organized as part of the overall systems design and tailored specifically for each system. Modern systems, however, recognize that data should be shared among systems; therefore, sophisticated linkages are often constructed to minimize redundancy. Even in these systems, however, the application is usually considered first, and the data are structured or acquired as needed.

In most linked personal applications, data structures should be treated as a separate, stand-alone systems project. The volatility, breadth, and unpredictability of the data needs of the personal computing applications make it impossible to tailor data structures for each individual application without extreme costs and control problems.

These separate data structures must be built in ways that anticipate these variations in use. This guideline highlights the considerations in the construction of data structures for use by linked personal computing and offers some suggestions to help the design process.

Goal of data structures

1. *Data structures are built only to serve the architecture of appropriate business applications.*

While data structures should be applications of their own for control purposes, they have no purpose in a business organization except to the extent that they serve the architecture of applications, which, in turn, serve the needs of the business; a data structure is not an end unto itself. Properly constructed, however, data structures become resources that allow the implementation of profitable and efficient personal computing applications.

The converse is also true; poorly constructed data structures act as barriers to the implementation of effective applications.

Components of a data structure

2. *For data to be used in several applications, the data must be compatible in both logical and physical attributes.*

The *logical* structure of data is defined in these terms:

- Data elements. Usually the smallest pieces of data identified separately.
- Records. An identifiable accumulation of data elements.
- File. A specified collection of records.
- Keys. Data elements that act as "handles" for records or files. Programs can "grab" (access) specified records or files based on the values of the keys.
- Data base. A collection of records where data elements can be accessed ("grabbed") independent of the other elements in the record or file.

The *physical* structure of data is important to the hardware used in an application. The physical structure is defined in these terms:

- Block. A group of records that is read into a computer at the same time. Since it usually takes longer to read/write data from a disk than it does to process it, larger blocks usually increase the speed of systems.
- Sequence. The way the records are arranged in a file as viewed by their keys. If a file is said to be in alphabetic order, it is understood that its keys are in alphabetic order. To understand sequence completely, the designer must also know the "collating" sequence of the machines and operating systems involved. For example, some systems will place letters before numbers and others will place numbers before letters.
- Binary representation. This is the physical way in which the magnetic impulses are translated into logical characters. There are two common codes which are used: ASCII (American Standard Code for Information Interchange) and EBCDIC (Extended Binary Coded Decimal Interchange Code). In addition, numeric data can be in a variety of forms, including "packed," display, floating point, and so on. The physical data are often displayed on "record dumps" in octal or hexadecimal representation.

The definitions and relative advantages of these physical representations are beyond the scope of this guideline, but for data to be exchanged among applications, they must be in the same physical format or go through a process that converts the data from one format to another.

Appropriate Goals for Linked Personal Computing Data Structures

3. *Appropriate goals are the following:*
   a. *Data elements should be usable by many applications.*
   b. *Minimize redundancy of data elements.*
   c. *Design for rapid entry/retrieval of data elements.*
   d. *Minimize computer file storage space.*
   e. *Provide adequate security and control.*
   f. *Provide adequate privacy.*
   g. *Provide adequate precision.*
   h. *Achieve compatability with other hardware and software systems.*
   i. *Achieve transferability among types of data storage media.*

Note that these goals focus on the data elements more than on the record or file structure. Personal computing applications tend to use different data elements at different times; therefore, the grouping of elements into records and files is less important than it is in conventional EDP.

Data elements should be usable by many applications—As noted in Guideline 5.2, data redundancy should be avoided; to do this, data structures should be highly flexible, both in terms of known systems and in anticipation of others that may be developed. This is usually accomplished by structuring the data elements in terms of their logical relationships rather than in terms of how they are to be reported.

For example, in conventional EDP, employee records might be stored in a file in sequence by employee number; a cross-reference to employee name might also be maintained. In personal computing, however, the logical structure of the data base might mirror the organizational structure, showing the employees within their departments within their divisions, and so on. Of course, the ability to access records by employee number and name must also be provided. Because of this goal, many personal computing applications use "relational data base management systems" to control data structures.

Minimize redundancy of data elements—The elimination of data redundancy is focused at individual data elements, not at records or files. The goal should be to have a data element exist only once in a system or network with indices, as needed, to point user applications to the physical location where the element is stored.

A corollary to this guideline is that data should be stored only in detail form; if summaries are needed, they should be computed from the detail elements each time they are needed. Abiding by this corollary improves the consistency of the data; if summaries are maintained separately from the detail, then, if the details are adjusted, the summaries must also be adjusted; otherwise, a reconciliation error will occur.

Sometimes, however, records that contain summaries of detail records are maintained to improve the speed with which users can obtain reports of the summary data. In this case, the performance gains may well offset the time and costs of synchronization.

Another way of dealing with this potential problem is to forbid changes to detail (and summary) data. If a detail record needs to be modified, an "adjustment" transaction is processed that corrects or offsets the original transaction. This adjustment transaction is, of course, also processed against any summary records being maintained.

This adjustment approach is common in accounting applications. For example, if a journal entry is made for $100 when the amount should have been $500, it is appropriate to process another transaction for $400 to correct the account, rather than electronically "erasing" the original $100 transaction and replacing it with one for $500.

Using this offset approach gives a clear trail of transactions; users or auditors who may be investigating "what happened" after the fact have an "audit trail" they can follow. Offsetting also prevents "changing the past." This is important when official reports have already been published based on the detail data as it then existed.

The disadvantage of the offset approach is that all records pertaining to a situation must be processed in order to receive the accurate information; looking at individual records might give incorrect, incomplete information. For example, in a credit-rating file, one record might be posted listing the person as a credit risk; later information might correct that rating; if the offset approach were used, the system must assure that any inquiry receives both the original and the correction record. Accessing only the original record will provide an incorrect answer. Offset transactions also take more computer file space than is needed when data are corrected by replacement, although this is usually a minor consideration.

Design for rapid entry/retrieval of data elements—Data should be received by or extracted from data bases fast enough to allow maximum productivity from the people working with the application. Appropriate times are usually described in terms of "response times." If response time is too slow, workers lose their concentration; both productivity and accuracy can suffer.

Satisfactory response times are usually in the range of 2 to 5 seconds, a long time for computers, but much processing must occur in that time period. (Some research, however, suggests that consistent subsecond response time will greatly improve data-entry productivity. See Werner L. Frank, "Personal Computers: Performance Paradigms, *Software News,* November 1984, p. 16, and "The Economic Value of Rapid Response Time," IBM document GE 20-0752, November 1982.)

Generally, flexibility and response time correlate negatively. That is, the greater the flexibility, the slower the response time. Response time is particularly important in applications where the user is interacting with customers, for example in banking teller applications or in telephone order-entry applications. People are accustomed to very rapid response in normal conversation; even 5 seconds of "dead air" can cause considerable discomfort. Try, sometime, to hold a conversation with someone, mentally counting to five before responding to a statement.

Minimize computer file storage space—Storage of data on magnetic tape is relatively inexpensive, but storage on tape is very inflexible. Therefore, most personal computing data structures are on a direct-access media, typically floppy or hard disks (although "bubble memories" and nonvolatile random-access memories are becoming more cost-effective). Storage costs are measured in dollars per kilobytes, and although costs for disk storage are decreasing, they are still high enough to be an important factor.

Besides cost, the number of data that fit on one floppy disk is limited and a large file may require manually changing disks, a slow and error-prone process. Use of disk space is also a factor in the system's average response time. The greater the number of records, the longer it takes for even a computer to access records.

Provide adequate security and control—Data must be protected from deliberate or accidental misuse. Controls such as those described in earlier guidelines in Part I can keep accidental errors from occurring and can detect errors or deliberate tampering rapidly if it has occurred. One very simple, but important technique, for example, is to simply "time stamp" all accesses to the data base and report the last access each time a user logs onto the system. Users should be trained to question any access that appears suspicious.

Note that the goal is to provide "adequate," not "perfect," security and control. Especially in personal computing applications, where the work is being done by people of widely varying technical skills, perfect security and control is an unrealistic goal.

An "adequate" goal, for example, may simply be to be able to reconstruct any file in case of damage to the original. On the other hand, in situations where security and control are vital system functions, "adequate" may require sophisticated magnetic keys, data encryption, personal characteristics for identity verification, signature authentication, and other state-of-the-art techniques.

Note, however, again with special reference to personal computing applications, that security is difficult to measure. This is especially true since successful security violations are probably never even detected. Managers are therefore hardpressed to know how much to spend on security, especially since the price paid for security is not only in money, but also in the convenience with which the systems can be used.

Linked systems are also vulnerable to vandalism—destruction of files for no apparent gain to the perpetrator. One novel and particularly dangerous form of vandalism is the so-called "program virus." This is a bit of code that reproduces itself in a file by writing over records already there. Further, a virus program can look at other files in a computer memory and "infect" those files if the virus is not there already.

Besides the normal ways of protecting systems from unauthorized users who may be vandals, the best protection is usually to have adequate backup files stored apart from the active files which may be used if the active files are destroyed in any manner.

Provide adequate privacy—Data must be easily available to those authorized to use them but should be restricted from unauthorized people. In my opinion, privacy is more critical than security, especially since breaches of privacy are even harder to detect than are breaches of security. Further, as discussed in Part I, personal computing equipment can itself be used as tools to violate security. Also, see Part I for guidelines on how privacy can be better achieved in personal computing.

Often "adequate" security and privacy can be achieved simply by locking up floppy disks in a desk or filing cabinet. Hard disks are more difficult to "lock up"; these should be controlled by a file management system that provides password control.

Provide adequate precision—Precision refers to the accuracy available when describing very large or very small numbers. Precision is often a factor in scientific/ engineering applications, but probably should be given consideration in commercial applications as well. Most commercial applications are satisfied with formats in dollars and cents, but intermediate calculations often produce fractions of cents which could, if accumulated, be significant. As is fairly obvious, the precision of a number is a function of the least precise number in intermediate calculations.

Achieve compatibility with other hardware and software systems—To the extent possible, the data structures should be consistent in logical and physical terms, as described above. The greater the natural consistency, the less conversion will be needed to use the data. Compatibility is also discussed in Part I.

Specialized data formats are used when special codes are needed to provide certain functions to the system. For example, the codes that provide underlining and boldfacing in word processing usually vary among programs. Special formats are also often used to compress data for more economical storage or transmission. For example, most data communications programs compress the data and insert (and later strip) special communications control codes. Programs that provide rapid file backups also compress data for storage economy.

When data files are built for use by specific applications, as is often the case in conventional EDP, the data structures are designed to be consistent among the programs and hardware used by those applications. In personal computing–linked applications, however, there usually is no way of predicting when a data base will be accessed by a particular application or used by a particular type of hardware. Therefore, there is value to setting standards that will increase the consistency of *all* company data structures. This consistency will not only enhance the ease of accessing data, but will also lower overall maintenance costs because users and EDP professionals will be more familiar with the data structures.

One simple guideline might be that all data be stored in American Standard Character Information Interchange (ASCII) format or be easily converted to ASCII format via utility programs which are provided. Often, however, these conversion programs delete some of the special control characters and thereby lose the benefit of their function. For example, converting the data produced by a word processing system to ASCII might cause the loss of underlining/boldfacing in the document.

Achieve transferability among types of data storage media—Personal computing vendors have not yet determined standard storage media that can be used by all equipment. Floppy disks can be found in various sizes, such as $3\frac{1}{2}$, $5\frac{1}{4}$, and 8 inches.

Even use of the same-size disks, however, does not guarantee compatibility, since different vendors use different data formats and directories on the same size disks. The situation is exacerbated when considering hard disks and tape cassettes offered by some vendors.

There are only a few techniques for achieving this compatibility, short of using identical equipment or equipment "guaranteed" to be compatible. Data may be converted by specialized programs. Another common conversion method is to transmit the data from one machine to another, using the communications system as the conversion mechanism. Data compatibility should always be tested as part of the development process of any system.

Types of data structures

4. *There are five types of data structures:*
   a. *Serial*
   b. *Indexed*
   c. *Hierarchical/network*
   d. *Relational*
   e. *Random*

With the exception of the relational structure, all the structures define the organization of data records. The structure defines the way the record keys are organized and, therefore, accessed. Because of this, relational data structures are becoming popular in linked personal computing applications. However, this structure requires the most complex software and takes the most media space. See Table 5.3 for a summary of these comments.

Serial—Records are simply arranged in the sequence of their keys. When records are added or deleted, a complete new file is written. This is the classic file organization, still widely used in conventional EDP applications for batch processing tasks. It is particularly efficient when transaction activity is well distributed among the records on the master file. Since a new file is created whenever updates are made, this structure automatically creates a file backup. Serial files may be on either tape or disk media.

Indexed—Initially, records are arranged in the sequence of their keys, as they are in a serial file. However, an index is maintained that tells the software the physical address at which keys are located. This index is used for directly accessing specific records. Records can be added (or deleted) without rewriting the entire file simply by telling the index where the additional records are. After a while, however, the file gets "messy" and slow to process and must be reorganized.

Indexed structures provide many of the benefits of serial structures while allowing reasonable direct access and therefore are used when sequential processing is the norm but occasional direct access is needed. Index structures require, however, that files reside on disks and require more space than similar serial files.

Hierarchical—Serial and indexed files are accessible only by predetermined major keys (although there can be several layers of subordinate keys). One way of accessing files through various elements is by defining "master" and "detail" records. The masters are, in effect, index records that tell the software how to access the detail data in terms of the particular key shown in that master. There can be many masters, and new masters can be added with minimum effort through a relatively painless reorganization of the data structure. This hierarchy of masters and details creates an inverted tree structure where the masters are the tree trunks and the details are branches.

A familiar example of hierarchical structures are the "product structure" file used in manufacturing materials requirements planning (MRP) applications. Here the final product is the master record and all the purchased parts and subassemblies form the hierarchical detail records.

This data structure is appropriate for applications where data are accessed by a nested set of keys, where one "master" record leads to others. This structure is common in many business applications. Besides the MRP application mentioned above, this data structure could be used for an order file where the order number leads to the line items on the order; for an invoice file, where the invoice number leads to the line items on the invoice; or to a personnel file, where the department number leads to the employee numbers of the people in the department.

One special case of the hierarchical data structure is the "network" structure. In a network structure, one data record leads to others in a predefined fashion as in the hierarchical structure, but no hierarchy exists; there are no "master" and "detail" records. Any record can be linked to any other via a chain of predefined key records.

Relational—In this, the newest and most complex structure, the data elements themselves are interlinked and data can be accessed without any preparation. As has been noted above, this data structure is most useful for personal computing applications that need data in an unpredictable manner. For example, a personnel file may contain data elements showing employees' department code, length of service, and job classification. Using a relational structure, reports can be prepared showing all employees in a given department or all employees with a given length of service or all employees in a given job classification, all from the same file, without sorting the file.

Random—This structure, rarely used in personal computing applications, places records in a physical location on the disk that has been calculated based on the major key of the record. Specific records are then accessed simply by recomputing that location. This method is particularly fast when reading or writing records accessed by the same key used for the physical location computation.

It is quite difficult to locate records based on any other key; this storage method, therefore, is extremely inflexible. The computed physical locations are rarely in the same sequence as the logical keys; for example, logical key A may be in physical location 30, while logical key B may be in location 17. Therefore, it is rarely practical to use a random file in a batch process, which generally expects the records to be in both logical and physical sequence.

Characteristics of various data structures

> 5. *From the standpoint of linked personal computing, the most important characteristics are direct access and access flexibility.*

The characteristics of the various structures are summarized in Table 5.3.

Most personal computing applications process events as they occur; transactions are usually not collected and batched for future (albeit efficient) processing. Direct access is, therefore, essential, since the "real-world" transactions will not obligingly come in according to record key sequence.

People are also notoriously reluctant to be forced to remember the key numbers the computer needs. For example, we may efficiently store orders on our file according to an order number key. It is convenient when customers know their order numbers, but we must be able to process their transactions when given other data such as their name and the transaction date. This, again, speaks to the need for relational data structures.

Data indices

> **6. If various data bases needed by linked personal computing applications are located at different nodes on the network, data indices are needed to direct applications to the appropriate node and file.**

In practice, these indices are hierarchical. Each node must contain an index that shows at which nodes other data elements are located. Also, each node contains an index showing which local file contains which data elements.

Ideally, then, an application will ask for a data element. The data management system looks in the local index to determine the node at which the element is stored. The system accesses the index at that node and determines the file in which the element is located, reads the element, and returns it to the requesting application for use. See Figure 5.7 for an illustration Of this process. Sometimes, an application will construct a local file which is built of data elements copied from other nodes; this local file is then retained for processing without taking the time to get the master data element each time.

This is an efficient process as long as two precautions are observed. First, the data element copies should never be updated. Such updates should be made only to the master data element, so that there is only one correct version. Second, the local elements should be "refreshed" frequently from the master element, so that any updates to the master are appropriately reflected on the copies.

Data dictionaries

> **7. Data dictionaries state the definitions of the elements in data structures both in business and in EDP terms, to minimize data redundancy and to help application writers use the data structures.**
> **8. This is a typical list of the entries made for each element in a data dictionary:**
>   **a. Data name**
>   **b. Data definition**
>   **c. Data format**
>   **d. Edit criteria**
>   **e. Source**
>   **f. Update frequency**
>   **g. Element owner, custodian**
>   **h. Relationships with other elements**
>   **i. When dictionary entry was last updated and by whom**

Data dictionaries state the definitions of the elements in data structures both in business and in EDP terms. The EDP definitions help the application writers use the data structures efficiently without rewriting data access programs. The definitions in business terms help application writers use the data correctly and minimize the tendency for writers to reinvent redundant data elements for private use in their applications.

This is a typical list of the entries made for each element in a data dictionary:

- *Data name.* Show the narrative name of the element as well as the "EDP label" used in programs. For example, an element might have the narrative name "Order Number" and the EDP name "ORDERNO."
- *Data definition.* Define the element in sufficient detail to differentiate it from other elements that might have similar names. For example, "Order Number" could refer to orders placed on our company by customers or could refer to

orders we place on our vendors. The definition should make the usage very clear.

- *Data format.* Show the format in something like a COBOL "PICTURE." For example, the order number may have a PICTURE of "A999-9999A" showing a 10-character field, including an embedded dash.
- *Edit criteria.* Show edit criteria for both format and content. Format edits check for field size and for the alphanumeric characteristics of each character. Content edits describe what characters are acceptable in each space. For example, we can say that the order number's alpha suffix indicates what country the order came from and should be edited against the official "country table." The first three digits may indicate the sales office to which the order is to be credited and must be verified against the official "sales office table." Sophisticated dictionaries can contain not only the edit criteria but also working computer language subroutines which can be used in programs to perform the necessary edits.
- *Source.* State where the data element came from. For codes, state both the source system and the way the code is derived. For example, the order number may come from the Order Entry System (OESYS), with the four digits after the dash generated from a sequential assignment table in OESYS. For data fields, merely state the source system, and if appropriate, the hard-copy backup. For example, "Units Ordered" stated that the data came from OESYS as transcribed from the Sales Order Worksheet.
- *Update frequency.* State how often and when the data element is updated. For example, general ledger account summary data elements might be updated every Monday and on the second workday of the month.
- *Element owner, custodian.* State who "owns" the data element, the department or person who can make changes to the definition and control of the element. For example, the owner of the Order Number field may be the order processing department manager. The custodian(s) are those systems and/or departments that process the field. Custodians for the Order Number may be the sales office order processing department, the OESYS system, and the company EDP department. Note that, typically, there is only one owner but there can be several custodians.
- *Relationships with other elements.* State the way this element is dependent on or feeds other elements. For example, we could say that the Order Number is the top-level key in a hierarchical file and Order Line Item Numbers are linked to this element. Or, we can say that an account summary record is the sum of Account Journal Transactions.
- *When the dictionary entry was last updated and by whom.* As noted below, dictionary items must be maintained. Showing information about the most recent update gives users confidence about the integrity of the dictionary entry and also gives the user the name of someone to call with questions about the specific entry.

Updating data indices and data dictionaries

9. All the data indices and the data dictionaries must be kept current.

All the data indices and the data dictionaries must be kept current, at least on a daily basis, although "real-time" would be better. If these guides to the data base are not current, the applications that depend on them will quickly fail, and applications writers will begin to use their own methods, which will duplicate and conflict with the "official" guides. The result will be frustration and expensive confusion.

It is better not to have the guides at all then to have them in a poorly maintained state.

Keeping these guides up to date generally requires two things: the assignment of resources dedicated to the maintenance of the guides, and controls to assure that only authorized people or systems can update the guides. These controls should be in written policies, but automated controls through the use of passwords or other security methods must also be used, if only to keep others from temptation.

Moving data around networks

10. *Usually, data are transmitted among nodes in a network or among information system applications as complete physical files.*

11. *In* **traditional transmission**, *records are passed directly from one system to another, and the record structure can be tailored specifically to the needs of the two systems.*

12. *Another approach is to establish* **application packets** *in which data elements are logically separated; this allows the sending and receiving applications to be "logically" decoupled.*

13. *Gateways can be a useful tool for linking application packets with applications.*

Usually, data are transmitted among nodes in a network or among information system applications as complete physical files. It then becomes the responsibility of the receiving system to select the data records or data elements specifically needed.

Application record packets—When records are passed directly from one system to another, the record structure can be tailored specifically to the needs of the two systems. For example, a record sent between systems A and B can be 278 characters long with the key in characters 12 to 20, while a record sent between systems F and G might be 323 characters long with the key in characters 35 to 42. Each sending and receiving system is written to expect the data in the specific formats shown. See the "traditional" transmission portion of Figure 5.3.

The advantage of this traditional communication method is that the data flow is trailored specifically for the applications involved. This results in two substantial benefits:

- Transmission volume is minimized. Only data elements needed by the receiving application need be sent; in addition, data can be coded in ways expected by the receiving application. Reduced transmission volume, of course, reduces transmission costs and transmission time as well as lowering record storage costs at both the sending and receiving applications.
- Progams are designed to process only the specific data used by the applications. The programs can be tightly focused and are therefore usually less expensive to write and maintain.

There are, however, several major disadvantages with this traditional system design:

- Both the sending and receiving applications must be synchronized with each other. Changes to data, codes, processing rules, edits, and/or run timing must be communicated and coordinated among applications.
- Major changes to data structures may require major changes to many programs in the affected applications, even those programs not directly using the

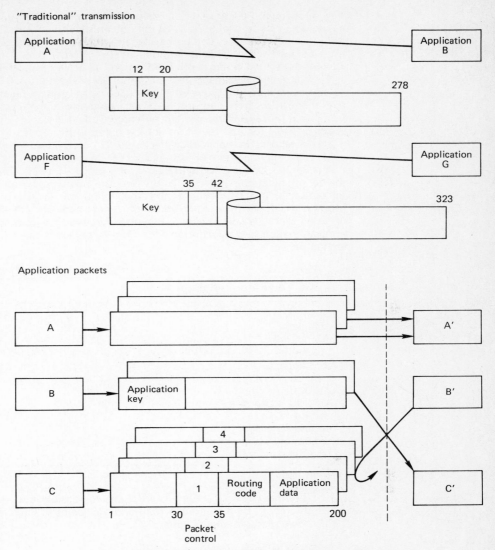

Figure 5.3 Application record packets.

new data elements. For example, if the length of a record is changed or if data element characteristics are changed, many programs may be at least recompiled and various processing steps may need to be rewritten.

Sometimes, however, especially in personal computing applications, much greater flexibility is needed. As computing capabilities proliferate in organizations, it is impractical, if not impossible, to reliably predict which applications will want to communicate with each other. Further, the problems of synchronizing changes to the various applications is either impossible or, for those who would attempt it, requires a bureaucracy that quickly strangles decentralized systems architectures.

A reasonable solution to this problem is to establish the concept of *application packets*. Application packets are fixed-length, fixed-structure records which are used for all communications in the company. There are two major portions of each packet, the control section and the application section.

The control section is usually at the front of the record and is in a format that is fixed for *all* records in the company. See Figure 5.4 for a typical format of an

The Application Packet (AP) is a corporation-wide standard mechanism for communicating business transactions between one entity and another. It includes a data record format, a file structure, and an interface method to the data communications network. It is designed to be application independent, in order that the communication system can correctly handle and route the files on the basis of standardized control records.

The record length and general format are standard for all Application Packets. The AP has specific record types which are used by the communication and routing systems to transmit files between entities. The Communication AP records are distinguished from other types of FC records by a Record Code that begins with "00", and it is these specific "00" record types that are the focus of this appendix.

All records in Application Packets have a standard length of 160 bytes. In the case of Communication APs, bytes 1–40 contain blanks, bytes 41–48 contain the "00" Record Codes described below, and bytes 49–160 contain necessary data for the communication network. It is the Record Code field, bytes 41–48, which is crucial for determining the function of the Application Packet. Currently, bytes 47–48 have been reserved for future expansion of the record code and are always blanks. The layout of an AP record is given below. The entries required for Communication System record are below each field description. The *Core Data* field is more fully described in the following pages.

Data Element	Length	Position
Application key	35	1–35
blanks		
Packet identifier	5	36–40
blanks		
Record code	8	41–48
000000 (Routing record)		
001000 (Additional Destinations)		
002000 (Long or extended File description)		
Core data	112	49–160
Routing record		
Additional destinations		
Long file description		

Core data descriptions—There are three possible layouts for *Core Data*, depending on the record type entered in the *Record Code* field. Each layout is presented with COBOL field pictures and explanatory text. The layouts show only the 112-byte *Core Data* area.

Routing record—000000:   This record is used by the communication system to determine the primary destination of the file and obtain other transmission-related data. There can be multiple routing records within a file. All records that follow a routing record will be considered part of that routing, until another routing record is encountered. The communication system reads an AP file sequentially and breaks it into separate routings each time a new routing record is encountered.

		Record/Element Number
05	*Routing-record*	000000
10	DATA-TYPE	PIC X(02).
	AS = ASCII	
	BI = binary	
10	NETWORK FILE-ID	PIC X (08).
	Unique name for each file type	
	COMSYS File ID used by routs	
10	DESTINATION-FILE-NAME	PIC X(26).
	Use standard file naming convention; optional	

Figure 5.4 Application packets.

		Record/ Element Number
05	Routing-record	000000

10	BLOCK-FORMAT	PIC X(02).
	F— = fixed-length records	
	FB = fixed-length, blocked records	
10	BLOCK-SIZE	PIC X(06).
	Multiple of the record length, 160 bytes	
	Preferably, block size equals or is less than 1920 bytes	
10	RECORD-SIZE	PIC X(04).
	Always "0160"	
10	CARRIAGE-CONTROL-TYPE	PIC X(02).
	A = ANSI control	
	N = no control	
	M = mainframe control	
	Blank = system default	
10	FILE-DESCRIPTION-1	PIC X(20).
	Optional; allows short description	
10	SOURCE-ADDRESS-CODE	PIC X(12).
10	DESTINATION-ADDRESS-CODE	PIC X(12).
10	ROUTING-SECURITY	PIC X(02).
	Blank = not specified	
	PR = company private	
	CO = company confidential	
	IU = internal use only	
10	ROUTING-PRIORITY	PIC X(02).
	Blank = normal	
	HI = high	
	LO = low	
	NX = never transmit	
10	VERSION-NUMBER	PIC X(02).
	Communication System Version number	
	At this time, the field is filled with blanks	
10	FILLER	PIC X(12).

Figure 5.4 (*Continued*)

application packet record. The control section identifies the application that created the packet record and contains record codes to allow receiving applications to uniquely identify a given packet record.

The application section contains the data portion of the record; several packet records may be needed to contain the data found in a traditional transmission record. See Figure 5.5 for an illustration of how application packet records relate to traditional transmission records.

The major advantage of the application packet concept is that the sending and receiving applications are now "logically" decoupled. The sending application creates a series of specifically structured records without any need to synchronize them with specific receiving applications. The receiving applications need look only for those specific packet records needed by that application. Other records can be ignored. Programs need only be changed when changes are made to the specific data elements needed by that application.

The example in Figure 5.5 illustrates the difference between the traditional transmission record format and the application packet. The traditional payroll record shown might be variable in length to accommodate a varying number of deductions, and contains both payroll and personnel information. Every application that needs some of the data on the record must read all the data. For example, an appli-

Traditional Record

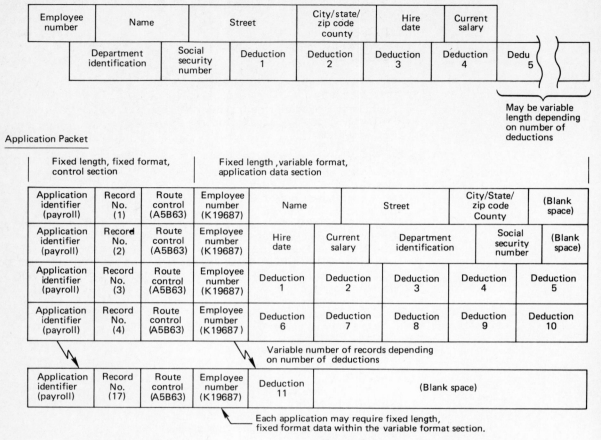

Figure 5.5

cation that simply prints an employee directory must also read (with the associated appropriate security) salary data. Similarly, changes to the structure of the deduction portions of the record will still require changes to the directory application so that it can read (and ignore) the deduction changes.

An application packet might be created in which packet record 1 contains the basic employee data, while record 2 contains the organizational data. Record 3 can contain basic payroll data, and additional records can be created as needed to accommodate the varying number of deductions. Now, the directory program need read only records 1 and 2. Payroll privacy can be maintained; changes to the deduction sections of the packet need not affect applications which read only records 1 and 2.

The flexibility offered by application packets comes at a price, however. Here are some concerns:

- Transmission volume increase. Application packets leave blank spaces and contain a much higher percentage of nonapplication control information than do traditional records. Transmission time and costs increase as do the costs of record storage.

- An organization is needed to assign and monitor the application codes so that they are uniquely identifiable. This same organization may also maintain a directory of applications and application owners so that potential data "vendors'' and ''buyers'' may talk to each other. In ideal situations, this organization might also maintain the data dictionary for both human- and machine-readable reference.

In the most flexible application of application packets, data records can be sent directly to using applications and can then be stored in a special ''read-only'' data pool from which personal computing applications can ''fish'' for specific data needed on an ad hoc basis. This becomes the company equivalent of public data bases. The ''hook,'' of course, is the control section of the application packet record, and the data angler knows where to fish because of the centrally maintained application code directory or the system data dictionary (see Figure 5.6).

Needless to say, data security for such a data pool is a critical consideration. Confidentiality can be maintained by the usual methods described in Part I, but care must be taken to be sure that the appropriate controls are not only installed, but also maintained.

Gateways—Gateways are hardware or software structures that link applications with the communications networks. The logical structure of gateways is discussed further in Guideline 5.1. Physical characteristics of gateways are discussed more fully in Chapter 6. Gateways are mentioned here, however, because they can be a useful tool for linking application packets with applications. Software gateways can be used to create application packets at the sending application and to restruc-

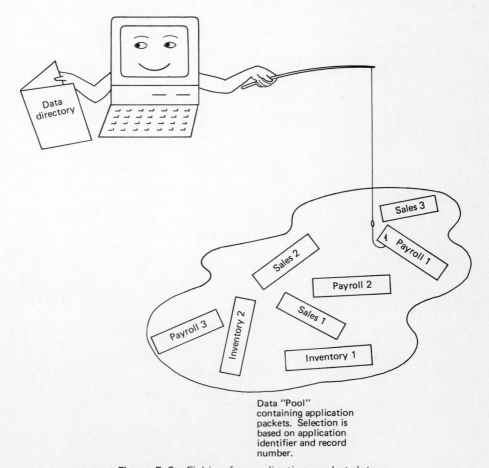

Data ''Pool'' containing application packets. Selection is based on application identifier and record number.

Figure 5.6 Fishing for application packet data.

ture the separate packets at the receiving application, stripping the redundant control data.

In many cases, basic gateway skeletons can be created by the central organization controlling application packets. These skeletons can be used by application developers, thereby increasing the ease with which the application packets may be used.

CHECKLIST

Guideline 5.3
Data Structures for Coordinated Personal Computer Applications

	YES	NO	N/A

1. **Goal of Data Structures**

   Are data structures built only to serve the architecture of appropriate business applications?

2. **Components of a Data Structure**

   For data to be used in several applications, are data compatible in both logical and physical attributes?

3. **Appropriate Goals for Linked Personal Computing Data Structures**

   Have these goals been established?

   a. Are data elements usable by many applications?

   b. Has the redundancy of data elements been minimized?

   c. Is the system designed for rapid entry/retrieval of data elements?

   d. Has computer file storage space been minimized?

   e. Does the system provide adequate security and control?

   f. Does the system provide adequate privacy?

   g. Does the system provide adequate data precision?

   h. Is this data structure compatible with other hardware and software systems?

   i. Is this data structure transferable among various types of data storage media?

4. **Types of Data Structures**

   Have these types of data structures been considered?

   a. Serial
   b. Indexed
   c. Hierarchical/network
   d. Relational
   e. Random

5. **Characteristics of Various Data Structures**

   For linked personal computing applications, have the most important characteristics been defined as direct accessability and access flexibility?

(Continues)

193

6. Data Indices

If various data bases needed by linked personal computing applications are located at different nodes on the network, are data indices used to direct applications to the appropriate node and file?

7. Data Dictionaries

Are data dictionaries established to state the definitions of the elements in data structures both in business and in EDP terms to minimize data redundancy and to help application writers use the data structures?

Does the data dictionary contain entries such as these for each data element?

a. Data name
b. Data definition
c. Data format
d. Edit criteria
e. Source
f. Update frequency
g. Element owner, custodian
h. Relationships with other elements
i. When the dictionary entry was last updated and by whom

8. Updating Data Indicies and Data Dictionaries

Are all the data indices and the data dictionaries kept current?

9. Moving Data around Networks

Are data transmitted among nodes in a network or among information system applications as complete physical files? (In *traditional transmission,* records are passed directly from one system to another, and the record structure can be tailored specifically to the needs of the two systems. Another approach is to establish *application packets* in which data elements are logically separated; this allows the sending and receiving applications to be "logically" decoupled.)

Are gateways used for linking application packets with applications?

Guideline 5.4: Host Computers in Coordinated Personal Computing Systems

Background

Sometimes we become so enthralled with the relatively low-cost convenience of personal computing that we forget that there are those "other" computers, the "big, expensive" ones that we have used for years. These "other" computers are usually called "mainframes" if they are really big, or mini- or superminicomputers if the systems are a bit smaller. In fact, there is a long, smooth continuum reaching from physically small and inexpensive home computers to the much larger, very costly so-called supercomputers used primarily for sophisticated scientific research or extremely large commercial operations.

As semiconductor technology makes increasing computing power available for less money in smaller packages, physical size and cost become less useful as measures of computer "size." Several factors usually become measures:

- Computing speed. In commercial applications, speed is usually measured in MIPS (millions of instructions per second), while scientific users often rate "megaflops" (millions of floating-point operations per second).
- Amount of internal "random-access" memory (RAM) available, usually measured in kilo- or megabytes (thousand or millions of bytes).
- Number of channels and/or ports available for use by peripheral devices such as disk and tape storage systems, printers, and terminals.
- Size and capability of the peripherals that can be attached to the system. Larger computers, for example, have access to larger, faster disk storage devices and faster, more sophisticated printers.
- The operating system used. The operating system dictates the ability of the computer to deal with many different types of work in what appears to be the same time. More complex operating systems, of course, require all the increased hardware resources mentioned above.

Interestingly, from one viewpoint, the power of all the personal computers in a company often exceeds the capabilities of the company's large mainframes. For example, a single mainframe may operate at 30 MIPS, while a typical personal computer operates at only 0.5 MIPS. At these rates, however, 60 personal computers will have raw computing power equal to that of a mainframe (at, by the way, substantially lower hardware costs).

It is easier, of course, to harness the power of a central mainframe than it is to harness completely the power of 60 widely distributed personal computers. There is great potential, however, in those personal computers, providing a significant challenge to the designers of distributed systems.

Some people differentiate between personal comput*ers* and other computers that are shared by many people. As noted in Part I, this is often an artificial distinction, since well-managed shared computers can give individuals many of the advantages of personal computing.

These generic labels, then, are really somewhat arbitrary. It is usually more useful to identify computers in a system according to their use in that system. Thus, in this guideline, we focus on computers used as "hosts" in a system, computers that provide significant services to other computers in the system. Although these hosts, because of the demands placed on them, are usually above the midpoint on the capability–cost continuum, many so-called desktop computers have the power and capabilities to provide hostlike services to other computers in a coordinated, linked system.

The other computing capability in the network/system are called "nodes." These nodes can be anything from "dumb" terminals which are totally dependent on the host computing capabilities to large mainframes, computers that can be, in fact, more powerful than the host itself.

The major difference between a "node" and a "host" is in the relationships of the systems. Nodes relate to the outside world, usually to people or to other systems. A node, for example, might be a personal computing station used for data entry. A node might also be the interface between an information system and a real-time system used for process control.

Hosts, however, have relationships primarily within the system, connections to the nodes; hosts, however, may also have specified connections to other systems. For example, a node might provide the linkage to a company-wide communication system.

Another difference is in the reality of independence that exists with personal comput*ers;* in a shared system environment, the main computer is, at best, a gracious host, and, at worst, a controlling dictator. System/network control responsibilities also vary, depending on the architecture of the system. In some systems, the hosts are passive, providing services only at the request of one of the attached nodes; in other systems, however, the nodes are "slaves" to the host, performing functions only when instructed to do so by the host. In these "master/slave" designs, the host may even provide the node with the programs and data it is to use through a process of "downloading." In these systems, the host can then "upload" the results of the activities at a node, again under host control.

These larger computers, of course, can be used for applications beyond "merely" supplying personal computing power to individuals. These host computers can be designed into coordinated personal computing systems in ways that allocate functions to the most appropriate hardware. This guideline describes, then, how the concepts for coordinated systems described in the first three guidelines in this chapter can be applied and, in fact, expanded by the use of the unique powers of both personal and host computing.

Economics are also a consideration. Because of the expense of a host system, there are large, step-function increases in cost (and capability) whenever a host computer is added to the system. Between these steps, incremental node capacity can be added at relatively low cost. When networks are constructed only with personal computing nodes, the incremental cost of each node is relatively small and relatively constant.

These cost models clearly affect the way the network charges for its services. In systems with only linked personal computing nodes, the cost of each incremental node can be stated accurately, within the usually broad limits of the network capacity. Because the cost per node is constant, this incremental can be fairly charged to the individual nodes.

When host systems are involved, however, someone must forecast the number of nodes that will eventually be used. This number is used to allocate the cost of the host to the individual nodes. If the estimated number of users is too high, the nodes will not pay the full cost of the host, but if the estimate is too low, the node users will overpay and will be encouraged to seek lower-cost services. One way of dealing with this dilemma is to have the host offer positive and negative rebates. If the host usage is higher than forecast, the host refunds money to the users, usually based on a usage formula; if, however, the host service is underutilized, the node users can be charged a "negative rebate," a surcharge, to allow the host to recover its costs fully.

Advantages to users from using hosts in coordinated personal computing systems

1. Hosts can provide:
   a. Economies of scale
   b. Personal computing convenience with host data, power, and controls.
   c. More complete edits
   d. The monitoring and enforcing of standards
   e. Both independence and involvement; individual self-determination together with the coordination of activities

Hosts provide economies of scale which at certain volume breakpoints, lower the total costs of the application. For example, large files may be managed on hosts at lower cost than on personal computers. Similarly, batch processing of many transactions might be more appropriate for certain applications than processing those transactions "on-line" in a personal computing environment.

Using hosts in a coordinated system provides a combination of personal computing convenience with host data, power, and controls. This advantage is especially valuable in applications where decentralized operations require:

- Local capabilities in addition to interaction with remote data bases. Airline reservation systems are typical of this type of application.
- Periodic access to powerful but expensive computing capability. This is common in many engineering applications where data may be entered and reported on personal computers but the sophisticated computations are best done on a powerful host.
- High levels of local service combined with the rigors of central control. Banking applications are good examples of this, where tellers in local branches need local computers to provide high levels of personal service but also need tight centralized accounting controls to minimize the possibility of serious financial errors. The tighter the central control, the closer the design comes to the "master/slave" relationship described above.

Another advantage available from using hosts is that transaction edits can be more complete. Edits can be improved not only by more thorough processing available by the power of hosts, but also because transactions can be processed against a central master file. For example, an order entered in a personal computing application in a local sales office can be edited for format and structure locally, but depending on the size of the company, edits against the corporate product file may require a host. Having these complete edits performed in a coordinated system means that errors can be corrected more rapidly and increase the speed with which valid transactions are processed.

As we have discussed before, standards facilitate intracompany communication and, by reducing duplication, lower costs. Standards can also institutionalize "best practices" and therefore improve the overall quality of the company's administrative practices. Personal computing, by its nature, tends to be difficult to standardize. Using hosts in a coordinated system, however, gives the systems designer a tool with which to monitor and, as necessary, enforce specific standards. For example, host computers can edit transactions in the system to assure compliance with data formats and business codes.

Personal computing gives users feelings of great control and involvement with their work, but a user may also feel isolated from the rest of the company, from others, for example, who are doing the same types of work. People working only with hosts, however, may feel "automated"; they feel (and may in fact be) paced by the program run by the remote, impersonal host.

A good compromise may be a coordinated system that allows users both independence and involvement—individual self-determination together with the coordination of activities that comes from use of a host. An example might be a travel agent who uses a personal system for some work but has the option of linking to larger networks to complete reservation transactions.

Advantages to systems designers from using hosts in coordinated personal computing systems

> 2. *Hosts can provide:*
>   a. *Access to specialized resources*
>   b. *The balancing of system processing loads to give consistent performance even under very high loads*
>   c. *Low-cost backup for both processing services and data*

The advantages to users, shown above, are, by themselves, sufficient justification for building coordinated host/personal computing networks. Since, in this context, users are customers, the advantages become first-order justifications, as described in Guideline 4.3.

Host/personal computing networks, however, also provide substantial advantages to the systems designers. Although these advantages are, in fact, second-order justifications, these advantages give the designers tools with which to better help the users in the long run.

The use of hosts in coordinated systems, for example, give the systems designers access to specialized resources. These resources can include:

- High-performance processing units and peripherals that provide efficient application operation. For example, technical writers can compose their documents on personal computing equipment and then efficiently and cost/effectively print the document on a high-speed, high-quality printer attached to a host.
- Specialized, centralized data resources which, because of their size, can be attached only to a host. For example, a personal computing-based product design system might well use a central file of parts and components showing quality and cost information.
- Specialized services, available only at hosts because of economies of scale. Typical services include technical consulting from systems programming or telecommunications experts.
- Access to special software which is usable only on hosts because of the computing resources required. Certain languages, for example, require the memory and speed of a host for reasonable operation. The same is true of some data management systems or security/audit control systems. Similarly, certain applications, particularly those which are computational intensive, as are many simulations, require host memory size and computational speed.

Capable designers can also use hosts to balance the system processing loads to give the user consistently high performance even under very high loads. In general, designers will allocate person–machine interface tasks to personal computing, sending processing tasks to a host, often within the response time of the user interface. For example, an order-entry system might collect the data via personal computing, editing each transaction on a rapid host during the time the (much slower) order entry continues. To the system user/operator, the system appears to perform smoothly very complex tasks.

Another service that a host can provide to personal computing systems is low-cost backup both for processing services and for data. For example, if appropriate programs exist on both a personal computing system and on a host, either can be used if the other is unavailable. There are, of course, trade-offs. Processing via personal computing is probably a bit slower than it would be on a host, but personal computing probably gives increased convenience and control.

As was discussed in Part I, backup for data is a major concern in personal computing applications. In a host/personal computing network, the personal computing data can be transferred periodically to the host. This is especially useful for personal computing systems which include hard disks which contain tens of millions of bytes of data. Now, relatively low-cost tape drives are becoming available for use in providing data backup; however, transferring data to the host may still be an economical, effective method of providing backup to the personal computing application.

Capabilities hosts must have to be used in coordinated personal computing systems

3. *To function as a host, a computer system must have hardware and software resources that can:*
   a. *Connect personal computing nodes and the host*
   b. *Automatically (sometimes remotely) initiate processing on the host*
   c. *Convert node data to and from host format*
   d. *Provide communication between the nodes and the host*

4. *To accomplish these four functions requires:*
   a. *Physical linkages*
   b. *Logical linkages*
   c. *Application design that uses these capabilities*
   d. *Compatibility of application development tools*
   e. *Operating system compatability*
   f. *Data structure compatabilities*
   g. *Security*
   h. *Privacy*
   i. *Expense allocation*
   j. *Specialized software to handle node/host linkages*
   k. *Directories*
   l. *Interfaces to environment outside the system*
   m. *Training for users*
   n. *System/network support*

To accomplish these four functions requires significant human and capital resources, together with a fair amount of technical sophistication. Chapter 6 is devoted to guidelines that provide more detail on these topics.

Physical linkages.   A physical network must be built that provides flexible bidirectional communication (i.e., communication between the nodes and the hosts and back). Depending on the systems architecture, connections may also be required between the individual nodes. These connections are usually some sort of electronic or fiber optic cable. Technology for "wireless" bidirectional communication exists (e.g., two-way radio transmission, cellular telephone), but is, at this time, too expensive for broad commercial use.

Logical linkages.   A network is defined not only by the physical linkages, but also by the "logical" linkages, the linkages defined by the architecture of the system. Architectural considerations are discussed more fully in the first three guidelines of this chapter.

Application design.   In general, the physical and logical capabilities of coordinated system technology is ahead of the abilities of application systems designers to make use of these technologies. Designers must use the techniques described in Guideline 4.3 to identify the first-order tasks of the enterprise and then use their imaginations to accomplish these tasks using the full capabilities available to them through coordinated personal computing systems. Designers must overcome the self-imposed limitations inherent in the traditional batch processing or on-line-to-a-central-computer application architectures.

Compatibility of application development tools.   Simply stated, it may take some planning to be sure that programs will run on the various physical devices in the network. Transportable programs are still more of a goal than a reality. One major consideration is the object language of the programs themselves. Depending on the systems, the source language of the programs must also be considered.

One way of ensuring compatability, of course, is simply to write the programs only on the physical systems on which those programs will run. This is the traditional way programs are written, but in these days of networks and programmer workstations, it may be an overly restrictive limitation.

Programming language, of course, is only one of the several factors that must be considered. Other factors include the system libraries which must be available to programs, system utilities, the physical resources (devices, memory, etc.) expected by the application programs, operating systems, and, of course, data structures (discussed a bit more below).

Operating system compatability.   This is a primary consideration because it affects all the issues described in this section. As a rule of thumb, programs will run only under one operating system. Two situations, however, may mitigate this rule.

First, with care and planning, programs may be written in a language or language subset that will run under a number of different operating systems. Subsets of popular languages such as BASIC, COBOL, FORTRAN, and Pascal may run well under several different operating systems, although subset users may not be able to use attractive, computer-specific language features. Some languages, such as C and Ada are designed specifically to allow program transportability.

A somewhat more complex approach, but one that is relatively common on large time-sharing hosts, is to run one operating system as an application program under the host computer's pimary operating system. The "real" application program then runs under the secondary operating system (which runs under the primary operating system). This "layered" approach, of course, lowers the overall efficiency of the system's operation, but it does allow some transportability between otherwise incompatible systems.

These layers are often called "shells" and are becoming more common on personal computers as the capabilities of personal computers increase. Some shells are implemented on personal computers in "windowing" systems which allow the users to manage the running of several programs at one time, viewing each concurrently through a portion of the computer/terminal screen called a window.

Data structure capabilities.   Application programs are usually written with a specific data structure in mind. The programs expect a given set of formats, coding conventions, data base organizations, and collating sequences. These are discussed more fully in Guideline 5.3.

Data can usually be stored on various systems by using a "lowest common denominator" such as American Standard Code Information Interchange (ASCII) format and sequential file organization, but the data may require substantial further processing before they can be used on the second system.

Data structures that give the user and the application maximum flexibility, such as relational data bases, are usually the most difficult to transport, since they usually take full advantage of the unique capabilities of a specific hardware/software environment.

Security/privacy.   By definition, system networks must allow access to system resources in a flexible, relatively unpredictable manner. It is this flexibility which creates the advantages to both users and systems designers.

One price for this flexibility is the technical complexity described in other items. Another price is the significant increase in the danger from security and privacy violations. The very flexibilities creating the advantages open the opportunity for violations.

These issues are discussed more fully in Chapter 6, but note that coming to grips with this problem is a vital necessity in coordinated applications, not an option. The absence of visible violations does not necessarily imply successful security; it may only imply inadequate detection capabilities.

Expense allocation.   The accounting for the costs of coordinated systems is a subject closely related to the management incentive and control structure of the company. One of two approaches is common. In the first approach, costs are allocated to users in direct proportion to use of resources, in much the same way that we are charged by utilities or by the telephone company for the amount of electricity or telephone services used by our homes. In this approach, the systems managers must establish pricing and billing systems.

The second approach is simpler. All the costs for the systems services are accumulated, charged to an overhead account, and then allocated to all departments based on some factor, such as headcount or floor space used.

Regardless of which approach is used, it is probably important to keep track of system usage by each user, if not for cost allocation purposes, then for an ongoing understanding of the changing needs of the users. Without such an understanding, the network cannot allocate its resources appropriately. Therefore, the system owners and custodians must identify the critical system resources; some type of application is needed, usually functioning as an operating system subset, which collects and reports the usage of those critical resources.

Specialized software to handle node/host linkages.   These systems are highly specialized programs designed to control both the communication and application aspects of the network. They are highly technical and provided usually by the hardware vendor or by a vendor that specializes in communications hardware and software. These systems are essentially subsets of the operating systems used by both the nodes and hosts which both affect and are affected by the applications operations. This software is discussed further in Chapter 6.

Directories.   Directories tell the various nodes where to find specific people, applications, data, and physical nodes. When a host is involved in a network, the directories for the network are usually installed on the host. Nodes access the directories on the host. The hosts may then automatically establish the connection between the requesting and destination nodes or may merely return the appropriate address, depending on the requirements of the application (see Figure 5.7.)

Interfaces to environment outside the system.   These interfaces are to people, sensors, instrumentation, and process control tools. Interfaces to people are usually

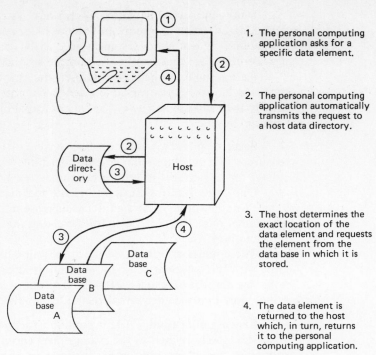

1. The personal computing application asks for a specific data element.

2. The personal computing application automatically transmits the request to a host data directory.

3. The host determines the exact location of the data element and requests the element from the data base in which it is stored.

4. The data element is returned to the host which, in turn, returns it to the personal computing application.

Figure 5.7   Finding a specific data element.

some sort of keyboard, but technology permitting "friendlier" relationships is becoming available. This will allow such tools as touchscreens, light pens, tablets, mice, and soon, even voice to be used as a means of people-to-computer communication.

In engineering/scientific applications, the computers need to interact with instruments and tools, sometimes devices which themselves contain sophisticated automation. In these "process control" and data acquisition applications, the interface must transmit and receive both digital and analog signals, as required, as well as timing signals to synchronize the signal or to create a reference for further analysis.

In host/coordinated personal computing systems, the interactions with the environment outside the system, whether human or automated, are usually accomplished by the nodes. These nodes can be specialized and even dedicated to specific interface tasks. For example, a data collection terminal can be set to record transactions from a factory floor. The terminal can be constructed with large keys or slides that can be used by workers with gloves or be built to withstand the "dirty" factory environment.

In systems such as these, the host can act as a controller, instructing the nodes what to do next, editing and storing and routing data as they are collected, and if properly programmed, changing the systems activities as a function of the data collected at the nodes.

Training for users.   Training for both new and experienced users on an ongoing basis is particularly required in network applications because of the complexities of the application interactions. In host/personal computing applications, the complexities (and, therefore, the need for training) are particularly acute because of the variety of technologies facing the users. To be successful, users must master the complexities at the node, at the host, and those of the network itself. On the positive side, having hosts in network provides designers with the computing power required to provide users with appropriate guidance and assistance.

System/network support.　While training helps users to be reasonably self-sufficient and confident in their use of the system, all users will encounter problems imposed by the nodes, the hosts, the network, the application software, or by the mistakes of the users themselves. Problems will be especially acute whenever changes are made to any aspect of the network.

At this point, the users must have some resource to call upon for help, a support group that will provide consulting and training for specific situations. The support group can also help adapt the system to the changing needs of the applications and the organization and can help implement the network technical modifications as new hardware and software become available. This support group is usually associated with the company's information systems department, since the problems of coordinated personal computing networks usually overlap with those of mainframe and voice/data communications networks. Technical support is discussed further below.

Management issues

5. *Management issues require decisions based on cost–performance trade-offs:*
    a. *Load control*
    b. *Host resource allocation*
    c. *Implementation of new technology*
    d. *Application architectures*
    e. *Use of proprietary versus commercial packages*
    f. *Technical support*
    g. *System audits and controls*
    h. *Testing policies*

Many of the issues regarding the use of hosts in coordinated personal computing systems must be satisfied by management evaluations of cost–performance trade-offs, in addition to appropriate technical considerations. Management decisions, of course, affect resource availability for all systems, but host/personal computing systems presents some unique opportunities. In centralized systems with mainframes or large minicomputers, the company's information systems department exercises relatively complete control, usually in accordance with management desires. In totally decentralized personal computing systems, management control is significantly diffused. It is relatively difficult to achieve consistent application of policies and standards. Host/personal computing systems offers a challenging mixture of decentralized authority (over the personal computing stations) with relatively significant control over the hosts and the network resources.

Next we look at some of the areas in which management can set policies with regard to cost–performance trade-offs.

Load control.　Systems loads are usually measured in terms of disk storage space, on-line response time, and/or job throughput time. Most technical managers try to keep normal operation in the range of 50 to 60 percent of capacity, with peaks approaching full capacity. Allowing normal loads to rise clearly lowers the unit costs of processing, but service levels will generally decrease and peak loads may actually cause the system to fail completely.

Host resource allocation.　The amount of host capability made available for use with personal computing is another potential trade-off. To the extent that hosts are used with personal computers, they are not available for use on normal production computing tasks. On the other hand, use of host/coordinated personal computing may lower the demands on the routine production computing tasks.

Implementation of new technologies.   The problems are caused by the opportunities presented by products that usually offer additional features and lower costs. Managers must decide, often in the face of ambiguous technical advice, when to implement or to remain with existing technology rather than waiting for or switching to something better.

Again, the complexity of the host/personal computing network complicate these decisions. Managers must examine the trade-offs available with the hardware and software available for the hosts, the personal computing nodes, and the communications network. In addition, the interactions between these elements must be evaluated.

As a result of these complexities, once a company has committed itself to a systems strategy, it is difficult, if not impossible, to change significantly. Vendors are therefore well advised to offer new products only after giving careful consideration to compatibility with and migration from existing systems.

Application architectures.   The systems architecture must match the management style and company culture. One major decision, for example, is the amount of authority allowed to decentralized nodes versus what authority is reserved for the more controllable hosts.

Use of proprietary versus commercial software packages.   In general, using commercially available software both for applications and for systems management provides capability at lower cost and more rapidly than if a company develops its own software. Commercial packages, however, will usually lack some of the features important to a specific company, as well as having some features that a company may not use or may wish to disable actively. Developing proprietary software can provide not only the initial custom fit with the company's needs, but this software will probably also be more adaptable to the company's needs as those change over time.

Again, these decisions require technical advice, but in the end, business managers must choose the appropriate mix of commercial and proprietary software based on their understanding of the availability of resources for both new systems and systems support. Business managers must also evaluate the ability of the organization to adapt its procedures to the structure of commercial software packages.

Technical support.   As has been noted before, ongoing technical support is needed at both host and node sites. Managers can choose from among several different support models:

- Totally decentralized to user nodes. This type of support tends to be expensive, but it can be tailored for and very responsive to the unique needs of each node. On the other hand, local support people may have to be broad in their knowledge and, therefore, not as deep in certain areas as a functional specialist would be.
- Totally centralized with phone in consulting and remote diagnosis, with local repair only when necessary. This model is the opposite of the first. It tends to be economical, but less responsive to the specific needs of any given user. On the other hand, under a central organization, specialists can be developed so that all questions can (eventually) be answered.
- Hierarchical support levels. Obviously, some mix of support resources is a good compromise, especially given the nature of a hierarchical host/personal computing network. Certain specialists can be stationed at the host, while more broadly trained support people can assist at local nodes.

There are, however, some concerns unique to this approach. First, over time, it tends to be the most expensive of all the approaches. Both the central and local support organizations will tend to justify their existence and to grow. Since no one group will have responsibility for both organizations, there will be at least some conflict and competition, especially if resources are rationed. Finally, and not least, communications among the various support organizations will be difficult and costly to maintain. If the communication is not maintained, however, the company will suffer from redundant and sometimes conflicting solutions, leading eventually to the erosion of the basic advantages of the systems being supported.

Systems audits and controls.　As has been mentioned elsewhere in this book, systems must have controls and audit trails for security, privacy, and for error prevention, detection, and correction. In addition, the controls and data are useful for management analyses aimed at simplifying and improving the processes.

The complexities of host/personal computing networks, of course, make audits and controls more difficult but also more necessary. In general, the need for effective audits and controls is directly proportional to the amount of decentralization and authority available to local nodes.

Testing policies.　Again, testing a host/personal computing system is particularly difficult because of the complexities of the networks. Fingerpointing between the system elements is common. Technical managers should have the responsibility of specifying what to test and how to perform those tests. Thorough tests should be completed whenever even the slightest change is made to *any* portion of the system, whether in the host, nodes, or network.

It falls to business managers to decide *when to stop testing*. From a technical standpoint, there never can be enough testing to assure completely reliable performance. Business managers must decide when the cost of further testing is greater than the costs involved in releasing the system (or the modifications) for use.

Another business decision is how much of the network can be shut down for how long in order to accomplish testing. Again, the business manager must balance the costs of continued scheduled testing with the risks and costs of failure, unscheduled disruption, and repair in later production.

Statements of guidelines

6. *Acquire data as close to the source as possible.*
7. *Time stamp all transactions.*
8. *Do as much editing as possible at the point of data acquisition.*
9. *Get data to the host as soon as possible.*
10. *Edit data at the host as soon as possible.*
11. *Notify the source of edit results (positive and negative) as soon as possible.*
12. *Store "official" data at the source.*
13. *Make corrections by offset, never by replacement.*
14. *Use global, shared, local architectures; stress logical and, as appropriate, physical system hierarchy.*
15. *Establish/manage standard business codes.*
16. *Use gateways to isolate nodes and applications from network.*
17. *Use application packets to logically isolate applications.*
18. *Use relational data bases where possible to allow maximum flexibility in uses of data.*

19. *Use performance analysis tools at the source to measure loads and report re*
    sults to users and MIS managers.
20. *Implement audit and security by:*
    a. Transaction/process logging
    b. "Windows" into systems
    c. Simulation capability
21. *Implement test policies by using:*
    a. Base of test data
    b. Simulation capability
22. *Charge nodes for host services; use the rebate method.*

These guidelines gather in one place the ideas, some of which have also bee
mentioned with regard to other topics, which are most appropriate for system
where hosts are used in coordinated personal computing networks. Since these sys
tems tend to be both complex and dynamic, management must pay specific attentio
to keep needs for control in balance with the advantages of flexibility. These idea
should therefore be managed as guidelines, not as bureaucratic rules.

Acquire data as close to the source as possible.   This usually means that da
acquisition is performed at a node. In some cases, however, especially where da
are acquired in machine-readable form from some other system, the data may l
acquired by the host. In these guidelines, we will assume, for literary convenienc
that data are collected at nodes.

These guidelines gather in one place the ideas, some of which have also bee
mentioned with regard to other topics, which are most appropriate for systen
where hosts are used in coordinated personal computing networks. Since these sy
tems tend to be both complex and dynamic, management must pay specific attentic
to keep needs for control in balance with the advantages of flexibility. These ide
should therefore, be managed as guidelines, not as bureaucratic rules.

Time stamp all transactions.   Time stamping automatically places on t
transaction the date and time it was entered into the system. In systems that a
distributed in several time zones, the time stamp should reflect the time at one pla
in the network, usually the host location.

Time stamps should also be applied at each step in the process. For examp
when a transaction reaches the host, a time stamp should be applied. Similar
when the transaction is returned to a node, it should be stamped.

By the very nature of the complexity of these systems, transactions to one d
base or one application will "compete" with each other for use of resources. I
example, in an airline reservation system, two ticket agents in different cities n
be trying to assign the same seat on a flight. Time stamping the transaction allc
the system to apply processing rules based on time of data entry.

Time stamping is also essential for the system's audit trail. Virtually any inv
tigation into the history of a transaction, whether because of a suspected secu
breach or simply for accounting verification, needs to know when a transaction v
entered.

The time stamps can be collected into a log showing the flow of transacti
through a system. These logs are very useful in analyzing system performance a
can become a metric for measuring system capacity.

Do as much editing as possible at the point of data acquisition.   The l
person to correct a data error is the person who entered the data. Further, it is n
effective for people to know of the edit problems as soon as possible so that
situations are still fresh in their minds. Another advantage of rapid editing is

the system need not waste its resources processing both incorrect transactions and the repaired transactions.

All this suggests, then, that transactions are best edited in the location and at the time of entry. Some edits, however, cannot be performed at the local node, which leads us to the next three guidelines.

Get data to the host as soon as possible. There are two major reasons for getting data to the host as quickly as possible. First, data can be edited at the host, as discussed below. Second, once at the host, the data can be made available to other applications.

Edit data at the host as soon as possible. The host can edit the transactions against master data bases and/or perform more complex edits than can be performed at the nodes. Some systems collect the transactions into batches for economy of further processing; if possible, however, the transactions should be edited quickly so that the edit results can be reported back to the node and corrections easily made, if necessary.

Notify the source of edit results (positive and negative) as soon as possible. Corrections must be made at the node, not at the host, even if the host knows what changes to make (see the next guideline). Getting the edit results back to the node allows any needed changes to be made quickly, ideally, by the person who initiated the transaction.

It is clearly more important to report errors back to the source so that corrections can be made. However, positive edit results should also be reported back in a reasonable time period. Positive reporting tells the node that the transactions have been received and processed and also gives the people at the nodes some positive reinforcement for their good work.

Store "official" data at the source. One of the dangers in systems where data are entered in one place and then forwarded to a host is that there then exist two copies of the data. Having two copies offers the potential for reconciliation errors, not to mention the cost of storing two copies of the same data.

For control, there must be one "official" data set; I recommend that the official set be the one closest to the people who created the data—that the official set be maintained at the local node. For example, if accounting transactions are generated at a division of a large company and then sent monthly to corporate headquarters for processing, the official transactions should be the ones at the division.

This implies that errors, even if detected at the host, be corrected first at the node. Then the corrections can be transmitted back to the host so that the two files are again synchronized. If in doubt, however, the local files should take precedence over the central files. This policy might cause a bit more transmission traffic than would a policy advocating central file management, but it clearly places data ownership authority and control in the hands of the people who are most affected by the data, the local people.

Make corrections by offset, never by replacement. As has been discussed before, corrections by offsetting transactions may take more space, but they do leave an audit trail that can be followed by investigators. This guideline is particularly useful when multiple files exist: for example, one at a local node and one at the host. Then if the files fail to reconcile, a review of the transactions and the corrections to transactions can easily be made. For example, if a transmission error occurs, the system managers can quickly determine which transactions were lost.

Use global, shared, local architectures; stress logical and, as appropriate, physical system hierarchy.   Host/coordinated personal computing systems are a form of architectural design that implies hierarchical function. It is therefore important to create both the logical and physical aspects of the systems in ways that support the hierarchical functions.

Three tools have been discussed in other guidelines which can be used to implement the desired hierarchical distribution. The first tool is the concept of systems owners, custodians, and users. Defining the way people use any system is a primary consideration. The second tool is the concept of global, shared, and local systems. These concepts provide an architectural framework that can provide the appropriate mix of central control and efficiency with decentralized operation and flexibility. The third tool involves hierarchical data structures, where applications are directed to data at nodes or hosts by directories within the system.

Implementing these concepts requires a mixture of hardware and software capabilities that is usually best implemented by combinations of host computers and personal computing systems, all linked by a communications facility. As personal computing nodes become more powerful, however, together with advances in rapid, flexible communications capabilities, the concepts of "peer" systems, systems in which all nodes are equal and there are no hosts, becoms more practical. This is discussed further in Chapter 6.

Establish/manage standard business codes.   As has been discussed before, standard business codes are a mechanism for helping systems communicate in a decentralized environment. This concept can be managed particularly well in host/personal computing systems by having the host edit the business codes against centrally managed master files.

The following systems design features are applicable to any networked application and are, therefore, specifically appropriate for host/personal computing systems:

- Use gateways to isolate nodes and applications from network.
- Use application packets to logically isolate applications.
- Use relational data bases where possible to allow maximum flexibility in uses of data.

Use performance analysis tools at source to measure loads and report results to users and MIS managers.   Performance is a key issue in host/personal computing systems. As discussed above, one advantage of the host/personal computing design is the ability of the systems operators to balance work loads dynamically by moving applications and data between nodes and hosts. This load switching should be accomplished based on predetermined performance metrics, and of course, the effectiveness of shifts in loads should be demonstrated by those same metrics.

Note that the guideline stresses performance measures at the data source, at the interface between the systems and people. It is probably important also to measure performance within the system, but the critical aspect is that perceived by the people who work with the system. To be useful, changes must be made visible to the users/customers.

Implement audit and security.   Control is particularly difficult in host/personal computing systems because increasing the effectiveness of controls usually compromises the flexibility which motivated the use of this type of systems architecture. The control measures shown below are particularly appropriate for network systems because they can be implemented with minimal impact on the system user instead, they can be implemented by a separate group of specialists in security an control issues. Using a separate group in this way helps maintain the desired flexibility, but it is also costly. Of more concern, approaches such as this clearly set a group of "watchers" apart from the group of "users," tacitly encouraging a hide-and-seek contest. Here are the suggested security/control methods:

- Transaction/process logging
- "Windows" into systems: programs that can be run apart from but concurrently with the primary system, allowing the auditors to capture system activities as they occur.
- Simulation capability: ability to use "dummy" accounts and ficticious entities to operate normal system processes in a controlled environment without affecting normal processing and real accounts and entities. This allows users to investigate "what if" alternatives and allows auditors to analyze the processes followed by particular types of transactions.

Implement test policies. Testing is a post-development, expensive screen which tries to find development errors before they are detected by users/customers. Ideally, the errors would not be made at all, thus reducing the need for testing. The evolving profession of software engineering focuses on reaching this ideal, but until it is realized, testing is the best mechanism available for protecting the customers.

As has been noted before, testing in network environments because of the essentially infinite variety of errors that can be created by the hardware and/or software in any individual node or host, is very difficult. Further, there is finger-pointing, as hardware, software, and network engineers each blame the others in cases of systems failure.

The following two methods are particularly useful in host/personal computing applications:

- Base of test data. A data set that is held reasonably constant. This "test suite" is run every time the system is modified in any way, and the results from the new run are matched against previously derived "correct" results; discrepancies between the two systems must be explained before the developers are allowed to proceed.
- Maintaining this set of base data is an expensive and complex operation. On the other hand, the test suite will live as long as the system is kept operational, and therefore, the test suite is usually prepared carefully and then enhanced as new features are added to the primary system.
- Simulation capability. These are again the "dummy" accounts, mentioned above. Testing modifications on the dummy accounts allows bugs to be found without causing disruptions to normal processing.

Charge nodes for host services; use the rebate method. Inside companies, multientity systems can be funded in several ways. In more centralized organizations, the costs of the system are simply charged to a central overhead account. The system is "free" to users. This method encourages use of the systems; it even encourages experimentation, since even failures cost nothing but the work time of the experimenters.

It is becoming increasingly common, however, for systems to charge their users for system services. The costs involved are usually linked to usage and encourage users to be efficient and effective in their use of system resources. As was mentioned above, especially in host/personal computing systems, charges must be based on some estimate of activity. Therefore, it makes sense to offer "positive" and "negative" rebates so that users are charged fairly for the systems. These costs should be sufficiently high that users take an interest in the system operation, sometimes even helping to manage the system through steering committees or advisory counsels.

One way of having the benefits of experimentation together with the discipline of cost allocation is to have the system costs centrally charged during its early operation, say for its first year of operation. During that year, users are encouraged to try different uses freely. Costs are not charged back, but information on systems usage is distributed so that users can estimate what the costs would be. After the first year, users would be charged for the system, presumably knowing by then what applications can be run on the system in a cost-effective manner.

CHECKLIST

Guideline 5.4
Host Computers in Coordinated Personal Computing Systems

	YES	NO	N/A
1. Advantages to Users from Using Hosts in Coordinated Personal Computing Systems Are host computers used to provide these capabilities? a. Economies of scale b. Personal computing convenience with host data, power, and controls c. More complete edits d. The monitoring and enforcing of standards e. Both independence and involvement, individual self-determination together with the coordination of activities			
2. Advantages to Systems Designers from Using Hosts in Coordinated Personal Computing Systems Are hosts used to provide these design features? a. Access to specialized resources b. The balancing of system processing loads to give consistent performance even under very high loads c. Low-cost backup for both processing services and data			
3. Capabilities Hosts Must Have to Be Used in Coordinated Personal Computing Systems Are hardware and software resources available that can: a. Connect personal computing nodes and the host? b. Automatically (sometimes remotely) initiate processing on host? c. Convert node data to and from host format? d. Provide communication between the nodes and the host?			

(Continues)

4. To Accomplish the Four Capabilities Shown in 3, Are These Functions Provided?
   a. Physical linkages
   b. Logical linkages
   c. Application design that uses these capabilities
   d. Compatibility of application development tools
   e. Operating system compatibility
   f. Data structure compatibilities
   g. Security
   h. Privacy
   i. Expense allocation
   j. Specialized software to handle node/host linkages
   k. Directories
   l. Interfaces to environment outside the system
   m. Training for users
   n. System/network support

5. Management Issues

Have these issues been reviewed based on cost–performance trade-offs?
   a. Load control
   b. Host resource allocation
   c. Implementation of new technology
   d. Application architectures
   e. Use of proprietary versus commercial packages
   f. Technical support
   g. System audits and controls
   h. Testing policies

6. Guidelines

Have these general guidelines been considered?

a. Are data acquired as close to the source as possible?

b. Are all transactions time stamped?

c. Is as much editing as possible performed at the point of data acquisition?

d. Are data sent to the host as soon as possible?

e. Are data edited at the host as soon as possible?

f. Is the data source notified of edit results (positive and negative) as soon as possible?

g. Are "official" data stored at the data source?

h. Are corrections to transactions made by offset, not by replacement?

i. Are global, shared, local architectures used?

j. Do architectures, stress logical, and as appropriate, physical system hierarchy?

k. Are standard business codes established and managed?

l. Are gateways used to isolate nodes and applications from network technology?

m. Are application packets used to logically isolate applications?

n. Are relational data bases used where possible to allow maximum flexibility in uses of data?

o. Are performance analysis tools used at the data source to measure loads and to report results to users and MIS managers?

p. Are audit and security policies implemented by
   1) Transaction/process logging?
   2) "Windows" into systems?
   3) Simulation capabilities?

q. Are test policies implemented by using:
   1) Test data bases?
   2) Simulation capabilities?

r. Are nodes charged for host services, preferably using the rebate method?

REFERENCES

DANIEL S. APPLETON, "Business Rules: The Missing Link," *Datamation,* October 15, 1984, p. 145.

JOHN BLACKFORD, "Strategic Connections," *Personal Computing,* May 1987, p. 131.

PETER A. BOYER, "Fitting Microcomputers into Manufacturing Systems Applications," Technical Paper No. MS84-191, Society of Manufacturing Engineers, Dearborn, Mich., 1984.

ROB CORDELL, "Rock Solid Office Architecture," *Computerworld on Communications,* October 3, 1984, p. 21.

ANDREAS DIENER et al, "Database Services for Personal Computers Linked by a Local Area Network," *ACM Conference on Personal Computers,* December 9, 1983, p. 217.

LEE W. DOYLE, "Micro-to-Mainframe Links: They Don't Quite Make It . . . Yet," *Today's Office,* May 1986, p. 34.

WILLIAM DURELL, "The Politics of Data," *Computerworld,* September 9, 1985, p. ID/25.

MICHAEL DURR, "Ins and Outs of Data Integrity," *Micro Communications,* January 1985, p. 18.

JANET FIDERIO and BECKY BATCHA, ed., "Microcomputer Networking," Executive Report, *Computerworld,* March 24, 1986, p. 59.

ANNE R. FIELD, "IBM's Software 'Road Map': A Magic Carpet to the Future?" *Business Week,* May 11, 1987, p. 159.

CLARE P. FLEIG, "The Hidden Corporate Resource: Applications Developed on PCs," *InformationWEEK,* March 31, 1986, p. 40.

MICHAEL GORMAN, "Getting Control of Data Base Systems," *Computerworld,* December 3, 1984, p. ID/1.

GIG GRAHAM, "Real-World Distributed Databases," *UNIX Review,* May 1987, p. 33.

JAMES HANNAN, "A Primer on Micro-to-Mainframe Links," *Infosystems,* February 1986, p. 32.

TOM INGLESBY, "Manufacturing Is Itself a System," *Manufacturing Systems,* Summer 1984, p. 26.

WILLIAM INMON, "Lifting the Fog on Subject Data Bases," *Computerworld,* October 24, 1984, p. 53.

International Data Corporation, "Information Systems for Tomorrow's Office," White Paper to Management in *Fortune,* October 15, 1984.

LESLIE C. JASANY, "Tying the Factory Together with PCs and Networks," *Production Engineering,* April 1984, p. 52.

R. MCCORD and M. HANNER, "Connecting Islands of Information," *UNIX Review,* May 1987, p. 25.

KEN MICHIELSEN, "Micro Applications Development," *Datamation,* April 15, 1986, p. 96.

ED MILLSAP, KEN SLOAN, and STEVE GERRARD, "Relational DBMS," *Computerworld,* March 4, 1985, p. ID/1.

JEFF MOAD, "IBM's SAA: Is It Fact or FUD?" *Datamation,* May 1, 1987, p. 19.

JOEL ORR, "Integrating the New Mix," special section on CAD/CAM, *Computerworld Focus,* March 19, 1986, p. 27.

MARY PETROSKY and DON CRABB, "Linking Up the Office," special report in *Info-World,* March 24, 1986, p. 25.

JUDITH A. QUILLARD et al., "A Study of the Corporate Use of Personal Computers," CISR WP No. 109, Center for Information Systems Research, Massachusetts Institute of Technology, Cambridge, Mass., December 1983.

WENDY RAUCH-HINDIN, "Distribution Databases Clear Hurdles," *Mini-Micro Systems,* June 1987, p. 61.

WENDY RAUCH-HINDIN, "True Distributed DBMSes Presage Big Dividends," *Mini-Micro Systems,* May 1987, p. 65.

RICHARD L. ROTH, "Making Connections in the Shadow of the Mainframe," *Computerworld,* October 15, 1984, p. ID/7.

RONALD SHELBY and RONALD DUBIEN, "Choosing Your First (or Second, or Third) DBMS," *Computerworld,* February 18, 1985, p. ID/7.

JACK SHOMENTA et al., "The Application Approach Worksheet: An Evaluative Tool for Matching New Development Methods with Appropriate Applications," *Management Information Systems Quarterly,* Vol. 7, No. 4, 1983, p. 1.

DON TAPSCOTT, "OA Banks on Connectivity," *Datamation,* March 15, 1986, p. 106.

J. VAN DUYN, *Developing a Data Dictionary,* Prentice-Hall, Inc., Englewood-Cliffs, N.J., 1982.

JOHN W. VERITY, "Grafting a Wonder Office System," *Datamation,* March 15, 1986, p. 88.

JESSE VICTOR, "LANs Link PCs to Mainframes," *Mini-Micro Systems,* May 1987, p. 91.

Chapter Six

Guidelines for Personal Computing Communications Networks

Goal of Communications Networks

A reasonable goal of all workers in an organization is to do their individual tasks in full coordination with but with minimum duplication of the work of others. Accomplishing this simply stated goal requires three additional steps:

- All workers have specified task assignments.
- Everyone knows what others are doing.
- The work output of each worker blends smoothly into the work input of others.

In practice, of course, achieving these steps is incredibly difficult. Groups have long tried to achieve needed coordination and cooperation by organizational structures, position descriptions, and group standards, guidelines, policies, and procedures. Presumably, if all people do exactly what they are supposed to, no more, no less, all work will blend together and be complete. However, the real world forces continual compromises and adaptations.

Problems increase greatly as orgnizations become separated geographically; time, language, and culture become critical factors. The degree of mutual dependence is also an issue. Where a stand-alone decentralized unit can provide the customer with full services, communications can be minimized. A good example of this is a hotel chain; a local hotel can meet virtually all of a customer's needs; communications are needed only to lower costs (perhaps by coordinating purchasing activities) or to provide enhanced services (making reservations in the customer's next destination).

Typically, however, manufacturing organizations are functionally organized, with, for example, sales offices geographically separated from the production facilities. Nothing can be accomplished for the customers until the communication and coordination is correctly accomplished.

217

Definitions

A network, as discussed in this chapter, is an organized system of channels by which communications can take place. Ideally, these channels can carry any type of signal, data, voice, or video. From a practical standpoint, however, especially in the short term, managers must choose specialized channels and ask people, who are more flexible and adaptable than is communications technology, to integrate the individual communications.

Local Computing versus Communication

From the very first days of automated data processing, the need for local computing power has competed for the technological spotlight with the need to communicate data among users. Clearly, of course, these two technologies are closely linked, since the local communication nodes also provide local computing power. These trends can, however, be mutually disruptive, since communication requires considering the needs and capabilities of other nodes, while local computing can optimize solutions to local problems regardless of the needs of others.

In batch computing, data communication is often accomplished simply by sending a file on magnetic tape from one application and/or location to another. In on-line applications, communication is achievable through the central host; a file can be sent to the host and accessed by a receiving application as needed.

The emphasis between local computing and communications depends heavily on the culture of the organization, the degree to which decentralization is stressed versus central control, and the degree to which individual work is stressed versus cooperative programs. Some degree of communication is always needed, even in the most decentralized of organizations; in fact, improved communications can allow greater individual independence without burdensome controls to assure the proper meshing of the individual work.

Although this chapter will focus on the communication of data between computer-based applications, we recognize that the boundaries are blurring between different communications media, data, voice, messages (mail), video, and facsimile. As communications technology improves, users will have more flexibility in using the media appropriate for each specific application's needs, and the need for compromise and adaptation will diminish. Further, the concept of ''computer-based applications'' is gradually expanding. Now, in general, computer-based applications are considered a separate, identifiable part of any job; gradually, however, because of the pervasive influence of personal computing, this separation is disappearing, and both personal computing and communications are as fundamental as office furniture.

Categories of Interapplication Communication

Communications in any organization or even within a given application can be grouped into categories (see Table 6.1).

Batch communication—Data are transmitted in a defined package such as letters in envelopes and data on tapes. The senders and receivers are completely independent of each other and are connected only by the communication medium (e.g., the postal service or a company's internal mail system or a book). Even in batch communication, however, there must be preestablished coding and decoding standards; in a letter, those standards may simply be the language in which the letter

TABLE 6.1

Categories of Interapplication Communications

Categories	Type of Linkage	What Is Transmitted	Data Communications Example
Batch			
Point-to-point	Address/directory	Usually a package	Mailing tapes/disks
"Mail drop"	Distribution system	Usually a package	
Synchronized			
Point-to-point	Directory and schedule	Usually a message	Mail networks
Broadcast	Distribution and schedule	Usually a message	Radio/TV networks
Buffered synchronized (includes factors for synchronized category)	Buffer mechanism	Usually a message	Computer-based bulletin boards

is written; on a data tape, the agreement must include the physical and logical format of the data on the tape.

In batch communications, a physical package is usually transferred from the sender to the receiver. There are, however, two types of potential linkages; communication can be from one point, directly to another. Mailing a letter is one example of this. The sender, however, can be buffered from the receiver by some sort of distribution system. A "mail drop" such as a post office box can serve as such a buffer. Similarly, bookstores provide both a time and a location buffer for communication between an author (the sender) and the reader (the receiver).

Synchronized communications—In this form of communications, the sender and receiver are both active at the same time. Usually, however, only a logical message is transferred; a specific package is not physically passed from one to another. Smoke signals, semaphores, and telephones are examples of synchronized message communications.

Synchronized communications can be point-to-point or broadcast. As with batch communications, point-to-point synchronized communications require the sender to know exactly how to reach the receiver through some sort of a directory, but synchronized communication also requires that the sender and receiver agree on a given transmit/receive schedule. Synchronized communications can also be broadcast. This places the burden for coordination on the receiver rather than the sender. For example, the receiver of a television show takes the responsibility for tuning in at the correct time.

Buffered communications—This is a means of communication that converts synchronized communication to batch communication. Buffering requires that there be an intermediary which acts as the receiver; the ultimate receivers then access the message at their convenience.

A primitive example is when a communications specialist transcribes a semaphore message onto paper as it is sent and then hands the paper to the addressee. Avant-garde examples include telephone answering machines, videocassette recorders, and other types of devices that electronically buffer the receiver from the sender.

Buffers can perform services other than just time shifting. Intelligent buffers can also perform, for example, editing or translation services. For example, a library can scan publications and send to patrons only those articles that the patrons have previously requested, or a publication service can translate magazine articles from the language of the author to that of readers.

Data communication can be accomplished in all these categories. In general, technological sophistication is least with batch communications and most complex with buffered synchronized communication. Communications convenience, however, is greatest when senders and receivers are most loosely coupled. Both batch and buffered synchronized communications physically decouple the senders and receivers, but a buffer can also perform logical translation as a service to the receiver. For example, a data buffer can convert the data from the sender's format to a format required by the receiver. This type of buffering is often called a "gateway" or a "bridge." Examples showing how data communications fits into these categories are given in Table 6.2.

Advantages to Communications Networks

Communications should allow the organization to achieve the goal stated above (i.e., interpersonal, interfunctional cooperation and coordination with a minimum of redundancy and rework). As described in Chapter 4, applications can be identified in terms of first-order tasks that directly affect customer needs and second-order tasks that help facilitate operations within the company. Communications systems can also be viewed in this way.

Communications systems have traditionally been second-order systems, allowing data to be transferred to various places in the company where specific processing occurred. In general, costs are reduced when communication is held to a minimum. For example, the same system that communicates an order from a sales office to the factory should also trigger transactions in inventory and in accounts receivable systems.

Similarly, communications on the factory floor should be minimized. Ideally, a system should, for example, transmit inventory control and process control information. Communications are often more useful in the factory than in the office because factories are already functionally organized and have defined requirements for interfunctional relationships. The communications networks need only automate those interfaces.

The problem, of course, is that the data interface for each of the various machines on the factory floor is different. One way of dealing with these differences is to develop a "protocol," a standard that each machine must meet. The Manufacturing Automation Protocol (MAP) is the best known of these protocols. A similar set of standards for office automation, called Technical and Office Protocol (TOP), is also being developed.

Since the interfaces between functions within an office are usually poorly developed, communications in the office environment usually refers to the sharing of specialized resources. Although this is a valuable cost-saving application, it may be making efficient something that should not be done at all; as with other systems, looking at the tasks that most closely affect the customers is the way to apply communications wisely.

Networks can also act as a translator among computing devices that normally cannot communicate. Some offices, for example, have personal computers that use different disk formats. Data in one disk format cannot be used by a personal computer expecting another format. A communication network can be used to create this linkage. Data flow from one disk, into "its" computer, from the computer, via

TABLE 6.2

Physical Structure Alternatives

Factor	Media								
	Twisted Pair	Coaxial Baseband	Cable Broadband	Fiber Optics	Microwave	Laser	Infared	Packet Radio	Satellite
Speed (MBPS)[a]	10	20	50	3000	200	1.5	0.25	0.1	200
Channels	Few	Many	Many	Many	Many	Few	Few	Many	Many
Topologies[b]	R, B, P	R, B, P	R, B, P	R, B, P	P	P	P, S	P, S	P, S
Distance	Unlimited (with modem)	10 km	50 km	50 km (with re-peaters)	10 km	100 m	100 m	Unlim-ited	Unlim-ited
Transmission integrity	Low	High	High	High	Medium	High	High	Medium	High
Noise	Medium	Low	Low	Low	Medium	Low	Medium	Medium	Medium
Crossover	Medium	Medium	Medium	Low	Low	Low	Low	Medium	Medium
Security	Low	Medium	Medium	High	Low	High	Low	Medium	Low
Media cost	Low	Medium	Medium	High	Medium	High	Medium	Medium	Medium
Connection cost	Low	Medium	Medium	Medium	Medium	High	Low	Low	Medium
Installation cost	Low	High	High	Low	Low	Low	Low	High	Low
Number of nodes	10s	100s	100s	10s	100s	10s	10s	1000s	1000s

[a]MBPS = million bits per second.

[b]R, ring; B, bus; P, point-to-point; S, star.

221

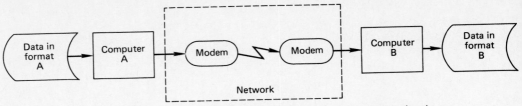

Figure 6.1 Converting data formats using communication.

the communications network to the other computer, which then writes the data to its disk, in its format (see Figure 6.1).

Standards

Although standards are appropriate in almost all endeavors, standards are absolutely crucial in communications because of the large numbers of diverse organizations that are involved. To establish an international communications network successfully requires the coordination of several government organizations and several public utilities, in addition to the hardware and software vendors involved in the systems and applications portions of the project. Because of this, several governmental and professional organizations have established standardization efforts that are guiding the communications industry. Some detail about these standards are discussed in the Appendix to this chapter.

The key point, however, is that, when you are considering a large investment in network technology, be sure that you are working with vendors who are following the appropriate standards, and, if at all in doubt, obtain expert advice to guide you through the technical complexities. Further, it is probably wise to choose a specific set of communications protocols (technical standards) and use that for all aspects of the network to which it applies. Insist that vendors either follow the protocol you have selected or have well-tested, demonstrable connections (gateways) to that protocol.

The word "demonstration" has particular relevance to communication situations. When in doubt about the ability of devices to work, insist on a demonstration. Vendors should be able to transmit and receive data (and voice and video, if that capability is also claimed) among devices. There should be two aspects to the demonstration. The first should simply demonstrate the ability to communicate. The communication "road" is either open or not. The second, however, is more difficult to demonstrate: the vendor should show the performance or capacity of the open channel, how many "lanes" are open on the road. Performance is greatly dependent on both load and noise, just as commute time on a highway depends on the number of other cars on the road (is it rush hour or very early morning?) and the weather conditions.

Chapter 6 Guidelines

Three groups of guidelines are offered in this chapter, following the sequence with which network decisions are considered. Guideline 6.1 discusses the logical aspect of the network, how the network appears to the users; Guideline 6.2 discusses how this logical framework can be physically built using hardware and software technology. Guideline 6.3 then focuses on network management considerations.

Most readers will find Guideline 6.3 directly applicable to their management of personal computing communications. Readers who have some experience with data communications and who understand the vocabulary of this specialized field may wish to skip directly to Guideline 6.3.

Readers who have little experience with any type of data communication, however, are advised to read Guidelines 6.1 and 6.2 first. These are designed to provide an overview of this complex technology, defining some concepts and terms. Some of the materials in these two guidelines may also be useful, even for knowledgeable readers, for explaining data communications to those less familiar with the subject.

The Appendix to this chapter discusses the characteristics of various communications standards. All of this technical complexity should be of interest only to those who wish to learn enough of the appropriate "buzzwords" to be able to better work with communications experts. On the other hand, the best communications experts should provide you with appropriate advice without overwhelming you with arcane terminology.

Guideline 6.1: Logical Structure of Personal Computing Communications Networks

> ***1. Keep the applications as high as possible on the OSI levels, always at level 7 if at all possible.***

This guideline discusses the way the network appears to the users, the "logical" design. The logical design and the physical design may match, but they need not. For example, from a logical standpoint, we use telephones for point-to-point communication, talking directly to another home or office. Physically, however, the phone system is usually a series of interconnected star networks.

Usually, the users of networks do not and should not be concerned with how the network works technically and whether or not International Standards Organization (ISO)/Institute of Electronics and Electrical Engineers (IEEE) standards are being followed. Note, however, that the technical designers and network managers must be concerned with these issues because the standards provide flexibility that will be essential during the network's life cycle. This flexibility is best achieved by keeping the applications as high as possible on the Open System Interconnection (OSI) model levels, always at level 7 if at all possible. Every step lower on the pyramid ties the application more closely to a specific hardware/software combination.

Note that users of network facilities can be either individual people (users) or specific application systems (applications). Users send/receive messages for tasks such as electronic mail or to use servers such as specialized printers or disk files. Applications may, in addition, send/receive specific transactions or full files of data.

Designers of logical communication networks should have, at least, these objectives:

- Maximum local independence of applications/workstations with minimum costs in redundancy and reconciliation. This implies:
- Easy, timely access of data by applications when needed.
- Data stored in a single, accessible location or routed in a specific fashion.
- Economic justification of expensive equipment and data banks by resource sharing.
- Application/workstation technical independence, so that local facilities can be logically and physically diverse and can evolve with minimum concern about effects on other applications or workstations.

Logical topologies

2. *Logical topologies are selected based on needs for recipient selectivity, cost per message, need for interaction/feedback, and whether the sender or receiver has message control.*

There are three different logical ways in which communications can occur. These are shown in Figure 6.2. Logical topologies are selected based on needs for recipient selectivity, cost per message, need for interaction/feedback, and whether the sender or receiver has message control. As Table 6.3 shows, point-to-point topologies are most direct, but also most costly; broadcast communications is lowest in unit cost but least controlled.

Note that both point-to-point and distributed topologies require the sender to have a unique address for the proposed recipients. Assigning and maintaining these addresses is a nontrivial task. These addresses should be in some directory, preferably machine-readable, that is available to all potential sending nodes. In some systems, such as electronic mail systems, names are used as at least a first approximation at a unique address. Similar names must then be qualified in some way to make them unique. In broadcast topologies, the control is in the hands of receivers. They must turn on their receivers or log on to the bulletin board; otherwise, even the most carefully constructed message will never be received.

There is always the question, of course, even in point-to-point transmission, as to whether or not the transmitted message was, in fact, received. Some systems, therefore, have an ''acknowledgment'' feature, in which the sender is notified when the message is delivered to the recipient. A variation of this can work even with a

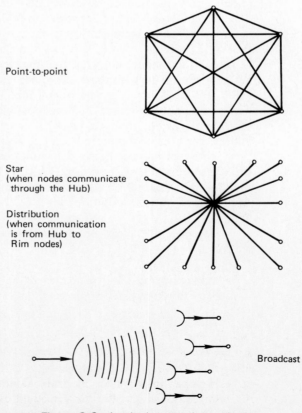

Point-to-point

Star
(when nodes communicate
 through the Hub)

Distribution
(when communication
 is from Hub to
 Rim nodes)

Broadcast

Figure 6.2 Logical network topologies.

TABLE 6.3

Choosing a Logical Topology

	Ability to Select Particular Receiver	Cost per Message	Interaction/ Feedback	Primary Control of Communication	Examples
Point-to-point	High; each node must have a unique address and directory	High; each message is sent individually	High; senders and receivers can communicate interactively if desired		Telephone, electronic mail
Star	High; each node must have a unique address.			Sender	
Distribution	Directory is needed only at hub	Medium. Same message to all receivers	Low/medium-receivers are known to sender, so some feedback can be arranged		"Junk" mail; electronic mail using distribution lists
Broadcast	Low; sender selects location (frequency), media, and time	Lowest; message sent only once	Very low; sender must ask receivers to identify themselves	Receiver	Radio, TV, electronic bulletin boards

bulletin board broadcast system. Systems can be constructed so that the message sender can determine which receivers have read the message and when.

The logical topology used should be the one that meets the application need at the lowest cost. It is appropriate, therefore, to specify the communication needs in terms of the four factors and then to select the topology that meets the needs at lowest costs. Personal mail, for example, clearly requires point-to-point capability. Sometimes, however, low-cost hybrid systems can be constructed. For example, an electronic bulletin board is a broadcast architecture. The sender merely posts the messages, and the recipients have the responsibility of accessing the bulletin board and reading the message. Some bulletin boards, however, provide an additional direct message capability in which one subscriber can send a point-to-point message directly to another subscriber. Thus most of the communications can be broadcast at low cost, with the availability of higher-cost point-to-point transmission as needed. Note, however, that, even with this hybrid system, overhead functions such as directory maintenance must be implemented.

Bridges

3. Bridges should be used for communications that are less frequent or of lower priority than those which are transmitted on the individual networks.

Bridges are design devices that allow networks to be joined. For example, two local area networks (LANs) may be joined by a logical bridge. Communications across bridges is usually at a performance level lower than that within the individual networks. For example, if communication within a network is interactive, communication across a bridge may be on a batch basis. Therefore, bridges should be used only for communications that are less frequent or of lower priority than those which are transmitted on the individual networks.

The directory process must also consider the use of bridges. As noted above, each receiver in a point-to-point or distribution network must have a specific address. Receivers in other networks, however, may be referenced only by their network address. Messages to these remote receivers are sent across the bridge where the receiver's specific address is determined.

Gateways

4. *The concept of gateways allows designers to segregate connection functions from others in the network and to provide for the specific capabilities needed at those connections.*

Gateways are logical places in the networks at which connections can be made to other networks (via bridges) or at which data can entered into the network or extracted from it. The concept of gateways allows designers to segregate connection functions from others in the network and provide for the specific capabilities needed at those connections. Individual users/applications need only deliver (receive) messages/files to (from) the gateway without concern for the specifics of communication technology. In fact, if the individual local networks are sufficiently capable, user/applications may simply address (receive) messages without concern if the receiver (sender) is within the local network or must be transmitted across a bridge. The directory of the local network determines whether this is a "local" or a "long-distance" call and uses the gateways if needed for long distance.

These are some of the functions typically provided by gateways:

- For incoming messages, directories of the data bases, nodes (users), and facilities (servers) available within the network. The directories should include the address of the network element and the formats or codes needed to access the element.
- For outgoing messages, directories of the networks in which the addressee exists, so that messages can be routed to the correct network.
- Security to limit/authorize the users/applications passing through the gateway. Controls may be imposed by specific users/applications or by some level-of-authority code that designates the types of elements which a user/application is allowed to access. Outgoing messages might also require authorization. Some user/applications may be restricted only to intranetwork activity.
- Logging of the messages for use in performance analysis or in transaction accounting. These logs provide audit trails in case of a later-detected problem and also provide the basis for charging user/applications.
- Communications interface activities required by the network technology. This may include assembling/disassembling of packets, applying/reading routing codes, setting/checking record counts, and so on.
- Reformatting outgoing data files for efficient use of the transmission or translating those transmission formats into those used by the individual networks for incoming messages. This is necessary, for example, if application packets are used.

Electronic mail

5. *Electronic mail may be justified as a replacement for paper memos, bulletins, and telephone traffic; however, as large numbers of people join the mail network, the system becomes a medium with its own unique communications characteristics.*

Electronic mail is the implementation of a point-to-point and distribution network for message traffic rather than for preformatted data files. Electronic mail is designed as a replacement for paper memos and bulletins and telephone traffic and can be justified on that basis alone; however, as large numbers of people join the mail network, the system becomes a medium with its own unique characteristics. Electronic mail is less formal than memos but provides a "hard copy" not available in telephone conversations. Further, because electronic mail is asynchronous, people can communicate at their own convenience without the intrusion of phone calls. Yet electronic messages, somehow, have greater "urgency" than do paper memos. In addition, electronic mail can be linked to electronic filing systems, electronic calendars, and electronic bulletin boards to provide a full service communications service among users.

There are, however, several problems. Electronic mail works best when all participants have personal computing equipment on their desks. This can be expensive unless the cost of the equipment can be justified by additional personal computing applications. Further, people are likely to use the system more effectively if they are reasonably comfortable with using keyboards. This may be a particular problem to engineers who took drafting courses while their liberal arts colleagues took typing, or to managers who are accustomed to having secretaries to perform keyboard functions.

Voice and video messages on networks

6. *Voice, video, videotex, and facsimile messages should share networks with data to the extent that total costs for all communications are reduced. From a logical standpoint, sharing presents even greater opportunities for creating new forms of communications in which voice, video, and facsimiles are combined with words and numbers. Videotex is an elementary example of the power of this combined communications technology.*

Currently, voice and video are discussed as part of communications only in terms of the way the physical network is used. As will be discussed in the Guideline 6.2, data can share certain physical networks with voice and/or video transmission. This sharing is desirable to the extent that total costs for all communications are reduced, but from a logical standpoint, sharing presents even greater opportunities.

Technologies are gradually developing in which voice and video communications are converted to digital forms in which they can be combined with data files. Once in this digital format, the networks can transmit voice and video just as it does data. Thus we can look forward to totally new forms of communications, such as talking and illustrated reports, rather than simply lists of words and numbers. As a first step toward this, for example, most networks can process illustrations or artwork built on personal computers.

This combination of words and pictures is sometimes called "videotex." It is especially useful as an advertising medium, as it has the ability to deliver both a verbal and a visual sales presentation. Laser disk technology is often linked with personal computing to achieve this capability.

Many videotex systems also allow limited but useful feedback from the reader to the sender. Using a menu, for example, readers can indicate their interest in particular subjects and can guide the presentations accordingly. Some systems even allow the readers to place orders directly through the videotex system.

Facsimile transmission—Transmitting facsimiles is really a small subset of the advanced capabilities promised in the voice/video area. Most facsimile transmission devices already convert the documents to digital form and send the resulting "message'' across public phone networks. Once converted to digital form, facsimile messages could be combined with other forms of data, again, to provide new forms of communication in which the facsimile is only one portion of the entire message.

Applications of personal computing communications technology

7. *Implement personal computing communications networks by keeping the people affected as closely involved as possible in all stages of the implementation.*
8. *Implement networks successfully within homogeneous groups before trying to link diverse groups or different companies.*

The purpose of this section of the guideline is merely to provide some examples of how logical personal computing networks can operate in typical business organizations. These examples are, at best, "hints" which will, hopefully, stimulate thinking and creativity to apply networks productively in your organization.

Table 6.4 presents application examples from the view of existing functions within a manufacturing organization. Office functions include such things as accounting, personnel, purchasing, and sales and marketing administration. Factory functions are those directly involved with product fabrication and assembly. Customer service refers to support of customers directly at the place in which the customers place orders or ask questions. Engineering/scientific functions usually occur in research and development departments, in product marketing sections, in manufacturing engineering, and in quality departments.

Implementing networks in the functions noted above is no easy task, requiring

TABLE 6.4

Network Applications Examples by Organizational Function

	Resource Sharing	Message Services	Data/File Sharing	Work/Project Coordination
Office	Printers, plotters	Electronic mail, teleconferencing, electronic bulletin boards	Use of global and shared files	Project schedules, work flow, production measurement
Factory	Tools, robots, test equipment	Automated storage and retrieval systems, status reports, "recipe" assignment	Specification data, routing data, quality data, inventory	Work order backlog, shipping schedules, work station/tool scheduling
Customer service	Configuration systems, order input systems, order scheduling, customer needs analysis	Inquiries order processing, customer feedback	Accessing factory files for marketing/sales use, coordination of deliveries	"Paperless" processing, faster communication of orders, sales accounting
Engineering/ scientific	Tools, lab equipment, measurement instruments, test monitors	Problem sharing, solution communication	Standard specifications, vendor data, library access, process models, metrics	Project schedules, status reporting, project accounting
Interfunction/ Intercompany	Network resources, very expensive equipment, network specialists	Vendor ↔ customer manufacturing ↔ marketing R&D ↔ manufacturing	Shipping schedules, purchasing forecasts, production schedules, quality data	New product release, shipment schedules, accounting close data

mastery of arcane technology and achieving the cooperation of people who are already successful at their (old) jobs and who do not have the time to invest in learning radical new ways to work. The problem of cooperation becomes more severe, however, when communication is attempted among groups. Some of these applications are shown in the section of Table 6.4 labeled "Interfunction/Intercompany." It is these applications which, when properly implemented, will reward the company with large returns on its communications investment.

Problems become even greater when different companies, usually vendors and customers or partners in a development project, attempt cooperative communications. The potential payoffs are great; rapid placement of orders, communication of status changes, and sharing of technical evaluations of product quality are just some of the potential benefits. The concept of "just-in-time" production scheduling, together with its sister concept, "zero inventory," are possible only with very close communication between vendor and customer.

Yet the problems in implementing network communications among companies are severe, technical as well as organizational. In addition, in some cases, legal advice will be needed to assure that cooperation does not become so close that it can be interpreted as collusion or conspiracy. Yet the benefits may be worth the needed efforts.

Implementing personal computing communications networks is best accomplished as any other major change; the people affected should be as closely involved as possible in all stages of the implementation. In addition, using networks successfully within homogeneous groups is probably essential before trying to link diverse groups, much less different companies.

Personal computing technology can also be used for applications that cross functional and organizational boundaries and provide unique opportunities and problems. The opportunities come from the potential for groups to work more closely with less overhead and less supervision. The problems arise from reduction in normal audit trails, reduction is work visibility, an the potential for work being released to other groups before it has been finished or properly reviewed.

Telecommuting

9. *Working at home using personal computing communications may be appropriate for tasks that can be well defined and for which all needed communications can take place electronically or via mail. To maintain necessary levels of social interaction, however, telecommuting for only a few days per week, working at the office during the other days, is a good compromise.*

The benefits of working at home, "telecommuting," can be significant. Employers save on the costs of office space and can retain employees (such as working mothers) who might otherwise be forced to resign. Employees save on commuting costs and time, have truly flexible working hours, can dress as they like, and can blend their work in with their personal lives.

There are, however, significant issues to resolve. Most jobs, for example, have significant amounts of social interaction which are needed to lubricate the organizational machinery. This socialization, of course, is missing from telecommuting work.

Training is also an issue. It is easy enough to invite a telecommuter into the office for a formal class, but it is much more difficult to replace the informal training that occurs among physically adjacent coworkers. Sometimes, telecommuting only for a few days per week, working at the office during the other days, is a good compromise.

All sorts of legal and administrative issues must also be considered; here are a few examples:

- Insurance coverage for both the employee and the equipment.
- Worker safety and working conditions laws.
- Zoning requirements at the telecommuter's home.
- Tax considerations, especially if the telecommuter can use the equipment for personal tasks.
- Worker performance evaluation.
- Salary administration; if some sort of "piecework" pay standard is selected, the earning of benefit credits must also be considered.
- Calculation and reimbursement of increased home expenses due to the telecommuting work (e.g., utilities, special furniture or fixtures, etc.).

Video/computer-based conferencing

10. Video/computer-based conferencing is a "real-time" medium which, although expensive, is the next best thing to being there and should be considered as an alternative to actual travel.

Technologies can be combined to allow people to hold conferences even when geographically separated. The current state of the art requires that each participant be in specially equipped rooms which hold all the video, audio, and computer equipment. Video/audio technology allows the participants to see and hear each other, while on-line computers control the network and facilitate message and data transmission as needed in the context of the conference. Although video/computer-based conferencing is expensive, mainly because of the high cost of the required communications room and the need for broadband transmission channels, the break-even point is rapid when compared to the time and expense of travel for all participants.

Electronic bulletin boards/teleconferencing

11. Electronic bulletin boards and computer-based teleconferencing allow people to communicate on their own schedules, providing the efficiency of a broadcast network design while allowing the relatively focused communications available in distribution or point-to-point architectures.

Whereas video/computer-based conferencing is real-time, electronic bulletin boards and computer-based teleconferencing are asynchronous, allowing people to communicate on their own schedules. Further, electronic bulletin boards/teleconferencing provide the efficiency of a broadcast network design, while allowing the relatively focused communications available in distribution or point-to-point architectures. Because of the need for everyone to share all discussion, bulletin board/conferences are usually physically operated on star networks, with the host at the center acting as the network operator.

In its simplest form, people can merely post messages on the host bulletin board and can also read the notices posted by others. Bulletin boards grow to electronic conferencing when the software allows users to organize themselves into private groups in which messages can be posted, read, and answered. These private groups are essentially ongoing conferences or discussions of the subjects of interest to the groups. Since the communication is asynchronous, participants can be located literally around the world, in dramatically different time zones.

Most bulletin boards also have public groups that anyone can join to discuss issues of general concern. One public group in almost all electronic bulletin boards is usually concerned with the operation of the bulletin board itself. Another common public conference is one focused on hints for using personal computing.

If the company culture permits, a public group usually also forms to discuss company policies, management philosophies, rumors, and other morale issues. Such a group can be a useful, open company grapevine. These electronic bulletin boards/ conferences also usually allow some form of private message transmission among participants, which gives these systems some of the characteristics of electronic mail.

The formation and maintenance of electronic bulletin boards are expensive and benefits are intangible, at best. Free interpersonal communication, however, is a keystone to individual motivation and creativity. If costs become a concern, users can be charged for bulletin board usage.

Application independence from and integration of hardware/systems software technology

12. *Communications networks can help technically different systems work together by acting as a technical "common denominator," allowing applications to communicate directly or to use the same data.*

13. *When changes (improvements) have been made in individual applications and/or personal workstations, it may be necessary to write a special program to convert data from the new format into the old one so that communications can continue properly.*

Communication between applications and individuals is the basic theme of this chapter. As you can see by now, this is complicated under the best of circumstances, but differences in the hardware and software create a Tower of Babel. Figure 6.3 summarizes the dimensions of the integration of applications and workstations.

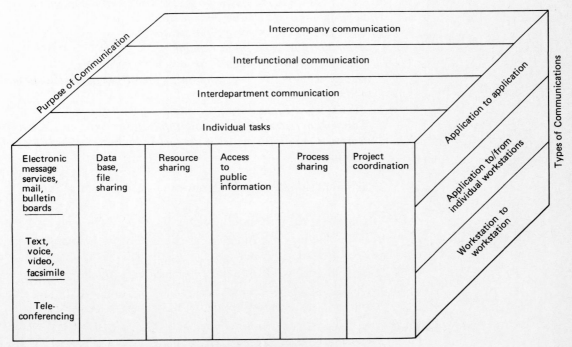

Types of Communications Applications

Figure 6.3   Application/workstation integration.

As noted above, communications networks can actually help different systems work together by acting as a technical "common denominator," allowing applications to communicate directly or to use the same data. Therefore, communications networks, on the one hand, allow applications to grow separately, using the specific hardware and software appropriate for that local application. On the other hand, however, through its "common denominator" the network will allow at least some integration of these diverse applications.

This "common denominator" effect is particularly important as the individual applications and workstations are modified to take advantage of rapidly advancing technology. In some cases where changes have been made, it may be necessary to write a special program to convert data from the new format into the old one so that communications can continue properly. This conversion may cause a loss of systems efficiency, but it does allow the necessary communication to continue.

Networks are also useful for linking a wide variety of devices that require specialized interfaces and data formats. Custom gateways can be constructed to link these devices to the network and therefore to other devices. In an office, this allows linkages between workstations and file and printer servers, to telephone communications, to document scanners, to copiers. In factories, this allows the linkage of automated tools, material-handling equipment, and data collection equipment. In laboratories, this allows the linkage of specialized analysis tools, instrumentation and measuring devices, and analog sensors.

Control structures built into the systems architecture

14. *Network controls should be a major consideration in the design process. Here are some of the issues that should be considered:*
   a. *Automatic logging of all messages*
   b. *Automatic logging of all routings*
   c. *Use of message sequence numbers*
   d. *Use of transmission batch or packet check total controls*
   e. *Identification of sending person/application*
   f. *Identification of sending physical node*
   g. *Availability of encryption capability*
   h. *Use of "dial-back system" for access to network*
   i. *Design different access capabilities for different users, applications, and nodes*
   j. *Availability of password protection*
   k. *Controls over transmission and applications error-correction processes*
   l. *Notice to a sending node of the last time that node was logged on to the network*

In communications networks, control implies these functions:

- Assuring that the data transmitted are received accurately and completely
- Assuring that network functions are used only by those appropriately authorized for unauthorized functions
- Assuring that network accounting functions are timely, complete, and accurate
- Providing the ability to reconstruct and/or recover data and other network resources in the event of accidental or deliberate losses

Controls are largely a management issue and are discussed in more detail in Guideline 6.3, but the controls are also of concern to the network systems' designers. Here are some of the design features that will aid in control of the network:

- Automatic logging of all messages. These logs can be used as backup in case of system failure, as well as for research in problems that may be detected after transmission. The logs can also be used for network usage accounting.

- One major design concern, however, is how long to keep the logs, since the data volume may rapidly become very large. If the data are at all voluminous, a special application system will be required to analyze the logs.

- Automatic logging of all routings. Networks often use different physical paths between two points, sometimes changing paths within one message. If problems are later detected, knowing the routings can often provide clues as to where or when the problems occurred.

- Use of message sequence numbers. This allows the receiving person or application to verify that all the messages sent were, in fact, received.

- Use of transmission batch or packet check total controls. Batch controls establish that all messages sent were received and that all messages contain the correct numbers of lines and values.

- Identification of sending person/application. Anonymous messages should be forbidden.

- Identification of sending physical node. The receiving application should be able to verify that the messages received came from appropriate, authorized physical locations.

- Availability of encryption capability. It is not necessary, not even desirable, to encrypt all transmissions, but the capability to do so should be available for sensitive messages.

- Use of "dial-back system" for access to network. One significant method for preventing unauthorized network access is to allow that access only when the network initiates the call to the (authorized) remote nodes. If a remote node wishes to communicate, it calls the network and requests access. The network then checks the access authority and location and returns the call to the appropriate location, granting it the appropriate access level.

- Design different access capabilities for different users, applications, and nodes. Users may be allowed access only to given files or to given network capabilities or resources. Users can also be given read-only access, be granted writing authorization, or have the full capability to modify the data already on the file.

- Availability of password protection. As with encryption, passwords need not be required but should be allowed, even encouraged. Passwords allow users/applications some amount of privacy.

- Controls over transmission and applications error-correction processes. Error corrections by definition allow changes to existing data; therefore, error-correction processes can cause deliberate or accidental distruction and must be carefully authorized and monitored.

- Notice to a sending node of the last time that node was logged on to the network. This allows users/applications to verify that their "name" was not used by someone else since that user/application last officially used the network.

CHECKLIST

Guideline 6.1
Logical Structure of Personal Computing Communications Networks

	YES	NO	N/A

1. Are applications kept as high as possible on the OSI levels, always at level 7 if at all possible?

2. Are logical topologies selected based on needs for recipient selectivity, cost per message, need for interaction/feedback, and whether the sender or receiver has message control?

3. Are bridges used for communications that are less frequent or of lower priority than those that are transmitted on the individual networks?

4. Are gateways used to allow designers to segregate connection functions from others in the network and to provide for the specific capabilities needed at those connections?

5. Is electronic mail justified as a replacement for paper memos, bulletins, and telephone traffic?

6. As large numbers of people join the electronic mail network, is the system justified as a medium with its own unique communications characteristics?

7. Do voice, video, videotex, and facsimile messages share networks with data so that total costs for all communications are reduced? (From a logical standpoint, sharing presents even greater opportunities for creating new forms of communications in which voice, video, and facsimiles are combined with words and numbers. Videotex is an elementary example of the power of this combined communications technology.)

8. Are personal computing communications networks implemented by keeping the people affected as closely involved as possible in all stages of the implementation?

9. Are networks successfully implemented within homogeneous groups before trying to link diverse groups or different companies?

10. Are employees allowed to work at home, using personal computing communications for appropriate tasks that can be well defined and for which all needed communications can take place electronically or via mail?

11. To maintain necessary amounts of social interaction, is telecommuting practiced for only a few days per week, with employees working at the office during the other days?

12. Is video/computer-based conferencing, an expensive "real time" medium that is the next best thing to being there, considered as an alternative to actual travel?

13. Are electronic bulletin boards and computer-based teleconferencing systems used to allow people to communicate on their own schedules, and to provide the efficiency of a broadcast network design, while allowing the relatively focused communications available in distribution or point-to-point architectures?

14. Are communications networks, which act as a technical "common denominator," used to allow application to communicate directly or to use the same data?

15. Are special programs written to convert data from the new format into the old one so that communications in individual applications and/or personal workstations can continue properly?

16. Are network controls managed as a major consideration in the design process?

Are these issues considered?
a. Automatic logging of all messages
b. Automatic logging of all routings
c. Use of message sequence numbers
d. Use of transmission batch or packet check total controls
e. Identification of sending person/application
f. Identification of sending physical node
g. Availability of encryption capability
h. Use of "dial-back system" for access to network
j. Design different access capabilities for different users, applications, and nodes
k. Availability of password protection
l. Controls over transmission and applications error-correction processes
m. Notice is routinely given to a sending node reporting the time that node was logged on to the network

Physical Structure of Personal Computing Communications Networks

> 1. *Work with someone who is a communications specialist.*
> 2. *Start communications with simple techniques, gradually moving toward more sophisticated technology.*

This guideline gives you an overview of the alternatives available when choosing the physical structure of a communications network. The guideline provides vocabulary, not expertise, but it will, hopefully, give you enough information to allow you to work productively with communications specialists. Note that although network data communications can be quite complex, some elementary forms of communication can be started slowly and easily, gradually moving toward sophisticated, complex systems.

- Simply sending physical disks or tapes from one computer to another is a basic form of data communication.
- Use of personal computing workstations hooked to a multitasking mainframe also allows communications, primarily by sharing files. This can also form the basis of what can later be a full-blown star local-area or wide-area network.
- Sharing resources among several personal computing workstations; communication is especially useful when data are shared using file servers. These resource-sharing systems form the basis of future local-area networks.
- Use of PBX for communicating between personal computing nodes, either locally or, using modems, over long geographic distances.
- Use of baseband local-area network technology.
- Use of broadband local-area and/or wide-area network technology.

Physical structures: topologies

> 3. *Separate the selection of logical and physical topologies, since they need not be identical.*
> 4. *Consider issues such as these when choosing a physical topology:*
>   a. *Performance for given logical topologies*
>   b. *Control/security considerations*
>   c. *Setup cost*
>   d. *Cost of incremental nodes*
> 5. *Choose hybrid physical topologies for redundancy and flexibility (at some cost, however, of efficiency).*

Physical topologies represent how the network is linked by wire or by broadcast media. The logical topologies discussed in Guideline 6.1 are laid on top of the physical topology. The physical topology creates limitations to the logical topology, but the logical and physical topologies need not be identical. Physical topologies are illustrated in Figure 6.4. For example, the logical topology can be point-to-point, but it can be implemented on any type of physical topology, except, perhaps, on the broadcast physical topology.

Performance, however, is a key issue; for example, if the network will usually be used by point-to-point logical networks, it probably also makes sense to have a bus physical network, since a physical tree or ring network may handle point-to-point communications, but with degraded performance. Physical networks, however, are rarely dedicated to one logical task, and optimum performance may not be possible for all the applications that will use the network. Table 6.5 shows some of the considerations that govern the selection of physical topology. Except for the

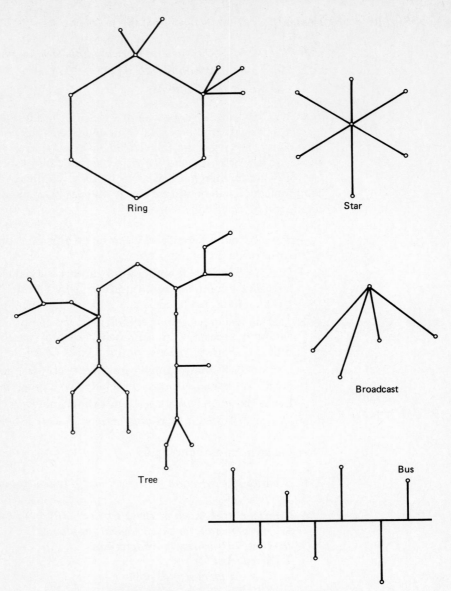

Figure 6.4 Physical network topologies.

TABLE 6.5
Choosing a Physical Network

Physical Topology	Logical Topology	Ease of Controls and Security	Performance (Speed Between Nodes)	Media	Cost	
					Setup	Per Node
Star	All	Easy	Medium	Wire	High	Low
Tree	All	Medium	Medium	Cable	High	Low
Bus	All	Medium	High	Wire, cable	Medium	Low
Ring	All	Easy	Low	Wire, cable, optical fiber	Medium	Medium
Broadcast	All but point-to-point	Difficult	High for appropriate applications	Microwave	High	Very low

broadcast topology, all logical topologies can be accommodated, albeit at different performance rates.

Controls and security are easier to implement when messages follow a known path, as with a ring topology, or go through a single point, as with a star topology. Broadcast topologies are the most difficult to control and secure. Usage logging and password protection are often useful, even in broadcast topologies, but for real message security, some form of encryption is probably required.

Data storage media must be related to topology in order to balance data rates between the network and the processor nodes. The host computer of a star network could be drowned in the data provided by many broadband cables, although data rates can be controlled through special gateways called "packet assembler-disassemblers" (PADs).

The ease with which nodes can be added is a function of the transmission topology selected. Setup costs are high when a large facility must be established independent of the number of nodes on the network. In star and tree networks, for example, a high-cost central switching facility is needed from the very beginning of the network. For bus systems, the main bus cable must be laid from the very beginning. Broadcast networks, of course, need the central transmission center regardless of the number of receiving nodes. Ring topologies are the least expensive to establish since all that are needed are the linkages between the adjacent nodes. Incrementally, however, additional nodes can be added inexpensively, with connections required only to one designated point on the network. Ring nodes are a bit more expensive to add since connections must be made to both adjacent nodes.

It is important to note that most real-world physical networks are really hybrids of the topologies shown in Figure 6.4. Most often, for example, tree or bus networks may exist in a local facility, supporting local-area networks, with the "root" of the tree attached to other trees through a wide-area-network star configuration through a central host (see Figure 6.5).

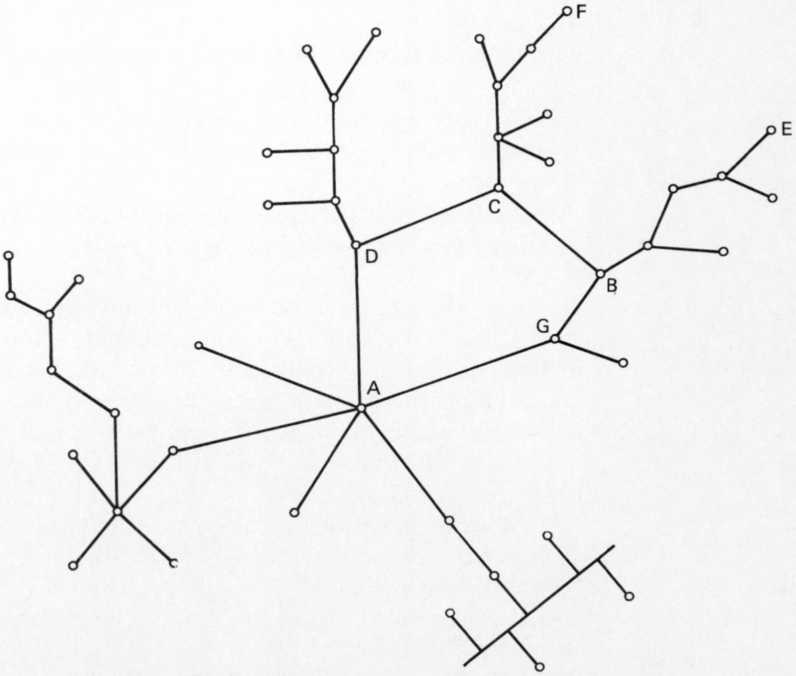

Figure 6.5 Example of hybrid physical topologies.

Figure 6.5 also shows how redundancy can be built into the topology of physical networks. For example, let us assume that the system's logical architecture calls for point-to-point communication between nodes E and F. The shortest physical path is E-B-C-F along the branch of a physical ring. Another path, however, uses tree and star topologies, following path E-B-G-A-D-C-F. The latter longer path may, in fact, be preferable if link B-C is broken or very busy. The longer path might also be necessary if the central node A performs some administrative and/or some control functions the benefits of which outweigh the loss of performance imposed by the uses of the star network.

Physical network capabilities

> 6. *Relate data storage media to network topology to balance data rates between the network and the processor nodes.*

The physical capabilities of a network are a function of the media used and the network technology selected. See Table 6.6 for a summary of these capabilities.

PBX technology is usually relatively easy and inexpensive to implement because existing wiring can be used. The PBX itself, however, may need to be replaced to accommodate data transmission. PBXs allow easy movement of nodes, and easy addition of users; on the other hand, the twisted-wire pairs used by PBXs are limited in the speed with which data can be transferred and in the number of different types of devices that can be used on the network.

Baseband technologies provide more transmission speed and allow more types of devices to be used on the network. Baseband networks are particularly useful in factory or laboratory environments, where the varieties of devices and the amounts of data are typically higher than those that exist in office applications.

Broadband is useful when data communication should be joined with voice and video on multiple channels. Broadband networks are expensive, however, both to set up and for incremental nodes. Further, the diverse capabilities of such a network require more sophisticated ongoing network supervision.

Long distance transmission: wide area networks

> 7. *For wide-area networks, select a cost mechanism that is independent of network variations and motivates the network vendor to provide the best possible service.*
> 8. *Use integrated services data networks (ISDNs) for wide-area networks where and when these networks become available.*

In a given local facility, the logical and physical topology of networks are often identical, since the actual wires or cables define the network. Transmission among buildings and certainly among cities, however, becomes subject to combinations of public and private communications systems which may bear no resemblance to the logical topology used. In fact, the physical topology may vary dramatically from time to time for the same physical network and may even change during a given transmission session!

Considerations for selecting physical wide-area networks are shown in Table 6.2. It is quite common, especially when using public networks, that various forms of transmission media will be used at different times. Performance over a given network will vary as a function both of the characteristics of transmission routes used and the number of other messages being transmitted over the network. When selecting a wide-area-network vendor, it is therefore important to establish a cost mechanism that is independent of network variations and, in fact, motivates the

TABLE 6.6
Capabilities of Physical Networks

Network Technology	Physical Topologies	Media	Factors			
			Media Maximum Speeds	Channel Capabilities	Maximum Network Distance	Reasonable Number of Devices in Network
PBX; used instead of LAN[b] or WAN[c]	Star, tree	Twisted-wire pair	3 MBPS[a]	1 voice, 1 data	20 m without modem; unlimited with modem	100s–1000s
Baseband; used for LAN	Star, ring, bus	Twisted wire pair or 50-Ω coaxial cable	10 MBPS	1 data channel or 10s of multiplexed voice and data channels	10 km	100s–1000s
Broadband; used for LAN or WAN	Tree, bus, broadcast	75-Ω coaxial cable, fiber optics, microwave	10 MBPS	100s voice, video, data channels	50 km	10s–100s

[a]MBPS, million bits per second.
[b]LAN, local area network.
[c]WAN, wide area network.

241

network vendor to provide the best possible service. Charging for connect time, for example, may be inappropriate, since on a congested network, it may take longer to complete a transmission successfully than it would when the traffic is light. The vendor is thus motivated to crowd the network, receiving more money from many (unhappy) customers who are connected for long periods.

Customers are usually better served by a cost-per-kilobit mechanism which charges based on volume of data transmission. Here the incentives are correct for both the network vendor and the customer. The vendor makes more money when the network is efficient, and the customer can control costs by keeping messages compact.

The problem, of course, is that much long-distance transmission capability is "analog" rather than "digital," and message length can be measured only in terms of connect time. As digital facilities, called Integrated Services Digital Networks (ISDNs) become predominant, however, more rational costing mechanisms can be established. ISDN will also allow the blending of voice, video, and data, will increase network capacity at lower unit costs, and will allow connections of all types of computer-controlled (digital) office, laboratory, and factory equipment. In essence, the advent of ISDN will provide wide-area networks with the same physical capabilities currently available to local-area networks. This will allow organizations to locate their physical facilities to provide maximum convenience to their customers and/or employees and still maintain efficient, effective interfacility communication.

Two major concerns about ISDN are costs and standards. As with many new technologies, the startup costs are high and the benefits seem elusive. ISDN offers far better capabilities to connect facilities which either cannot be connected or can be connected only at great cost or complexity. The business applications that take advantage of these improved connections are still undefined.

Further, again typical of new technologies, many approaches for ISDN implementation are struggling to define a standard. Regional Bell operating companies (RBOCs) and the Consultative Committee on International Telephone and Telegraph (CCITT), an international communications standards organization, are two of the organizations struggling with ISDN standards. A set of standards published by CCITT, called the I-series of recommendations, is gradually emerging as the basis for ISDN technology.

To maximize the performance of the physical networks (and if the charging mechanism is appropriate, to minimize costs), combinations of expensive high-speed and inexpensive low-speed transmission media may be established with concentrators at the linkage between the two media to promote efficiency. Low-speed transmission is appropriate close to nodes, while high-speed transmission is appropriate across long distances (see Figure 6.6).

Protocols: access methodology

9. *Select protocols for either local- or wide-area networks, using statistical studies performed by experts in which message traffic is simulated.*
10. *Use protocol converters to link networks of different topologies and protocols when additional flexibility in capacity and performance is needed.*

Once the network topology is designed, for either local- or for wide-area networks, it is necessary to select the appropriate "protocol," the mechanism used to send messages across the network. For bus or tree topologies, common protocols are token ring, carrier-sense multiple access (CSMA), carrier-sense multiple access with collision detection (CSMA/CD), and collision avoidance. Ring topologies may use token ring, register insertion, and slotted ring protocols.

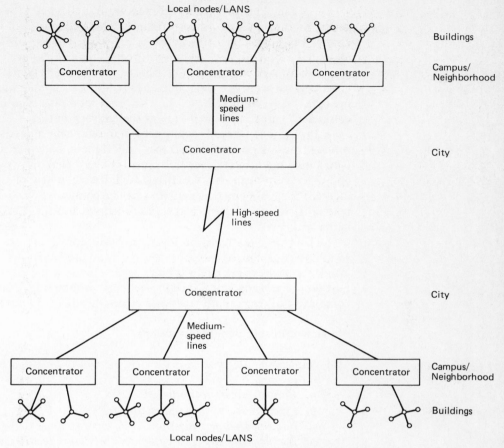

Figure 6.6 Wide-area networks.

Selection of the protocol appropriate for given applications requires consideration of factors such as:

- Number of sending/receiving nodes
- Number of messages being sent at once
- Length of messages and message packets
- Variation in work load
- Network speed and capacity
- Speeds and capacities of nodes
- Length of network
- For token ring, token processing time (size of token)
- For slotted ring, overhead bits per slot (size of slot)
- For register insertion, register size

Proper selection of a protocol usually involves statistical studies in which message traffic is simulated. Expert advice is needed to set the study assumptions, to use the simulation software, and to analyze the results. One of the most difficult assumptions to make is that of load, since successful networks will quickly grow as people find benefits from increased communication.

Making decisions based on careful assumptions and simulations is better than just guessing, but the real world may require changes to accommodate increased needs for capacity and/or performance. These changes will ideally be made in the context of the installed topology and protocol, but use of "protocol conversion" may allow some needed flexibility. Protocol converters are complex software programs that allow messages to be transferred among networks with different protocols. This software is usually implemented on a computer which is a node in all the networks to be connected. Often, the conversion task is so large that a specialized computer is used, dedicated only to the conversion task.

Protocol converters usually accommodate such things as synchronous/asynchronous transmission, access protocol differences, code conversion (e.g., ASCII to EBCDIC), and network speed. Protocol converters allow networks to grow in stages and allow continued use of existing facilities while new ones are tested and implemented. Then old and new networks can be connected when appropriate. Similarly, networks can be tailored to specific functions and then linked together by a converter as needed.

As with everything, however, protocol converters are not free. In addition to the obvious cost of the converter hardware and software, converters reduce the efficiency of the overall network and usually increase the message transmission time. Further, diagnosing and correcting network problems is greatly complicated by the complexity of tracing messages and errors through the converter.

Physical controls over the network

11. Implement physical controls over networks by using techniques such as the following:
   a. Control access to nodes.
   b. Place nodes in shielded enclosures.
   c. Use shielded or fiber-optic transmission lines.
   d. Use network analysis equipment to detect security violations.

Network security will be discussed in some detail in Guideline 6.3, but some physical controls are appropriate to this guideline. Controls should be over all portions of networks, including all nodes, transmission media, buffers, converters, repeaters, and concentrators. Here are some ways in which physical controls can be implemented:

- Control access to nodes. Place terminals in locked or guarded rooms or use locking devices on the terminals.
- Place nodes in shielded enclosures. Computing equipment emits electromagnetic radiation that can be detected and analyzed with appropriate equipment. Shielding is expensive and often creates difficulties in easily using the equipment, but it is necessary in high-security applications.

    In some environments, the network nodes must be placed in shielded enclosures to protect the network from electromagnetic emissions from the environment. Disks, tapes, and other magnetic data storage media are especially vulnerable, but computer memories and transmission lines may also be affected. Damaging radiation may come from such things as large motors, electronic laboratory equipment, other computing equipment, radars, and high-frequency communication devices.
- Use shielded or fiber-optic transmission lines. Twisted-pair wires are easiest to tap and also most sensitive to electrical noise in the environment; coaxial cables are significantly more secure, but may still be affected. Fiber-optic lines are most secure, and new installations requiring security or in which lines are exposed to electrical noise should use fiber optics where possible.

Radio/microwave transmissions can easily be intercepted and are also easily disrupted by deliberate or accidental interference. Laser transmission is extremely secure but is still novel and expensive and useful only in applications where the nodes are within line of sight.

- Use network analysis equipment to detect security violations. The same equipment that can locate network breaks or faults may also be used to detect changes in network performance that indicate taps or interference. Logs should be maintained and reviewed routinely to detect these changes, and operators should be trained to notice suspicious changes and to take appropriate action.

CHECKLIST

Guideline 6.2
Physical Structure of Personal Computing Communications Networks

	YES	NO	N/A
1. Is a communications specialist working on the system design?			
2. Have communications applications been implemented first with simple techniques, gradually moving toward more sophisticated technology?			
3. Are logical and physical topologies selected on their individual merits, as they need not be identical?			
4. Are issues such as these considered when choosing a physical topology? a. Performance for given logical topologies b. Control/security considerations c. Setup cost d. Cost of incremental nodes			
5. Are hybrid physical topologies selected when redundancy and flexibility are more important than efficiency?			
6. Are data storage media related to network topology to balance data rates between the network and the processor nodes?			
7. For wide-area networks, is a cost mechanism selected that is independent of network variations and that motivates the network vendor to provide the best possible service?			
8. Are integrated services data networks (ISDNs) used for wide-area networks where and when these networks become available?			
9. Are protocols selected for either local or wide-area networks based on statistical studies performed by experts in which message traffic is simulated?			
10. Are protocol converters used to link networks of different topologies and protocols when additional flexibility in capacity and performance is needed?			
11. Are physical controls over networks implemented by using techniques such as the following? a. Control access to nodes b. Place nodes in shielded enclosures c. Use shielded or fiber-optic transmission lines d. Use network analysis equipment to detect security violations			

247

Management Considerations for Personal Computing Communications Networks

1. Take responsibility for managing data communications development and operations regardless of whether you are personally an expert in this technology or depend on the advice of others for technical expertise.

By now you should be convinced that data communications is a technology of its own, related to but really quite different from other computer science and information systems technologies. You should also be convinced that the success of personal computing in most organizations depends, to a significant extent, on the proper management of this technology.

You may decide to become expert in data communications, in which case, materials in this chapter will serve as a very light introduction. More likely, you will work with some staff member or consultant who is a specialist in this technology. In either case, however, the *management* of data communications and the application of the technology to personal computing and to information systems that include personal computing is *your* responsibility, not the responsibility of the expert. This guideline, then, provides some ideas on the general management of data communications development and operations, with special emphasis on the application of data communications to personal computing networks.

Planning for networks

2. Develop a plan; consider the elements shown in this guideline.
3. Involve functional users in the development of the plan; user managers and councils have final authority to review and approve the plan.
4. Develop functional plans first; then worry about the interconnections of the functional networks.
5. The plan should include discussion of issues such as these:
   a. Business goals and objectives
   b. Information systems architectures
   c. Utilities to be offered
   d. Technical strategies and tactics needed to implement the business goals
   e. Inventories of existing and planned devices
   f. Profiles of users
   g. Profiles of application systems that will use the network
   h. Statement of performance required under assumed volumes
   i. Justification
   j. Implementation and operation issues

As with any complex, comprehensive project, a plan is essential for successful implementation and operation of personal computing communications networks. Ideally, functional staff people will work with information systems specialists to develop the plan, but user managers should have final review and approval authority. The actual construction of the communications plans is the responsibility of information systems management, but user managers *must* be heavily involved. If there are functional committees such as a manufacturing council or a finance council, they should review and approve all plans. Clearly, any information systems-related councils, such as the personal computing steering committee, should be involved.

The plan should include discussion of issues such as these:

Business goals and objectives.   Discuss the communications that will be required in office, administration, manufacturing, factory marketing, sales office, and research/development applications. See Figure 6.7 for examples of how networks can be applied to functional business applications. Each of these areas may require specialized networks. Plans for these functional networks should, of course, be approved by functional management.

Once the functional plans are developed, consideration must be given to linking the functional networks. Note that the linkage issues should be considered even

---

Office Applications (applies to office applications in all functions)
    Electronic mail
    Teleconferencing
    Computer bulletin boards
    Company directories
    Shared office equipment (printers, copiers)
    Facsimile transmission
    Voice
    Video (videotex)
    Access to ''official'' company data bases
Administrative Functions
    Linkage of accounting with applications that create initial transactions
    Personnel data
    Training data
    Facilities scheduling (e.g., conference rooms, company pool cars)
    Consolidation and distribution of budgeting/expense reporting
    Cash management among various dispersed banks/lockboxes
Manufacturing Functions
    Access to inventories
    Work location scheduling, loading
    Central programs/downloading for automated tools
    Process routing
    Collection of production and performance data
    Collection of process statistics for quality reporting
    Maintenance applications
    Linkages to vendor inventories, shipment status
Factory Marketing Functions
    Access to central product configuration files
    Access to consolidated customer records
    Field office performance status
    Status of orders in factory production
    Credit management
    Consolidation of market research
    Consolidation of proposal/quotation status
Sales Office Functions
    Status of orders in factory
    Consolidated information of orders from various divisions of decentralized, geographically dispersed customers
    Comparing performance statistics from various field offices, by product line, by salespeople
    Comparative pricing by sales office, by product line
    Status of quotations, proposals
Research/Development Functions
    Consolidation of experiment results
    Centralized programs and downloading for automated instruments
    Consolidation of project status
    Performance statistics on vendors of various components
    Material quality data
    Information about quality of products during manufacture
    Information about quality of products after shipment to customers

---

Figure 6.7   Example network business applications by organizational functions.

while developing individual functional networks, but only as a background issue. It is more important to have effective functional networks than it is to have effective interfunctional linkages; in the worst cases, functional interconnections can be accomplished through bridges, gateways, and protocol converters.

Office networks are basic to all functions since all functions have some type of office operations. The group who develops the office network probably should, therefore, contain representatives from all functions.

Information systems architectures.   This factor involves discussion of how personal computing relates to the overall information systems structures of the company. Common types of architecture models have been discussed elsewhere in this book and include such things as decentralized computing, centralized computing, global-shared-local models, centralized data with decentralized read-only capabilities, levels of detail models (low-level operational systems, supervisory systems, management/staff systems, executive/strategic systems).

Utilities to be offered.   Many of these utilities are really part of the office functional network. Common network utilities include electronic mail, teleconferencing, bulletin boards, shared network hardware and software facilities (e.g., broadband capability, gateways, teleconferencing rooms), shared data resources (e.g., employee, application, data, node directories; files of standard company codes), and access to shared office resources such as specialized copiers/printers and facsimile transfer.

Technical strategies and tactics needed to implement the business goals. These are all the issues covered in the first two guidelines in this chapter. Topics should include integration of data, voice, and video; use of PBX versus LAN; baseband, broadband; and digital versus analog transmission facilities. Note again that different technical strategies may be appropriate for different functions and that an appropriate strategy may be required for linking the functional networks through bridges, gateways, and converters.

Inventories of existing and planned devices.   Few organizations have the luxury of planning their network with a clean slate; most have nodes already in place to which the planned network must adapt and serve. It is necessary, therefore, to take an inventory of those devices noting their characteristics and the limitation that they impose on the planned network.

The most common of the existing "devices" involves the telephone systems found in most companies. Many have analog PBXs which would require replacement if telephones are to be linked to the planned networks. Some companies, however, have already invested in digital phone switching systems and wish to use this rather than implementing a higher-speed LAN.

Profiles of users.   Figure 6.8 provides a checklist of the types of data that should be collected about potential network users. Remember, however, that the taking of surveys of people's plans, especially when population samples are selected, is a science of its own. Therefore, after you have drafted the survey form, you should seek expert advice both about the questionnaire and as to the size and composition of the sample to be surveyed. Such expert advice can often be found in your company's market research department and is readily available from outside consultants.

Profiles of application systems that will use the network.   Networks will be used also by application information systems; in fact, the greatest data volume will usually be imposed by systems. Figure 6.9 provides a sample checklist to be used for collecting data about these systems. Although sample data may be satisfactory for user profiles, profiles of systems should include all the systems that will use the

Geographic Location
    City:
    Building (address):
    Location in building:
Organizational Function
    Organization:
    Job title:
    Describe job:
Check/Describe Specific Needs:
    Electronic mail
    Teleconferencing
    Bulletin boards
    Access to company data
        (list examples)
    Access to office equipment
        (list examples)
    Access to information systems
        (list examples)
    Access to company networks from home/other remote sites
    Access to noncompany networks
        (list examples)
Describe needs with relation to the following subjects; be specific:
    Privacy
    Security
    Flexibility (volitility of equipment, system needs, equipment location movement)
    Peak- and slack-period projections
    Tolerance to downtime
    Tolerance to response time
    Personal data storage needs on the network
    Forecast of usage growth

Figure 6.8 Network planning: user profile checklist.

Application name:
Application owner:
Application custodian:
Data volumes to be communicated:
    When:
        Day of month
        Time of day
        Frequency
        When peaks/slack times
    Number of records:
    Number of characters/bytes:
    Volumes of peaks/slacks:
Number of sending nodes by location:
Number of receiving nodes by location:
Data storage requirements on the network:
    Data volume:
    Retention requirements:
Sensitivity to transmission error:
Sensitivity to network downtime:
Sensitivity to user downtime:
Number of users accessing the application: average, peak, slack:
Priority of this application versus other applications:
Privacy requirements:
Security requirements:
Logging/accounting requirements:
Backup/recovery requirements:

Figure 6.9 Network planning: information systems application profile.

network and should also include the profiles of systems that are planned for near-term implementation. Advice from survey experts is usually not needed for developing the profiles of application systems.

Statement of performance required under assumed volumes.   After analyzing the requirements defined in the user/applications system profiles, the network plan should estimate message volumes at various times of day and on various different days of the month and year. Based on these estimates and on the sensitivity of the users to network responsiveness, the plan should state the network performance goals. Recognize, however, that these goals may require modification when the costs for achieving that goal are calculated. Note also that systems users will usually tolerate some diminished performance if the network provides required functional capabilities and is reliable and consistent in its performance. Personal users, however, become frustrated with poor network performance and revert quickly to substitute methods of achieving communications functions or will simply refrain from communicating.

Justification.   The network plan should describe the economic and noneconomic benefits that the network may achieve and the economic and noneconomic costs that may be incurred. Both long- and short-term effects should be considered. Costs of technological obsolescence should also be considered; it is likely that major expense will be incurred to keep the network functioning even close to the ever-advancing state of the art. Figure 6.10 lists some of the factors that might be considered in the justification of networks.

Implementation and operation issues.   The plan should include many of the people and facilities considerations described later in this guideline. Include the schedule both for the initial network implementation and the implementation of network services to geographically dispersed company units. Carefully describe the ongoing support organization that is anticipated.

This section of the plan should be quite detailed, anticipating concerns that user managers may have. These concerns, especially in nontechnical organizations,

---

Potential Economic Benefits
    Less travel
    Use of shared resources instead of replicating resources
    Less paper
        Lower paper costs
        Lower mail processing costs
        Lower storage, retention costs
    Less voice traffic (expensive voice communication replaced by less expensive data communication)
Potential Noneconomic Benefits
    Less rework due to miscommunications
    Improved personal relations among people
    Better, more complete consideration of issues
    More rapid implementation of new technologies, processes
    Better information available to decision makers, more rapidly
    May lead to "flatter" organization structures
Potential Economic Costs
    Initial costs for network implementation: hardware, software, staff, space
    Ongoing support costs
Potential Noneconomic Costs
    Distraction of people from main tasks (spend too much time communicating)
    Focus on technology rather than on fundamental customer needs
    Increased centralization with resulting bureaucracy, loss of flexibility

Figure 6.10   Justifications of networks.

are usually focused on staffing and training. Therefore, these two issues should be carefully planned and described.

Establishing technical objectives

6. *Translate business plans into the technical project of establishing networks by establishing tactical goals and objectives for the network(s). These are some of the subjects for which objectives should be stated:*
   a. *Local-node independent operations*
   b. *Local-node access of "public" data and equipment resources*
   c. *Internode, interapplication transfer of data, processing, and control*
   d. *Systems reliability and systems availability goals*
   e. *Support of a wide variety and diversity of business, manufacturing, engineering, and scientific applications*
   f. *Geographic dispersion*
   g. *Communication outside the company*
   h. *Volume and flexibility goals*
   i. *Network message capability*
   j. *Types of equipment accommodated on the network*
   k. *Security and privacy issues*
   l. *Statement of special needs*

The business-oriented planning process may be translated into the technical project of establishing networks by establishing tactical goals and objectives for the network(s). These are some of the topics that should be considered while setting the network objectives:

Local-node independent operations.   To what extent can the nodes function as stand-alone personal computing or local computing facilities rather than as terminals for the network? When networks are superimposed on organizations in which personal computing is already established, this objective merely ratifies what exists. However, where telephone systems are the basis for a network, the capability of nodes becomes a fundamental functional and economic decision.

Local-node access of "public" data and equipment resources.   To what extent will resources be shared? Resource sharing is a primary justification for networks, but implementing this sharing requires a strategy of building accessible data bases and selecting hardware and software that allows the sharing to exist.

The alternative, of course, is to make each node functionally independent. This builds a network that is highly reliable because of its inherent redundancy, but it will be very expensive, highly inefficient (since much equipment will be used only occasionally), and functionally confusing since there will be inconsistencies between similar, but separate data bases.

Again, in practice, there will be combinations of shared and independent nodes. It is important, however, to establish a policy preference, treating inevitable exceptions with management judgment.

Internode, interapplication transfer of data, processing, and control.   How closely linked will be application processing? This is really an organization question that results from the types of process analyses described in Chapter 4. Early in the use of personal computing networks, work is performed, as in prenetwork times, with functional and individual independence. As networks and applications become more sophisticated, however, work tasks can be integrated across geographic and organizational boundaries, eliminating the intermediate, overhead tasks.

For example, in most organizations a "receiving document" is generated by the material-handling organization when a vendor delivers an order. This receiver is transmitted to accounting, where it is linked to the purchase order and vendor invoice and paid. This process can be duplicated and improved through the use of personal computing in each department, but networks can improve the overall process by eliminating the separate paperwork, by allowing the purchasing, receiving, and accounting functions to share a common data base, even extending the network to vendor data bases when the appropriate controls are in place.

Systems reliability and systems availability goals.   How reliable must the system be to meet the business goals? Reasonable reliability (availability of about 95 percent) is feasible from all reputable vendors. Greater reliability is also available but only at increasing costs and by designing systems appropriately.

Support of a wide variety and diversity of business, manufacturing, engineering, and scientific applications.   What functions are to be supported by network operations and in what priority? In what priority are these separate functional networks to be linked together?

Geographic dispersion.   In which geographic areas will the network be implemented? In practice, this is really a question of priorities; that is, which geographic operations will be implemented with what capabilities, in what order? For example, some outlying areas can be given dial-up access to company networks, with broadband capabilities scheduled for implementation at a later date.

Communication outside the company.   There are really several steps in this goal. First is the availability of network access by employees working at home. Next comes the ability to access public networks; a variation would be to allow access to public, broadband cable networks, allowing data, voice, and video interorganizational linkages.

The most sophisticated step is allowing systematic intercompany communications, perhaps through Electronic Data Interchange (EDI) standards. The sophistication lies not in the technical issues, but in the solution to management questions of control, security, coordination of data codes and formats, and so on.

Volume and flexibility goals.   How many nodes per employee should be anticipated? For what message volume should the network be designed? If volumes are really not estimated well, it may make sense to design a network that can easily be expanded, although placing priority on this goal may require other trade-offs. This goal might also address the need for accommodating node volitility and the need for flexibility to add or move nodes and/or to change the capabilities of nodes without affecting the overall network.

Network message capability.   Should the network accommodate data, voice, video; conversations, messages, files? Again, there is a priority and growth question; what types of messages should the network accommodate first?

Types of equipment accommodated on the network.   Again, in what priority? Should the network accommodate personal computing stations, terminals mainframes, and smart dedicated equipment (copiers, laboratory instrumentation)? The key to the linking of all these types of equipment is the implementation of hardware and software standards, the selection of equipment that meets those standards, or the construction/acquisition of appropriate bridges, gateways, and converters.

Security and privacy issues.   What trade-offs should be made between open, flexible use of network facilities versus the need to keep transactions and information private and secure from inappropriate use? It is important to state whether the same levels of security/privacy need be applied to all network facilities or whether flexibility is required. Flexibility obviously increases network functionality but probably also increases network implementation and support costs.

Statement of special needs.   What significant special needs were identified in the business plan (e.g., need for portable terminals, facsimile transmission, connection of special equipment, peak volumes, telecommuting, etc.)?

Managing network development projects

7. *Manage the implementation of network systems as you manage the development and implementation of all other major information systems, with, however, these special concerns:*
   a. *Multiple vendors*
   b. *Prototypes, pilots, and technical experiments*
   c. *Network testing*
   d. *Version control*
   e. *Physical/site planning*
   f. *Implementation issues*

The implementation of network systems should be managed as are other major information systems projects. Shown below, however, are some of the special concerns required by the development of networks.

Multiple vendors.   At the very least, you must coordinate the systems of different vendors of computing equipment and that of communications equipment. Usually, however, there are several vendors in each category. For example, you are likely to have several vendors for mainframe, mini-, and personal computing equipment. Similarly, you may have one vendor for network connection equipment (modems, multiplexers) and another (perhaps several) for transmission services. Different vendors for hardware and software provide still another dimension of complexity.

There are two requirements to managing this complex environment properly. First, you must establish a central coordinator who is responsible for the overall network implementation. This coordinator should report either to the company's chief information manager or to the manager of the PCIC. Second, the central coordinator must establish both application and technical standards that define the interfaces between vendors and between the vendors and internal systems development. The central coordinator should also coordinate the selection of vendors and determine policies which state when vendor contracts should be established centrally versus those which may be set locally.

In general, agreements should be set centrally both to achieve volume discounts and to achieve standardization. Implementation, however, is almost always better accomplished by local people; therefore, vendors should be selected who have offices near the sites in which network facilities will be located.

Communication services and regulations vary dramatically among different countries; it is usually appropriate, therefore, to select communications vendors familiar with the problems in given countries. Again, the coordination of transmission among countries becomes a significant task for the central coordinator.

Prototypes, pilots, and technical experiments.   Because of the complexities of communications networks, it is almost impossible to consider all the issues and interactions while designing the network. One useful, theoretical approach is the use of mathematical models to simulate key characteristics of the network. By necessity, however, simulations must use simplifying assumptions.

Networks must be developed, therefore, in empirical, incremental steps. Limited function technical experiments can be used to test specific network features; prototypes can be established by the design group to test specific application interactions with the network. Pilot operations are the last of the application tests because, although it is by definition limited in scope, pilot operations allow real-world users access to the network, and real-world users almost always do "dumb" things not anticipated by the network designers.

All these design experiments must be carefully monitored both qualitatively and quantitatively. Performance statistics should be collected and plotted on statistical control charts to determine the normal characteristics of the network process.

Network testing. Testing network systems is complex because of the inherent multiple vendor and multisite nature of networks. Test coordination becomes a major concern. This concern is best met by performing the tests in a very formal manner, by a specially designated test group, separate from the development group, which formulates test scenarios, implements tests among the appropriate sites, and evaluates the results.

Testing is especially complex when multiple versions of hardware or software exist at various sites. Also, as changes are implemented or as new versions of hardware/software are installed, regression tests (tests to see that previously correct features are still functioning properly) must be performed, again considering the capabilities of the various versions.

Version control. The multiple-site and multiple-vendor nature of networks exacerbates the normally difficult task of control over different versions of the system. It is important:

- That the network coordinator develop a standard way of identifying versions of network hardware/software facilities
- That all hardware/software be identified by version
- That the central coordinator keep an inventory of the versions that exist at each node
- That version implementation be scheduled so that nodes operate in a predictable fashion
- That network managers not trust the central inventories or the version implementation schedules and that the version identification automatically be displayed on all messages and reports processed through a node so that managers know what version is really installed

As noted above in the paragraph on testing, version control is particularly vital when testing various new or modified facilities.

Physical/site planning. Although physical planning is an appropriate, but minor, requirement of all information systems, it is a complex and essential requirement for computer networks. Space in each site must be allocated for antennas, multiplexers, and concentrators. More complex, however, is the planning for intrasite wiring, so that new personal nodes and personal computing devices can be added flexibly.

Flexibility is often obtained by stringing wires through false ceiling spaces (with "drops" down to desk nodes), through interstatial spaces, or by having intrasite, strategically located multiplexer wiring blocks, minimizing the amount of wiring needed to connect new or moved locations. Be aware of new, novel means of linking nodes within sites. Some new buildings (so-called "smart buildings") have special channels and intrasite multiplexers that facilitate network wiring. Some local networks, for open office and factory areas, utilize centrally located infared transmitter receivers, bypassing wiring entirely.

As has been mentioned before, networks are very sensitive to electrical interference which may be generated by manufacturing machinery, by some laboratory equipment, and by some communications equipment. Site planning must consider these situations and, as required, provide proper shielding or use fiber-optic cables.

Implementation issues. Implementing all information systems, especially personal computing systems, requires the proper management of changes in the organizational environment; however, implementation of networks is even more complex because of the interactions between remote organizations which have not previously worked together closely. Complex changes such as these are best implemented by:

- Involving the user organizations in early planning decisions and in all development, testing, and implementation activities.
- Thorough user training and documentation.
- Having, as part of the implementation team, a "network evangelist," a "technical missionary," who is a "champion" for the benefits of the changes that the network will bring. This person will create emotional excitement which will keep up user (and development team) enthusiasm even when the inevitable technical problems cause hardship and confusion.

Network accounting

8. *Maintain records of network usage.*
9. *Keep these records private, especially the records of detailed network transactions.*
10. *Use the accounting records to charge users for network services.*
11. *Use the accounting records to provide the trails needed for accurate post-event audits to detect security/privacy violations and to determine who committed the violation and how.*
12. *Use the accounting records to provide data about the performance of the network, compared to user and management expectations.*

Charging for network services—Network usage must be recorded and analyzed for three reasons:

- To detect and investigate security and privacy violations
- To allow managers to study performance characteristics of the network
- To allow the network costs to be charged to users in an equitable manner

Records should be kept by the network control center (see below) on an automated network accounting system. These types of records are often maintained:

- Who/what application logs on the network, when, and from what physical location
- The destination node of the various messages/files
- The length of time the user/application is connected to the network
- The length of time the user/application actually uses the network
- The number of messages/files transmitted
- The number of cumulative characters transmitted
- The amount of network storage resource used
- The special network services (e.g., directories, mail, conferencing) used (if any)

Note that these accounting records themselves can be used (or misused) to trace the activity of individual employees. These accounting records should, therefore, be kept private. I strongly recommend that they be used only in the aggregate for legitimate performance and financial accounting. Detailed network transactions should be reviewed only for security investigations and, even then, only with the explicit permission of the Chief Information Manager. The security and performance uses of network accounting are discussed below; this section focuses on charges to users.

As noted before, there are significant initial network costs followed by ongoing expenses for support and to fund system maintenance and enhancements. The initial expenses should be funded from research or overhead funds, since users will not be willing to pay until they can actually use the network. These initial costs, however, can be recovered by a surcharge on the ongoing usage fees.

Charges to users are generally itemized, but are included together with charges for other EDP services and charges from the PCIC. The following types of charges should be considered:

- Charges for personal communications equipment, such as modems and multiplexers; these are "lease" charges determined in the same way as are charges for personal computing equipment.
- One-time account setup charges. These charges should cover the incremental costs of establishing the communications account and may also include some amount to offset the amortization of the network implementation costs.
- Connect-time charges. These charges often vary to encourage use during off-peak periods.
- Network usage charges. Charges by message number and length are preferable to simply calculating time on the network, since users have more control over message sizes.
- Data storage charges. Charges should be sufficiently high to encourage storage off the network, on disks or tapes at the node.
- Charges for the use of special devices and for special, manual services. Typical charges are for use of special printers or plotters or for mounting special tape files or for placing special forms on printers.
- Charges for the use of special software. Some widely used services, such as directories, may be bundled with the normal network charges, but you may want to charge separately for expensive, specialized software such as computer-aided-design software, special data banks, and so on.
- Charges for support and consulting services from the network customer/user support group (see below).

Network managers must collect and maintain a data base that records all the transactions on which the charges are based and allows users and auditors to examine, analyze, and confirm the basis of any charge. This usually means that a detail log must be kept in which each network transaction is recorded. The routine bills need not show the detail, but the detail must be available on request.

Controls, security, and privacy—The security and privacy measures discussed elsewhere in this text are critical for network applications. The network accounting records shown above, however, provide the trails needed for accurate post-event audits to detect security and privacy violations and to determine who committed the violation and how. Audit trails should also record access from one network to others to verify that internetwork transactions are valid.

Although this type of detection is after the fact and is therefore not as desirable as are prevention techniques such as passwords, just the knowledge that such detection methods exist may be enough to discourage violations.

These audit trails are also useful in case of accidental damage to the system and for locating and recovering "lost" messages. The accounting records can also record modifications made to programs used in the network, not only to detect security violations, but also to verify that the modifications were made with proper authorization and only after proper testing.

Performance measures and statistics—Data are collected about the performance of the network and compared against user and management expectations. When changes are made to the network, performance can be monitored to verify that the expected changes, and only the expected changes, occur. These are the types of performance measures that can be determined from network accounting records:

- Node usage
- Usage of network hardware and software resources per time period
- Average message throughput time (perhaps normalized by message volume)
- Network availability; also mean time to failure and mean time to repair
- Network volumes (in numbers of message and data volume) per time period
- Number of backup/recovery operations required by application

Networks are most cost-efficient when the flow through the network is balanced, when network resources are neither overload nor idle. Performance statistics can be used to calculate load balancing and to suggest which resources or nodes need adjustment. Network demand can sometimes be adjusted through the manipulation of connect-time charges or by actually modifying the ability of certain nodes to access the network at certain times.

Sometimes, performance accounting will show that certain network resources are not used to the extent expected. Resource usage can be motivated through advertising, training on the benefits and use of the resource, favorable pricing, and the publishing of success stories.

Administration and support of network operations

13. *Provide excellent network administration and support services.*

14. *Implement a network control center (NCC) as an operational unit within the information systems function.*

15. *Take special care in the implementation of fault management services, for communications hardware, software, and media, and for the application systems that operate on the network.*

16. *Establish a customer/user support organization, reporting to the same manager as does the head of the NCC, which provides ongoing assistance and consulting to network users.*

17. *Establish and enforce policies that define the proper, legal use of proprietary software and data on the network.*

18. *Where economically feasible, purchase site licenses that allow unrestricted internal use of proprietary software and data.*

Ongoing administration and support literally create the environment for network success or failure. Good support can compensate, at least to some extent, for mistakes in development, and poor support can destroy even the best developed network.

Network control center—The network control center (NCC) is the heart of network operations. The NCC has the responsibility for both network administration and network monitoring. In small networks, the NCC can be simply one person who performs whatever administration is needed and who is the liaison with vendors of communications services. In large networks with significant resources internal to the company, the NCC may be a large department with dedicated, special-purpose network monitoring and control equipment.

NCCs may be centralized, or regionalized, depending on the organization of the company and the topology of the network. It is essential that no part of the network be hidden from the view of some NCC. These are some guidelines for NCC organization:

- Every node should be under the control of one and only one NCC.
- All internode lines should be under the control of at least one NCC; sometimes responsibilities for lines overlap; if so, one NCC should have responsibility for resolving any administrative conflict.
- All NCCs should have the ability to communicate quickly with each other.

The NCC is an operational unit, not a development, project-oriented group. The NCC should be in the information systems department but be either in a separate telecommunications group or in the data processing operations group. NCCs should have the responsibility to perform the following tasks:

- Operate network switches and lines; reconfigure the network as appropriate to maintain network quality and performance.
- Monitor network usage/traffic; identify and alleviate bottlenecks; balance loads.
- Monitor/maintain network quality.
- Provide user installation, moving, removal services (connection services).
- Provide linkage with other communication services.
- Handle complaints about services, such as recording message charges, mounting library data tapes or printing messages, and teleconferencing.
- Detect and correct faults (see below); monitor alarms.
- Replace defective terminals or other network components.
- Record charges.
- Maintain security/privacy features of the network.
- Provide disaster recovery services.
- Maintain auditability of network.
- Maintain inventories of network hardware assets (for billing and for network analysis).
- Implement and test software versions/updates.
- Periodically run diagnostic tests on network components and capabilities.
- Record network process/performance statistics.
- Assign and adjust priorities to appropriate users.
- Manage queues waiting to use scarce, shared resources.
- Manage gateways, bridges, converters among local- and wide-area networks.
- Perform routine operation/administration services such as:
  - Checkpoint/restarts
  - Backup/recovery procedures
  - Daily network turn-on, turn-off procedures

- Perform maintenance on both network hardware and software.
- Manage information systems and data bases associated with network operations. These systems should provide:
  - Network performance statistics
  - Use of sharable resources
  - Inventory/location of network components and configurations
  - Record of defects, incidents, and alarms
  - Symptom, diagnosis, and suggested repair file
  - Network expenses
  - Network charges to users
  - Inventory/status of software
  - Library of data files stored in network libraries
  - User/node/facility directories
- Implement and manage directories of people, nodes, sharable resources, and public data bases. This may appropriately be one of the information systems mentioned above, since although it is a separate service, directories are "merely" ways of displaying information about the physical status of the network and about transactions/changes that are occurring to the network.

Fault management.   Detection and correction of network failures and defects is a significant part of the NCC functions that deserves special comment. For those networks that operate strictly with vendor-provided services, the vendors usually provide fault management services. However, when an organization uses private lines, has many geographically dispersed nodes, and/or coordinates the activities of many different vendors, the fault management responsibilities become significant. Well-trained specialists should be hired to provide fault management services.

Network fault management is so complicated because of the wide variety of defects that can occur, because of the wide geographic area over which defects can occur, because of the problems that can be caused by complex interactions of hardware, software, and transmission media, and because problems are often intermittent rather than being "hard" failures.

Fault management requires that these steps be carried out:

- Isolate and identify the problem.
- Determine how to make the repair.
- Implement the repair.
- Determine that the problem is solved and that the repair has not created additional problems.

Specialized diagnostic tools such as protocol analyzers, signal analyzers, and network analyzers are needed for these tasks; depending on the network, the instruments must analyze both analog and digital signals. Proper fault management requires three steps: measurement, test, and control.

Measurement is the first step, usually taken when the network is established or after significant network changes. Data are collected about the process and experiments are performed to determine the optimum parameters or settings for the network.

Testing involves continuously checking the network facilities against design specifications/standards and sounding alarms when the network drifts outside predetermined tolerances. Monitoring is a form of testing in which network conditions are "sampled" at prescribed intervals and the resulting data are analyzed and compared against redefined specifications.

Control involves "closing the loop," in which corrective actions are taken together with testing until the network is stable and operating again within design limits.

One important class of instruments allows models of network components to be constructed and conditions and problems to be simulated. This allows both problem diagnosis and the testing of the sometimes extremely complex effects of alternative corrections. Note, however, that models are really abstracts of the real world, and although models can be a valuable tool, they cannot substitute for carefully monitored tests performed on the real network.

Although fault management is usually focused on communications hardware, software, and media, there are similar concerns over the management of defect detection and correction made to application systems. Unique problems occur because these systems cannot be shut off for significant periods of time; final systems testing must often be performed (in fact, should be performed) while the network is live, while users are performing routine transactions.

Great care must be taken with authorization of modifications and version control. One good mechanism is to have well-controlled "phantom," "dummy" accounts which live on the live network and which can be used for controlled tests. (Needless to say, these phantom accounts should be considered in all systems audits lest test transactions somehow be confused with real ones.)

Customer/user support services—In addition to support of the physical network operations, network users require ongoing consulting and assistance. The support organization is usually separate from the NCC, reporting to the same manager as does the head of the NCC. Costs for routine services are usually bundled into normal NCC charges; however, customer/user who require unique support should be charged specifically for those services. Support services include:

- Maintenance/enhancement support for application systems that run on the network.
- Consulting on network usage. Helping users get the best cost/performance from the network.
- Managing conferencing, bulletin-board services.
- Providing training both when new services are implemented and on an ongoing basis to help new people learn network functions.
- Assisting project managers in the testing of applications systems which will use network functions.
- Encouraging collaborative activities between different network users. This can be accomplished by providing system libraries, by arranging meetings between people working on similar problems, and by promoting and publicizing best practices.
- Helping users receive cost-effective services from vendors of network services. Records of vendor performance can be maintained, central contracts can be established, and/or standard contract forms can be provided to users who hire contractors locally.
- Providing users with data and information for use in presentations describing or justifying network functions.

Network legal issues—Network managers need to be especially concerned with the legal implications of the use of proprietary software and data, on the network. These problems occur because programs and data, once on the network, can easily be transferred to other nodes. Yet many software vendors and almost all public data base vendors restrict the use of the materials to the specific person who purchased the software or service. Each different person using the software or data should pay for it separately.

These are some of the issues:

- Unauthorized copying of copyrighted, proprietary programs or data
- Transferring copies of the programs or data to unauthorized users
- Incorporating proprietary programs or data into other, internal work which is then distributed freely

Usually, "backups" of data or programs are allowed as long as such a backup is used only by the original licensee and is not copied for profit, but some vendors might even limit this process. Read the contracts that come with software and are part of the applications for access to public data bases, and get legal advice, if necessary.

These problems can be eliminated by negotiating site licenses with vendors which allow broad use of the programs or data within an organization. Some companies will use only those vendors who are open to negotiating reasonable site licenses. If such licenses cannot be negotiated economically and you still want to use the proprietary data or software, you should implement the legal restrictions through firm policies stating that compliance with copyright laws and contractual agreements is required. Supervisors and auditors should be asked to verify compliance with policy.

CHECKLIST

Guideline 6.3
Management Considerations for Personal
Computing Communications Networks

	YES	NO	N/A
1. Are user managers taking responsibility for managing data communications development and operations regardless of whether they are themselves expert in this technology or if they depend on the advice of others for technical expertise?			
2. Have user managers developed a plan, considering the issues shown in this guideline?			
3. Are functional users involved in the development of the plan with user managers and councils who have final authority to review and approve the plan?			
4. Have functional plans been developed first with interconnections of the functional networks considered next?			
5. Does the plan include discussion of issues such as these? a. Business goals and objectives b. Information systems architectures c. Utilities to be offered d. Technical strategies and tactics needed to implement the business goals e. Inventories of existing and planned devices f. Profiles of users g. Profiles of application systems that will use the network h. Statement of performance required under assumed volumes i. Justification k. Implementation and operation issues			

(Continues)

265

6. Have the business plans been translated into the technical project of establishing networks?

Have tactical goals and objectives for the network(s) been established?

Have objectives been stated for these subjects?
a. Local-node independent operations
b. Local-node access of "public" data and equipment resources
c. Internode, interapplication transfer of data, processing, and control
d. Systems reliability and systems availability goals
e. Support of a wide variety and diversity of business, manufacturing, engineering, and scientific applications
f. Geographic dispersion
g. Communication outside the company
h. Volume and flexibility goals
i. Network message capability
j. Types of equipment accommodated on the network
k. Security and privacy issues
l. Statement of special needs

7. Is the implementation of network systems being managed as is the development and implementation of all other major information systems, with, however, these special concerns?
a. Multiple vendors
b. Prototypes, pilots, and technical experiments
c. Network testing
d. Version control
e. Physical/site planning
f. Implementation issues

8. Are records maintained showing network usage?

9. Are these records kept private, especially the records of detailed network transactions?

10. Are the accounting records used to charge users for network services?

11. Are the accounting records used to provide the trails needed for accurate post-event audits, to detect security/privacy violations, and to determine who committed the violation and how?

12. Are the accounting records used to provide data about the performance of the network, compared with user and management expectations?

13. Is emphasis placed on providing excellent network administration and support services?

14. Has a network control center (NCC) been implemented as an operational unit within the information systems function?

15. Has emphasis been placed on the implementation of fault management services, for communications hardware, software, and media, and for the application systems that operate on the network?

16. Has a customer/user support organization been established, reporting to the same manager as does the head of the NCC, which provides ongoing assistance and consulting to network users?

17. Have policies been established and enforced that define the proper, legal use of proprietary software and data on the network?

18. Where economically feasible, have site licenses been purchased that allow unrestricted internal use of proprietary software and data?

REFERENCES

MARSHALL D. ABRAMS, "Observations on Operating a Local Area Network," *IEEE Computer,* May 1985, p. 51.

PAUL W. ACCAMPO, "MAP Pilots: Promises and Pitfalls," *CIM Technology,* Spring 1986, p. 19.

HOWARD ANDERSON, "IBM's LAN Impacts the Telecom Professional," *Telecommunication Products plus Technology,* January 1986, p. 19.

HOWARD ANDERSON, "Moving toward Intelligent Networks," *Telecommunications Products plus Technology,* February 1986, p. 32.

PETER G. BALBUS and BRIAN M. NESMITH, "Digital Network Strategies," *Datamation,* July 1, 1985, p. 102.

JENNIFER E. BEAVER, "TOP: New Standards for the Office?" *Computer Decisions,* January 28, 1986, p. 46.

LOUIS BECKER, "Network Control Centers," *Computerworld on Communications,* September 5, 1984, p. 51.

BRUCE BORDEN, "Lines of Communication," *UNIX Review,* April 1985, p. 42.

JAMES C. BRANCHEAU and JUSTUS D. NAUMANN, "A Manager's Guide to Integrated Service Digital Network," *ACM Data Base,* Spring 1987, p. 20.

DALE CABELL and DOUG CABELL, "Bridges and Gateways," *Micro Communications,* July–August 1985, p. 28.

"Communications Glossary," *Micro Communications,* September 1984, p. 49.

Communicating with IBM, an HP-to-IBM Communications Primer, Part Number 5957-4623, Hewlett-Packard Company, Palo Alto, Calif., 1984.

SAM DICKEY, "The Lid Is Off ISDN—Tomorrow's Communication Connection," *Today's Office,* April 1986, p. 32.

JOHN DIX, "SNA Communications: The (LU 6.2) Glacier Advances," *Network World,* April 7, 1986, p. 31.

JOHN DOHERTY, "LU 6.2 Meets SNA," *Computerworld Focus,* January 15, 1986, p. 57.

TERRY L. DOLLHOFF, "Manufacturing Communications: Local Area Networks for the Integrated Factory," *Production Engineering,* February 1985, p. 68.

JOHN DOUNIS, SHARON EFROYMSON, and LYLE ANDERSON, "Multiuser System versus Local-Area Network: There Is a Right Choice," *Computerworld,* March 3, 1986, p. 51.

MICHAEL DURR, "Administration Revealed," *Micro Communications,* July–August 1985, p. 37.

MICHAEL DURR, "Network Software Bridges Gap between Local Area Network," *Mini-Micro Systems,* January 1985, p. 117.

JUDITH ESTRIN, "Hybrid Technologies Rewrite the Rules for Local Area Networks," *Mini-Micro Systems,* January 1985, p. 195.

STEVEN A. FAROWICH, "Communicating in the Technical Office," *IEEE Spectrum,* April 1986, p. 63.

DAVID FERRIS and JOHN CUNNINGHAM, "Local Nets for Micros," *Datamation,* August 1, 1984, p. 104.

HOWARD FRANK and IVAN FRISCH, "Local-Area Nets: What Matters Most to Users," *Computerworld,* November 5, 1984, p. ID/1.

JOHN GANTZ, "Systems Integration: Living in a House of Our Own Making," *Telecommunication Products & Technology,* May 1987, p. 35.

JOHN GANTZ, "Special Feature Section White Paper, ISDN: How Real? How

Soon?'' *Telecommunications Products plus Technology,* Vol. 4, No. 1, 1986, p. 33.

CHARLES J. GARDNER, "On the Road to MAP and TOP," *Telecommunications,* March 1986, p. 94.

LOUIS GIGLIO, "IBM's Disoss Runs the Office but Is It Running over Users?" *InformationWEEK,* July 29, 1985, p. 24.

MARK HALL, "Factory Networks," *Micro Communications,* February 1985, p. 14.

JAMES G. HERMAN, "Network Management: Old and New," *Telecommunications,* August 1987, p. 57.

BRIAN JEFFERY, "A Look at IBM's Token-Ring Network," *Computerworld Focus,* January 15, 1986, p. 33.

MICHAEL A. KAMINSKI, "Protocols for Communicating in the Factory," *IEEE Spectrum,* April 1986, p. 56.

ERIC H. KILLORIN and PAULA J. MUSICH," "A Master Strategy for Local Networking," *Telecommunications Products plus Technology,* March 1986, p. 30.

MIRIAM LISKIN, "How Computers Communicate," *Personal Computing,* January 1986, p. 39.

ROBERT N. MACHLIN, "Managing a Local Area Network, *Telecommunications,* November 1984, p. 84.

Making the LAN Connection, a Local Network Primer, Part Number 5957-4624, Hewlett-Packard Company, Palo Alto, Calif., 1984.

N. DEAN MEYER and DAVID LITWACK, "PC–Mainframe Linkage: The Five Connections," *Today's Office,* January 1985, p. 24.

THOMAS MILLER, "High-Performance Telework Helps Companies Compete," *Computerworld,* February 24, 1986, p. 69.

THOMAS MILLER, "Telecommuting Benefits Business with DP's Help," *Computerworld,* February 17, 1986, p. 51.

OLGA M. M. MITCHELL and THOMAS BROWNE, "ISDN: Switching to the Future," *Telecommunications,* March 1986, p. 96h.

JOHN P. NELSON, "Data Integrity in Factory Integration," *Manufacturing Systems,* March 1985, p. 48.

L. DAVID PASSMORE, "The Networking Standards Collision," *Datamation,* February 1, 1985, p. 98.

K. L. PHILLIPS, "Telecommunications in the Year 2000," *Telecommunications,* August 1987, p. 90.

JIM PRUITT, "Software That Helps Reduce Costs and Improve Services," *Telecommunication Products & Technology,* May 1987, p. 63.

STEPHEN J. RANDESI, "Whether or Not You Have an IBM Shop, Bone Up on IBM Office Automation Basics," *Network World,* April 7, 1986, p. 38.

LURA K. ROMEI, "More for the Money with Multiuser Systems," *Modern Office Technology,* October 1985, p. 109.

CHARLES RUBIN, "Finally . . . Computer networks That Really Work," *Personal Computing,* July 1985, p. 68.

OMRI SERLIN, "Departmental Computing: A Choice of Strategies," *Datamation,* May 1, 1985, p. 86.

ERIC SPIEWAK, "Networking Schemes Integrate Islands of Automation," *Telecommunications Products plus Technology,* February 1986, p. 18.

WILLIAM STALLINGS, "Standards: The New Fiber Diet," *Datamation,* March 15, 1987, p. 61.

WILLIAM STALLINGS, "Beyond Local Networks," *Datamation,* August 1983, p. 167.

WILLIAM STALLINGS, "Local Networks." *ACM Computing Surveys,* Vol. 16, No. 1, 1984, p. 3.

WILLIAM STALLINGS, "The IEEE 802 Local Network Standards," *Telecommunications,* March 1986, p. 40.

GARY STIX, "Is There a PBS to the Promised LAN?" *Computer Decisions,* March 26, 1985, p. 98.

Touring Datacom, a Datacommunications Primer, Part No. 5957-4622, Hewlett-Packard Company, Palo Alto, Calif., 1983.

SATISH K. TRIPATHI, YENNUN HUANG and SUSHIL JAJODIA, "Local Area Networks: Software and Related Issues," *IEEE Transactions on Software Engineering,* August 1987, p. 872.

JESSE VICTOR, "Micro-to-Mainframe Choices Expand," *Mini-Micro Systems,* May 1985, p. 91.

VALERIE WOODBURN, "An Update on PC LANs," *Telecommunication Products & Technology,* June 1987, p. 35.

Appendix: Some Details about Communications Standards

Because of the need for coordination and cooperation in communications technology between vendors, communications utilities, and users, standards are needed on both a national and international basis. To accomplish this, both the International Standards Organization (ISO) and the Institute of Electrical and Electronics Engineers (IEEE) have established very active committees which are publishing standards. In addition, some vendors have such significant presence in the communications marketplace that their products form a de facto standard.

Open Systems Interconnection Model

The best known communications product from the ISO is the Open Systems Interconnection (OSI) model. This model defines seven levels into which all aspects of communications technology, both logical and physical, can be separated. The OSI model defines the tasks to be performed at each level and also outlines the rules (called "protocols") by which the various levels communicate with each other. The details of the protocols are being established by working standards committees.

The OSI model provides communications hardware and software vendors with a structure in which to operate. To the extent that vendors follow the protocols defined by the OSI model and the standards committees, their products will also work together. This will allow users to select the products from several vendors to accomplish the specific tasks needed by the user with reasonable confidence that the products from the different vendors will function together.

From top to bottom, this is the OSI model:

Level 7: application layer.   This is the user's interface to the network, where the application programs will contact the communications system. For example, word processing programs or electronic mail systems contact networks at this level.

Level 6: presentation layer.   Data are translated to and from the format most appropriate for use by the network. Typically, in this layer, data are formatted, codes are converted, and text may be compressed and encoded. For example, this is the level at which the codes from various different terminals are converted to a format compatible with the communications network.

Level 5: session layer.   Communication paths with specific nodes are established and terminated. The work done by each node is known as a "process," and coordination between processes occurs at this layer. For example, a session might be established to allow a user to log on to a remote node.

Level 4: transport layer.   This layer is the main interface between the communications network software and its hardware. This layer provides a buffer between the hardware and software and, ideally, allows the network to switch among various physical transmission methods with no impact on the user. One primary function of this layer is to assure the integrity of the data being transmitted. Acknowledgment messages and error messages from the communications network are usually routed in this level.

Levels 4 to 7, the topmost layers, are usually implemented in software by the operating system of the node computer or by a special communications control program invoked by the node. Level 3, below, the network layer, is, however, usually implemented by a special communications "driver."

Level 3: network layer.   This layer controls the actual switching and routing of the network. It also functions as the gateway linking one network to others. It is in this level that the system decides which message gets physical control of the communications channel. It is here that "tokens" are passed or message collision control is established, depending on the message control mechanism used. For a packet network, the X.25 protocol is established at this level.

Level 2: data link layer. The physical data are controlled by this layer. Data bits are converted to/from character representations, and error checking and correction are applied. Transmission speed is also controlled at this level. It is at this level that the physical connection to the network is made via a serial "RS 232" connector, for example, or an "IEEE 488" parallel connector, or some other device.

Level 1: physical layer. This is the layer that provides the electrical and mechanical means of transmitting and receiving the data bits among devices. It is at this level that the actual transmission medium, wire, coaxial cable, microwave, fiber-optics cable, and so on, must be considered.

These two lowest levels, levels 1 and 2, are usually implemented by specific hardware products.

Systems Network Architecture Model

In 1974, IBM introduced the Systems Network Architecture (SNA) communications model. This model has six layers, which are similar to but do not correspond directly with the OSI model. These levels are:

Services Manager Layer
Function Management Services Layer
Data Flow Control Layer
Transmission Control Layer
Path Control Layer
Data Link Control Layer

Before the SNA architecture was introduced, IBM used a Binary Synchronous (BSC or bisync) protocol, which uses various transmission control characters to mark transmission blocks and to check for communications errors. Many BSC networks are still in active use.

In contrast to BSC, SNA networks use a synchronous protocol called Synchronous Data Link Control (SDLC). With SDLC, the transmission need not send extra control characters to coordinate the network, but with SNA, as with the OSI model, sophisticated hardware and software are needed to keep the transmissions synchronized.

As an oversimplification, BSC networks are more flexible and can communicate with more different types of devices; the synchronized models require more linkage precision, but have far greater capacities and speeds than are possible with BSC networks. The SNA and OSI layers also shield the applications programmers from the details of network management, while BSC networks are usually more closely involved with the applications programs.

Related to SNA, IBM offers Advanced-Program-to-Program Communications (APPC) software, a Document Interchange Architecture (DIA), a Document Content Architecture (DCA), and SNA Distribution Services (Snads). Within APPC, IBM has defined a series of Logical Unit (LU) protocols which describe how physical units (PUs) on the network relate to each other. PU 2.0 describes general-purpose nodes, PU 4 is a communications node, and PU 5 describes a host processor.

LU 0 is used for product-specific devices, while LU 1 describes a protocol for printers and remote-job-entry nodes. LU 2 and 3 are specific to 3270-type terminal devices; LU 2 describes a protocol for the 3270 terminal themselves, while LU 3 is used for 3270-type printers. LU 4 was to be used for communications on low-cost topological or star networks; LU 4 has been superseded by LU 6.2. LU 6.0 and 6.1 are protocols for intersystems communications. For most companies, protocol LU 6.2 is the most significant. LU 6.2 combines the standards described in LU 0, LU 4, LU 6.0, and LU 6.1 to provide a single protocol for interprogram communication within an SNA environment.

DIA is an architecture that describes how documents (files) can be transferred among different systems. Theoretically, DIA can be implemented independent of SNA, but most IBM products implement DIA using SNA technology.

DCA describes the data used to describe documents in this architecture. DCA is generally designed for text, but data formats can be described for graphics to be embedded in the text, and user-defined data in binary formats can also be included. DCA allows transfer of documents among devices that would otherwise be incompatible.

Snads provides software tools that allow asynchronous communications on the otherwise synchronous SNA network. Snads provides the software buffers to communicate using the LU 6.2 protocol. These buffers, called Distribution Service Units, are located strategically around the network to provide required store-and-forward services.

IEEE 802 standards

The Institute of Electrical and Electronics Engineers (IEEE) is developing several standards based on the OSI model. IEEE 802.0 and IEEE 802.1 are documentation and are not part of the actual standards.

- IEEE 802.2 defines the upper half of the Data Link layer (level 2). This upper half is called the Logical Link Control, while the lower half is called the Medium Link Control.
- IEEE 802.3 defines a standard similar to the Ethernet protocol invented by Xerox and Digital Equipment Corporation. Ethernet and IEEE 802.3 devices can coexist on the same network, but they cannot talk to each other. This standard defines a CSMA/CD bus local-area network (LAN). CSMA/CD means "carrier-sence multiple access with collision detect"; it is a technology that allows multiple messages to attempt to use the same facility. If two collide, the carrier senses the collision, retransmits both messages, and holds other messages until the carrier appears available. "Bus" refers to the network topology, where there is one long cable strung through the facility with devices connected to the cable at various points.
- IEEE 802.3 networks are usually implemented on the "baseband," a single channel of up to 10 million bits per second; coaxial cable is usually used, but fiber-optic links are becoming popular. LANs are usually relatively short in range, about 500 meters, but various LANs can be linked to cover greater distances, if necessary.
- IEEE 802.4 defines a token-passing bus network that can be on either a baseband or a broadband. Token passing is another way (other than CSMA/CD) in which a message can be given permission to use a network. Here the carrier gives a device a "token," which then allows the device to transmit.

    A broadband network has much more capacity than does a baseband network and can also transmit several signals at once. Broadband networks are usually subdivided to send voice and video as well as data.
- IEEE 802.4 networks can cover up to 25 miles. This standard is becoming

important because it is used in the Manufacturing Automation Protocol (MAP) sponsored by the General Motors Corporation.

- IEEE 802.5 is the protocol for the token-passing baseband ring LAN being developed by IBM. A "ring" is another network topology in which devices are connected to their immediate neighbors in a circular manner. Data travel in only one direction around the ring.
- IEEE 802.6 is the standard for metropolitan area networks (MANs), networks that operate over an area the size of several city blocks.
- IEEE 802.7 is a technical advisory group that is preparing a manual on the installation of broadband LANs.
- IEEE 802.8 is a technical advisory group that is considering the uses of fiber optics on token ring LANs and on repeater links in CSMA/CD LANs.

Manufacturing Automation Protocol

The Manufacturing Automation Protocol (MAP) is an implementation of the standards shown above for a manufacturing environment. The MAP implementation is sponsored and led by General Motors Corporation and involves seven vendors in a joint development effort: Allen-Bradley, Concord Data Systems, Digital Equipment Corporation, Gould, Hewlett-Packard, IBM, and Motorola. MAP architecture shows how the OSI models and the IEEE 802 standards can be combined into a physical and logical network which will allow devices that perform many different functions from many vendors to work together. General Motors will be able to select and utilize the equipment from any vendor who follows the MAP architecture.

MAP specifically defines the lower three OSI levels:

Level 1: physical: MAP uses a token bus topology following the IEEE 802.4 standard. Broadband cable is the recommended physical medium.

Level 2: data link: The upper (logical) portion of this layer follows the IEEE 802.2 standard. The lower (physical) level follows the token bus IEEE 802.4 standard.

Level 3: network: This is the layer in which all the devices match each other; all network devices must have protocols and drivers that communicate at level 3.

Levels 4 to 7 are left to the discretion of the individual vendors, with the proviso, of course, that they maintain the interface at level 3. Vendors who wish to communicate at these higher levels (which usually increases performance) must agree on common implementations of these levels or must develop hardware or software gateways which translate data from one format to another to compensate for the way different vendors implement the various levels.

Technical and Office Protocol

The Technical and Office Protocol (TOP) has been proposed as the standard for communication in offices, analogous to MAP in the factory. The standards for TOP are the same at each OSI layer as MAP except at level 1, the Physical Layer, TOP uses IEEE 802.3 (baseband LAN standard) instead of the IEEE 802.4 (token bus LAN standard).

MAP/TOP steering committee

Both MAP and TOP are "consensus standard," standards that companies must adopt voluntarily, rather than standards imposed by regulatory agencies. To implement this consensus, the Society of Manufacturing Engineers (SME) has organized a MAP/TOP steering committee to negotiate technical details and to stimulate implementation and pilot projects. Much of this work is being accomplished by MAP and TOP users groups.

As noted, MAP is aimed at data communication on the factory floor, while TOP is focused on office communications. A primary concern of the MAP/TOP steering committee, however, is the linkage between MAP and TOP, that is, the integration of factory and office automation. The organizations represented on the MAP/TOP steering committee are Boeing Company, John Deere & Co., E. I. du Pont de Nemours & Co., Eastman Kodak, Ford Motor Co., General Motors, Inland Steel, McDonnell Douglas, Procter & Gamble, and the U.S. Air Force.

Chapter Seven

End-User System Development

Introduction

All information systems eventually serve people doing the work of the organization. These "end-users" have long built their own "manual" systems using paper, pencils, typewriters, and calculators, but until the advent of personal computing, users have had to depend on "technical intermediaries" in order to harness the power of computers. These technical intermediaries are the systems analysts, programmers, systems administrators, and data processing operations people, computer professionals who surround the computer-room temple.

The costs and physical size of computers have continually decreased, but it is only in the recent past that computers which can accomplish significant business tasks have become small enough and sufficiently inexpensive to be dedicated to the use of a single person. Personal computing, of course, includes the personal use of both a stand-alone "personal computer" and the personal use of a "piece" of a larger computer through "time sharing."

Even today, however, most personal computing requires the involvement of computer professionals. Most people use personal computing through the creative use of fixed-feature software packages or simply by using an already functioning system to accomplish a task or application.

Technology is evolving, however, which allows (encourages) people to go beyond using tools programmed by others. Many users now have the capabilities needed to develop their own programs and systems, although some may still be advised to seek the assistance of professionals.

This chapter provides guidelines which will, first, help users decide whether to develop their own programs and systems or whether to seek professional assistance. Then, for those who decide to develop their own software, the guidelines offer advice on how to do this in ways that will provide the maximum benefit to the overall organization.

Definitions

To place boundaries on the guidelines in this chapter, I offer appropriate definitions of the terms "end user," "program," and "system."

What is an end user?

An *end user,* in this chapter, is simply a person who uses computers and systems for doing specific tasks related to the business of the organization; the computer/system is a tool for this person. Information systems people are *not* end users in this context; they are the designers, builders, and operators of the tools. (I recognize that it is quite possible, appropriate, and even desirable for information systems people to use computing power as a tool for building systems; however, because of their technical expertise, I consider information systems people a special class of end users; this chapter is, therefore, oriented toward those generally less expert in computing and systems topics.)

Systems versus programs?

A *program* is a series of instructions to a computer which causes it to perform some function. Programs can be purchased as packages or can be custom developed by the users themselves or by specialists in accordance with the specifications provided by the specific users.

A *system* is a group of programs, together with appropriate procedures and documentation, that allows groups of people to perform some task related to the function of the business. Systems are supersets of programs and relate as much to people as they do to computers. Systems can also be purchased but almost always must be modified to fit specific user environments, at least in their manual portions and in their people–system interfaces.

End-user systems usually fit one of these categories:

- Reports: materials developed from access to a data base; extract or summarize in ways that communicate information meaningfully to a reader. Reports need not only be tables of numbers; reports may be in narrative or graphic form or in innovative combinations of words, graphics, and numbers.
- Models: tools for analysis through the use of mathematical simulations, spreadsheets, or graphic illustrations.
- Personal processing programs: specialized programs that perform specific tasks unique to both the job and the individual. These programs can be commercial packages, custom-written programs, or custom modifications of existing programs/packages.

Figure 7.1 shows factors that differentiate complete information systems from programs that are written for controlled or private use.

End-User Systems Development versus End-User Programming

As mentioned above, the advent of low-cost, powerful computers has given many people the opportunity to use a computer, even to write programs. End-user programs may be simple or sophisticated but are, by definition, written for *private* use and are generally not usable without the person who created them. These programs generally have weak data edits and are limited in scope, in the volume or type of

Computer programs that operate correctly are necessary both for programs for personal use and for information systems. The factors shown below are optional in personal programs. Information systems, however, *must* include these factors or, at least, consciously consider each factor and omit it. (The factors are repeated in all the categories in which they apply.)

A. Design/Development Factors
1. Data format and content edits
2. Transaction audit trails
3. Input data, transaction balancing ("batch") controls
4. In-process, interprogram balancing controls
5. Output data, report balancing controls
6. Security/privacy
7. Checkpoint/restart capabilities
8. Data integrity, nonambiguity; data reconciliation
9. Documentation: training, reference, program, user, operator
10. Backup/restart/recovery capabilities
11. Standards applied to programs and development process
12. User (manual, interface) procedures
13. User procedure testing
14. Integration/linkage with other systems
15. Integrity/control of codes used in system
16. User steering committee for development guidance
17. Error correction/suspense control processes
18. Adequate performance under production data/transaction loads

B. Implementation Factors
1. Training users/operators
2. Parallel/pilot testing
3. Conversion of files from existing systems
4. User procedure testing

C. User Factors
1. Transaction audit trails
2. Designation of system/data owners/custodians
3. In-process, interprogram balancing controls
4. Output data, report balancing controls
5. Security/privacy
6. Checkpoint/restart capabilities
7. User (manual, interface) procedures
8. User procedure testing
9. Ongoing training for new, replacement users
10. System administration activities
11. Integrity/control of codes used in system
12. Error correction/suspense control processes

D. Data Factors
1. Data format and content edits
2. Maintenance of transaction/data history files
3. Input data, transaction balancing ("batch") controls
4. In-process, interprogram balancing controls
5. Output data, report balancing controls
6. Security/privacy
7. Data integrity, nonambiguity; data reconciliation
8. Adequate file space for production data
9. Integration/linkage with other systems
10. Integrity/control of codes used in system

E. EDP Operations Factors
1. Transaction audit trails
2. Maintenance of transaction/data history files

Figure 7.1 Factors that differentiate information systems from programs for personal use.

3. Transaction/data schedules, cutoffs
4. Input data, transaction balancing ("batch") controls
5. In-process, interprogram balancing controls
6. Output data, report balancing controls
7. Security/privacy
8. Checkpoint/restart capabilities
9. Data integrity, nonambiguity; data reconciliation
10. Backup/restart/recovery capabilities
11. System usage reporting
12. User accounting, charges
13. System run schedules for file updates, reports
14. Integration/linkage with other systems
15. Error correction/suspense control processes
16. Data library procedures
17. Operations run logs

F. Support Factors
1. Documentation: maintenance and enhancement
2. Management of modification requests and implementation
3. Standards applied to program modifications and to support process
4. Production system version control
5. Ongoing training for new, replacement users
6. User steering committee for support guidance
7. Consistency of integrity/control of codes used in system

Figure 7.1 (*Continued*)

data handled, in the speed with which they operate, or in the documentation provided.

End-user programs provide entertainment and training, and can often provide their specific authors with personal tools to do their jobs better. A personal computing "system" may also have entertainment and training characteristics and definitely helps people do work. However, personal computing systems are *organizational assets,* helping not only the individual work/programmer but also others in the organization who do the same type of job and others who may succeed the original system's author.

Often, personal computing systems begin as personal computing programs and go through several interations until their use is repetitive and stable. At this point, the writer should be encouraged to document the procedures for using the system and offer it to others doing similar tasks. The goal for creative people developing personal computing systems should be to allow others to use their systems to do their jobs. Then the creative people can go on to work on other tasks.

This does not necessarily mean that the person who receives the system need use it only as written. It is reasonable to expect the other people to start with the borrowed system and then to modify it to suit the borrower's style and specific tasks. A great deal of work is saved, of course, because the borrower can build on the work of others, not having to "reinvent wheels." The modifications to the system can also be made available to the community of people using the system so that everyone can benefit from everyone else's ideas, creating a powerful form of organizational synergy.

Maintenance of end-user programs and systems

In general, if an end user writes a program, that end user maintains the program. When the programs are organized, enhanced, and documented and become a system used by others, the maintenance responsibilities may be accepted by the PCIC or by a support group in the information systems department. The support group has the right to review the system and insist that, before the system is accepted for maintenance, the author modify the system or its documentation so that it complies with information systems department standards.

This policy encourages end users to develop their work into systems and to follow information standards. However, the policy does not in any way inhibit people from buying packages or writing their own programs in any way or for any purpose, as long as they remain fully responsible for them.

Alternatives to writing end-user programs/systems

When faced with a problem or a business procedure, it makes sense to consider alternatives in this sequence. Proceed from one step to the next only if there are clear benefits from the investment of time and equipment cost.

- Do the task manually, using pencil, paper, and calculators.
- Write down the manual steps into a procedure so that you can replicate the process each time the task is performed.
- Use general personal computing software such as a word processor or a spreadsheet to automate appropriate steps in the procedure.
- Purchase a commercial software package, such as an accounting or an inventory system, to do the task.
- Modify the commercial package to meet your specific needs more closely.
- Write your own programs to perform the tasks.
- Link the programs together and write the appropriate documentation to create an end-user *system* that is suitable for support by the information systems department.

Following these steps has several benefits. First, the task will be performed in the simplest, least costly manner. Second, the worker can experiment inexpensively with many different ways of performing the task. Third, when and if it becomes economical to automate, the end user really understands the task and can create, with minimum reworking, a program or system to do the right job.

See also Guideline 2.3 which discusses alternatives to personal computing, in general.

Ownership issues with regard to end-user programs
and systems

Ownership issues with regard to personal computing, in general, are also discussed in Guideline 2.3. Guideline 2.3 suggests that software written by employees (including end users) belongs to the company if any one or more of these conditions is present:

- The software was written using company resources or equipment.
- The software was written during the employee's normal working hours.
- The software is useful for the company's business functions.

Under these guidelines, end-user programs and systems almost always belong to the company.

Guidelines in this Chapter

The guidelines in this chapter provide a structure under which end users can create systems effectively, with minimum bureaucratic interference but in such a way as to create a company asset, when appropriate. To this end, Guideline 7.1 describes "End-User Responsibilities in Developing End-User Systems." This guideline discusses differences between end users in office, administrative, factory, field, and laboratory settings. End-user development life cycles are discussed and the need for reporting integrity, controls, and documentation are stressed.

Guideline 7.2 discusses "Tools to Facilitate End-User Systems Development." Both packages and programs are discussed, introducing also the concepts of reusable code and templates so that end-user programmers may build on their own experience.

The ultimate "tool" for the end user is the PCIC. The very reason for the existence of the PCIC is to convert personal computing into an economical, productive company asset; encouraging end-user systems development should be a major branch of PCIC activities. Guideline 7.3, "Role of the PCIC in End-User Systems Development," shows what resources might be made available to end users to help them grow in their knowledge, creating systems for their own use and for the use of others in the company.

Guideline 7.1: End-User Responsibilities in Developing End-User Systems

General

As noted above, end-user programs and systems are company assets, even when they are written for the private use of the author. These tools should be developed such that they produce high-quality, reliable results, helping other people, not confusing them.

In addition, ideally, even private tools should be available to others who are doing similar jobs or who can learn (or even simply copy) from the personal programs. At the very least, these programs should be available for use by people who take over the author's job on a temporary or permanent basis.

Types of end-user computing

1. *End-user computing usually involves these levels:*
   a. *Using programs specifically written for the application task being performed.*
   b. *Using flexible but limited function program packages (products).*
   c. *Writing individual programs to accomplish personal tasks.*
   d. *Modifying preprogrammed systems to suit their specific needs.*
   e. *Designing, writing, and implementing a full system, meeting the specific needs of a specific end user.*
2. *People undertake the different levels of end-user computing based on a variety of factors, such as these:*
   a. *The technical aptitude of the end users.*
   b. *The willingness of end users or managers to spend the time apart from their normal job to learn or implement personal computing technology.*
   c. *How much this application will be used.*
   d. *Whether or not the system will be used independent of its initial author.*

End-user computing usually involves the levels shown below, stated from the most straightforward to the most complex. In general, the straightforward methods are less expensive, but less flexible; usually, the users must adapt their preferred working techniques to the specific system. As the end users become more technically involved, the costs increase but the users have more control over the systems and can tailor them to their specific work environments.

- Using programs specifically written for the application task being performed. Usually, these programs are written by information systems specialists specifically for the task. These programs usually require the user to learn only the application; users need learn very little about the computing technology involved. Often, these are conventional information systems written, ideally, with heavy involvement of some users, often developed at great time and expense. As time goes on, however, these systems require maintenance by the information systems group, or the system's limitations will restrict the ongoing flexibility of the users.
- Using flexible but limited-function program packages (products). Word processing, spreadsheets, and data base packages fall into this category. Users must learn the capabilities and limitations of the software packages they use, but they may not need to learn any of the underlying complexities of the hardware or operating systems.
- Writing individual programs to accomplish personal tasks. In this case, users need to learn specific programming language and enough about their hardware and operating systems to use some files and, perhaps, some specific communications capabilities.
- Modifying preprogrammed systems to suit their specific needs. These preprogrammed systems may be generalized applications; packages from vendors, such as accounting or inventory packages; or a system written by the company's information system department for a specific application which now requires modifications.
- End users who undertake the modification of a system must understand both the construction and the use of the system and must know enough to modify it without damaging anything else. The noncomputer aspects of the system, such as user interfaces, documentation, and audit trails, must also be reconstructed, as required. Refer again to Figure 7.1 to see what is involved in a system versus a program.
- Designing, writing, and implementing a full system, meeting the specific needs of a specific end user. This requires full knowledge of information systems and reasonable knowledge of the languages, hardware, and operating systems being used. Figure 7.1 lists the considerations.

Given that the decision has been made to implement a personal computing application, people undertake the different levels of end using computing based on a variety of factors, such as these:

- The technical aptitude of the end-users. If the users have no interest or ability in the technologies of computing, they will opt for one of the simpler, less flexible forms of end-user personal computing.
- The willingness of end users to spend the time apart from their normal job to learn or implement personal computing technology. The person's manager, of course, may also be reluctant to see competent employees diverted from their primary tasks. The fear, of course, is that end users will become so fascinated by the intricacies of computing that they will ignore their basic job.

- How much this application will be used. This usually depends on the number of people who are likely to use the application and the length of time it will be used. The greater the use, the greater the benefits to be derived from taking care to make the personal computing application a more complete information system.

- Whether or not the system will be used independent of its initial author. If the author is the only user, or if the author is easily available to all users, some looseness in the personal computing application can be tolerated. If, however, the application will be used over time and in places far from the developer, the system will require more complete development. Sometimes, of course, even where the developers are readily available, the developers enhance the systems just to keep from being perpetual references for other users.

In this chapter the term "program" will imply personal use programs, while "systems" will imply "information systems." End-user "software" will be used when the guideline applies to both programs and systems.

Different end users need different capabilities

3. *All end users need office support tools.*

4. *Administrative end users need specialized tools and applications, including access to central company files, customized CRT screen forms, and communication with other groups.*

5. *Personal computing in factory applications usually involves communications and interfaces between automated machines that talk different languages and which have different communications protocols.*

6. *Communications are also crucial in field office applications. Often, portability is required.*

7. *Laboratory scientists and engineers use personal computing for creating models, collecting and analyzing data, and controlling experimental processes.*

End users are simply defined as people who use computing/information systems technology for the basic functions of the organization. End users in different functions, however, have varying needs.

All end users need office support tools. These usually include word processing for memos and simple spreadsheets for budgets and expense calculations. Office support may also include electronic mail and access to company directories, certain general data bases, bulletin boards, and conferencing systems.

Administrative end users, those in accounting, personnel, or in forms processing applications, also need specialized tools to process their particular tasks. These include access to central company files that pertain to their applications, customized CRT screen forms, and communication with other groups involved in their process. Communications needs are usually high; in frequency, in volume, and in geographic dispersion. Administrative end users are usually involved in all the types of personal computing mentioned above.

Personal computing in factory applications usually involves communications between various workstations and between the workstations and the factory administrative areas, such as production control and inventory storage areas. Successful factory personal computing applications must also solve problems of interaction between automated machines that talk different languages and have different communications protocols.

Communications are also crucial in field office applications, whether those field offices are for sales, administrative, or work site management. Here the communications focus on field-to-home-office interactions and between individual workers or salespeople and the field office. Communications between field offices is often difficult to implement because such communication requires that a network be established; field-to-home-office communication can use simpler star networks or personal computer-to-host configurations. Field office applications often also require the use of portable computing for use by people working away from the office. Communications between customers and field offices is also increasing, both for order processing and for inquiries against the status of an order or project.

Laboratory scientists and engineers use personal computing to create models that can be analyzed more economically than constructing real-world experiments. In addition, personal computing can be used to collect data from measurement instrumentation and for analyzing the data collected. Laboratory end users can also use personal computing to control experimental processes by collecting data, comparing those data against expectations, and changing the conditions of the process in accordance with a predetermined program.

End-user development methodologies

8. *Rather than submit to the temptation to have no development discipline, end-user developers should use these approaches:*
    a. *Use prototyping as the development methodology.*
    b. *Plan for supportability as a primary attribute of the program/system.*

Supportability in end-user software can best be achieved by:

- Constructing the software with a defined structure.
- Documenting heavily within the software.
- Using information systems/PCIC experts to review the software at significant steps in the construction.

Most software is built in accordance with a development process often called the software development life cycle. A life cycle is methodology, a process that helps managers control development; assures a minimum of interaction between developers, managers, and end users; and forms the basis for a general software quality program.

The traditional systems development life-cycle model is often called the "waterfall model" because the process moves in only one direction. See Figure 7.2 for a simplified illustration of the model. The process begins with an investigation, and proceeds through design, system construction, testing, implementation, and finally support and maintenance.

This model can be used for end-user systems development projects but rarely is because of its formality. The waterfall model structures the communication between developers, managers, and users, but in end-user computing, these three roles are invested in one person. Close communication is simple, and the formality of the model becomes confining.

The obvious temptation is to follow no process, but simply to dive into the work with minimum organization and planning, filling in holes as they appear. This, of course, can cause several problems: the development task may take far longer than first estimated as new situations which require rework are discovered late in the development. Some problems will not be found in the development period at all and will be discovered only in the operation of the software. Further, the software may be much more difficult to support, since the original program is likely to be a "patch work," not following an understandable, logical structure. Our memories

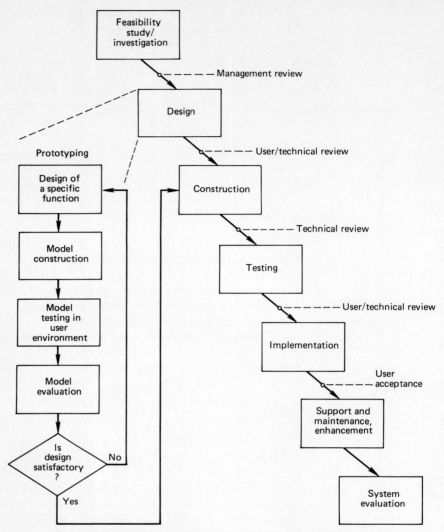

Figure 7.2 Traditional systems development life-cycle model.

fade rapidly, and when we make modifications, even to our own programs, long after the programs were written, we are likely to cause as many problems as we correct.

Rather than submit to the temptation to have no development discipline, I suggest that all end-user software use this approach:

Use prototyping as the development methodology. A prototype is a model of the final software, something that illustrates certain key functions but which is not yet complete. Several prototypes may be constructed to display and test various portions of the software. The advantage of prototypes is that they can actually be used and tested to find areas in which the design or construction is incomplete or inadequate.

Prototyping is really part of the design step. A final, well-constructed, well-tested version is almost always appropriate. Prototypes usually should not be placed in operation for any length of time because they generally are inefficient to operate, unreliable, and costly to support and maintain.

Plan for supportability as a primary attribute of the software. Some end users want their programs to exhibit exotic functionality, contain lots of "bells and whistles." Other end users strive for high performance, to make their programs operate more rapidly than comparable programs.

There is nothing wrong with these goals, but I strongly recommend that the primary goal be supportability, the ability to use and modify the software in the "real," rapidly changing world. Given that supportability is achieved, other appropriate attributes can also be built into the software.

Supportability in end-user software can best be achieved by:

- Constructing the software with a defined structure. The exact type of structure should be chosen by the developer to meet the needs of the specific application; what is important is that there be an explicit structure, that the structure be described, and that the structure be followed consistently. Structure increases supportability because it is easier for the maintenance person to locate the portions of the software that require modification and to minimize the impact of the modification on other portions of the software. It is critical that modifications be implemented in the same structure as that used in the development in order to maintain consistency for future modifications.

- Documenting heavily within the software. Documentation must, of course, accurately represent the code and data in the software. Documentation that is separate from the software tends to become obsolete, while comments within the software itself are usually kept accurate.

- Some external documentation is useful, especially for complex software or for software developed over long time periods. One effective, yet simple technique is to record all project events and decisions in a "lab book," a hard-bound book of blank, lined, usually numbered pages. This book becomes a diary for the project, a chronology that can be used to reconstruct significant events. Besides, in later stages of the project, these books make fascinating, often embarrassing reading.

- Using information systems/PCIC experts to review the software at significant steps in the construction. End-users should take advantage of the technical expertise in the company by inviting specific experts in either the application or in the hardware/software being used to review the end-user software. These reviews should be made at various stages in the development, but always in time to allow easy implementation of the suggestions. As these reviews can bruise even the most sturdy egos, everyone should approach them with appropriate expectations. The "experts" should remember that they are reviewing end-user software, not the work of a software professional. The end users, however, should sincerely appreciate the constructive comments of the experts and not enter the review with preset defensiveness.

Accuracy of end-user software

9. *Since it is usually impossible to distinguish at sight between "official" and "personal" computer-produced reports, these suggestions should be considered:*
   a. *Use special paper for official reports.*
   b. *Adopt a reader-beware attitude for* **all** *computer-produced reports.*
   c. *Use "official" data whenever possible.*
   d. *Learn and implement techniques for improving report data integrity.*

Until the advent of personal computing, computer-produced reports, although not always accurate, were at least "official;" they were produced from "official" company data by "official" company systems. Although perhaps inaccurate, they were at least consistent with other reports used in the company.

Now, of course, it is impossible to distinguish at sight between "official" and "personal" computer-produced reports. These suggestions should be considered:

Use special paper for official reports. This suggestion was offered in previous guidelines and merely gives readers the ability to distinguish visually between "official" and "unofficial" reports. Use of special paper, however, is only an aid to wary readers; readers are still obligated to examine all reports intelligently, and end-user developers are still obligated to exercise practices that improve accuracy.

Adopt a reader-beware attitude for *all* computer-produced reports. Readers should examine *all* reports for reasonableness and consistency. Readers should:

- Test at least samples of the data on the reports to verify that suggestions for report integrity, shown below, have been followed.
- Cross-check data with other reports.
- Duplicate some of the computations manually.
- Rearrange samples of the data into different sequences to see if the data still seem logical and consistent.
- Use approximations to verify that the data in the report are in the "ballpark."
- Ask developers to specifically state their assumptions and the rules and algorithms (formulai) used in the reports.
- Especially if the report comes from an automated spreadsheet, try different data values in the spreadsheet and verify that the results change in the manner expected.
- Explore the details of the highest and lowest values on the report to verify their accuracy; determine especially the effect that these extremes have on any statistical calculations shown.
- Ask developers to describe specifically the data bases used, the organizational groups included, and the time periods covered by that data. Even when official data sources are used, reconstruct samples of the data on the report to confirm that the version used by the developer coincides with reader expectations. Ask specifically about any omissions or inclusions from the "standard" data base.
- Insist that all reports be dated; different versions of the same report may require both date and time stamping.
- Insist that detail backup be available for all data on the reports.
- Test the reasonableness of numbers by translating them into the physical items they represent. For example, translate salaries into people, occupancy costs into floor space, and inventory costs into number of units.

End-user programmers should use "official" data whenever possible. End users should avoid developing and maintaining separate, special files. If the end users do not need all the fields on the official data bases, processes must be developed to extract the needed fields.

Having used official data sources, the end-user should state both the name and date of the official file used so that the readers can, if they wish, confirm data on the report by going back to the official sources. If, for some reason, the developers must use private data, they should carefully state, on the report, the data used, how they differ from official sources, and, if possible, should reconcile the private data to the official data.

End-user developers (and readers) should learn and implement techniques for improving report data integrity. These techniques include:

- Cross-footing (adding both column and row summaries).
- Use of control totals on files and reports; use of item counts, value totals, and "hash" totals for control.
- Use of consistent formats and units of measure (e.g., all data on the reports shown in thousands, all measures in metric, all volumes in liters, etc.).
- Accurate labeling of report rows and columns.
- Proper footnoting of specific elements which are inconsistent with the other data on the report.
- Use of percentages and proportions as well as raw data to verify the reasonableness of the data.
- Comparison of this report to the same reports for different time periods or for other organizations to see that differences are reasonable.

CHECKLIST

Guideline 7.1
End-User Responsibilities in Developing End-User Systems

	YES	NO	N/A

1. Has end-using computing been defined in terms of these levels and in this sequence?
   a. Using programs written specifically for the application task being performed
   b. Using flexible but limited function program packages (products)
   c. Writing individual programs to accomplish personal tasks
   d. Modifying preprogrammed systems to suit their specific needs
   e. Designing, writing, and implementing a full system, meeting the specific needs of a specific end user

2. Are people working on the different levels of end-using computing based on a variety of factors such as these?
   a. The technical aptitude of the end users
   b. The willingness of end users or managers to spend the time apart from their normal job to learn or implement personal computing technology
   c. How much this application will be used
   d. Whether or not the system will be used independent of its initial author

3. Have all end users been given office support personal computing tools?

4. Have administrative end users been given specialized personal computing tools and applications including access to central company files, customized CRT screen forms, and communication with other groups?

5. Have factory applications of personal computing included communications and interfaces between automated machines that talk different languages and have different communications protocols?

6. Have communications been considered in field office applications?

   Is the requirement for portability also considered?

(Continues)

291

7. Are laboratory scientists and engineers given the opportunity to use personal computing for creating models, collecting and analyzing data, and controlling experimental processes?

8. Are end users encouraged to use these types of development disciplines?
   a. Use of prototyping as the development methodology
   b. Planning for supportability as a primary attribute of the program/system

9. Is supportability in end-user software being achieved by these methods?
   a. Constructing the software with a defined structure
   b. Documenting heavily within the software
   c. Using information systems/PCIC experts to review the software at significant steps in the construction

10. Are the following methods used to distinguish "official" computer-produced reports from "personal" computer-produced reports?
    a. Use special paper for official reports
    b. Adopt a reader-beware attitude for *all* computer-produced reports
    c. Use the same "official" data whenever possible in both personal and official reports
    d. Learn and implement techniques for improving report data integrity in all reports

Guideline 7.2: Tools to Facilitate End-User Systems Development

Types of Tools

1. *End-user development tools may be grouped into these categories, listed from easiest to use to most sophisticated:*
   a. *Modifiable application packages*
   b. *Data base inquiry software*
   c. *Specialized software*
   d. *Application generators*
   e. *"Simple" programming languages*
   f. *Sophisticated programming languages*
2. *End users should use the system highest on the list in guideline 1, the tool that is easiest to use.*
3. *The complexity of data bases is usually inversely proportional to the complexity of the development tools.*
4. *Read-only data bases reduce controls needed on end-user systems, but "reader-beware" precautions are still appropriate.*
5. *If the application is likely to be used on hardware other than that on which it is developed, the end-user developer should seek advice from the PCIC on compatibility guidelines.*

The basic development tool of the computer professional has long been the computer language. The first programmers wrote in "machine language," actually communicating with the hardware in its native dialect of 1's and 0's. Then came assembly language, which buffered the programmer from some of the hardware details. Soon after came "higher-level" languages and their related compilers, languages that were further from the hardware and closer to the natural language of the user/programmer. Then came operating systems, which provided utilities and services to the developer, relieving programmers of many of the details involved in system development and operation.

All of these, languages, compilers, and operating systems, are development tools, and all of these are also available to the end-user software writer. Also available, however, are tools specifically appropriate for end users, although these tools are often also used by computer professionals. End-user tools, however, are specifically designed for use by relatively unsophisticated people. The price for this friendliness, however, is usually limited performance or capability.

End-user development tools may ge grouped into these categories, listed from easiest to use to most sophisticated:

- Modifiable application packages
- Data base inquiry software
- Specialized software
- Application generators
- "Simple" programming languages
- Sophisticated programming languages

"Easiest to use" usually implies increased automation and maximum number of fixed-function features; the software assumes the maximum amount to be about what the users want. Most sophisticated software generally gives the user great flexibility, with minimum inherent defaults or fixed functions. Most powerful languages, however, allow developers to customize their tools so that each developer has a set of default functions unique to the developer's individual needs and environment; in fact, the developer could build several tools from the same language, each customized for particular tasks.

Tools are also categorized by "procedural" versus "nonprocedural" functions. Nonprocedural tools are usually more oriented to the needs of the users, allowing the developers to work in their natural language and in the jargon and logic of the application; the developer need not translate the application needs into the "procedures" required by the computer (hence, nonprocedural).

Procedural tools are those which developers use, in which the sequence of actions written in the tool defines the sequence in which they occur in the computer. Most well-known computer languages, such as BASIC, FORTRAN, and COBOL, are procedural, since the sequence of instructions as eventually executed by the computer follows exactly the sequence (procedure) written in the original program (although instructions can be executed out of sequence through the use of "branch" or "go to" routines).

Clearly, a developer must know more about the underlying computer technology in order to use procedural tools. Information systems are procedural combinations of programs built with either procedural or nonprocedural tools. Information systems can also contain procedures performed manually.

While the taxonomy defined above refers mostly to the way the developers' needs are translated into computer language, the categories also affect the way data are organized and used. Data structures, as described in Chapter 5, may be simple or extremely complex. In general, simple structures must be used in the way preconceived by their designer, while more complex structures are amenable to the changing needs of various users. Complex structures are, of course, more difficult to establish and manage. End-user programmers must, therefore, be appropriately knowledgeable themselves and must use appropriate programming packages, usually called "data base management systems."

In addition, end-user applications can be greatly simplified if the responsibility for data base update and maintenance is removed from the end-user application and segregated to applications built for the specific data maintenance functions. These simplified applications use data bases on a "read-only" basis. Since such applications cannot create problems for other users of the data base, controls over these read-only applications can be reduced significantly, limited mainly to concerns for security and privacy. Even with read-only applications, however, the "reader-beware" precautions described in Guideline 7.1 are appropriate, since the end user can read selective extracts and incorrect summaries.

End users usually develop their software on the same hardware on which the system will be operated. If, however, the application is likely to be used by other people on other hardware, or if the application is likely to be used after the currently used hardware is replaced, the developer must be concerned with compatibility issues and should request guidance from the PCIC or other appropriate information system professionals.

When using personal computing, the goal of most end users is to accomplish their business task in the most effective and productive manner. Therefore, end users should use the system highest on the list above, the tool that is easiest to use. These tools are listed in Figure 7.3

Modifiable application packages

6. *End users should minimize changes to complete application packages in order to get maximum leverage from the vendors' systems.*
7. *For complete applications packages, the end user retains responsibility for op-*

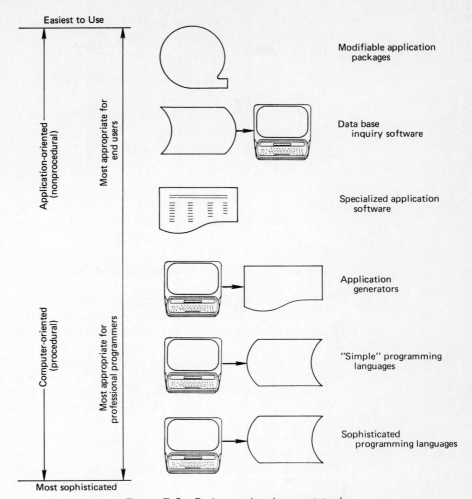

Figure 7.3   End-user development tools.

erational/user documentation and for documenting any modifications made to the vendor's basic package.

These are systems that completely perform a given application. Examples include payroll, inventory control, statistical analysis, purchasing, order processing, and so on. Often, vendors will offer a fully integrated family of applications that can be implemented all at once or in pieces. Examples might be a complete general accounting family, complete material control systems, and so on.

The application usually includes everything needed, including programs, data structures, and documentation. All the end-user needs add is the specific data and the people needed to operate the system. At this, the easiest level of end-user development, the vendor takes responsibility for virtually all aspects of the information systems task, data as well as programs. The end user must, however, retain responsibility for operational/user documentation and for documenting any modifications made to the vendor's basic package. Often, vendors provide sample operational/user documentation, and the end users can simply tailor the samples to suit their specific environment.

In practice, however, the user usually has some options; here are the options usually allowed, in order of significance. The first options are relatively benign;

changes made further in the list require more control and consulting with both the vendor and with in-house information systems experts. Obviously, end users should minimize changes in order to get the maximum leverage from the vendors' systems.

- Modifying operating/user documentation
- Modifying report formats
- Modifying input form/input screen formats
- Modifying report content
- Modifying definition of data fields
- Modifying programs at predefined places (''user exits'')
- Modifying input/processing edits
- Modifying content/structure of data base
- Modifying content of input forms/screens
- Modifying processing logic of the system

Data base inquiry software (also called report generators)

> 8. *When using inquiry packages, the end user is responsible for the precautions shown in Guideline 7.1 for report integrity, for documenting the timing and logic of the inquiry, and for the uses and distribution of the reports.*

In these applications, the developer uses a specialized software package to write specific reports from read-only data bases. The developer must know the details of the data base, although even this responsibility is usually softened through the use of specialized data dictionary software in conjunction with the inquiry package.

Specific reports are created by following the prompting given by the inquiry packages. Instructions are given to the users in their own language, often by allowing the user merely to give the software an example of what is wanted.

Some report-generating systems also allow users to modify the packages to attain capabilities not inherent in the package. When this is done, the end-user developer must assume all the responsibilities described above under ''Modifiable application packages.'' In any case, the end user is responsible for the precautions shown in Guideline 7.1 for report integrity. The end user, of course, is also responsible for documenting the timing and logic of the inquiry and for the uses and distribution of the reports.

Specialized software

> 9. *When using ''specialized software,'' end-user developers are responsible for tasks mentioned above under ''inquiry software,'' and are also responsible for locating the data to be placed in these systems and for entering them accurately into the system. It is also critical to document the assumptions and formulas used in the specific application of this package. If ''programming'' is done through the use of ''macros'' or ''logic statements,'' the user developer must take responsibility for the full scope of documentation and control issues.*

Often these software tools are computer metaphors of well-known manual processes. Spreadsheet systems are the most common of these packages, but others include data base systems, decision analysis and modeling tools, and graphics software. Even some word processing systems might be included in this category when the tools are used as part of a system rather than simply as a personal tool.

Most of these systems are extremely useful when used in their simplest form.

Users are responsible for tasks mentioned under "inquiry software" above, but significantly, users are also responsible for locating the data to be placed in these systems and for entering them accurately into the system. Most of these tools have weak input edits, so that data integrity is completely the responsibility of the data-entry person. It is also critical to document the assumptions and formulas used in each application, both for reader understanding and for making modifications later.

Some vendors offer applications packages called "templates," which turn one of these specialized packages into modifiable application software. These templates allow user development with only the concerns described above. On the other hand, some specialized packages also allow relatively sophisticated programming within the package metaphor through the use of "macros" or "logic statements." Using these tools greatly increases the power of the system but makes the user developer responsible for the full scope of documentation and control issues.

Application generators

10. When using application generators, the developer has full responsibility for all aspects of the information sysems task, data, programming logic, and documentation, except for the structure of the programs themselves.

These systems are the point at which professional programming and end-user systems development overlap; either group can use these tools effectively. Application generators are essentially complete programming languages, sometimes called fourth-generation languages, either tailored for specific applications or which can be applied to any application but make many decisions for the developer. The generator makes assumptions on how systems should be structured and extensively use preprogrammed libraries of subroutines for standard functions. These programming tools are often related to data base tools such as dictionaries, so that entire families of applications can be developed consistently.

An application generator performs the following tasks:

- Allows rapid construction of programs, thereby encouraging use of prototyping methodologies.
- Removes the need to learn a computer language. Tasks are specified by completing forms and answering computer-generated questions.
- Eliminates many language syntax, grammar, and punctuation errors.
- Standardizes structure, increasing supportability.
- Increases compatibility between applications.
- Increases potential for standard modules which can be reused in many applications.
- If the tool is available on several different computers, increases portability of applications. Programs can be transported between those computers simply by recompiling the high-level source instructions.
- If the tool produces, as an intermediate output, procedural language statements, professional programmers may alter the procedural code to accomplish functions not possible in the application generator. In addition, this procedural code can provide examples for use in programmer training and for use as subroutines in other applications.

When using application generators, the developer has full responsibility for all aspects of the information systems task, data, programming logic, and documentation. The developer is still, however, buffered from many of the details of hardware and systems software, and the actual structure of the user software is defined by the applications generator.

"Simple" programming languages

11. *When using simple languages, developers must assume full information systems responsibilities for their software, with the possible exception of some hardware and operating system considerations. Developers take full responsibility for proper use of language, proper verbs, labels, syntax, and punctuation, and for program and data structures.*

The word "simple" is placed in quotes because no programming language is truly simple. What I am calling simple programming languages, however, are those that can be learned quickly and which are relative hierarchical in their complexity. A person can do simple things quickly, using easily learned subsets of the language, delaying learning more sophisticated aspects until they are needed. BASIC and FORTRAN are common "simple" languages.

At this point, the end user is working as a programmer. Simple languages usually have sufficient power to do any task, although sometimes inefficiently; simple languages also have enough power to create any possible problem; therefore, developers must assume full information systems responsibilities for this software, with the possible exception that the developer may be buffered from some hardware and operating system considerations. Developers must take full responsibility for proper use of language, proper verbs, labels, syntax, and punctuation and take complete responsibility for program and data structure. In fact, because of the simplicity and limitations of these languages, it may be difficult to create really good, supportable data and program structures.

Sophisticated programming languages

12. *End users should not use sophisticated programming languages.*
13. *Sophisticated programmers may act as a special class of end users by using personal computing technology to improve their work.*

Sophisticated programming languages are those that give the programmer full control over the computer environment, including all portions of the computer and its peripherals, communications, data, and operating systems. Sophisticated languages give programmers control and flexibility at the cost of extreme complexity. Most computers, for example, have an assembly language that allows programmers very careful control, at the price of the need to focus on every detail of logical and physical systems operation. Languages that are somewhat less machine specific include Pascal and C. In artificial intelligence environments, programmers often use LISP or PROLOG.

Sophisticated programming languages are used when some aspect of hardware use is of prime importance. For example, most compilers are written in a sophisticated language so that the compiler will use minimum computer memory and perform rapidly. Games are usually written in assembly language to maximize the speed of the program while using a minimum amount of memory to keep the costs of the game hardware low.

End users should not use sophisticated programming languages. Any who do use them are either acting as professional programmers, not as end users, or are likely to use the language poorly. End users, even if they know the rudiments of a sophisticated language, will be more productive in accomplishing their basic task by using one of the simpler methodologies mentioned above; furthermore, the simpler tools will usually generate code that uses computer resources more efficiently than the sophisticated code that can be generated by most end users.

Anyone using sophisticated languages (even professional programmers) should use many of the program development tools available. These include program skeletons, sometimes called templates, which offer predefined, pretested structure for many applications. Whenever possible, programmers should reuse already written and tested subroutines.

Sophisticated programmers may act as a special class of end-users by using personal computing technology to improve their work. Personal computing tools available to professional programmers include source program text editors, precompilers, test-data generators, and program version managers. Programmers can also use personal computing to measure their work by performing tasks such as counting lines of code. Entire applications, called computer-assisted software environments (CASE), are available to serve the professional programmer as an end user.

CHECKLIST

Guideline 7.2
Tools to Facilitate End-User Systems Development

	YES	NO	N/A
1. Have end-user development tools been grouped into the following categories, listed from easiest to use to most sophisticated? a. Modifiable application packages b. Data base inquiry software c. Specialized software d. Application generators e. "Simple" programming languages f. Sophisticated programming languages			
2. Do end users follow the methodology highest on the list above, the tool that is easiest to use?			
3. Is the data base methodology considered separately from the development methodology? (The complexity of data bases is usually inversely proportional to the complexity of the development tools.)			
4. While read-only data bases reduce controls needed on end-user systems, are "reader-beware" precautions still implemented?			
5. If the application is likely to be used on hardware other than that on which it is developed, has the end-user developer obtained advice on compatibility guidelines from the PCIC?			
6. Do end users minimize changes to complete application packages in order to get the maximum leverage from the vendors' systems?			
7. For complete applications packages, does the end user retain responsibility for operational/user documentation and for documenting any modifications made to the vendor's basic package?			
8. When using inquiry packages, is the end user held responsible for the precautions shown in Guideline 7.1 for report integrity, for documenting the timing and logic of the inquiry, and for the uses and distribution of the reports?			

(Continues)

301

9. When using "specialized software," are end-user developers held responsible for tasks mentioned above under "Inquiry Systems," and are end users also held responsible for locating the data to be placed in these systems and for entering them accurately into the system?

10. Have the assumptions and formulas used in the specific application of this package been documented?

11. If "programming" is done through the use of "macros" or "logic statements," has the user developer taken responsibility for the full scope of documentation and control issues?

12. When using application generators, has the developer taken full responsibility for all aspects of the information systems task, data, programming logic, and documentation, except for the structure of the programs themselves?

13. When using simple languages, have developers assumed full information systems responsibilities for their software, with the possible exception of some hardware and operating system considerations?

14. Do developers take full responsibility for proper use of language, proper verbs, labels, syntax, and punctuation, and for program and data structures?

15. Do end users use sophisticated programming languages? (It is better if they do not.)

16. Are professional programmers using personal computing technology to improve their work, thus acting as a special class of end users?

Guideline 7.3: Role of the PCIC in End-User Systems Development

General

1. *The role of the PCIC in end-user systems development is essentially a specific case under the general policies described in Guidelines 2.3 and 2.4.*
2. *Two major tools available to the PCIC for influencing end-user developers are training and guidelines.*

The role of the Personal Computing Information Center (PCIC) in end-user systems development is essentially a specific case under the general policies described in Guidelines 2.3 and 2.4. End-user systems development affects many aspects of a company's information systems function; therefore, in many companies, some of the PCIC functions suggested in this guideline will appropriately belong to other groups in the company's information systems department.

Goals

The PCIC should set policies and guidelines and offer services to accomplish these goals with specific regard to end-user systems development:

- Help end users develop systems that increase benefits to company customers and increase the value of company assets.
- Help end users, through the development of personal computing systems, be more innovative and productive in their primary business functions.
- Integrate the work of all end-user developers with the overall information systems efforts of the company.
- Help end users benefit to the maximum extent possible from the experiences of others in the company.
- Protect company data and systems assets from accidental or deliberate damage from end-user systems development.

These goals are stated in what I consider to be an appropriate priority sequence; however, the priority is not absolute and might appropriately be changed in specific situations. For example, I do not believe that rigid rules and controls need be set to provide absolute security and privacy, since most end-user developers will exercise reasonable self-imposed restraints. However, individual innovation should not be allowed to excuse a security abuse committed by an aberrant employee.

Note, too, that efficiency is not set as a goal. Rarely will end-user computing lower information systems costs or even be the least expensive information systems alternative. End-user computing must be justified in terms of effectiveness, innovation, and productivity, not in terms of absolute costs.

Two major tools available to the PCIC for influencing end-user developers are training and guidelines. Both these subjects are covered extensively in Chapter 2, but there may be special applications to accommodate end-user systems development. For example, the PCIC can influence the tools used by the end-user developers by offering training only on recommended tools and methods. Similarly, the PCIC can offer education (as opposed to training) on the concepts and philosophies underlying the role of end-user systems development. Training can also be offered on design and architectural issues as well as on the details of specific packages and tools.

Guidelines can be published as means of communicating to end-user developers what others in the company have learned. Standards and policies can increase the rigidity of the guidelines and are appropriate in those areas in which the work of an end-user developer may affect other people. For example, violating a guideline by using a nonrecommended software tool may only increase the developers' costs. However, a rigid policy may be appropriate to keep developers from writing to company-wide data bases without appropriate approvals.

Helping end users develop systems that increase benefits to company customers and increase the value of company assets

These are some of the specific techniques that the PCIC can use to help end-user developers. The PCIC can:

3. *Advise both end users and their managers on appropriate applications for end-user systems development.*

4. *Suggest and evaluate alternatives.*

5. *Help end users justify their project to management.*

6. *Assure that end-user developers use data base and communications assets correctly with minimum duplication and corruption.*

7. *Inform end-user developers about the limitations of company-wide data and systems and offer suggestions as to how end-user applications might overcome these limitations.*

The PCIC can advise both end users and their managers on appropriate applications for end-user systems development. The PCIC can also suggest alternatives, estimating the relative costs and benefits of each alternative. When appropriate, the PCIC can help end users justify their project to skeptical management.

The PCIC can also guide end-user developers toward increasing the value of other information assets. The assets that can be most affected by end users are the company-wide data bases and company-wide communications networks; PCIC advice can assure that end-user developers use these assets correctly, not duplicating them and not corrupting them with inaccurate, inconsistent data. End-user developers can also benefit from knowing the limitations of company-wide data and systems, with the PCIC offering suggestions as to how end-user applications might overcome these limitations.

Helping end users, through the development of personal computing systems, be more innovative and productive in their primary business functions

8. *Suggest specific applications that are not now being approached by others in the company and in which the developer can therefore make unique contributions.*

9. *Encourage end-user developers toward business and organizational innovation, not clever use of computers with limited business applications.*

10. *Help developers and their managers measure and evaluate the success of end-user applications from business, not technical viewpoints.*

11. *Attend application walkthroughs and conduct application reviews and inspections.*

As with the previous goal, the PCIC can offer both end-user developers and their managers with advice and justification about appropriate end-user applications and alternatives. In support of this goal, the PCIC might also suggest specific applications which are not now being approached by others in the company and in which the developer can therefore make unique contributions.

The PCIC should encourage end-user developers toward business and organizational innovation, not clever use of computers with limited business application. Often, the best ways of communicating these concepts is by highlighting the successful experiences of others in the company. The PCIC can also help developers and their managers measure and evaluate the success of end-user applications from business, not technical viewpoints.

Often, the PCIC can keep end users focused on the business problem by providing end users with strong technical support so that the end users do not feel that they must become technical experts themselves. This support can be provided when PCIC consultants attend application walkthroughs and conduct application reviews and inspections.

Integrating the work of all end-user developers with the overall information systems efforts of the company

12. *Issue guidelines recommending compatible hardware and software.*
13. *Encourage the use of consistent architectures for end-user-developed systems.*
14. *Encourage the use of standard company codes.*
15. *Encourage the use and maintenance of official company data dictionaries and directories, especially when using communications networks.*
16. *Offer end-user developers prewritten subroutines or full packages that will link user systems to company networks.*

The emphasis here should be on the way end-user applications work with both the applications developed by the information systems department and those developed by other end users. One major way of accomplishing this is by issuing guidelines (such as the "Recommended Lists" described in Part I) recommending compatible hardware and software.

Coordination can also be achieved through the use of consistent architectures for end-user-developed systems. The architectures should focus on the way data are used and stored and in the ways in which controls and data are communicated among applications. Consistent architectures are especially important in factory applications, where data and programs are communicated between automated tools and information systems.

Compatibility is also improved by the use of standard company codes rather than having developers invent their own. The PCIC can make these codes available to the developers and also, in systems reviews, verify that these codes are being used when appropriate. As discussed in Chapter 6, one major coordinating function when using communication networks is the use and maintenance of official company data dictionaries and directories.

Control of interfaces to company communications network and services can be improved by offering end-user developers prewritten subroutines or full packages that will link user systems to company networks. These programs buffer the users from the complexities of communications protocols and also may provide the gateway functions that allow data to be transmitted and received among applications developed by individual end users.

**Helping end users benefit to the maximum extent possible
from the experiences of others in the company**

17. *Create group learning, using techniques discussed in Chapter 2, with special
    emphasis on topics of interest to end-user system developers. Important issues
    to share include:*
    a. *Use of development tools*
    b. *Evaluation of specific vendors*
    c. *Management of development projects*
    d. *System testing considerations*
    e. *Use of assistants in systems operation*
    f. *Use of the system by others*
    g. *System maintenance and enhancement*

As discussed in Chapter 2, a major function of the PCIC with regard to general personal computing is the creation of group learning, allowing all members of the company's personal computing community to benefit from individual experiences. This can be accomplished on a broad basis through guidelines, newsletters, contributed libraries, and users groups, and on an individual basis through technical advice and by attending reviews and walkthroughs.

This sharing is particularly appropriate for end-user system developers, since they are generally working in unfamiliar technical territories. End-user developers can learn both from other end users and from professional information systems people, and the PCIC should strive to use both sources for advise, as appropriate.

Here are a few issues, important to end-user systems development in which experience sharing can help.

- Development tools that have been used successfully (or tools that should be avoided or used with caution) for specific situations.
- Evaluation of specific vendors and their products.
- Management of development projects: estimating time and costs.
- System testing considerations.
- Training others to assist in the operation of personal systems. In particular, how to use administrative or paraprofessional assistance in entering data, performing routine operations tasks, and performing audit and control functions.
- Distributing the system for use by others in the company.
- System maintenance and enhancement techniques.

**Protecting Company Data and Systems Assets
from Accidental or Deliberate Damage from End-User
Systems Development**

18. *Publish security and privacy guidelines.*
19. *Help end users seek and correct security and privacy violations, whether accidental or deliberate. Conduct audits and reviews to verify that violations are not occurring.*
20. *Provide end-user developers with training to help them do their work in appropriate ways.*
21. *Help end-user developers to implement adequate operational logs to show how, when, and by whom the systems are being used to verify that the systems are not creating violations.*

22. *Help developers make their work understandable to others so that the system can continue in use even if the developer leaves the company.*

23. *In case someone does leave behind a poorly documented and constructed system, furnish the user managers with technical assistance that will permit the use of the application after the developer leaves the company.*

As noted above and in previous chapters, security and privacy guidelines should be published by the PCIC so that both users and system developers know what proper conduct is expected of them. However, users and developers should be considered innocent until proven guilty, and controls that interfere with open development and use of systems should not be implemented unless problems have become rampant. Even then, I suggest that the problem be considered more as a personnel problem than as a technical issue. On the other hand, systems should not be so lax that undue temptation is created, and all systems should seek to find and correct accidental security and privacy violations.

Security and privacy issues are discussed in Chapter 3; end-user system development provides for greater potential damage than does mere system use; the PCIC should provide end-user developers with training to help them do their work in appropriate ways. Audits and reviews should focus on these applications to verify that accidental violations are avoided, and if deliberate violations are discovered, these applications, rightfully or not, become prime suspects. For their own protection, end-user developers should therefore have adequate operational logs to show how, when, and by whom the systems are being used.

One subtle but important class of "damage," unique to end-user-developed systems, may be incurred when the developer leaves the company. The company can keep the system, but the software may be useless without the private knowledge kept by the developer. The PCIC can help mitigate this problem in two ways: first, by working with developers, in general, so that their work is reasonably well documented and can be understood by others, and second, in case someone does leave behind a poorly documented and constructed system, it can furnish the user managers with technical assistance in "deciphering" and perhaps enhancing the application, thus permitting its continued use by the company.

CHECKLIST

Guideline 7.3
Role of the PCIC in End-User Systems Development

	YES	NO	N/A

1. Is the role of the PCIC in end-user systems development considered a specific case under the general policies described in Guidelines 2.3 and 2.4?

2. Are training and guidelines two major tools made available to the PCIC for influencing end-user developers?

3. Does the PCIC advise both end users and their managers on appropriate applications for end-user systems development?

4. Does the PCIC suggest and evaluate hardware and software alternatives?

5. Does the PCIC help end users justify their projects to management?

6. Does the PCIC assure that end-user developers use data base and communications assets correctly with minimum duplication and corruption?

7. Does the PCIC inform end-user developers about the limitations of company-wide data and systems and offer suggestions as to how end-user applications might overcome these limitations?

8. Does the PCIC suggest specific applications that are not now being approached by others in the company in which the developer can therefore make unique contributions?

9. Does the PCIC encourage end-user developers toward business and organizational innovation, not clever use of computers with limited business application?

9. Does the PCIC help developers and their managers measure and evaluate the success of end-user applications from business, not technical viewpoints?

10. Does the PCIC attend application walkthroughs and conduct application reviews and inspections?

(Continues)

309

11. Does the PCIC issue guidelines recommending compatible hardware and software?

12. Does the PCIC encourage the use of consistent architectures for end-user-developed systems?

13. Does the PCIC encourage the use of standard company codes?

14. Does the PCIC encourage the use and maintenance of official company data dictionaries and directories, especially when using communications networks?

15. Does the PCIC offer end-user developers prewritten subroutines or full packages that will link user systems to company networks?

16. Does the PCIC create group learning, using techniques discussed in Chapter 2, with special emphasis on topics of interest to end-user system developers?

17. Are these important issues shared among end-user systems developers?
    a. Use of development tools
    b. Evaluation of specific vendors
    c. Management of development projects
    d. System testing considerations
    e. Use of assistants in systems operation
    f. Use of the system by others
    g. System maintenance and enhancement

18. Does the PCIC publish security and privacy guidelines?

19. Does the PCIC help end users seek and correct security and privacy violations, whether accidental or deliberate?

20. Does the PCIC conduct audits and reviews to verify that violations are not occurring?

21. Does the PCIC provide end-user developers with training to help them do their work in appropriate ways?

22. Does the PCIC help end-user developers to implement adequate operational logs to show how, when, and by whom the systems are being used to verify that the systems are not creating violations?

	YES	NO	N/A

23. Does the PCIC help developers make their work understandable to others so that the system can continue in use even if the developer leaves the company?

24. In case someone does leave behind a poorly documented and constructed system, does the PCIC furnish the user managers with technical assistance that will permit the use of the application after the developer leaves the company?

REFERENCES

JOHN CONNELL and LINDA BRICE, "Rapid Prototyping," *Datamation,* August 15, 1984, p. 93.

End User Microcomputing, A Federal Survey Report and Resource Guide, Information Resources Management Service, U.S. General Services Administration, May 1986.

JAMES E. FAWCETTE, "All You Need to Learn about Programming," *Personal Computing,* December 1984, p. 319.

WILLIAM R. FENNEY, "Systems Analysis and Small Computers," *Creative Computing,* November 1980, p. 43.

JOHN C. HENDERSON and MICHAEL E. TREACY, *Managing End User Computing,* CISR WP No. 114, Center for Information Systems Research, Massachusetts Institute of Technology, Cambridge, Mass., May 1984.

HENRY LEDGARD, "Programmers: The Amateur vs. the Professional," *Abacus,* Vol. 2, No. 4, 1985, p. 29.

I. STEVEN KERNS, "What End Users Don't Know May Hurt You," *Computerworld,* October 8, 1984, p. ID/31.

STEPHEN KIMMEL, "Don't Write That Program," *Creative Computing,* August 1980, p. 64.

JAMES MARTIN, *Application Development without Programmers,* Prentice-Hall, Inc., Englewood-Cliffs, N.J., 1982.

PIETER MIMNO, "Power to Users," *Computerworld,* April 8, 1985, p. ID/19.

STEPHEN L. PRIEST and WILLIAM A. NORKO, JR., "Information Resources in User Hands: When, Where, and How Much," *Computerworld,* October 8, 1984, p. ID/45.

H. RICE and D. RAKER, "So You Want to Buy a Micro CAD System?" *Manufacturing Systems,* April 1985, p. 18.

JOE L. WILLIAMS, "Microcomputing: Production Planning's Liaison," *P&IM Review and APICS News,* April 1984, p. 54.

RONALD A. ZINK, "The Tilt to End-User Computing," *Computerworld,* July 23, 1984, p. ID/5.

NICHOLAS ZVEGINTZOV, "Front-End Programming Environments," *Datamation,* August 15, 1984, p. 80.

NICHOLAS ZVEGINTZOV, "Nanotrends," *Datamation,* August 1983, p. 106.

Chapter Eight

Where We Are;
Where We Are Going

Introduction

In this final chapter I offer some perspectives, summarizing the status of personal computing in corporate environments and describing some major technological trends. These trends, when joined with our imaginations and energies, can literally alter the form and content of all organizations in our world.

I believe that the application of personal computers will become increasingly industry specific; therefore, in this chapter, I am not suggesting guidelines. Rather, I have included several sections that contain some general recommendations, and some discussion of the substance and implications of significant, emerging, personal computing technologies. From these, and the firm base provided by the guidelines in the earlier part of this text, I expect that you will have productive and enjoyable use of these powerful tools.

Focus on customers

The promise of personal computing can best be realized, in any organization, if you focus on the basic ways in which you serve your customers. As the needs of those customers evolve, the organization must exercise flexibility and imagination as to the specific ways in which it meets those changing needs. Following the guidelines in Chapter 4 will help you recognize second-order processes and alter them to reduce costs, improve communications, and reduce organizational complexity. Equally important, however, will be the application of your creative marketing skills to find ways in which to harness this technology to alter the very products and services you provide.

Changes are simple but not easy

The ways to achieve these changes are simple but not easy, and have been well defined by business professors and consultants. Ideas on both what to change and how to accomplish the changes can be gained from continually reading—reading

315

© 1988 by Prentice Hall, A Division of Simon & Schuster Inc., Englewood Cliffs, NJ 07632 the books and articles that your customers are reading so that you see how their expectations are being formed. Read journals and attend professional meetings to learn the state of the technology and how it is being applied in other leading organizations.

Use the PCIC as a technical monitor; ask the PCIC, as a specific task, to prepare annual technological forecasts and recommendations. (Get these forecasts and recommendations during the middle of your fiscal year so that you have enough time to develop the ideas into plans for the next year.)

Encouraging innovation

Deciding what ideas to implement is crucial; one reasonably inexpensive way of doing this is to encourage experimentation within your existing organization. Allow people to divert small amounts of company resources to self-motivated experimental projects; explicitly fund these experiments only as they demonstrate useful results. Personal computing experiments, with the exception of some communications applications, are specifically amenable to this small-scale approach.

By definition, of course, some, perhaps most, of these experiments will fail. Although it is important to reward success, it is equally important not to penalize disappointments, so that you create an environment in which creativity becomes fertile and in which risk taking is encouraged.

Change as a process

Once an idea is adopted, it must be implemented; change is difficult and costly but is best accomplished through the participation of everyone who will be involved, at all levels of the organization, with the explicit, unwavering backing of management. Publicize the successful examples in your organization and in others in your industry, and set realistic but firm goals for implementing the changes in all appropriate groups.

As described in the guidelines in this book, personal computing is both a cause for change and a means by which other changes can be managed. Whatever the cause, forces will buffet your organization, requiring either adaption or dissolution; change is therefore a process that should operate continually in your organization, and like any other process, can be managed and improved continually.

Status of Personal Computing in Corporate Environments

Progress in corporate environments

Many good things are happening in personal computing in corporate environments. Many companies are well into the Sanction Phase of personal computing use and some are in the early steps of the Promulgation Phase (see Figure 1.3). Personal computing is an acceptable tool, emerging from novelty status into the most conservative applications. Specific applications, such as word processing and spreadsheets, are even institutionalized in some applications in some companies.

Personal Computing Information Centers (PCICs) are being established, either explicitly along the lines described in this text or on an ad hoc basis, by specialists in the information systems function or by self-educated, experienced users who offer their consulting services to others in the company.

Personal computing progress is most advanced either in stand-alone form or in personal-computing-to-host applications as described in Chapter 5. Personal computing communication networks are just being sanctioned, even in the most advanced organizations, and most companies are in experimental or hobbiest stages. Application architectures are just being developed to fully exploit the capabilities of distributed personal computing and hosts linked with networks. Information systems are just being conceived in which the users interact with their personal computing station and neither know or care about where data are stored and processed.

Maturing of the personal computing industry

Standards are beginning to emerge within the industry; as a result, investments in both hardware and software are less likely to become obsolete, and new equipment, selected for additional features or capability, is likely to be at least upward compatible with existing equipment (i.e., existing software will run on the newer equipment, although software for the new hardware may not run on the older units).

Standards are also causing the prices of hardware to plummet. Low-cost manufacturers can build terminals, computers, and peripherals as commodities. The PCIC will be challenged to provide good advice to its customers, comparing the benefits of installing a "name brand" personal computer to its "generic brand," low-priced competitor. Above all, however, the PCIC will be responsible for testing and advising users on both software and hardware compatibility issues as the variety of available low-cost hardware increases.

Currently, separate standards seem to be evolving for office personal computing and engineering personal computing. Both users and their advisors, the PCIC and information systems managers, need to consider carefully the major uses of personal computing equipment before acquiring it. The problem for engineering applications is more complex because engineers and scientists often need office-type applications such as word processing and spreadsheets, while office users rarely need scientific or mathematical software.

One evolving solution to the dilemma is the ability to build a "shell" in the operating system normally used for engineering work. The office programs, together with their operating system, can then execute within that shell. This approach gives engineers the needed application flexibility, but the office applications often operate more slowly than they would in their "native" hardware environment.

The advent of standards will channel both industry and user resources into continuing improvements rather than into competitive alternatives for accomplishing similar tasks. Standards cause the varieties of alternatives, as perceived by users, to decrease; users have more time to absorb technology into their primary business functions. Standards will also increase the breadth of hardware and applications to which the users can apply general personal computing education, lowering the time and expense needed for specific training on each item of hardware and software.

Increased personal computing power

Personal computing power is becoming increasingly available at costs affordable by normal business operations. Processors have the speed and internal memory space to be effective even with complex systems, and megabyte external file storage is also available for reasonable prices. All this power means that software writers can increase the sophistication of programs while maintaining rapid interactions with people. This power allows artificial intelligence and decision support systems, discussed later in the chapter, both of which require significant computing resources, to be implemented in personal computing applications. Increased power will become apparent to users in the form of increased "friendliness."

Human factors

The inability for people to interact easily with personal computing is a major barrier to the promulgation of the technology. Personal computing does not yet adapt itself to the people it presumably serves; rather, people must still adapt, grasping the technology in order to harness personal computing power.

Methods of interacting with people are not as standardized as are other aspects of personal computing technology. Although widely criticized, keyboards are still the primary input device, and reports are still the primary means by which information is displayed.

Many alternative input devices have been offered; none has become standard. The most successful alternative has probably been the "mouse," coupled with on-screen icons to allow rapid selection of processing options. Even less successful than "mice" are light pens, touch screens, and touch pads. Voice input is just now emerging from the laboratory.

Output technology is even lower on the development curve. Vocal output messages are possible at reasonable cost, but this technology is widely implemented only in simple inquiry applications. Graphics software is available, and many users can print charts as alternatives to tables of numbers. Personal computing can help produce pictorals for use as illustrations in presentations. Visual literacy, however, is quite low; people are not being educated in the syntax and grammars of visual communications. The results are as motley as would be articles written by authors who were never educated in writing tecniques.

On the other hand, the "metaphor" architecture appears to be a successful model for use in packaged software. The most popular packages are word processing, designed on typing and publishing models, spreadsheets, modeled after accounting spreadsheets, and data base systems, following the concept of the ubiquitous filing cabinet.

Information systems, however, have not yet adopted the metaphor architecture; we are just evolving personal computing models of such things as factory cells, and factory and office work flows, which may raise the power of the metaphor concept to use in systems. As a result of these human interaction limitations, personal computing has been most accepted when dedicated to a specific function (e.g., the ever-popular word processing and spreadsheets). Yet the potential of personal computing lies in its application to broad-scale, general processes.

This dilemma will be resolved to some extent by increasing user education, but the real solution lies in powerful, general-purpose hardware which is sufficiently low in cost that it can be dedicated to a single, perhaps tailored use. Software will create the tailoring, in a heuristic manner, starting with some general function, and modifying itself to suit the specifics of unique users and environments. An intermediate step before heuristic software is available would allow support organizations to modify (perhaps iteratively) a software package and implement it on a tailored hardware configuration so that the combination meets the needs of unique users.

Organizational effects: economies of information

Personal computing is currently most successful at operational, middle-management, and staff levels of organizations. Personal computing has not yet made significant dents in the executive suites (although personal computing may be easily seen on the desks of the executives' secretaries and staff assistants). This lack of penetration is generally attributed to:

- The unstructured nature of executive work
- The highly personal nature of most executive work

- The lack of comfort most executives have with keyboards
- Executives' need for data outside the organization

The artificial intelligence/decision support system trends discussed in this chapter will bring at least some personal computing applications into the executive suite, but the rapid application growth will still be at lower levels, where problems are more structured and where (usually internal) data are historic and precise.

Much staff and middle-management work involves the restructuring of data and the communication of data among other people. Some of this work will be automated by personal computing applications, allowing line managers to operate effectively in flatter, shorter organizational structures. Fewer people will have only internal customers, bureaucracy will decrease, and successful organizations, even large ones, will become more responsive to their external environment.

To achieve some of these benefits, organizations must focus on performing tasks that directly affect customer satisfaction, not necessarily tasks that improve only internal organizational efficiency. Traditional organizational structures should be reexamined, especially at the functional boundaries. Personal computing can improve the interfunctional linkages, such as those between research and development (R&D) and manufacturing, between sales and manufacturing, and between all functions and accounting.

The key to improving these interactions is to focus on the data flow, not on the organizational structure. Product structure data, for example, is vital to R&D, manufacturing, and cost accounting; a common product structure file should be available to all these functions. Computing hardware, systems software, and even applications, may come and go, but data live forever.

Personal computing has the potential of changing the work and information flows *between organizations* as well as those within organizations. Again, the focus should be on data flows, allowing each separate group to process those data in its unique manner. For example, vendors may be given access to a customer's production schedule to allow the delivery of purchased parts on a "just-in-time" basis. Obviously, each company uses the same data in different ways, but rapid communication is required to accommodate changing production requirements, on the one hand, and parts availability on the other.

All this integration may also have an effect on the size and location of organizations. Although economies of scale will still be a major factor, especially in capital-intensive industries, economies of information flows will become important, especially in distribution and service industries. Organizations will, on the one hand, be physically close to their customers to provide rapid delivery of goods and services, but on the other hand, organizations will need to share information. Because of this, for example, local travel agencies are joining together into large organizations to share information about the increasing variety of travel services available. Such linked agencies can also help customers who are also geographically dispersed. Similar trends are occurring in other industries, such as real estate, banking, and insurance, where local personal services can be greatly augmented by rapid communication among highly dispersed data bases.

Some of these linkages will occur through trade associations; others will be created through franchise structures; still others will occur through the acquisition of small, local companies by large national firms. Eventually, linkages may be limited only by the application of society-imposed antitrust laws.

Geopolitical boundaries are also falling to the technology of data flow. These boundaries, however, will probably prove more durable than company structures. People in various countries, because of differences in legal and cultural environments, require different types of service products, thus limiting the utility of shared information.

Economies of information can also change the nature of the service products themselves; much more integration becomes reasonable. This is most obvious in the financial services industries, where we can purchase all sorts of investments, from real estate to certificates of deposit, as easily (and in some cases, in the same location) as we can buy a pair of shoes.

Note that most of the examples of integration are focused on service industries, not on manufacturing products. Because of their "intangible" nature, service products are more amenable to the power of economies of information than are manufactured products. Impacts on manufactured goods are likely to occur, albeit slowly, because of two strong trends. The actual composition of manufactured products will change because of "group technology," where new products are designed from already developed parts and subassemblies. Group technology lowers the cost and increases the speed of product design, making custom products more economical, providing increased functionality and reliability at lower prices. Group technology is feasible, of course, only to the extent that information about the nature of parts and subassemblies is available to designers.

The second trend is the advent of "flexible manufacturing systems" (FMS), which will create dramatic changes in the production process itself. FMS information flows will allow rapidly modifiable "work cells" and flexible routings to allow economic production of custom products. FMS is related to "computer-integrated manufacturing" (CIM), in which many steps in the production process are linked with computers and networks. Eventually, CIM will allow full integration of all production processes, including the initial sale to a customer, the R&D design step, manufacturing, and finally, shipment back to the customer.

Technological integration

As discussed in other chapters, there are strong trends toward linking all forms of quantitative data: voice, video, text, and numeric. Even those data currently in analog form (such as voice and video) are being converted to digital format and transmitted via emerging services such as the Integrated Services Digital Network (ISDN), discussed briefly in Chapter 6.

We are still, however, limited in our ability to describe, much less integrate, qualitative, "fuzzy" data. Some of these data can be converted into quantitative form through the use of probability mechanisms, but we are a long way from applying personal computing to problems requiring inferences and intuition. Artificial intelligence and decision support systems can be very helpful, as described in the following sections, but the inability to work with qualitative data will remain a major differentiation between human and personal computing abilities.

Computer education/computers in education

Application of personal computing technology, in its current form, is limited by the "computer literacy" of users, the ability of users to adapt themselves and their problems to the language and structure of the computing hardware and software. Those people who can, through formal or informal training, learn about computing are therefore able to take advantage of current capabilities. I believe, therefore, that computer literacy courses should be made available to people, so that those who are willing to learn can do so effectively.

As I have noted above, however, we in the personal computing industry cannot expect the world to adapt to our limitations; rather, we must increase the technology to the point that user needs are met without requiring those users to undergo special education or training. On the other hand, education (on any subject) is a service product similar to many others described above, and the power of personal computing and economies of information can be well applied to education and training processes. Current products offering "computer-assisted instruction" or "computer-based training" are mere hints of what is possible with improved people-computer interfaces and the application of artificial intelligence. Multimedia presentations using voice, video, text, and numbers will become common, and simulation capabilities will allow people to practice even complex tasks by compressing experience into short, low-cost laboratory sessions.

Artificial Intelligence in Personal Computing in Corporate Environments

In this section I offer an extremely brief overview of artificial intelligence (AI) focusing primarily on the effects that AI technology will have on personal computing applications. AI, as a distinct application, should never really be obvious to users. Rather, application systems should increase their functionality and performance by using embedded AI techniques.

Let us look at some very basic definitions and contrasts. Information systems are traditionally focused on data and on transactions that affect those data. Processing occurs according to a sequence of steps defined in a systems design and implemented through a series of computer programs which are executed on computer processing units and related peripheral devices. Automated information systems are most useful when the data are voluminous and the processing steps are highly repetitive. Modification to the processing requires carefully controlled changes to the programs and/or the hardware used.

Artificial intelligence, on the other hand, is a blatant attempt to harness the tools of computer science in ways that simulate or even duplicate human skills and behavior. AI is usually divided into three major categories: expert systems, natural language, and robotics. Robotics was the first of these technologies to reach the commercial marketplace; expert systems are just now becoming relatively widely used. Natural-language systems are still restricted to laboratory and limited function applications.

Expert systems

Most common expert systems are designed to respond to stmuli in the same ways that a human expert would respond to those same stimuli. The most familiar expert systems are diagnostic systems, where the system is presented with a series of observations, can ask for additional data, and then presents both a diagnosis and a prescription. Expert systems have been written, for example, for certain medical diagnoses and for diagnosing and repairing computer hardware.

Information systems are based on sets of manual and automated procedures. See, for example, Figure 8.1, which shows an information system–style flowchart showing the decisions involved in going to lunch. Most common expert systems, however, are based on discrete rule statements. Figure 8.2 shows rules for going to lunch at a level of detail comparable to that of the information system flowchart in Figure 8.1. These rules are developed by a new class of computer professional called a "knowledge engineer."

Major differences between the two approaches are obvious when changes are required. For example, let's say that Paul's Pizza Place moves into town. To accommodate this change in an information system, we would have to modify several

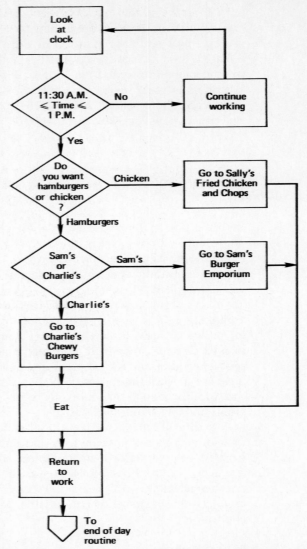

Figure 8.1 Information systems flowchart for going to lunch.

1. Lunch time is between 11:30 a.m. and 1 p.m.
2. Lunch involves eating food at a location away from the workplace.
3. Hamburgers are lunch food.
4. Chicken is lunch food.
5. Chicken for lunch may be eaten at "Sally's Fried Chicken and Chops."
6. Hamburgers for lunch may be eaten at "Sam's Burger Emporium."
7. Hamburgers for lunch may be eaten at "Charlie's Chewy Burgers."
8. After eating lunch, you return to work.

Figure 8.2 Oversimplified rules for an expert system for going to lunch.

decision loops and recompile the program. For our expert system, we merely add two rules:

4a. Pizza is food.
7a. Paul's sells pizza.

Because of the ease of adding and modifying rules, expert systems can be made heuristic; that is, they can learn from "experience" and modify their own rules. For example, if our lunch expert system "noticed" that we go to lunch at exactly 12:15 every day, the system could modify lunchtime rule 1.

Expert systems are also usually programmed to display the rules used to allow them to reach a decision, basically to answer the question: Why did you reach that decision? Expert systems allow "expert observers" to be available automatically to all personal computing users. For example, an expert disk drive diagnostician could monitor disks and warn users that the drive is about to fail, before losing any data. Or an expert accountant could be built into spreadsheet programs to create crossfoot and audit trail techniques automatically, to verify the accuracy of the application.

Natural language

"Speaking" and "hearing" are usually considered robotics functions; differentiating among homonyms is a skill that bridges the natural language/robotics boundary. However, the "understanding" of language, no matter how entered, is a "natural language" task.

Understanding human languages is probably the least advanced of the AI disciplines because of the subtleties and context problems related to language. It is difficult, for example, to define rules that allow a system to differentiate among "The ball is *blue*," "Susan is (feeling) *blue*," and "The baby is (turning) *blue*." Sentences such as "The White Sox murdered the Yankees," thoroughly confuse non-American English-speaking human beings, much less mere computers.

The applications of natural language are fairly obvious. Allowing people to interact with systems in both cultural and professional terms will greatly increase the "friendliness" of systems. Systems, however, will be required to learn the implications of imprecise remarks. For example, the president might ask the system how best to improve short-term profits. A nonintuitive system might determine that the highest short-run profits can be achieved by firing all the employees and selling from inventory—not, perhaps, what the president had in mind.

In addition, specific language-oriented applications are very useful. Language translation systems will greatly facilitate international communication, even if the translations are not perfect and require some polishing by a human translator. Given speaking and hearing capabilities, we could simply dictate letters to our computers.

Robotics

Early applications of robotics were simply mechanical tools programmed to accomplish specific functions. More advanced applications require greater anthropomorphic capabilities. The five senses are the most widely sought abilities; touch skills are reasonably available, and vision is coming into commercial applications. Hearing is being studied in connection with natural-language processes. Smell and touch are not widely available in AI applications, but sophisticated chemical analysis instrumentation is available and is often linked to systems to provide reasonable emulation of the data gathered by human beings with their smell/taste senses.

Challenges in robotics, of course, exceed the simulation of the senses. All physical activities become robotic tasks; for example, controlled movement, especially over uneven terrain, is quite difficult. Robotics becomes especially powerful when expert systems are linked with sensing and transport mechanisms to provide a reasonably generalized, mobile, reasoning tool. Although this combination has interesting science-fiction applications, tailoring robots to special purposes by restricting motion and sensory capabilities is probably more productive and efficient, at least in the near future.

Integrated AI applications

AI will ultimately provide personal computing with the ability to "close the loop," to provide feedback against an expected situation and order the necessary corrections. See Figure 8.3 for a general diagram of this process.

AI can support and enhance all steps in the closed-loop process. Decisions can be enhanced by expert systems and natural-language capabilities. Operations can be supported by robotics. Process evaluation can be accomplished using expert systems techniques, especially if the evaluations must be made on "fuzzy" criteria such as "better" or "worse." Expert systems can then, heuristically, decide how the process should be corrected and implement those corrections through robotics mechanisms.

This type of closed-loop process is reasonably obvious for manufacturing or repetitive administrative operations, but the concepts can also be applied to less precise tasks, such as selling, R&D projects, or personnel management. For example, expert programs have been developed that ask questions about a person's behavior and then offer suggestions on how best to work with that person in selling or negotiating situations.

AI can also be integrated with traditional information systems applications. Expert systems can determine what data should be collected, processed, and reported. Other expert systems can analyze data and extract from them information tailored to specific managers and specific situations. Data can be collected by natural-language and robotic systems, and processing efficiencies can be achieved by using expert systems to optimize complex communications and data storage situations.

Decision Support Systems in Personal Computing in Corporate Environments

Decision support systems (DSSs) are means by which complex decisions can be made or improved based on innovative uses of information systems and computer science

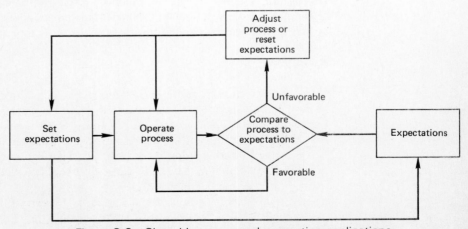

Figure 8.3 Closed-loop personal computing applications.

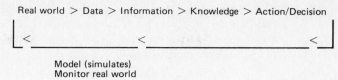

Model (simulates)
Monitor real world

Figure 8.4

technologies. DSS is a popular topic in personal computing for two main reasons. First, these systems require a synergistic blend of information systems, AI, and human intelligence; as such, DSS is an ambitious, worthy objective. Second, well-functioning DSS would carry personal computing into the executive suite, supporting strategic managers not now directly served by any aspect of computer science technology.

Information systems tend to be passive, after the fact, dealing with large volumes of specific, organized data. DSS should be active and predictive, based on general, nonspecific, often poorly organized knowledge. DSS is therefore more sophisticated, more intuitive, almost philosophical, compared to the comparative "brute force" of typical information systems.

It may be, however, that the achievement of the ultimate DSS is less important than the work performed in pursuit of this goal, for by striving for this goal, we are forced to examine a wide variety of problems in systems integration and human interface. The knowledge gained in the study of DSS can be used to improve all systems, and even decision support itself can become a feature buried within specialized, integrated applications.

DSS components and flow

The flow from the activities of the real world to the decision is shown in Figure 8.4. The new factor in this flow is "knowledge," the extraction from information of "understanding" that can be applied to a specific set of circumstances. To achieve this the flow requires five distinct types of systems, as shown in Figure 8.5.

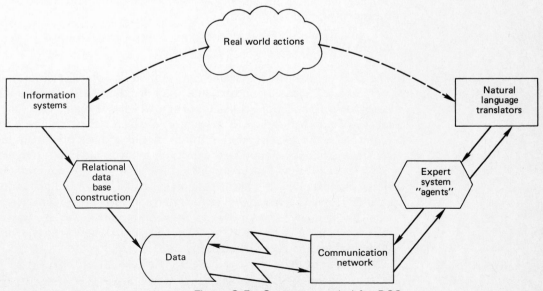

Figure 8.5 Systems needed for DSS.

The flow is in two parts. First are the systems that place the data into a relational data base. Data flow from the real world to the data base:

- Information systems to collect, edit, and file data which represent activities in the "real world."
- Relational data base systems which place the data into a structure in which they can be accessed in varying ways.

Once the data are filed, various inquiries can be made against it. As shown in Figure 8.5, the flow is two-way:

- A problem arises in the real world. A system is needed to collect that problem statement from the manager responsible for the decision. Ideally, this will be a natural-language system so that the manager can describe the circumstances in business rather than computer terms.
- An expert system translates the request into specific data processing terms, requesting specific data elements with specific time and organizational attributes. For example, the system might request specific orders for the month of July for the chemical analysis product line.
- Expert systems that perform this translation task are often called "agents," since they perform specific functions at the request of their principal, the responsible manager.
- The requests are funneled to a communications system that uses a directory to locate the needed data, extract them from the data base in which they are filed, and transport them back to the agent system.
- The agent expert system now analyzes these data using modeling and simulation techniques based on expert system rules.
- The agent system then presents the knowledge back to the manager, perhaps in the form of recommendations, with explanations.

This flow might occur several times as the manager refines a strategy and needs additional information. The agent system, through this process, "learns" the types of knowledge used by this manager, modifies its rules, and improves both its extraction and modeling tactics so that useful recommendations can be provided in the future with fewer iterations.

Group DSS

The DSS process is complicated by situations in which decision making is shared with others. These situations include joint decisions in which several managers must negotiate a final action, consultations in which one manager seeks the nonbinding advice of another person, concurrence in which a decision made by one manager requires the approval of another (often another group), or second-guessing in which someone attempts to modify the decision made by another after the fact.

The DSS flow can be modified in several ways to accommodate these situations. For example, the agent system can make the recommendations available to several people or even to the agent systems of the other managers so that the situation can be analyzed according to their unique rules. Where approval is required, the criteria for that approval can often be built into the agent system and considered when making the recommendation.

Different managers can have private data bases, updated periodically by extracts provided by their expert systems agents. For group decision situations, each executive can ask for individual analysis and then the results can be mediated by an expert system whose rules were formulated to reach a group consensus optimized toward a particular objective.

Another, less sophisticated but often-effective approach would simply be to post the situation and recommendation on an electronic bulletin board that can be accessed by everyone involved. These managers can then review the recommendation and post their comments for all to see and consider. In this environment, one manager should take responsibility for organizing the discussion, for ensuring that everyone participates appropriately, and for summarizing the discussion conclusions.

Developing DSS

Since a key to effective DSS is the still-new concept of the expert systems agent, there are few working DSS from which to learn. Academically, however, it seems that there are two distinct approaches to DSS development.

The first approach uses the traditional systems development model described in Figure 7.2. The analysis and design phases focus on the types of data and decisions made by the executives being served, and the tools needed to provide this information are built. This method is effective in situations where the types of decisions to be made are well defined and reasonably repetitive. This methodology might be appropriate for DSS that serve middle managers, whose work tends to be more repetitive and focused.

The second approach, ad hoc development, makes no assumptions about the specific information that will be required or the types of decisions that will be made. Instead, the techniques for extracting, communicating, and analyzing any data are built and are made available to various manager-users. The managers are trained to use the techniques for individual problems. Knowkedge engineers help the managers build, maintain, and use their expert system agents.

This second methodology is generally more expensive to build, to maintain, and to operate than is a DSS built for a specific purpose and audience. However, it is considerably more flexible than the single-purpose model, can handle a wide variety of situations, and therefore, is more likely to be used by senior executives whose work tends to be unstructured.

One compromise methodology would be to use a traditionally developed system to build the data bases from which a DSS can extract information. Ad hoc methods could then be used to formulated questions and create analyses as needed by specific managers in specific situations. The analyses, of course, are limited by the data that are placed in the extract data base.

Criteria for decisions are set in rules in the expert system agent. Quantitative decisions are relatively easy to set, although the priority of values often clouds decisions. In a common example, it may be easy to compute net profits and the increase in a company's assets, but it may be difficult to choose between strategies that maximize one at the expense of the other.

Qualitative factors are much harder to set, especially at strategic management levels where no top-down expectation exist against which a recommendation can be evaluated. Often managers will choose to set their own goals, seeking "merely" to continually improve their own performance.

Limitations on DSS

The major limitation on achieving DSS is, of course, the availability of the technology described so blithely above. Even small, but essential design elements such as dictionaries are incredibly difficult to build in organizations of any size.

Further, data for most strategic management decisions simply are not available from data bases. Many decisions require data about the external world, data that are even less available than are data on internal operations. Further, decisions are usually needed before adequate data can be collected. Often, some (perhaps, most) of the data needed are not available; approximations are almost always needed.

Finally, strategies are often set, not on rational criteria, but on the subjective values of the decision maker, values that may eventually be simulated by the expert systems agent, but which will be difficult to quantify. As I said above, the benefits from DSS may be not in actually building such software but in the intermediate benefits that accrue from working toward such systems.

Impact on Society from Personal Computing in Corporate Environments

Perspective

Viewing society through the kaleidoscope of personal computing is a fitting way to end this book. As with all major technical advances, personal computing is merely the pebble in the pond, creating ripples with unknown consequences. In fact, personal computing itself is really an unpredicted wave created by the convergence of innovations in computing, semiconductor physics, electronics, and communications technologies.

All technical advances are two faced, offering opportunities to some and discomfort to others. From blacksmiths to telegraph operators, society has paid for technology with job displacement, requiring both vendors and customers to adapt to new environments. Rarely does the company that dominates one technology dominate in the successor technology; the old company has too much to lose, and is too large to grasp initially illusive opportunities.

Personal computing is no different; the irony, however, is that many of the people being displaced are middle managers and staff professionals, the very same people who were the beneficiaries of the last technical wave in business, the wave that introduced information systems through large computers. Once released, however, the forces of change cannot be denied. The marketplace rewards entrepreneurs who build new companies to replace the old. The personal computing transition is even more rapid because of the competition offered by other countries, some of whom, as with new companies, have little to lose and much to gain. If our companies do not harness the power of personal computing, the companies of other countries will, allowing them to manufacture products and provide services that will draw dollars and jobs from our economy to theirs.

Changes, however, have secondary effects. The automobile brought freeways, suburbs, shopping malls, and pollution, none of which could have been foreseen by the Henry Fords and Louis Chevrolets who built the industry. Some of the initial effects from personal computing are introduced below. These issues should be viewed as questions without absolute answers, or more precisely, questions with many answers, with each of us having the chance to grade the test.

Jobs and leisure

Personal computing–based jobs will provide more power to individuals in functionally structured organizations. People will have greater horizontal scope of control and greater vertical depth to what they can do themselves. Some of this will be exciting; for example, more people will have direct contact with customers and products, less need to simply follow prewritten policies and procedures. Some of this will require the personal management of mundane details, writing and typing one's own memos, opening one's own (often electronic) mail.

Personal computing also provides the linkage to communication with others, the ability to exchange messages with people all over the world without regard to time differences, an ability that allows geographic dispersion of work groups in ways which provide close customer support while maintaining contact with colleagues and supervisors. One example of this capability, more common in Europe than in the United States, is videotex, a technology in which pictures and data are combined with communications to provide a wide variety of customized services. Using video-tex, people can dial a store from their home and view a catalog that contains actual demonstrations of products. The customer can view several products and then place an order.

This combination of video and text can be used in virtually any industry. Travel agents can display maps or pictures of accommodations; sales presentations using tailored graphics can be displayed. Applications in education are limitless, since students will be able to interact with a lesson, with video, audio, text, and computing all available to emphasize the subject material.

Interestingly, personal computing affects leisure also. For one thing, the productivity gains accomplished by personal computing may increase the amount of leisure time available to people. Others, however, may simply use the available time to do more work.

Personal computing can also provide recreation in its own right. Computer-based games are one obvious form of recreation, but personal computing can be used to enhance all sorts of other hobbies. Photographers can use personal computing to calculate darkroom formulas and to maintain records of how negatives were processed. Personal investment strategies can be tested and evaluated relatively quickly and painlessly. Computers can be used as a fine art tool creating colorful images directly or by writing programs which, in turn, create the images. Music, education, and creative writing are all affected by the potential of this very personal tool.

Security and privacy issues

As noted throughout this text, much can and should be done by users of personal computing to assure the appropriate control of equipment and data. The specter of these problems, however, remains a limitation to the promulgation of the technology.

Increased, low-cost computing power can allow the use of more sophisticated techniques which give users more personal control over their equipment and data. The price for that control, however, is usually restrictions in ease of use, in "friendliness."

Furthermore, that same power is also available to those who wish to break security and invade privacy. Technology, at best, provides a standoff. The crooks usually have the advantage, however, since they are willing to spend full time at their craft, while the rest of us view security as overhead, preferring to spend most of our time on productive tasks.

I do not foresee a simple solution to computer crime any more than I see a simple solution to crime in general; rather, I hope that society begins to treat computer-based violations as seriously as it does noncomputer crimes, with comparable sanctions and penalties. It will help when security violations are viewed as the felonies they often are rather than as intellectual pranks.

Some privacy violations have been forbidden by force of law; these can be treated as security issues. Most privacy problems, however, raise ethical concerns and are included in the discussion below.

Ethics

Personal computing provides power, power that can be used productively—or misused. Criminal (mis)use of personal computing should be controlled as described in the various discussions of security. Privacy is a more complicated matter; it is clearly inappropriate to use the power of personal computing to break into an employee personnel file, for example, to read someone's performance evaluation. But is it appropriate to use computing power to improve the accuracy of a direct-mail campaign? Is it appropriate, for example, to search for names of people who subscribe to a fishing magazine and who also own an expensive automobile, so that these people can be solicited for a membership in an exclusive fishing club? Although most of us are annoyed by the amounts of "junk mail" generated by this focusing, such direct-mail activity is rarely considered unethical.

How ethical is it, however, to apply these techniques to political campaigns? In state and national elections, the amount of data to be processed requires the power of large computers (although ethical issues are usually the same, whether we are discussing mainframes or personal computing). In local elections, personal computing power can be translated into money and votes. For example, precinct lists can be entered on files and then matched against lists of people who subscribe to issue-related publications or who previously contributed to specific causes. These people can then be solicited with computer-generated letters tailored to their specific interests. Is it appropriate that one candidate have access to this power by virtue of that candidate's money or technical expertise, while others must use less sophisticated methods?

What happens if someone uses personal computing to scan public-news data bases to search for embarrassing data about an opponent? This leads to the very essence of privacy, the society-sanctioned right that each of us has to keep certain facts about ourselves from the view of others. What privacy society grants through laws, society can also remove, allowing, for example, police officers to delve into a person's past criminal activities. How does the "public's right to know" compare with a person's ability to leave behind past embarrassments and "make a fresh start"? Personal computing puts these decisions in the hands of many more people than have ever had this power in the past.

Interestingly, ethics must walk where science fears to tread. Since medical science has few definitive data or prescriptive advice on the various ailments attributed to personal computing, managers must approach the circumstances ethically. Most physical complaints fall into two general categories: radiation dangers from the video display terminals (VDTs) inherent in most personal computing workstations, and the orthopedic and optometric problems from working continually in one place, staring at the VDT screen.

Studies of radiation dangers are inconclusive, but some of the allegations, especially by pregnant women, are quite serious. The science of ergonomics suggests many solutions to the problems of muscle and eye strain, but the solutions range in cost from simple work breaks or stretching exercises to the purchase of sophisticated, expensive workstation furniture. Advice from PCIC experts should be sought and heeded, but cost and effectiveness of various solutions do not necessarily correlate, and department managers must make ethical decisions, balancing the well-being and productivity of their workers with the responsibilities for maintaining a cost-effective environment.

Consequences of personal computing results

Who is responsible for the effects of computing? In simpler times, it was always relatively easy to look past the machine to the person who controlled that machine.

The causes of the legendary errors on computer-generated bills, for example, could usually be focused on incorrect data entry, or incorrect computer operation, or in more subtle cases, incorrect programming or systems design.

What happens, however, if, because of the speed or complexity of computing, an innocent error causes physical damage? For example, even after extensive testing a defect could remain in a factory machine control program which, in an unusual circumstance, could cause injury to an operator. Who is at fault?

What about the consequences of decisions based on computer simulations? Or, as artificial intelligence becomes a reality, who is responsible for the behavior of a computer program that has modified itself to perform actions never imagined by its original programmer?

Some of these consequences may be positive. Who, for example, owns the patent rights to a product designed by an artificial intelligence package, a product that was not imagined by either the author of the AI program or the user who purchased the operated the program? On the other hand, who is responsible for any damage caused by subtle flaws in the design of this AI-invented product? These questions alone will provide income for generations of lawyers.

All-electronic files

Personal computing applications are encouraging the elimination of paper. Communication of information and the retention of records is increasingly electronic. The costs saved by these developments are huge, involving tangible economies in materials, typing, copying, mailing and distributing, filing, and storage space. There are further intangible economies brought about by the speed of communication and by the ability to retrieve and analyze electronic information.

There are also potential dangers, resting primarily with the ease with which electronic files can be altered and deleted. Historical records are easily eliminated or modified, leaving no detectable trail. Documents used as legal evidence can disappear or be modified. Electronic files are generally vulnerable to the same types of treats as are hard-copy files (e.g., fire, water) but are also subject to damage by more subtle treats, such as radiation, electrical storms, or static electricity.

One set of solutions lies in the use of "intermediate" technologies such as microfilm/microfiche, or nonerasable laser-written images. The most promising of these laser-based technologies comes to computing from the audio recording industry. The compact disks which are revolutionizing the music recording industry are being introduced to computing as compact-disk read-only memories (CD ROMs). CD-ROMs can contain nearly 600 million bytes of information, about 250,000 text pages. Encyclopedias of information can be stored and quickly accessed using CD-ROMs. Another nonerasable laser device, particularly useful as an archival media, is the WORM, a disk that is *written once* and *read many* times.

It seems ironic that personal computing, this tool that gives each of us a better chance to influence our own small world, may also, by its very nature, leave no durable trace of its own existence. What will be left are the products *we* create with its help. Personal computing is merely a better hammer for some, a better spade for others. It is up to us to build our small cottage and till our colorful garden, doing our individual tasks in ways that are just a bit better because we have harnessed the power of personal computing.

Information as an infinite resource

Most of the world's economy has been developed around the concept of allocating scarce resources. Raw material, capital, and labor are all considered finite, and different economic systems have been developed to allow people access to these resources. Ultimately, the world economy is limited by the basic attributes of the planet on which we live: its land, its minerals, and its organic resources.

Information, however, is theoretically infinite. Information is never exhausted or worn. Information, however, becomes obsolete; its value can diminish rapidly with time.

Communication can overcome that weakness. As long as timely information is closely held by a small group of people, those people have an advantage over others. Wide distribution of information, however, can create new, unpredictable effects. The use of the information can interfere with the process that originally generated the information, in a personal computing application of the Heisenberg uncertainty principle (which holds that measurements interfere with the process being measured).

Stock market strategies are a good example of these principles. Once, professional traders had access to computer-driven data bases and models unavailable to less wealthy amateurs. This power allowed professionals to rapidly employ complex tactics to take advantage of market anomalies. Now, however, thanks to the power of personal computing, that many more people have access to the same data and the same models. When many people react to situations in similar ways, the market swings can be exacerbated, often creating self-fulling prophesies. For example, if many people follow a model that recommends that a stock be sold, the heavy selling pressure will, by itself, drive the stock price down.

It may be that just as laws are passed to control the allocation and distribution of products, laws may be needed to control the allocation and flow of information, creating an artificial scarcity of this infinite resource. Or, we will develop an economic system based on the scarcity of creative uses of information, for no matter how wide spread the power of personal computing, it is still people who differentiate wealth from poverty, people who define the basis on which that wealth is based, and people who use the personal computing tool, rather than being a mere servant to technology.

REFERENCES

General

JAMES DIEBOLD, "The Information Age Still in Its Early Stages," *Information Systems News,* October 1, 1984, p. 86

WILLIAM GATES, "The Future of Software Design," *Byte,* August 1983, p. 401.

JAMES MARTIN, *An Information Systems Manifesto,* Prentice-Hall, Inc., Englewood Cliffs, N.J., 1984.

JIM SEYMOUR, "The Micro of 1990," *Today's Office,* July 1985, p.45.

"Technology in the Workplace," a special report in *The Wall Street Journal,* September 16, 1985, Sec. 3.

CONNIE WRIGHT, "Waves of the Future," *Interact,* January 1985, p. 34.

Artificial Intelligence

JAMES S. ALBUS, *Brains, Behavior, and Robotics,* Byte Books, Peterborough, N.H., 1981.

ROBERT BERNHARD, "AI Researchers Need to Rethink Human Thinking," *Systems & Software,* October 1984, p. 97.

JOHN KRUTCH, *Experiments in Artificial Intelligence for Small Computers,* Howard W. Sams & Company, Inc., Indianapolis, Ind., 1981.

DONALD MICHIE and RORY JOHNSTON, *The Knowledge Machine,* William Morrow & Company, Inc., New York, 1985.

DANIEL R. PFAU and BARRY A. ZACK, "Understanding Expert System Shells," *Computerworld Focus,* February 19, 1986, p. 23.

OTIS PORT, "Computers That Come Awfully Close to Thinking," *Business Week,* June 2, 1986, p. 92.

WENDY RAUCH-HINDIN, "Bankers and AI Experts Team Up for Greater Revenues," *Systems & Software,* October 1984, p. 105.

KAREN SORENSEN, "Expert Systems Emerging as Real Tools, *InfoWorld,* April 21, 1986, p. 33.

Decision Support Systems

MICHAEL W. DAVIS, "Anatomy of Decision Support," *Datamation,* June 15, 1984, p. 201.

GERARDINE DeSANCTIS and BRENT GALLUPE, "Group Decision Support Systems: A New Frontier," *ACM Data Base,* Winter 1985, p. 3.

ROGER A. GOLDE, "Sharpen Your Number Sense," *Harvard Business Review,* July–August 1966, p. 74.

WALTER E. LANKAU, "Decision Support Systems Clearly Explained," *Computerworld Extra,* August 31, 1982, p. 5.

C. LAWRENCE MEADOR and RICHARD A. MEZGER, "Selecting an End User Programming Language for DSS Development," *MIS Quarterly,* December 1984, p. 267.

BERNARD C. REIMANN and ALLAN D. WAREN, "User-Oriented Criteria for the Selection of DSS Software," *Communications of the ACM,* Vol. 28, No. 2, 1985, p. 166.

JOHN F. ROCKART and MICHAEL E. TREACY, "The CEO Goes On-Line," *Harvard Business Review,* January–February 1982, p. 82.

Impact on Society

J. BAAL-SCHEM, "Societal Implications of Modern Information Tecnology," *IEEE Technology and Society Magazine,* December 1985, p. 20.

JOEL S. BIRNBAUM, "Toward the Domestication of Computers," speech delivered at the Columbia Computer Science Building Convocation, Columbia University, New York, October 10, 1983.

"Compact Disk Technology," *Personal Computing,* April 1986, p. 25.

Michael C. Gemignani, "Who Owns What Software Produces?" *IEEE Software,* September 1985, p. 48.

ROBERT MEAGHER, "Videotex Plus Mainframe Equals Distributed Information Delivery," *Computerworld,* March 17, 1986, p. 71.

JERRY POURNELLE, "CD-ROMS Are Facing a Limited Life Span," *InfoWorld,* March 17, 1986, p. 21.

JANET E. ZEIDE and JAY LIEBOWITZ, "Using Expert Systems: The Legal Perspective, *IEEE Expert,* Spring 1987, p. 19.

Appendix A

Sample Forms

SAMPLE FORM 3.1A
PERSONAL COMPUTING EQUIPMENT SELECTION LIST
(SEE GUIDELINE 3.1)

This selection list is published monthly by the company PCIC and is accurate as of the publication date. All equipment is immediately available unless otherwise noted. Prices, availability, and recommendation status are all subject to change without notice. (Because of the volatility of the marketplace, the Selection List probably should be published monthly and should therefore be in machine-readable as well as paper form. The Selection List could even be available as a text file for on-line look-up with personal computing equipment. Orders and justifications can also be entered on-line, but care should be taken to provide for the necessary authorizations and audit trails.)

Prices shown are for company purchases only. Employees may purchase for their personal use Recommended Equiment and Approved Equipment, if available, for the prices shown + 10 percent (see Guideline 3.6).

Purchase orders received by the PCIC will be updated to reflect prices and availability at the time of the order. If the recommendation status changes, the PCIC will call to discuss appropriate substitute equipment.

For current availability and prices, as well as advice on ordering situations, please call the PCIC. (Unless there has been a really drastic change in price or availability, the PCIC can usually take the responsibility for adjusting the internal order to reflect current conditions. Drastic changes, of course, should be discussed with the users before their orders are processed. Sometimes during a month, the recommended status of equipment will change, requiring some conversation between the PCIC and the users. To minimize these adjustments, users should be encouraged to call the PCIC to verify their information just before the order is placed. When the appropriate communications facilities are in place, the Selection List might also be available to users on an on-line file.)

Recommended List

(The Recommended List is organized by application so that users can easily see what equipment is appropriate to their use. The recommendation shows the equipment, its features, its price, and its availability. Several different configurations may be shown if several are recommended.)

1. For people using personal computing primarily as an electronic desk (some word processing, some spreadsheet, electronic mail, filing, calendar functions).
   a. Hardware
      (1) Configuration A: Total price (w/o options = $xxxx.xx). Consists of:
          CPU A ($xxxx.xx) with (list features)
          Disk AD ($xxx.xx) with (list features)
          Printer AP ($xxx.xx) with (list features)
          •
          •
          •
          (may show several configurations)
          •
          •
          •
          Options:

(Optional equipment for the various configurations may be shown separately. Option features and applications should also be explained.)

      Hard disk for configuration A ($xxxx.xx) with (list features) (available two weeks after order)

      Additional memory modules
         For CPU A ($xxx.xx) with (list features)
         For CPU B (none recommended)
         For CPU C ($xxx.xx) with (list features)
-
-
-

b. Software Packages. (The recommendations are organized by computer, since different software may be needed for different systems.)

(1) For CPU A and CPU C:
      Word processor AW ($xxx)
      Spreadsheet AS ($xxx)
      File system AF ($xxx)
      Scheduling system AP ($xxx)
-
-
-

(2) For CPU B
      Word processor BW ($xxx)
      Spreadsheet BS ($xxx)
-
-
-

(In each application area, there may be special needs that require special equipment. The examples shown, graphics and communications, are two common specialties.)

c. Special equipment for graphics applications
      Plotter P for use with CPU A and CPU C ($xxxx) with (list features)
      Graphics software package GSP ($xxx)
-
-
-

d. Special equipment for data communications
      Modem MM for all configurations ($xxx) with (list features
      Communication software package CSP ($xxx)
      Special cable kit SCK ($xx)
-
-
-

(Separate sections are needed for each distinct application area. The ones shown in these sections are typical.)

2. For people who use personal computing primarily for support and/or accounting/financial applications. (Primary use is for word processing or spreadsheets, some graphics for presentations.) Show lists as in section 1. The major differences in this section will be in CPU memory (to hold larger spreadsheets), integrated software, letter-quality printer options.

3. For people using personal computing primarily for engineering, scientific, and mathematical applications. (Primary use is in computer-aided engineering, modeling, statistical analyses, design; also equipment that connects with laboratory or manufacturing equipment via sensors.) Show lists as in section 1. Primary differences are in the types of CPUs recommended—need as much memory and speed as possible. Software is specialized for the application; utility software tends to be more technical; graphics, often in color, are highly desirable.

4. For programmers using personal computing primarily as a system development workstation. (Primary use is for prototyping, libraries of source code modules, preedit/precompiler systems, test data generation and analysis, source program text management, documentation generation.) Show lists as in Section 1. Primary differences are in the abilities to communicate to larger host computers and the amount of disk storage needed on the local workstation. Also, specialized software is required for these applications.

5. Specialized data-entry devices such as light pens, touch pads, bar code readers, and mice. Show prices and configurations to which the devices can be attached. (A separate section is probably needed for accessories that are unusual but which may be useful in a variety of application areas.)

6. Furniture and supplies. Because so much is available in this category, it is usually best simply to refer to either a recommended vendor or a recommended set of catalogs. (Any that are recommended can be shown here, but as stated in the guideline, this is usually best left to an outside vendor. At best, the PCIC may wish to attach the catalog of a recommended vendor to the selection list.)

7. Special systems for dedicated applications common to the company. These may be special engineering test equipment, word processors, portable systems, training systems, and so on. (If the PCIC recommends special equipment for specific uses, it can be listed here.)

Approved List

This equipment does not receive the full PCIC support given to equipment on the Recommended List. See Guideline 2.6 for more discussion of the differences between Recommended and Approved Equipment.

Equipment on this list may not be available from the PCIC, since depleted supplies are not replenished. Therefore, prices and availability shown below should be considered as guides only. (The differences between the approved and recommended lists are mentioned. Since the Approved List is usually the home of new equipment working toward recommended status, or old equipment being discontinued, the price and availability data are less firm.)

Equipment on this list is shown by type; configuration groupings are not suggested. (The format of the Approved List is basically two columns: product descriptions and comments. The products are arranged by product type rather than by application as is the Recommended List. The product types shown are a fairly inclusive list, but the categories can, of course, be adjusted as appropriate. The product description should be as specific as possible, showing not only vendor, price, and availability but also compatibility information. In the comments column should be the status of the equipment, whether it is being phased in or phased out, and what, if any, precautions are appropriate.)

Products	Comments
(Show name/number, vendor, price, availability)	(Precautions)

1. Hardware
   a. CPU's
      -
      - (list)
      -
   b. Disk storage
      -
      -
      -
   c. Printers
      -
      -
      -
   d. Tape drives
      -
      -
      -
   e. Plotters
      -
      -
      -
   f. Modems
      -
      -
      -
   g. Data-entry devices
      -
      -
      -
   h. Sensors/laboratory attachments
      -
      -
      -
   i. Other
      -
      -
      -

2. Software packages. (The basic two-column format is the same, but the categories are different, organized primarily about the application for which the software is used. The product description should, of course, describe the hardware and/or operating system required.)
   a. Word processing
      -
      - (list)
      -
   b. Spreadsheets
      -
      -
      -
   c. Integrated systems
      -
      -
      -

d. Graphics
-
-
-

e. File managers
-
-
-

f. Data communication
-
-
-

g. Programming languages/development aids
-
-
-

h. Project scheduling
-
-
-

i. Training aids
-
-
-

j. Statistical analysis
-
-
-

k. Mathematical functions
-
-
-

l. Desk management (calendars, list managers)
-
-
-

m. Other (list by application)
-
-
-

Not-Recommended List

(The format of the list is the same as that of the Approved List. Note that the guideline describes the recourse available to people if they decide that they want to purchase not-recommended equipment. The control is loose, merely an explanation, probably after-the-fact to the CIM and the vice-president, administration. Some companies might want to change this paragraph to require prior permission before such purchases are allowed. Also, if people feel that an item is on the Not Recommended List unfairly, they are welcome to discuss the matter with the manager, PCIC.)

The equipment shown on this list is expressly not recommended for use in the company. The specific reasons for this rating are shown in the comments section next to each item.

Purchase of equipment on this list requires specific explanation to the Chief Information Manager and the vice-president, administration. Anyone having additional information on this equipment that would mitigate the unfavorable rating is invited to discuss the subject with the manager, PCIC. (Use the same format shown in the Approved List.)

Index

(As time passes, the Selection List will become so large that an index will be helpful. The index should have two sections, one organized by product and one by vendor. A third classification, by function, is also common.)

1. By Product Name   Vendor   List (Recommended, Approved, Not Recommended)
2. By Vendor   Product Name   List

When ordering personal computing equipment, please complete this form, and attach the original to the completed and signed company internal order form. Keep the copy for your reference. (The form should be printed as a two-part set; the original is attached to the internal order and goes to the PCIC; the copy stays with the users for their reference. Additional sheets to elaborate on comments can be attached if necessary.)

Name:_____

Title:_____

Department/Division:_____

Address/Bldg/Mail Stop:_____

_____

Telephone Number:_____

Describe how you plan to use personal computing; check the boxes shown below and describe the applications in more detail in the comments section below.

_____ Word processing (describe types of documents in comments)
_____ Spreadsheets (describe types of documents in comments)
_____ Electronic mail
_____ Desk services (list in comments; e.g., calendars, lists)
_____ Engineering/scientific (describe applications in comments)
_____ Statistical (describe applications in comments)
_____ Use with other systems (give details in comments)
_____ Need for portability (describe applications in comments)
_____ Other (list applications and describe in comments)

Comments (attach additional sheets as needed).

Justify your need for personal computing equipment by listing the business benefits you expect from the use of personal computing; be as specific and quantitative as possible. (Attach additional sheets as needed.)

343

What specific equipment do you have in mind? (If you do not know, leave this section blank and someone from the PCIC will assist you.

    Hardware:
    Software:
    Other:
    Expected initial cost:
    Expected monthly cost of ownership:

___

Other services needed: (e.g., training, consulting)

___

Submitted by: _____ Date: _____

Approved:_____ | _____ _____ | _____
       Department Manager   Date   Manager, PCIC   Date

___

Management Comments:

___

PCIC Comments:

Index

A

Access controls, 90
Accounting ownership, 66
Addresses, directories, 160
Application architectures, 204
Application development tools, 200
Application evaluations, first-order
    personal computing, 141–
    43
Application record packets, 186–91
Application structure, directories,
    160
Architecture, 155–68
  components of, 156
  design/maintenance responsibilit-
    ies, 155–56
  directories, 160
  gateways, 163–65
  global systems, 157
  local systems, 159
  objectives of, 157
  shared systems, 157–58
  standard business codes, 150–62
  system management, 158
Artificial intelligence:
  expert systems, 321–23
  integrated AI applications, 324
  natural language, 323
  robotics, 323–24

Auditors, security, responsibility of,
    92
Audit trails, 120–21

B

Basic operating guidelines:
  acquiring personal computing
    equipment (guideline 3.1),
    57–64
    checklist, 63–64
    equipment ownership, 61–62
    equipment services, 61–62
    fundamental philosophy, 57–58
    guideline for, 58
    inventory control, 52
    justification, 60
    ongoing services, 61
    Personal Computing Informa-
      tion Center (PCIC), buy-
      ing from, 59–60
    selecting equipment, 58–59
  nonbusiness applications of per-
    sonal computing (guideline
    3.6), 101–3
    checklist, 103

Basic operating guidelines (*cont.*)
  generally acceptable situations,
    101–2
  generally unacceptable situa-
    tions, 102
  PCIC support of employee-
    owned equipment, 102
  primary guideline, 101
offsite personal computing (guide-
    line 3.5), 95–100
  checklist, 99–100
  hardware control, 95
  home workers, 97
  personal use, 96
  security considerations, 96
  software control, 95–96
ownership issues (guideline 3.2),
    65–72
  accounting ownership, 66
  checklist, 71–72
  equipment inventories, 68–69
  guideline purpose, 65–66
  retention issues, 67–68
  software purchases, 66–67
  user department responsibilities,
    66
  user-developed software/data,
    67
security guidelines (guideline 3.4),
    83–94
  basic guideline, 84
  checklist, 93–94
  equipment, security of, 84–88
  minimum policy, 83
  misuse of equipment, protection
    from, 88–90
  privacy violations, 90–91
  security issues, 83
  security responsibilities, 91–92
  violations, 84
sharing technology (guideline
    3.3), 73–82
  basic policy, 73
  consulting, 78
  expert services, 78–79
  newsletters, 76–77
  PCIC role, 73
  personal computing standards,
    76
  reference library, 76
  training, 73–75
  users' groups, 76–77
Batch communications, 218–19
Batch systems, definition of, 154

Bridges, 225–26
Buffered communications, 219–20
Business goals/objectives, 250
Business management of personal
    computing, 25–32
Business task applications, first-
    order personal computing,
    140–41

C

Central computers, linkage through,
    154–55
Change controls, 115–16
Communications networks:
  advantages to, 220–22
  definitions, 218
  goal of, 217
  interapplication communication,
    categories of, 218–20
  local computing versus communi-
    cations, 218
  logical structure of (guideline 6.1),
    223–36
    application independence, 231–
      32
    bridges, 225–26
    checklist, 235–36
    communications technology ap-
      plications, 228–29
    control structures, 232–33
    electronic bulletin:
      boards/teleconferencing,
        230–31
    electronic mail, 226–27
    gateways, 226
    logical topologies, 224–25
    telecommuting, 229–30
    video/computer-based confer-
      encing, 230
    voice/video messages, 227
  management considerations
    (guideline 6.3), 249–67
    checklist, 265–67
    establishing technical objec-
      tives, 254–56
    managing network development
      projects, 256–58
    network accounting, 258–60
    network operations, administra-
      tion and support of, 260–
        64

network planning, 249–54
physical structure of (guideline
    6.2), 237–47
  capabilities, 240, 241
  checklist, 247
  physical controls over network,
      244–45
  protocols, 242–44
  topologies, 237–40
    wide-area networks, 240–42
  standards, 222
Compatibility, 181
Components, decision support sys-
    tems (DSSs), 325–26
Computer-based conferencing, 230
Conferencing, computer-based, 230
Consulting, 78
Control guidelines:
  first-order personal computing
      (guideline 4.3), 135–46
    application evaluations, 141–43
    business task applications, 140–
        41
    checklist, 145–46
    decision support systems, 137
    first-order tasks, definition of,
        135–36
    fundamental principle, 135
    guideline purpose, 137
    program evaluation, 143–44
    task identification, 137–40
  operational controls (guideline
      4.1), 108–25
    audit trails, 120–21
    basic guideline, 108
    change controls, 115–16
    conventional EDP controls,
        similarities to, 108
    data format controls, 121–22
    documentation, 114–15
    equipment controls, 111
    error controls, 119–20
    file protections, 117–18
    general goal, 108
    identification code controls, 121
    ownership/custodian/user con-
        cepts, 108–9
    personal/organizational con-
        trols, 111–13
    process controls, 118–19
    regression controls, 116–17
    report authenticity, 110–11
    responsibilities, 109–10
    routine jobs/schedules, 113–14

operational controls (guideline
    4.1), checklist, 123–25
total quality control:
  application to personal comput-
      ing process, 131
  checklist, 133–34
  elements of total quality con-
      trol, 127–30
  fundamental principle, 127
  personal computing application,
      130
  personal computing as part of
      (guideline 4.2), 127–34
Control structures, communications
    networks, 232–33
Coordinated personal computing
    systems:
  benefits of, 150
  coordination accomplishment,
      149–50
  data structures (guideline 5.3),
      177–93
    characteristics of, 183
    checklist, 193–94
    components of, 177
    data dictionaries, 184–86
    data indices, 184–86
    data transmission, 186–92
    goal of, 177, 178–82
    types of, 182–83
  definitions, 154–55
  disadvantages of, 150–52
  linkage characteristics, 154
  logical network design (guideline
      5.2), 169–76
    basic rules, 170–72
    checklist, 175–76
    interface levels, 169–70
    ISO levels, 172
    logical servers versus dedicated
        equipment, 173
    networks, 169
    network structures, 172
    responsibilities, 173–74
    servers, 170
    workstations versus terminals,
        172–73
  system architecture (guideline
      5.1), 155–68
    architecture contents, 156
    checklist, 167–68
    design/maintenance responsibil-
        ities, 155–56
    directories, 160

computing systems (*cont.*)
gateways, 163–65
global/shared/local systems, 157–58
objectives of, 157
standard business codes, 150–62
system management, 158
Corporate environments:
status of personal computing in, 316–21
computer education, 320–21
human factors, 318
increased personal computing power, 317
maturing of personal computing industry, 317
organizational effects, 318–20
progress in, 316–17
technological integration, 320
Corporation guidelines:
authority for, 12–13
justification for personal computing checklist, 39
model assumptions, 11
Personal Computer Information Center (PCIC):
background, 41
checklist, 53
goals of, 43
guidelines for (guideline 2.4), 41–53
PCIC organization, 41–43
purpose of, 41
responsibilities of, 44–52
personal computing:
administrative responsibilities, 35–36
background, 25
business management of personal computing, 25–32
checklist, 37
employee-written software, ownership of, 33–34
possession versus ownership, rights of, 32–33
responsibilities for (guideline 2.3), 25–37
support functions, responsibilities to, 34–35
personal computing guidelines (guideline 2.2), 19–23
background, 19
checklist, 23

guidelines as living documents, 19–20
guideline statements, 20–21
purpose of, 19, 25
personal computing program:
background, 13
checklist, 17
guideline distribution, 14
guideline maintenance, 14
guideline statements, 14–16
objectives of (guideline 2.1), 13–17
responsibilities for, 13–14
technological breakthroughs, 13
purpose of, 13
sanction period, transition to, 12
structure of, 12

D

Data, security of, 86
Data communications, security of, 88
Data dictionaries:
entries, 184–85
updating of, 185–86
Data elements, 177
minimized redundancy of, 179
rapid entry/retrieval of, 179–80
usability of, 178
Data format controls, 121–22
Data indices, 184–86
host computers (guideline 5.4), 195–213
background, 195–96
capabilities, 199–206
checklist, 211–13
guideline statements, 215–10
systems designers, advantages to, 198–99
users, advantages to, 197–98
Data storage media, achieving transferability among types, 181–82
Data structures:
capabilities, 200–201
characteristics of, 164
logical attributes, 117
physical attributes, 117–18
types of, 182–83
hierarchical, 182–83
indexed, 182

random, 183
relational, 183
serial, 182
Data transmission:
  application record packets, 186–91
  gateways, 191–92
  traditional transmission, 186
Decision support systems (DSSs),
    137
  components/flow, 325–26
  development of, 327
  group DSS, 326–27
  limitations on, 327–28
Demonstration centers, marketing
    of, 48
Department manager, security, re-
    sponsibility of, 91–92
Device inventories, 251
Directories, 160, 201
  application structure, criteria for,
    160
  directory addresses, 160
Documentation, security of, 86

E

Electronic bulletin boards, 230–31
Electronic mail, 226–27
Employee-written software, 33–34
Encryption, 90
End-user systems/programs:
  alternatives to writing, 281
  capabilities, 284–85
    checklist, 291–92
    end-user software, accuracy,
      287–89
  definitions, 278
  development tools (guideline 7.2),
    293–302
    application generators, 297–98
    checklist, 301–2
    data base inquiry software, 296
    modifiable application pack-
      ages, 294–96
    simple programming languages,
      298
    sophisticated programming lan-
      guages, 298–99
    specialized software, 296–97
    types of, 293–94
  end-user responsibilities in devel-

opment of (guideline 7.1),
    282–92
  computing, types of, 282–84
maintenance of, 280–81
ownership issues, 281
Personal Computing Information
    Center (PCIC):
  checklist, 309–11
  company data/systems protec-
    tion, 306–7
  end-user/information systems
    applications coordination,
    305
  experience sharing, 306
  goals, 303–4
  role in systems development
    (guideline 7.3), 303–11
  versus end-user systems develop-
    ment, 278–80
Equipment:
  acquisition of, 57–64
    justification for, 60
    Personal Computing Informa-
      tion Center (PCIC), buy-
      ing from, 59–60
    selecting equipment, 58–59
  equipment ownership, 61–62
    equipment services, 61–62
    inventory control, 52
    ongoing services, 61
  inventories of, 68–69
  misuse of, 88–90
    access controls, 90
    encryption, 90
    operational controls, 89–90
    personnel controls, 89
  purchasing of, 45–47
    PCIC and 45–47
    software acquisitions/site li-
      censes, 46–47
  security of, 84–88
    data, 86–88
      data communication, 88
      input data, 86–87
      machine-readable files, 87–88
    hardware, 85
    procedures/documentation, 86
    software, 85–86
Equipment controls, 111
Equipment ownership 61–62
  leases, 62
Error controls, 119–20
Evaluation:
  of application, 141–43

Evaluation (*cont.*)
    criteria, 142–43
    performance of, 142
    setting expectations, 141–42
  of program, 143–44
Experimentation phase, 5
Expert services, 78–79

F

Files protection, 117–18
  storage space, minimizing of,
    180
First-order personal computing,
    135–46
  application evaluations, 141–43
  business task applications, 140–
    41
  decision support systems
    (DSSs), 137
  first-order tasks, 136–38
  fundamental principle, 135
  program evaluation, 143–44
  task identification, 137–40
Flow, decision support systems
    (DSSs), 325–26

G

Gateways, 163–65, 191–92
  communications networks, 226
Global system, 157
Group decision support systems
    (DSSs), 326–27
Guidelines:
  implementation process, 4
  reaction to, 3–4

H

Hardware, security of, 85
Hierarchical data structures, 182–
    83
Hobbiest phase, 5–7
Home workers, offsite personal
    computing and, 97
Host computers:
  capabilities of, 199–203

application development tools,
    compatibility of, 200
data structures, 200–201
directories, 201
expense allocation, 201
interfaces to outside environ-
    ment, 201–2
logical linkages, 200
operating system compatibility,
    200
physical linkages, 199
security/privacy, 201
specialized software, 201
system/network support, 203
user training, 202
Host resource allocation, 203

I

Identification code controls, 121
IEEE 802 Standards, 273–74
Independent personal computing,
    definition of, 154
Indexed data structures, 182
Information systems:
  hierarchy of, 159
  linkage characteristics, 154
Information systems architectures,
    251
Innovation:
  implementation of, 5–9
    departmental effect, 9
    Experimentation phase, 5
    Hobbiest phase, 5–7
    Institutionalization phase, 7–
      8
    Personal Computer Informa-
      tion Center (PCIC), 9
    Promulgation phase, 7
    S curve, 5–9
Input data, security of, 86–87
Institutionalization phase, 7–8
Interapplication communication:
  categories of, 218–20
    batch communications, 218–19
    buffered communications, 219–
      20
    synchronized communications,
      219
Inventory control, 52
  PCIC and, 52

L

Linkage:
  through central computers,
    154–55
  through hierarchical hosts, 155
  through topological network,
    155
Load control, 203
Local computing versus communi-
    cations, 218
Local system, 159
Logical linkages, 200

M

Machine-readable files, security of,
    87–88
Management issues:
  application architectures, 204
  coordinated personal computing
    system, 203–5
  host resource allocation, 203
  load control, 203
  new technology implementation,
    204
  proprietary versus commercial
    software packages, 204
  systems audits/controls, 205
  technical support, 204–5
  testing policies, 205
Manufacturing Automation Proto-
    col (MAP), levels of, 274
MAP/TOP steering committee, 274–
    75
Misuse of equipment, protection
    from, 88–90

N

Network accounting:
  controls, 259–60
  network services, charging for,
    258–59
  performance measures/statistics,
    260
  privacy, 259–60
  security, 259–60

Network development projects:
  implementation issues, 258
  managing of, 256–58
  multiple vendors, 256
  network testing, 257
  physical/site planning, 257–58
  pilots, 256–57
  prototypes, 256–57
  technical experiments, 256–57
  version control, 257
Network operations:
  administration and support of,
    260–64
  customer/user support services,
    263
  legal issues, 263–64
  network control center, 261–62
    fault management, 262–63
Network planning:
  issues involved in, 249–54
    application system profiles,
      251–53
    business goals/objectives, 250
    device inventories, 251
    implementation/operation is-
      sues, 253–54
    information systems architec-
      tures, 251
    justification, 253
    performance statement, 253
    technical strategies/tactics, 251
    user profiles, 251, 252
    utilities, 251
Networks, *See* Communications net-
    works.
Newsletters, 76–77
Nonbusiness applications of per-
    sonal computing:
  generally acceptable situations,
    101–2
  generally unacceptable situations,
    102
  PCIC support for employee-
    owned equipment, 102
  primary guideline, 101

O

Obsolete equipment:
  compatibility/conversion, 52
  management of, 52

Offsite personal computing, 95–100
  hardware control, 95
  home workers, 97
  personal use, 96
  security considerations, 329
  software control, 95–96
On-line systems, definition of, 154
Open Systems Interconnection (OSI)
    model:
  application layer, 271
  data link layer, 272
  network layer, 271–72
  physical layer, 272
  presentation layer, 271
  session layer, 271
  transport layer, 271
Operating controls, inventory con-
    trol, 52
Operating system compatibility,
    200
Operational controls, 89–90, 108–
    22
  access controls, 90
  change controls, 115–16
  conventional EDP controls, simi-
      larities to, 108
  data format controls, 121–22
  documentation, 114–15
  encryption, 90
  equipment controls, 111
  error controls, 119–20
  file protections, 117–18
  general goal, 108
  hardware control, 95
  identification code controls, 121
  ownership/custodian/user con-
      cepts, 108–9
  personal/organizational controls,
      111–13
  personnel controls, 89
  process controls, 118–19
  regression controls, 116–17
  report authenticity, 110–11
  responsibilities, 109–10
  routine jobs/schedules, 113–
      14
  software control, 95–96
Ownership issues, 65–72
  accounting ownership, 66
  equipment inventories, 68–69
  retention issues, 67–68
  software purchases, 66–67
  user department responsibilities,
      66

user-developed software/data,
    67

P

Personal Computer Information
    Center (PCIC), 9
  chief information officer,
      responsibilities of, 42–43
  goals of, 43
  PCIC organization, 41–43
  responsibilities of, 44–52
    accounting/inventory control,
        49–50
    application justification and
        evaluation, 48–49
    equipment purchases, 45–47
    equipment selection, 44–45
    equipment support, 49
    management of employee-use
        purchases, 51–52
    management of obsolete equip-
        ment, 52
    personal computing services,
        marketing of, 47–48
    pricing arrangements for users,
        50–51
    security, 92
    self-sufficient operations, 51
    standardization, 51
    training/consulting services, 49
Personal computing:
  future of, 315–32
    artificial intelligence, 321–24
    changes/innovations, 314–15
    corporate environments, status
        in, 316–21
    decision support systems, 324–
        28
    focus on customers, 314
    society, impact on, 328–32
Personal computing services:
  marketing of, 47–48
    demonstration centers, 48
    placing orders, 48
Personal/organizational controls,
    111–13
Personnel controls, 89
Physical linkages, 199
Possession versus ownership, 32–33
Precisions, provisions for, 181

Privacy:
  host computers, 201
  provisions for, 181
  violations of, 90–91
  See also Security.
Procedures, security of, 86
Process controls, 118–19
Program evaluation, first-order personal computing, 143–44
"Program virus," 180
Promulgation phase, 7
Protocols, communications networks, 242–44

R

Random data structures, 183
Reference library, 76
Regression controls, 116–17
Relational data structures, 183
Retention issues, 67–68
Routine jobs/schedules, control guidelines, 113–14

S

S Curve, 5–9
Security:
  guidelines for, 83–94
    basic guideline, 84
    equipment, 84–88
    minimum policy, 83
    responsibilities, 91–92
    security issues, 83
    violations, 84
  host computers, 201
  offsite personal computing, 96
  provisions for, 180
  responsibility of, 91–92
    auditors, 92
    department management, 91–92
    Personal Computing Information Center (PCIC), 92
    user, 91
Serial data structures, 182
Shared system, 157–58
Site licenses:
  importance of, 46–47
  seeking advantages, 47
  types of, 46

Society:
  all-electronic files, 331
  consequences of results, 330–31
  ethics, 330
  impact of personal computing on, 328–32
  information as infinite resource, 331–32
  jobs/leisure, 328–29
  security/privacy issues, 329
Software:
  purchases of, 66–67
  security of, 85–86
  specialized, 201
Sophistication, levels of, 1–2
Specialized software, 201
Standard business codes, 150–62
Synchronized communications, 219
System management, coordinated personal computing systems, 158
Systems Network Architecture
  model compared to Binary Synchronous (BSC) protocol, 272
  levels of, 272
  software, 272–73

T

Task content:
  changes in, 2–3
  change to business functions, 2–3
  needs, 3
  organization changes, 3
Task identification, first-order personal computing, 137–40
Technical objectives:
  communication networks, 254–56
    applications support, 255
    geographic dispersion, 255
    internode/interapplication transfer of data, 254–55
    local-node access of public data/equipment resources, 254
    local-node independent operations, 254
    network message capability, 255
    outside communication, 255
    systems reliability/availability of goals, 255

Technical objectives (*cont.*)
   volume/flexibility goals, 255
communications networks:
   equipment accommodated on
      network, 255
   security/privacy, 255–56
   special needs, statement of, 256
Technical and Office Protocol
      (TOP), 274
Technical strategies/tactics, 251
Technical support, 204–5
Telecommuting, 229–30
Teleconferencing, 230–31
Testing policies, 205
Topological network, linkage
      through, 155
Total quality control:
   application to personal computing
      process, 131
   elements of, 127–30
      alternatives evaluation, 129
      data analysis, 129
      data collection, 129
      improvements/changes, imple-
         mentation of, 129–30
      measurement points identifica-
         tion, 128–29
      metric specification, 129
      monitoring of process, 131
      operation, choice of, 127–28
      work task project description,
         128
   fundamental principle, 127

Training, 202
   PCIC and, 49
   sources, 74–75
   training coordination, 74

U

User-developed software/data, 67
Users:
   profiles, 251, 252
   security, responsibility of, 91
   training of, 73–75
Utilities, 251

V

Version control, 257
Video conferencing, 230
Video messages, 227
Voice messages, 227

W

Wide-area networks, 240–42